Controlling Urban Events

How does order emerge out of the multiplicity of bodies, objects, ideas and practices that constitute the urban? This book explores the relation between space, law and control in the contemporary city – and particularly in the context of urban 'mega events' – through a combined geographical and normative analysis. Informed by the recent spatial, affective and material 'turns' in the humanities and social sciences, Andrea Pavoni addresses this question by pursuing an innovative and trans-disciplinary approach, capable of accounting for the emergence of order in urban space both at the conceptual and empirical levels. Two overarching objectives are pursued. First, to account for the increasing convergence of logics, techniques and technologies of law, security and marketing into novel, potentially oppressive spatial configurations. Second, to envisage a consistent ethico-political strategy to counter this evolution, by rethinking originally and in radically spatial terms the notion of justice. Forging a sophisticated and original analysis, this book offers an analysis that will be of considerable interest to those working in critical urban geography, critical legal studies, critical event studies, surveillance and control studies.

Andrea Pavoni is post-doctoral fellow at DINAMIA'CET, Centre for Socioeconomic and Territorial Studies, at the University Institute of Lisbon, Portugal. He completed his PhD at the University of Westminster, London, in 2013. He is a fellow at the Westminster Law and Theory Lab, co-editor of the *Law and the Senses* Series (University of Westminster Press), and associate editor at the journal *Lo Squaderno, Explorations in Space and Society*.

Space, Materiality and the Normative

Series Editors: Andreas Philippopoulos-Mihalopoulos and Christian Borch

Space, Materiality and the Normative presents new ways of thinking about the connections between space and materiality from a normative perspective. At the interface of law, social theory, politics, architecture, geography and urban studies, the series is concerned with addressing the use, regulation and experience of space and materiality, broadly understood, and in particular with exploring their links and the challenges they raise for law, politics and normativity.

Titles in the series:

Spatial Justice
Body, Lawscape, Atmosphere
Andreas Philippopoulos-Mihalopoulos

Urban Commons
Rethinking the City
Edited by Christian Borch and Martin Kornberger

Border Security
Shores of Politics, Horizons of Justice
Peter Chambers

Forthcoming:

Law, Art and the Commons
Merima Bruncevic

www.routledge.com/Space-Materiality-and-the-Normative/book-series/SMNORM

Controlling Urban Events

Law, Ethics and the Material

Andrea Pavoni

Routledge
Taylor & Francis Group
LONDON AND NEW YORK

First published 2018
by Informa Law from Routledge

2 Park Square, Milton Park, Abingdon, Oxfordshire OX14 4RN
52 Vanderbilt Avenue, New York, NY 10017

Routledge is an imprint of the Taylor & Francis Group, an informa business

First issued in paperback 2019

British Library Cataloguing in Publication Data
A catalogue record for this book is available from the British Library

Library of Congress Cataloging in Publication Data
A catalog record for this book has been requested

ISBN: 978-1-138-64514-1 (hbk)
ISBN: 978-0-367-26435-2 (pbk)

Typeset in Baskerville
by Fish Books Ltd.

Contents

Acknowledgements vii

Introduction 1

1 Space matter event 11

2 Atmosphere rhythm tuning 45

3 Law space justice 69

4 Control urban event 108

5 Tuning the city 152

6 Law profanation justice 211

Conclusion 253

Bibliography 270

Index 301

Acknowledgements

Much respect to the hidden writers of this book, for stated and unstated reasons: **danilo** (for the presence) **andreas** (for the lines of flights) **mubi** (for the territories) **la cherie** (for the patience) **cate** (for being cate) **christian** (for the atmosphere) **cod** (for the nest) **val senales** (for the whiteout) **joburg** (for keeping it real) **matteo** (for the weeds) **nicola** (for the pessimism) **david** (for the form) **peter** (for the interior) **marco** (for the swing) **tulu** (for the pages) **blub** (for the disruptions) **ubu** (for the meticulousness) **pedro** (pra capa) **chris** (for kick-starting) **steven & vijay** (for the control), **alex** (for the shelter) **michiyo** (for the koto) **mb** (for keeping on) **madre e padre** (for the support) **david & kirstie** (for the brandscape) **guy** (for the encouragement) **andrew** (for the pragmatism) **giorgio** (for the profanation) **ai** (for the seeds) **gilles** (for making this happen) **the others** (who, though unmentioned, were indispensable).

Não cantes tua cidade, deixa-a em paz.[1]

Carlos Drummond de Andrade

A force de souffrir, je perdis les limites de mon corps et me démesurai irrésistiblement.[2]

Henri Michaux

Jede derartige Grenze bedeutet Defensive und Offensive; oder vielleicht richtiger: sie ist der räumliche Ausdruck einheitlichen Verhältnisses zwischen zwei Nachbarn, für das wir keinen ganz einheitlichen Ausdruck haben, und das wir etwa als den Indifferenzzustand von Defensive und Offensive bezeichnen können, als einen Spannungszustand, in dem beides latent ruht, mag es sich nun entwickeln oder nicht.[3]

Georg Simmel

1 'Don't sing your city, leave it be.' (Drummond de Andrade, 2012[1936]: 11).

2 'By dint of suffering I lost the limits of my body and gave up my shape, irresistibly.' (Michaux, 1966: 48).

3 'Each border means defensive and offensive, or more precisely: it is the spatial expression of the unitary relationship between two neighbours, a relationship for which we lack a unique term, and that we may define as the state of indifference between defensive and offensive, a state of tension in which both persist at the dormant state, may it or may it not unfold.' (Simmel, 1908).

Introduction

1. City is contradictions, and seeking to overcome them is bad utopia: the city cannot be their peace.[1]

At the turn of the millennium, Pierre Bourdieu and Loic Wacquant defined neo-liberalism as the 'new planetary vulgate'.[2] About ten years later, Neil Brenner described urbanisation as a planetary process.[3] In the meanwhile, as the early definition by Paul Crutzen and Eugene Stoermer is increasingly accepted in both the fields of science and humanities, the concept of Anthropocene indicates the extent to which the human has become a 'planetary force' in its own right.[4] Were it not such an ugly term, perhaps the *urbanocene* would be a more precise approximation of the age we are in.

In 1867, coining the notion of *urbanisation*, Ildefons Cerdà described it as a natural, trans-historical and universal process, 'an essential category of humankind', immanent to the coming-together of human beings in co-habitation, and coessential with civilisation.[5] He had a point. As soon as the human begins walking upright, the stability, and 'intense sense of security', that the four-leg square provided is lost. Plunged into the disequilibrium and insecurity of verticality, the need to build a roof becomes paramount. 'The very first cogito' – Michel Serres writes – 'was a plan for a refuge to recover the lost ball': architecture is born as an ontological necessity.[6] However, if the Neolithic signals the advent of the new condition of inhabitation within a designed and built environment,[7] the urban may be understood as a precise socio-historical condition, one which corresponds with the affirmation of capitalism. It is not the factory, but the contemporary metropolis, to be the quintessential locus of capitalism, both in the

1 Cacciari, 2009: 42 (my translation).
2 Bourdieu and Wacquant, 2001.
3 Brenner, 2013.
4 Crutzen and Stoermer, 2000; Castree, 2014.
5 Adams, 2014.
6 Serres, 1999 (my translation).
7 Wilson, 2007.

urban as a form devoid of quality and determinations, as well as, at the same time, in the historically situated socio-spatial relations *in* and *through* which it is actualised.[8]

What is the urban, then? This was the title of an Iowa State University symposium held in April 2016. Its poster asked the following question:

> Considering recent work in the humanities, what happens when we consider the urban to be a political ecology in its own right – a dense, complex, relational entanglement of human and non-human natures, embodied energies and materialities?[9]

This book emerges as an attempt to respond to this question, looking at the urban as, simultaneously, the immanent coming-together of bodies that such a post-human ecological understanding unfolds; a spatio-political project tied to the ever-expanding space of neo-liberal capitalism; and the planetary process that the relentless urbanisation of the Earth expresses. An attempt that prompts a reorientation of the initial question itself: trying to capture what the urban *is*, fundamentally means trying to understand how the urban *works* or, more precisely, how the urban *holds together*.

2.

> Robinson believed that, if he looked at it hard enough, he could cause the surface of the city to reveal to him the molecular basis of historical events, and in this way he hoped to see into the future.[10]

This is not a new question, admittedly. Perhaps, it is *the* question, implicitly underlying urban theory since the early, visionary reflections of pioneering urban sociologists. The question that, from the 1970s, a bunch of critical urban thinkers tied indissolubly to the structures, apparatuses, spaces and temporalities of capitalism. In the writings of Henri Lefebvre, David Harvey, Manuel Castells, Ed Soja and others, the investigation of the urban was understood as crucial to detect the contradictions of capital, unfold its hidden structures of power, ideology and exploitation, and eventually open the possibility for constructing a more just, equal, and sustainable urbanism.

This fundamental advancement in urban theory, however, was often obtained at the cost of overlooking that *everyday life* which had been fleetingly captured before in the writings of Siegfried Kracauer, Walter Benjamin, George Simmel, and so on. Not simply as a dimension opposed and reactive to the oppressive structures of the capital, but rather productive in its own terms, and thus inexplicable only through such

8 Toscano, 2004; Cunningham, 2005.

9 Retrieved from www.whatistheurban.org/about/

10 In *London*, 2014.

lenses.[11] This lack was what the so-called 'cultural turn' in urban theory set up to address. Animated by a postmodern ethos of hermeneutics, interpretation and deconstruction, it shook urban theory from its self-assured comfort, prompting a more accurate attention for everyday life in its trivial, flowing and unpredictable character, as well as destabilising the rigidity of supra-structures in the face of the moving and flowing complexity of the world.[12]

The clash between these two perspectives however would soon produce an impasse.[13] If Marxist structures (especially in their more 'orthodox' connotation) appeared to be too rigid to grasp the turbulent, common and conflictual materiality of the urban, postmodern hermeneutics proved far too loose. Among the consequences would be the propensity to confine instances of alternative and emancipatory political action into the supposed concreteness of embedded, localised and face-to-face direct action, somewhat understood as more authentic and genuine vis-à-vis cold, reifying and oppressive capitalistic abstractions. More pessimistically, this sometimes led to apocalyptic narratives of 'loss of control' in the face of an increasingly globalised and de-localised world of flows. More optimistically, to the excessive exaltation of temporary, actual or imaginary counter-spaces where to unleash the liberating and chaotic potential of urban life against the forces of domination, via the troubling celebration of disorder, dislocation and unpredictability as emancipatory *per se*.[14] More problematically, to the yearning for a different or 'differential' urban space where the contradictions of the contemporary metropolis would be dialectically overcome, and a post-conflictual utopia of peaceful and diverse deliberation would be created where more authentic forms of human agency would be restored: a mythical space indeed, still conceived under the hypnotising effect of the nostalgia for the ideal form of the Greek *polis*.

Either irremediably over-determined and dislocated by the capital, or de-constructed and re-imagined by its inhabitants and their practices, however, the city was equally assumed as 'a bounded unity and a stable object' of research, an ontological unity, that is.[15] A contradictory notion of space underlined these assumptions. Space is 'simultaneously too soft and too hard', in Eyal Weizman terms, too hard since built realities are understood as 'solid, fixed and unchangeable', too soft since assuming 'the

11 Hence the relatively little attention that critical urban theory gave to such thinkers, as was the case for some key parts of Henry Lefebvre's oeuvre, subordinating his works on 'everyday life' to the 'politico-economical' ones. See Goonewardena, 2008.

12 E.g. Dear, 2000; Watson *et al.*, 1995.

13 Thrift, 1993.

14 Storper, 2001: 155.

15 Farías, 2010: 12.

possibility of agency existing in the mere literal subversion of the existing', in other words, in interpretative 're-imagining'.[16]

The last two decades, however, have seen promising moves beyond this impasse. Recent turns in humanities (spatial, affective, material, post-human...) fostered a radical rethinking of the urban as a *multiplicity*, an immanent being-together of tangible and intangible, human and non-human bodies, a materiality of objects, people, ideas, sounds, noises, expectations, structures, affects: a dynamic and turbulent spatiality unaccountable either through the determinism of structural-functionalism or the anarchism of postmodern flows.[17] This theoretical direction that allowed, in Ash Amin's words, 'uncovering the material geographies of urban provision, and the intricate ways in which nature and culture fold into each other'.[18] Urban networks, socionatures, assemblages, infrastructures, materialities, ecologies, metabolism ... many and variously different are the intersecting tendencies that have been emerging in the last few years, designing a vibrant, trans-disciplinary field of research for urban theory. This is the thick theoretical breeding ground out of which this book emerges.

3.

> Spatial images are the dreams of society. Wherever the hieroglyphics of any spatial image are deciphered, there the basis of social reality presents itself.[19]

Whilst researcher try to grapple with their changing nature in the global urban condition, the cities are incessantly and internally reformulated around the needs of business and financial sectors, consumption and tourism, safety and speculation, shaped by the rhythm of privatisation, commercialisation, beautification, securitisation. In this context a novel, all-encompassing aesthetics emerges, in which security and entertainment merge and converge shaping everyday life within safe, comforting, capitalised and entertaining spaces, relations, and practices. Making sense of the urban, in this context, appears as paramount. What is the problematic field in which we are entangled vis à vis the current planetary urban condition? Which concepts may help us to make sense of, and indeed challenge, this situation?

These are some of the questions that justify the theoretical and terminological effort this book carries out, by piercing through the urban and its materialities through the angles of philosophy, geography, and law. Different reasons convinced me to embark on this feat. Primarily I intended to

16 Weizman, 2010: 276.
17 Latham and McCormack, 2004.
18 Amin, 2007: 108.
19 Kracauer, 1997: 60.

develop a theoretical trajectory which would intersect the invaluable insights of the thought of Gilles Deleuze, with some of those coming from the recent directions of 'new materialism' and the 'speculative turn' in contemporary philosophy,[20] on the one hand, by using invaluable philosophical allies such as Félix Guattari, Giorgio Agamben, Peter Sloterdijk and on the other, by avoiding the conceptual and strategic quicksand of so-called *relationalism* (or correlationalism), namely, the tendency to absolutise relation, or correlation, as the basic ontological component of reality.[21]

Whilst welcoming the spatial promises that the 'relational turn' in social science and humanities brought about, I thus criticise relational ontologies insofar as producing a totalising and suffocating image of reality that ends up being troublingly consistent with the post-political landscape of contemporary capitalism. It is the concept of *event*, I argue, that is ultimately missing from the picture, and thus requires to be rescued, and mobilised: *ontologically*, as the very potential for any urban assemblage to be otherwise; *genealogically*, in reference to the ever-increasing use of events (especially so-called mega events) as a precise strategy of urban branding and development; *strategically*, in relation with the promising notion of 'spatial justice'.

At the same time, as the book's title reminds us, urban events are inextricably tied up with the attempt to control, or *prevent* them. Thus, besides elaborating a novel conceptualisation of (urban) space, and critically discussing its problematic relation with normativity, as well as gesturing towards the ethical and political potential of spatial justice, the book explores the other side of the coin, namely the configuration of power that characterises the contemporary city in the context of contemporary neo-liberal capitalism: *control*, employing the term Deleuze borrows from the American writer William Burroughs. There is an enormous amount of literature dealing with the contemporary processes of juridification, securitisation, and commodification, through which urban life is increasingly shaped, captured, and exploited. The book attempts to traverse this dense theoretical context, without surrendering to the temptation to provide yet another paranoid account of our doomed condition, and yet avoiding naïve exaltation of the supposedly unlimited potentialities for resistance. The task instead is that of exploring the evolution of new, potentially oppressing logics of control, as well as delineating a radically material, ethico-politically worthwhile and strategically adequate concept of justice, in the hope to inform relative debates in the philosophical, urban and legal field.

The introduction ends with a brief outline of the book, intended to provide readers with a compass to orient themselves through the chapters,

20 Bryant *et al.*, 2011.
21 Meillassoux, 2009.

as well as with the possibility to retrace the impulses, inspirations and doubts which have influenced the building-process of the book itself.

4. Rather than new critiques, cartographies are what we need.[22]

Moving beyond the unproductive opposition between modern structures and postmodern chaos does not mean evading the primary question: how does the urban hold together, how is it *tuned,* and how are we to address its immanent ordering(s)? As mentioned, recent trajectories of theoretical thinking provide stimulating impulses in this direction, at times however falling short of fully addressing the consequences that overcoming traditional dichotomies entails. To simply abandon transcendence for the supposedly liberating immanence of networks, extensive connections, dislocating assemblages and vibrant matter is not enough, if a proper understanding of the 'mechanism of immanence' is left untold.[23] Otherwise, the risk is that of displacing dualisms only to fall into the cul-de-sac of relationalism: namely, the flattening of the social into a horizontal ontology without event, mirroring, and indeed contributing to reproduce, the closed horizon of post-political assimilation in which capitalism thrives.[24]

Chapter 1 begins to unpack this observation by putting in communication the concept of relation with that of event, a veritable blind spot in otherwise significant approaches such as Bruno Latour's *actor-network theory*, or Sloterdik's *spherology*. Engaging, among others, with the thought of Latour and Sloterdijk, Gabriel Tarde, Martin Heidegger, Graham Harman, Félix Guattari, and Gilles Deleuze, the chapter sketches the contours of an ontology able to account both for the relational character of being-together, as well as for the material excess that prevents any situation to be reduced to its *relations.* To do so, the Deleuzoguattarian concepts of *virtual, machine* and *event* are mobilised, so as to delineate what I term a 'demonic vitalism', through which I seek to overcome the impasses of relationalism as well as the perils of nihilism, without falling into the contradictions of (naïve) vitalism. The social is accordingly understood as a space populated and constituted by bodies that are human and non-human, tangible and intangible, simultaneously singular and in relation, always taken into concatenations and yet never exhausted by them, always virtually exceeding the actuality of social, physical, biological, psychological relations into which they are caught.[25]

22 Tiqqun, 2010: 216.
23 Barnett, 2011b; DeLanda, 2005.
24 Negarestani, 2011a.
25 Here, the use of the term 'body' follows with the Spinozist definition provided by Deleuze: 'a body can be anything: it can be an animal, a body of sounds, a mind or idea; it can be a linguistic corpus, a social body, a collectivity'. Deleuze, 1988: 127.

Chapter 2 aims to apply this understanding to the urban first, by engaging in a critical discussion with novel tendencies in urban theory, especially at the intersection with the concept of assemblage[26] and second, by engaging with recent works on concepts of atmosphere and rhythm, and proposing to articulate their folding within the (urban) space through the notion of *tuning*. Urban tunings are the immanent, emergent wavelengths in which the multi-scalar getting-together of bodies is 'ordered' in the city. This concept allows for building a simultaneously phenomenological and ecological, material, post-human and 'assembled' angle, whereby to observe the urban by emphasising simultaneously its *affective*, *dromological* and *normative* quality. Not a mere aesthetic device, this concept has a profoundly strategic nuance: it is around the creation, shaping and contestation of these tunings, I argue, that urban politics rests.

Chapter 3 further excavates the normative question of urban tunings, by constructing a way to understand its immanent and material quality. To do so, it merges the notions of law and space so as to delineate a *spatiolegal* understanding of the social. This requires a genealogical effort, tracing the articulation of the relation between law, space, and their eventful excess, in other words justice, within legal theory. In particular, I deal with recent works within so-called 'critical legal geography', the writing of Jacques Derrida on justice, and Andreas Philippopoulos-Mihalopoulos' Deleuzoguattarian notion of *lawscape*. On the one hand, this chapter sets the stage for the extensive discussion on spatial justice carried out in Chapter 6. On the other, it builds a bridge between the urban ontology developed in the previous two chapters, and the discussion of the biopolitical forms of contemporary 'control' pursued in the following chapter.

Chapter 4 provides an extensive description of the spatiolegal articulation of *control,* how it functions by retuning the urban into a juridico-economical configuration that materialises the logic of contemporary neo-liberal capitalism in the city. The chapter is a pragmatic attempt to make sense of converging tendencies in the field of marketing, security and law, by looking at the configuration they take into the contemporary metropolis. Here, a peculiar contradiction is emphasised. The logic of control appears as fundamentally centred on prevention, that is, the preemptive defusion of events from the urban, so as to guarantee its functioning as a safe and comfortable space of socio-economical transactions. At the same time, events of any kind and size, from neighbourhood festival to the Olympics, have become a key strategy for cities to generate the symbolic and affective capital on which they thrive.[27] To capture this conundrum, and building on Sloterdijk's concept of *interiorisation,* I

26 See Anderson and MacFarlane, 2011; Brenner *et al.*, 2012.
27 Richards, 2010.

introduce the notion of *brandscaping*, as a way to account for the material and spatial convergence of strategies and practices of marketing, security and law towards the common objective of producing commodified experiences of safety and safe experiences of consumption in the city. This is a convergence that, however, is never flawless or a priori, and rather requires to be explored in its contingent, eventful unfolding. This is what the following chapter does.

The original conceptualisation of the urban, the central role of the event, the complex diagnosis of contemporary control: these three overlapping directions converge in Chapter 5, where a case study grounds and expands the former conceptualisations. The chapter is based on an ethnography set in the city of Johannesburg, in South Africa, in the context of the 2010 FIFA Football World Cup. Guiding the chapter is the assumption that 'mega events' (such as the World Cup or the Olympics) are not exceptions, but rather explicitations of emergent configurations of urban control. They are thus invaluable tools to explore the way urban neoliberal capitalism functions, through standardised and aggressive reformulation of the legal, economical and physical texture of the urban space. At the same time, this chapter enters into dialogue with the field of event studies, proposing a novel critical as well as a methodological approach to the study of mega events and, *through* them, the urban in general.

Chapter 6 draws together and projects forwards the various threads surfacing in the preceding pages. Informing it is the question posed by Richard Sinnerbrink: how to construct 'a political philosophy and practice adequate to the deterritorialising dynamic of global capitalism'?[28] This is addressed by critically assessing recent accounts of *spatial justice*, and proposing a personal elaboration at the intersection between Deleuze's notion of event, Agamben's strategy of profanation, and Philippopoulos-Mihalopoulos' own work on spatial justice. Provided it is taken in its most radical acceptation – thus avoiding it being a redundant terminological supplement to the notion of social justice or, worst, a cooptable concept to be misused by conservative politics – the concept of spatial justice harbours the possibility of rearticulating the relation between law and justice into a strategy that, moving beyond both socio-legal and critical angles, though without abandoning critical sharpness, does not fall into simplistic anti-normative positions. Spatial justice, in other words, allows for doing *justice* to space, whilst rescuing justice from its dissolution into consensual procedures. This means restoring the original meaning of justice as a constant incompatibility with the status quo, never a matter of its simple rearrangement (e.g. distributive justice), but rather what holds the potential to open up the status quo by showing the possibilities of its reorientation. The concept of profanation is crucial in this sense, pointing to the simultan-

28 Sinnerbrink, 2006: 85.

eously modest and strategic task to unplug power relations in which a given situation is imbricated, and reorient their residual power towards alternative tunings. Thus the seemingly inescapable alternative between a 'justice within law' and a 'justice without law' is overcome, to unfold an ethico-political strategy which tries to *stay* at the radical interspersion of law and justice, in their immanent, material and excessive spatiality, without moving beyond the terrain of the spatiolegal, but rather *forcing* law to transform *sur place*, to *reorient* itself, that is, to the inescapable situatedness to the event of its taking place: its justice.

This book does not aim to sublimate relevant differences into an all-encompassing, homogenous trajectory. It rather seeks to provide space for different ideas, positions and disciplines to encounter, so as to generate productive frictions, and generate the sufficient intensity for the creation of new conceptual assemblages. It is not the internal and organic coherence between its parts to count here, but 'whether the product formed from these parts manages to attain some degree of consistency in the formation of a new object'.[29] I thus relied more on the conceptual intensity the concatenations of this book may generate, than to the possible destabilisation to its coherence they could provoke. Not all the tools required the same degree of sharpness, then. Some appear only in a singular combination; others are repeatedly and yet differently handled, deterritorialised and reterritorialised along the book, so as to gain complexity, theoretical depth and strategic edge. As will be evident to the reader, such rhizomatic combinations and re-combinations are not meant to deny structure and order, but rather to propel a productive oscillation within the book, one that would hopefully keep it open to its *outside*. To be sure, this oscillation always runs the risk of dissolving this effort into inconsistency, and yet is a necessary risk, I believe, to keep it alive, open and flexible enough to produce something new.

The book's structure is thus conceived as a spiralling movement, oscillating between its inside and its outside, at times returning back to its steps, addressing different concepts more than once, only to propel itself forwards yet again, adding at each step more theoretical sedimentations and stability, as well as boring each time new holes in its texture, new lines of flight averting its closure. This is, incidentally, the purpose of the quotes opening each section, often seemingly out of place vis-à-vis the section they introduce, insofar as pointing somewhere else within the book, or beyond. Lars Lerup once proposed an architectural practice which would strive to avoid the urge to produce a given, self-sufficient and finished work. He termed it 'building the unfinished', a practice that eschews a result-oriented ethos, yet without abdicating the task of building something: an

29 Bryant, 2011: 28.

inoperose architecture, that is, aimed to make buildings able to make space for the irruption of the potentialities, conflictuality and excesses of being-together, rather than preventively closing them off.[30] This book wishes to do something similar, not simplistically and cowardly averting the task of achieving *a* result, yet pursuing its trajectory freed from the anxiety of *the* result.[31]

30 Lerup, 1977: 31.
31 Masciandaro, 2010: 52.

Chapter 1

Space matter event

The relational turn in social sciences and, more deeply, the philosophical age of *correlation*, is the theoretical battleground this chapter engages with, in order to sketch the ontological approach which grounds the book. This is done through three steps.

First, I begin sketching the unorthodox sociology of Tarde, tracing its indirect influence into the 'sociology of association' of Latour's Actor-Network Theory (ANT), traversing Heidegger's spatial intuition and following their explicitation in Sloterdijk's *Sphereology*. Whilst I emphasise the relevance of these approaches in decisively moving beyond the binary impasse of contractualist (or individualistic) and organicistic (or holistic) understandings of the social, a question keeps resonating: *where is the event? Networks* and *spheres* produce flat and uneventful ontologies, as such drastically de-politicised and thus cooptable by conservative thinking.

Second, taking inspiration from Quentin Meillassoux's cry against *correlation*, I engage in a brief confrontation with Harman and, via a brief parenthesis on Parmenides, I explain how the claustrophobic outcomes of relationalism are archetypically retraceable to the paradigmatic split introduced by the Philosopher of Elea. Following Agamben, I do not understand the 'paradigm' as a hypothesis through which explaining 'modernity by tracing it back to something like a cause or historical origin', or as a 'signifier' whereby joining heterogeneous phenomena into a smooth syncretism. Instead, I assume it as a 'singular case that is isolated from its context only insofar as, by exhibiting its own singularity, it makes intelligible a new ensemble whose homogeneity it itself constitutes'.[1] A specific example, that is, by means of being exposed, 'gives life to a new problematic context', and therefore enters in *analogical* (and thus non-dichotomous, i.e. beyond the general/particular dichotomy) relation with other examples, not by flattening their differences but rather expressing the shared problematic fields out of which they strategically emerge. In this sense I explain the Parmenidean separation as the production of a

1 Agamben, 1993: 250.

problematic field in which politics is reduced to a post-political praxis of manipulating a matter (a life, a space, a common…) which is negatively posited as neutral and innocent (i.e. beyond power relations).[2]

Third, through Deleuze's elaboration of the notions of *virtual* and *event*, I introduce *demonic vitalism*, an ontology of being-together that assumes bodies as simultaneously singular *and* in-relation, always taken into concatenations and yet never 'exhausted' by them. The chapter may present at times an excessive degree of theoretical density, which however will gradually rarefy as the book progresses, and its methodological and ethical implications become apparent

1.1 To exist is to differ.[3]

In the last decades, many critical and innovative works have contributed to a move decidedly beyond contractualist and organicistic understandings of the social. The first de-spatialises social relations, by projecting in an ideal co-existence of rational individuals engaged in enlightened deliberations aimed at harmonising and safeguarding particular interests, a de-politicising vision today actualised in neo-liberal rhetorics of inclusion and participation. The second assumes society as an autonomous organism encompassing and subsuming its members via institutional apparatuses. Classic is Émile Durkheim's conception of society as a transcendent, monospherical container, to which individuals are bound by means of sharing 'social facts', collective representations which are external to them, pre-existing – and thus unexplained – conditions for human agency.[4]

A long-forgotten, lately rediscovered and recently popularised figure of late-nineteenth century French thought, Gabriel Tarde developed a social theory resolutely transversal vis-à-vis the binary just exposed. A contemporary and leading opponent of Durkheim, Tarde denies the existence of 'transcendent' social facts, collectively shared among human beings as result of the existence of a 'society' which would supersede them.[5] Against

2 Alberto Toscano, in a critique of Agamben, observes that a genealogical work should be about 'discontinuities' rather than 'continuity and concealment' (Toscano, 2011a). I think instead that any genealogical effort should be simply concerned with unfolding the problematic fields out of which the phenomena under investigation emerge. This, importantly, not in the 'revelatory' sense of aiming to uncover 'hidden rules' beneath them, but rather in the pragmatic sense of accounting for the strategic rationale they seek to address. If this entails unfolding continuities between apparent discontinuities, or *vice versa*, it cannot be known, let alone presupposed, in advance. In fact, it is an effort that 'makes the inquirer's present intelligible as much as the past of his or her object' (Agamben, 2009b: 24).

3 Tarde, 2012[1893]: 40.

4 Durkheim, 2008[1912].

5 '[I]nstead of saying, like Durkheim, that we "should treat social facts as a thing", Tarde says that 'all things are society', and any phenomenon is a social fact' (Latour, 2002: 122).

the presupposition of a uniform, coherent and homogenous society, he asserts that 'facts (including social facts) are contingent compositions emerging out of a complex of difference and repetition'.[6] Against the presupposition of a self-contained, self-identical individual, he assumes 'difference' as the original condition of existence, with identity being only a modality of difference, thus wholly inadequate as explanatory principle. Employing Leibniz's term, Tarde suggests that monads, rather than individuals, are the minimal component of society: monads are not given subjects, but rather agencies, such as notions and prejudices, perceptions and expressions, knowledge and desires. As Latour summarises:

> In the same way as Tarde refuses to take society as a higher, more complex, order than the individual monad, he refuses to take the individual human agent as the real stuff out of which society is made: a brain, a mind, a soul, a body is itself composed of myriads of 'little persons', or agencies, each of them endowed with faith and desire, and actively promoting one's total version of the world.[7]

There is no society at all, in fact, but rather *sociality*, in other words, an immanent and contingent process of emergence of social formations, heterogeneous agglomerations of human and non-human bodies, affects, ideas, opinions, traditions, assumptions, things. This does not imply chaos, however. The social always crystallises around stable distributions of ideas, feelings, opinions, practices: orderings, or *tunings*. Differently from Leibniz's monadology, there is no transcendent God who guarantees universal harmony. In Tarde's neo-monadology orderings emerge out of the 'immanent and constitutive action of every monad'.[8] Under the influence of late-nineteenth-century studies on hypnotism, Tarde controversially gives the notions of imitation and repetition a crucial role in accounting for the way ideas ('inventions') spread and order emerges in the social: 'any specific innovation – for example the pronunciation of a word or behavioural patterns for standing in line – may radiate and create resonances by being repeated by many humans or other species, over and over again'.[9] Thus we have a 'socio-biological' model: as in multi-cellular organisms, sociality is constituted by the imitative repetition and propagation of singular acts, or events, generating assemblages which are always potentially variable (they are not given), to some extent unpredictable (we are never able to fully forecast if a single act, or idea, will spread enough to form a crystallisation), performative (dependent on repetition, movement,

6 Toews, 2003: 93.
7 Latour, 2002: 121.
8 Lazzarato, 2004a: 23 (my translation).
9 Kullenberg and Palmås, 2009; Borch, 2005.

action), contingent (immanent to a spatio-temporal situation, to certain human and non-human agglomerations), and exposed to processes of standardisation through routinisation, hierarchisation and reification into rules.

1.2 Heterogeneity, not homogeneity, is at the heart of things ... things are not born alike, they become alike.[10]

A few years after Tarde's death, the Portuguese philosopher Leonardo Coimbra was developing a similar neo-monadological theory. His 'rythmontology', suspended between Georg Wilhelm Friedrich Hegel and Henri Bergson, assumes every being, or monad, as vibrating according to a given rhythm, oscillating between the slavery of the monotonous rhythm of sensation, and the potential of a superior synthetic activity, which would allow the overcoming material limits by releasing the 'rhythmical excesses' where free and creative activity lies. Although the concept of rhythmical excess is relevant, Coimbra's dialectical understanding of creation, invention and change remains within the boundaries of individualism, situating these processes firmly within the single monad, and its synthetic capacity to transcend its own limits. [11]

Tarde's approach seemingly avoids this impasse. His microsociology, by means of refusing notions of collective consciousness and pre-existent social laws in favour of the continuous co-interactions of sociality, offers a promising way beyond the individual/society binary.[12] An opposite problem however surfaces, when aligning the functioning of social interaction around suggestion and imitation. Namely, the implicit assumption of social beings as passive automatons, taken into processes of social contagion as some sort of hypnotised sleepwalker.[13] As Andrea Mubi Brighenti notes, moreover,

> The corollary of the idea of automatic obedience is the idea of an individual origin of the repeated elements ... What is repeated

10 Tarde, 1903: 71–2.

11 Coimbra, 1912.

12 Tarde's microsociology assumes the individual as a macro extension of micro-processes. It is thus different from Ervin Goffman's microsociology, which instead looks at inter-subjective relations between already-formed individuals, assuming a dichotomy between 'represented' and 'inner' self, and defusing society's conflict into a fluid and smooth interaction order. See Borch, 2005; Law, 2004: 56.

13 When assessing the use of these notions, we should also take into account the role played on Tarde's work by the contemporary surfacing in Europe of the turbulent, fascinating and frightening phenomenon of *urban crowds*, in a context in which rapid urbanisation was being matched by ever-increasing political demands. See, e.g. Borch, 2012; Brighenti, 2010c.

> through imitation, for Tarde, has an origin somewhere, and such origin is deemed to be individual and private.[14]

Seemingly unable to leave behind the heritage of positivist criminology and hypnotist psychology, Tarde would ultimately relapse on an 'implicit methodological individualism'. The individual has been fragmented in multiple 'little persons', yet in this 'neuro-horizontal' model of a 'society of minds' composed of a population of 'autonomous agents', the axiom of individual origin is left unchallenged, and merely shifted into a smaller dimension.[15] An a-spatial understanding seemingly predating the naïvety of the network-society theory in which, either praising or regretting the 'elimination' of space supposedly brought about by ITs, the ontological materiality of the social is unaccounted for. This problem often surfaces in recent strands of Tarde's revival, where the reliance on psychological automatism reproduces 'bodily closures' typical of individualistic models.[16]

In fact, there is a debate over who is responsible (Tarde or his 'followers') for reverting into individualism. Certainly the spatial blindness of recent mentalist interpretations did not help unfolding the ontological quality that notions such as 'imitation' and 'suggestion' assume in Tarde's thought.[17] This is a quality that Nigel Thrift and Christian Borch among others have recently emphasised, stressing the relevance of Tarde's theory play vis-à-vis a properly material exploration of urban processes.[18] In any case, the purpose here is not that of embarking on an in-depth exploration of the French sociologist but rather, whilst keeping these considerations into account, to trace his re-surfacing in one of the most interesting contemporary attempts to make sense of the social: Latour's Actor-Network Theory (ANT). By now the reader will be accustomed to this theory, dissected, endorsed, applied, criticised and dismissed countless times in the last decade. For this reason too there is no intention of presenting or analysing ANT yet another time, but rather to emphasise an aspect which I believe particularly relevant for the discussion to follow, namely, its relation with the key issue challenging Tarde's model: how to explain change, the surfacing of the new, without resorting to (pseudo) individualism.

14 Brighenti, 2010c: 301.
15 Bonta and Protevi, 2004: 6.
16 For a critique of this tendency in contemporary literature see Blackman, 2007.
17 Blackman, 2008: 46–7.
18 Thrift, 2007: 230; Borch, 2005.

1.3 Non si teme il proprio tempo, è un problema di spazio.[19]

According to Latour – who invested him as 'forefather of actor-network theory'[20] – ANT follows indirectly the footsteps of Tarde, seeking to account 'for how society is held together, instead of using society to explain something else', that is, without resorting to transcendental supra-structures or hidden social forces which would determine social action, as well as without relying on a subjective and anthropocentric understanding of the individual.[21] Stuck on a world of only-human actors, sociology has been myopic as regards the number of participants in the associations forming the social. Instead, especially in the case of critical sociology, Latour's favourite target, it has resorted to all sorts of hidden structures of power and exploitation as social explanations – structures which would guide the action of social members without them being aware, and that the social scientist would nevertheless be able to uncover by following the right method.[22] The resulting vision was that of a society made up of isolated subjects acting in a vacuum, a Newtonian world organised around frictionless laws (we are soon to see the crucial influence this assumption has played on legal thought). ANT's well-known way out of this impasse is a 'flat ontology', based on the principle of 'generalised symmetry' between human and non-human entities.[23] This does not intend to provide objects with agency, but rather to deny agency as much to humans as to non-humans, looking at the associations they form, and the way agency emerges as 'distributed' across these networks.

This flat ontology is able to avoid falling into the axiom of (whatever micro) 'individual origin' of the new, at the same time denying any status to a transcendent notion of 'society', and rather prioritising *relation* as the elementary social fact.[24] However, other sets of problems emerge. Whether any entity is reduced to its relation with other entities, can we still speak about 'entities' as such? Harman replies negatively, arguing that in this way an entity is 'exhausted' 'in its presence for another, with no intrinsic reality held cryptically in reserve'.[25] If the social is reduced to the relational with no excess 'held in reserve', Bryant therefore asks whether we are not left with a 'frozen universe without any change'.[26] Whilst undeniably useful when describing 'the steely accumulation' of social associations – namely the way social components get together crystallising in assemblages – is

19 CSI, 1996.
20 Latour, 2002.
21 Latour, 2005: 13.
22 Latour, 2005: 250.
23 Callon, 1986.
24 Barry and Thrift, 2007.
25 Harman, 2011: 12.
26 Bryant, 2011: 271.

Latour's networked ontology able to account for the 'lightening strikes' of change?[27] In fact, why is this so important?

The mission of Latour is to wage a radical attack on social sciences' project of Enlightenment, and its *will to know* society by reducing it to hidden laws to be uncovered and explained via the right method. A project as Foucault exhaustively explained, which informs the various (biological, sociological, economical, legal) *savoirs* shaping modern biopolitics.[28] If these are the stakes, it is clearly crucial to ask whether Latour's relationalism is fit for the task, or conversely runs the risk of becoming an unwitting ally of the biopolitical project itself.

ANT, Thrift argues, is informed by an 'attenuated notion of the event': insofar as assuming the event as the immediate and concrete moment of performance, ANT is unable to account for the overflowing potential that every event carries within, that is, the *eventfulness* of its taking place.[29] As a consequence, Marcus Doel diagnoses, this theory is unable 'to conceive of difference as such', that is, to think the *taking place* of difference itself, and thus to differentiate itself from the post-political play of 'equal differences' that capitalism is about.[30]Although I aim to deal extensively and clarify these points in the next pages, their relevance should be stated already: any approach grounded on the systematic reduction of beings to relations (i.e. relationalism), and thus the flattening of the social into a horizontal ontology, eventually defuses the social itself, neutralising its eventful potential. In other words, it removes the political from the social. How are we to overcome the ethico-political impasse of relationalism without falling back into either individualisms or deterministic structuralism? How could we conceive the spatiality of being-together beyond 'isolation', at the same time attending to a notion of non-relational, eventful excess, irreducible to the relation itself? Answering these questions will require briefly stepping back to where ANT's origins lie (Heidegger), and where they find their most 'spatially conscious' explanation (Sloterdijk).[31]

1.4 Our body is not primarily in space, it is of it.[32]

Notwithstanding he is mainly known as a temporal thinker, with Martin Heidegger the notion of space, or rather, 'spatiality', takes a fundamentally ontological relevance. Overcoming the understanding of space as

27 Thrift, 2007: 110.
28 Foucault, 1998.
29 Thrift, 2007: 110.
30 Doel, 1999: 46–7.
31 On Latour's debit to Heidegger see Harman, 2009. On ANT's relation with Sloterdijk's theory, see Latour, 2009a.
32 Merleau-Ponty, 1995: 131.

extension (René Descartes) and *a priori* background (Immanuel Kant), phenomenology turned the attention to the 'concrete' experience of the subject's involvement in space among things, thus seeking to bring the cogito down to earth, that is, to *throw* it into the contingency of lived experience. Edmund Husserl developed a quasi-performative understanding of space as a life-world emerging out of a subject's pre-theoretical interaction with the world. Likewise, the early Maurice Merleau-Ponty conceived a notion of pre-reflexive, incarnate consciousness expressing the subject's pre-representational experience of *Erlebnisse,* i.e. everyday life.[33] A key limit of phenomenology, however, was its reduction of space to an epistemological question (the manifestation of phenomena to a subject), which meant leaving unquestioned the subject/object separation and thus the ontological unity of the subject itself. By simply shifting from a-spatial, transcendental consciousness to the spatially embedded, everyday experience, Husserl still maintained a *factual* understanding of contingency: the subject was 'brought back onto space', but still kept ontologically separated from it, while *experience* became an all-encompassing substance swallowing up space as such.

To go beyond the impasse of Husserl's 'factuality', Heidegger introduces the concept of *facticity,* a veritable turning point for Western thinking towards a properly spatial ontology. Facticity means that there is no transcendental being isolated from space: every being is always-already a being-in-the-world. The original condition of being is a dislocating *being-thrown* onto the world, a being-there (*Da-sein*). Differently from earlier phenomenology however, for Heidegger this does 'not mean simply being contingently in a certain way and a certain situation'.[34] In Merleau-Ponty's words, 'our body is not primarily in space, it is of it'.[35]

> Da-sein 'is-in' the world in the quite specific sense of being-together-with the world or taking care of it ... the spatiality of Da-sein is therefore existential presence, not mere 'insideness' ... space cannot be an absolute, fixed structure that is the same for everyone – like for example Descartes' res extensa or Kant's a priori space. Rather, space is best understood as spatiality (Räumlichkeit),[36]

The quality of Da-sein is that of blurring any distinction 'between life and its actual situation. Being and its ways of Being', subject and object, thus folding essence into (co)existence.[37] Hence the late Merleau-Ponty's obser-

33 For an insightful account of the relation between Merleau-Ponty and Husserl see Schmidt, 1985.

34 Agamben, 1998a: 150.

35 Merleau-Ponty, 1995[1945]: 131.

36 Stramignoni, 2004: 189, 190.

37 Agamben, 1998a: 87.

vation: '[Husserl] has persuaded us that we are flux of individual Erlebnisse, whereas we are a field of Being'.[38] Isolation is a mere illusion, as beings are inescapably entrapped into the relational immediacy of the being-in-the-world. Yet, differently from phenomenology, Heidegger's approach cannot be easily fit within the category of relationalism.

1.5 To inhabit always means to build spheres.[39]

As Da-sein, the human being goes 'out of himself, out of the merely factual and biological character of its condition'.[40] Da-sein is according an *'e-motion'*:

> [B]eing in the world ... is a precious formula for saying that the fact of being in a movement of extraversion towards things always precedes our reflection.[41]

This being-outside-oneself (*ek-stasis*) as an original dislocation, or dispersion (*ursprungliche streuung*), is the ontological condition of being and the key of its constitutive *räumlichkeit*. Surely an ontology of space – contra his appreciations as mere temporal thinker – Heidegger's is also, quintessentially an ontology of movement: spacing.

In his *magnum opus*, Sloterdijk seeks to make explicit such 'spacing' by posing a seemingly trivial question: where is the Da-sein when it is thrown into the world? Sloterdijk's answer evocatively makes explicit the materiality of Da-sein's ek-static movement through a terminological invention: the Da-sein is in a sphere, or rather, its being-in-the-world is better understood as *being-in-a-sphere*, since space-creating beings is what we are. Being-in-a-sphere means diving in a 'medial mode of being [that] implies that the surrounding medium loses its object status'.[42] According to Sloterdijk, during the evolution of his thought Heidegger gradually 'misunderstood the act of diving as resolution to take over the fate of being', abandoning the promising analysis of the *where* of existence, to embark instead on the investigation of the *who*, with infamous consequences.[43] Sloterdijk wants to obviate for this deviation by developing further these spatial intuitions. Since we are always out-of-joint, always going-outside-oneself as well as always inside-a-situation, the very condition of being is that of 'inhabiting the dislocation'. Yet, and this is the crucial question of Sloterdijk's project:

38 Merleau-Ponty, 1968: 240, quoted in Schmidt, 1985: 56.
39 Sloterdijk, 2009: 82 (my translation).
40 Berardi, 2010: 81 (my translation).
41 Sloterdijk, 2005: 231.
42 Ten Bos, 2009: 77–8.
43 Quoted in Ten Bos, 2009: 77. See also Sloterdijk, 2009: 330.

how do we inhabit this dislocation or, how do we inhabit the outside?[44] I do not think, as Latour rather too abruptly states, that the significance of Sloterdijk's project lies in spatialising an otherwise a-spatial Da-sein.[45] Heidegger was not blind to space as it is sometimes suggested, and Sloterdijk in this regard simply provides an interesting spatial vocabulary useful to unfold these implicit premises.[46] In fact, the relevance of his *spherology* rather rests on having made explicit that being-in-the-world, as inhabiting-the-world, always entails a *praxis of world-making*: 'to inhabit always means to build spheres' and this occurs in the always co-constitutive coming together of humans and non-humans.[47]

Sloterdijk employs the metaphor of foam so as to convey the peculiar quality of being-together in the contradictory dynamic engendered by the tension between the necessity to 'produce and occupy a – to take – place', and the impossibility for two bodies to occupy the same place.[48] Bodies are always in *ek-static* movement, co-producing a space, spacing through their involvement with other (human and non-human) bodies. A bus, an assembly, a residential building, a city: foam is a way to account for sociality beyond the atomism of contractualist models and the homogeneity of holistic ones: not a contract, but rather a co-traction, a concatenation of heterogeneous elements 'held together' immanently, by the sum of their singular, mutual tensions. Like Buckminster Fuller's tensegrity structures, 'foam sociality' is only accountable for through-immanent, co-constitutive imbrications of semio-material relations.[49]

By merging Heidegger's spatial intuition with Tarde's multi-cellular sociality Sloterdijk produces a spatial ontology which comes very close to Latour's project, providing an extremely useful methodological approach to study urban agglomerations. Moreover, by accounting for the oscillation between the movement of being-together and the necessity of co-existence and thus co-immunity, Sloterdijk makes explicit the implicit spatiality of Latour's somewhat 'anemic' networks.[50] Finally, his approach overcomes also another limitation of ANT, namely the tendency, through the prioritisation of networks and multi-scalar prolongations, to overlook the phenomenological consistency of the here-and-now. If Brighenti stresses the need to complement ANT's 'ecological sensibility to the prolongation of the here-and-now' into concatenations of ontologically heterogeneous

44 Accarino, 2009: 25.

45 E.g. Latour, 2009a.

46 On Heidegger and space see for instance Schatzky, 2007; Malpas, 2006.

47 Sloterdijk, 2009: 82 (my translation).

48 See Philippopoulos-Mihalopoulos, 2011a: 199.

49 Accarino, 2009: 49. See also Serres, 1990. Tensegrity structures (tension integrity structures) are buildings without bearing walls, made stable by the co-traction between their internal tensions.

50 Latour, 2009a: 139.

elements, with a 'phenomenological sensibility to the here-and-now', in the direction of an 'ecological phenomenology' – then Sloterdijk's spherology appears particularly relevant in this sense.[51]

Sloterdijk's foams however, just like Latour's networks, imply a picture of the social in which entities are 'relata ... [with] no independent existence outside of the relation'.[52] Also in this model the impasse of relationalism seems to be reproduced. How could we gesture towards a notion of event as the excess that overflows both the 'phenomenological here-and-now' as well as its 'ecological prolongations' into other locales? It is by coming back to Heidegger that we may begin sketching a potential answer.

1.6 Even a single note can swing.[53]

The notion of being-in-the-world seemingly posits relation as its ontological foundation. With the concept of Da-sein the subject/object distinction is dissolved into the original, situational relationality of the being-there: accordingly, beings are 'bundles' of situated relations, pure *relata*. This is not all, however.

Especially in the *Beitrage zur Philosophie*, whose spatial relevance has already been emphasised,[54] Heidegger progresses from establishing the notion of the thrownness of Da-sein, to actually investigating the modality of that original being-thrown, its *event*.[55] The hyphenation plays a key role here: Da-sein is not to be reduced to a given state of affairs – a merely relational being-there – but is to be understood as the ontological 'event' of being-the-Da, being-*the*-there, a singular, eventful taking-place: the 'Da-sein is never objectively present in space, not even initially', it rather *takes place*.[56] Each being is the centre of a radical oscillation 'between' Being and Da-sein.[57] Or, Being is better understood as a becoming-Da-sein, neither static nor dynamic, neither isolated nor relational but paradoxically beyond these dichotomies: a swerving taking place, an eventful event.[58]

51 See Brighenti, 2010a: 37, 70.
52 Morin, 2009: 61.
53 Count Basie, jazz pianist, quoted in *Jazz*, 2001.
54 Elden, 2005.
55 Berardi, 2010: 15.
56 Stramignoni, 2004: 202. 'Dasein is its opening', Heidegger, 2008[1927]: para. 28.
57 Provided, of course, that we neither understand it as a static position 'between' two separated poles (Being and Da-sein) nor as a coincidence, but rather as a 'fold': there is no separation between Being and Da-sein, they are rather folded together in an inextinguishable tension: 'this difference is not "between" in the ordinary sense of the word. It is the Fold, *Zwietfalt*' (Deleuze, 2004[1968]: 78). See however Severino, 1980.
58 Berardi stresses the relevance of the notion of event in the late Heidegger, by noting that the caption of the *Beitrage Zur Philosophie*, that is, *Vom Ereignis*, usually translated as 'on the event', should be instead translated as 'from the event', so that to emphasise the event as the key locus of thought itself. Berardi, 2010: 6.

This nuance encapsulates an exceeding potential vis-à-vis networks and foams, postulating a being-together which is never merely relational, populated and constituted by beings that are taken into concatenations as well as never exhausted by them. The becoming-Da-sein in fact is not a linear, processual passage from a possibility to a reality – one in which the possible would be fully realised (and thus extinguished) into the reality of relations. It is rather a nonlinear swerving, a 'swinging' [*kehrig*] event or, more precisely, an *eventing* that is not exhausted by the relationality of its actual being-in-the-world.

2.1 Thinking is neither a line drawn between subject and object nor a revolving of one around the other. Rather, thinking takes place in the relationship of territory and earth.[59]

In Heidegger there is always a 'movement of being' which lies 'deeper', an ontological dispersion which the relationality of Da-sein cannot exhaust it in any way.[60] On the escort of this non-relational intuition Harman has developed an ontological approach, heretically joining Heidegger and Latour into his own brand of *Object-Oriented Ontology* (OOO). Harman accepts the key insights of Latour's philosophy, whilst striving to avoid falling into its problematic relationalism. Following ANT's crucial de-prioritisation of the human-world relation in favour of a post-human relationalism, he pushes this perspective further by seeking to account for beings regardless of 'our access to them', denying, *contra* ANT, that relations can fully define and exhaust them.

This attempt requires being contextualised within the more general surfacing, in the last decade, of the philosophical project of *Speculative Realism* (SR), kick-started by the publication of Meillassoux's *After Finitude.* It is a somewhat incomplete and almost programmatic text which traces a precise mission for philosophical thought: the breaking open of *correlation.* The Kantian revolution, Meillassoux explains, overcomes the Cartesian dichotomy between the thinking subject (*res cogitans*) and extended object (*res extensa*). This results in the crucial shift from the notion of substance to that of correlation as the central category of thought:

> by 'correlation' we mean the idea according to which we only have access to the correlation between thinking and being, and never to either term considered apart from the other.[61]

59 Deleuze and Guattari, 1994: 85.
60 Harman, 2009: 141–2.
61 Meillassoux, 2009: 5–6.

Whereas Kant would foreclose access to reality (*noumenon*), Hegel would absolutise this foreclosure by preventing not only the knowledge, but also the possibility to think of a noumenal outside. Heidegger and Derrida would further erase this possibility through ontological and linguistic means. For all its simplifications (and as we just saw for what concerns Heidegger, for instance, the matter is rather more complex), the intuition of this narrative is a powerful one: the various ground-breaking philosophies of the last century, in the end, betray a congenital incapacity to actually break any ground. Thus Claire Colebrook lists the *experience* of phenomenology, the *Da-sein* of Heidegger, the *pre-conscious* and *non-representational* involvement in the worlds of neuro-cognitive studies, the *networks* of ANT, the *life* of vitalism, all the way to the *feeling* and *affection* of contemporary posthumanism. All these approaches differently betray the same all-too-human weakness, namely, the need to posit 'some ground from which all relations emerge' and thus, ultimately, to reduce the world to a world *for us*.[62] Hence the paradoxically 'ultra-humanist' nature which, she argues, is

> masked by what passes in theory today for many modes of posthumanism: we no longer believe in the exceptional distinction of privileged white 'man', for *everything that lives* is an agent – subjected to the one norm of unity, community, communication, reciprocity and ecology: deep down we are all human.[63]

Determined to overcome this tendency, the project of SR intends to reinsert 'a concern with the Absolute' and 'a renewed attention to reality itself' against their anti-realist positions.[64] The Speculative Turn gathers various and different authors that, following (as well as often harshly criticising) the lines of flight opened by Deleuze and Guattari, Latour, Alain Badiou and others, are joined by the common attempt to break open the human-world correlation, so as to reorient thought towards a world assumed as utterly independent from human existence, cognition, imagination: a world *not for us*, that is. Here there is no room to even attempt to delineate the at times very different (and very much in-progress) trajectories of thinking currently traced by the likes of Reza Negarestani, Ray Brassier, Meillassoux, Ian Hamilton Grant, Bryant, Harman, and so on.

Instead, in this section I will focus on the latter. This is not for his particular merits vis-à-vis his fellow speculative realists, but rather for the strategic relevance his thought plays vis-à-vis the argument I am developing. Harman's theoretical architecture, informed by the post-human insights of

62 Colebrook, 2014b: 25.
63 Colebrook, 2014b: 33–4.
64 Bryant *et al.*, 2011.

ANT, and at the same time seeking to overcome the latter's suffocating relationalism via Heidegger, appears in fact rather consistent with the trajectory this book has been building so far. Analysing the core limits of this attempt, therefore, will allow me to position and clarify more precisely my approach.[65]

2.2 Poetic words do not originally belong to men nor are they created by them.[66]

Both Harman and Latour assume that every human and non-human, tangible and intangible being is equally material, in the sense that 'everything exists differently, but everything equally exists'. In Deleuze's terms, 'a body can be anything: it can be an animal, a body of sounds, a mind or idea; it can be a linguistic corpus, a social body, a collectivity'.[67] When we assume that the beings (bodies, objects) constituting reality are equally 'material', we should pursue this affirmation in its deeply ontological sense, beyond any trivial dichotomy between word and world, text and context, thought and matter, representation and reality, abstraction and concreteness. From classical materialism to postmodernism, the difference between a given, concrete, hard 'matter-stuff' and an immaterial, abstract or textual flow of representations and narrative has been mostly left unchallenged.[68] The hard-core materialist pragmatically suggests looking at the 'concrete' reality so as to uncover its laws through the appropriate scientific method, and the sceptical post-modernist who frowns upon this suggestion by affirming the infinite hermeneutical dissemination of interpretations which such an enterprise would produce, secretly agree: they both oppose the concrete materiality of the 'hard stuff' *out there*, to the immaterial abstraction of thinking and the impalpability of representations. Their disagreement is epistemological rather than ontological. Instead, the 'orientation' towards objects of OOO is an attempt, in the vein of the Latourian enterprise, to produce a properly ontological move, namely flattening the material/immaterial division into a horizontal ontology.

65 To be sure, the question of whether OOO's somewhat simplistic dismissal of correlation ultimately entraps its thinkers into a tangle of problematic contradictions is not crucial here. What I find more interesting is the 'orientation' its very name suggests. As Brighenti argues, the act of positing the fundamental philosophical question (*ti esti*, 'what it is'), avoiding at the same time modern certitude and postmodern renunciation, is already significant in itself (Brighenti, 2009: 301). The answers provided are obviously important and always susceptible to critique. Yet, what particularly counts here is the attitude which the question produces in those who are willing to really formulate it, and thus to follow its consequences. For a sagacious critique of OOO, see Wolfendale, 2014.

66 Agamben, 2006[1982]: 78 (indirectly quoting Plato).

67 Deleuze, 1988: 127.

68 Latour, 2007.

As already discussed, however, how could we think of the possibility of a genuine change, excess or event when everything is reduced and exhausted into relations? If beings are fully defined by their relations, are we not implying the possibility, by tracing these relations, to ultimately being able to define, produce and manipulate any entity? Politically, as we are to see, this relational closure is consistent with the ontology of contemporary capitalism, whose kernel is exactly the reduction of everything into both a measurable value and a traceable relation. Against this outcome, Harman contends that 'an object might be measured or registered by its relations, but can never be fully defined by them'.[69] The ethico-political consequences of this reasoning are vast. Yet, is his proposal satisfying?

To put it simply: Harman contends that an object is at the same time real and sensual, autonomous and relational.[70] Through a thought-experiment, he seeks to explain what such a non-relational autonomy means. Let us take three entities: a 'private' and intangible human product, such as an object of my imagination only known to me – Harman imagines a 'monster X', (MX); a 'public' human product, such as a well-known philosophical movement (e.g. the SR movement); a human-independent object, such as his cats. Harman states: 'if I fall tonight into a dreamless sleep, the monster will cease to exist. Monster X is entirely dependent on my thinking of it. The same is by no means true of the cats'.[71] The cats have both a real (non-relational) and sensuous (relational) existence, whilst the MX has not, existing only insofar as in relation to my mind.[72] The case of SR is different: though being a human-produced object, it can become a '*real* object independent of its creators and consumers', in other words, autonomous. The discriminant is the following: 'real objects exist "whether we like it or not", but intentional [i.e. sensual] objects can be vaporized by a simple act of shifting our mind elsewhere.'[73] An important presupposition is implied: the purely individual and private origin of thoughts, as well as the capacity, for the thinking subject, to wilfully possess, control and 'vaporise' them all, at will. A proprietary assumption, therefore, seems to guide this reasoning: the lack of possession and control over an object (e.g. SR) appears to sanction its status as autonomous, non-relational, and thus fully 'real'.

In fact, it only takes a shift of scale to make this equation explode. If MX is 'dependent' on its correlation with me who 'thinks' it, is not at the same time SR dependent on the correlation with, say, mankind? According to

69 Harman, 2009: 143.

70 Harman, 2011.

71 Harman, 2009: 190.

72 Cats have both a real and a sensuous existence as objects with respect to his mind, differently from the monster, they 'will remain autonomous forces unleashed in my apartment despite my lack of awareness of their activities' (Harman, 2009: 190).

73 Harman, 2009: 195.

the reasoning above, my death would make MX vaporise just as human extinction would make SR disappear. In fact, whatever their differences vis-à-vis longevity, number and variety of bodies they can affect, MX and SR must be understood as ontologically equal, equally material. If we really are to embrace a radical understanding of materiality, we need to avoid re-introducing subterranean dichotomisations. This is the case since Harman postulates not simply the fact that a 'being must be free of all relations', but the possibility of this being *actually* so. Let me explain. As I elaborate below, bodies are never fully exhausted into relations in the sense of harbouring a non-relational 'virtual impotentiality' whereby they are able to persevere in what they are exactly insofar as ultimately irreducible to the relations of which, unavoidably, they are part. According to Harman, this 'non-relational' quality must be 'fully actual'. Describing metaphorically this purely non-relational status as 'a state of perfect sleep, in which an entity would be real without entering further relations at all', he thus relates such a 'dormant object' to a drop of water, which in the depth of the ocean is 'perfectly real without ever being discovered, caressed or capitalised'.[74] Evidently, this position is only tenable, ironically, from the very anthropocentric perspective Harman seeks to displace: the dormancy of a drop of water here is postulated *qua* human-independent, yet it remains a mystery how a drop of water can 'actually exist' without ever being 'discovered or caressed' by other drops of water, for instance. Likewise, how could a cat survive without its relation to, at the very least, the air it breathes, the soil on which it stands?

Virtually non-relational, bodies are always *actually* involved in relations. To contend otherwise would be to suggest that both the cat and the drop of water are like those individuals of liberal tradition, understood as actually abstracted from space into the realm of rational deliberation. Moving from an attempt to de-prioritise the 'correlation to humans', we are ultimately served with a perspective that seemingly prioritises the 'independence from humans'. In his anxiety to preserve the 'autonomous reality' of the object against its dissolution into relations, Harman infers an untenable analogy between 'actuality' and 'reality', ultimately abstracting objects from their own spatiality. Against the contradictory outcome into which he falls, the material ontology I propose entails the acceptance of the materiality of every being, both humanly produced and human-independent: between MX, SR and cats, or whatever human-independent object, there is no ontological difference: they are all material, all dependent on (very different) sets of (either human or non-human, tangible or intangible) relations for their existence, though never fully definable and exhausted by them. Even more radically, this entails accepting that not only rocks or cats, but even our more private

74 Harman, 2009: 123.

thoughts are never fully 'ours', i.e. never fully *for us*. Thus two questions appear to be at stake with the attempt to challenge the human-world correlation: *first, that of dismantling the proprietary and immunitary logic of possession that underlines it; second, that of opening it up to the inhuman contingency of its 'event'.*

Instead, in his immunological attempt to guarantee the self-sufficiency and concreteness of objects, Harman's 'actualism' projects a frozen ontology made of only-actual beings which is as unable to account for change as Latour's relationalism.[75] Even more problematically, the uneventful 'closure' that Harman's ontology of 'being without event' produces ultimately implies a conservative acceptance of the status quo: in David Berry's words, this is

> not so much philosophy as *philosography*, where rather than *understanding* the world, there is an attempt to *describe* it, and a worrying tendency towards the administration of things through a cataloguing operation.[76]

How can one simultaneously exceed both the perils of relationalism and actualism? An answer to this question requires Deleuze's concept of the virtual, key to pursue the seemingly paradoxical task of thinking simultaneously beyond relation as well as separation, towards the conception of a *non-relational* side of beings, not actual, and yet fully material, concrete and real.

2.3 A life is never fully actualised, but endures a real virtuality, as a real multiplicity.[77]

Through the notion of 'virtual' we are able to ride the line of flight opened by Heidegger's swerving all the way onto Deleuze's concept of event. Although I believe that there is more in common between the two authors than the French philosopher would like to admit, here I do not aim to produce posthumous philosophical friendships. Instead, I wish to join their insights into a conceptual assemblage whereby delineating the ontology I have in mind.

The virtual could be (partially) defined as the field of the possible ways-of-being of a given 'body', a multiplicity expressing the potential modes of *a* being, 'the structure of a space of possibilities ... the space of all the possible states that a given system can have'.[78] Deleuze, through the philosophy

75 See Bryant, 2011: 122.
76 Berry, 2012.
77 Deleuze, 2004[1968]: 165.
78 DeLanda, 2005: 83–4.

of Bergson and the mathematics of Bernhard Riemann, distinguishes between discrete and continuous multiplicities: whilst the former can be counted, since numerical and quantitative, the latter are non-numerical, qualitative, continuous and heterogeneous.[79] When discussing the 'virtual multiplicity' then, we are not referring to a numerical multiplicity, according to which the virtual would simply indicate a set of already-given, possible states already possessed within by an actual body. This misunderstanding, which freezes space into actual relations, results from a typical confusion between the concept of 'virtual' and that of 'possible', is a major mistake indeed, since it is exactly in order to challenge the classical dichotomous opposition between 'possible' and 'real' that the concept of virtual was created in the first place. Differently from the possible, which is by definition not real, the virtual *is* real, although non-actual. It is real since it has real effects on the actual. In this sense it is *material*: though being non-actual, and it continuously 'haunts the actual'.[80] This does not mean that actual and virtual are separated, or that a pacific symmetry can be postulated among them: they affect each other, in a nonlinear, swerving asymmetry, between the real potentialities of the virtual and their relational actualisation. Actual and virtual are 'the two sides of the Real', only formally but not ontologically distinct: neither dualism, nor univocity, but rather a *double-structure*.[81] Thus Parmenides' archetypal split is revoked:

> Being is univocal ... A single voice raises the clamour of being ... There are not two 'paths', as Parmenides' poem suggests, but a single 'voice' of Being which include all its modes.[82]

Let us qualify this does not imply a static separation between a 'univocal', virtual Being, and the actual, relational 'modes' in which it unfolds. In fact, if we understand actual and virtual as two separated 'realms', then the consequences are two equally untenable solutions: a frozen actuality without virtuality (as either in the relationalism of ANT or in the actual dormancy of Harman), or an ascetic, immaterial escape into a pure (virtual) chaos in which no actuality takes hold. The latter, according to some, would be exactly the deadlock that Deleuze's philosophy of the virtual leads to. Badiou accordingly argues that Deleuze assumes the virtual as an all-encompassing and undifferentiated 'bare substratum' out of which actual

79 See Deleuze, 1991a: 38–42.

80 Gordon, quoted in Thrift, 2007: 110.

81 'The reality of the virtual consists of the differential elements and relations along with the singular points which correspond to them. The reality of the virtual is structure. We must avoid giving the elements and relations that form a structure an actuality which they do not have, and withdrawing from them a reality which they have' (Deleuze, 2004: 209).

82 Deleuze, 2004[1968]: 35.

entities would emanate – a sort of Plotinian God.[83] Were this the case, actual beings would be no more than 'sterile abstractions from a deeper movement of flux or becoming', as such lacking a proper ontological status.[84] Troubling consequences would follow, the critique goes, in both philosophical and political terms.

In the final chapter I will deal extensively with this critique, emphasising its value vis-à-vis certain strands of contemporary post-structural thought, as well as its limits vis-à-vis the eccentric philosophical trajectory drawn by Deleuze. At this stage, however, it is important to rescue the notion of the virtual from a major misunderstanding: namely, its confusion with an 'undifferentiated substratum', or 'bare origin' of all entities. To do so, we need to open a brief parenthesis on the notion of *undifferentiated* itself.

2.4

> What shows itself on the threshold between Being and non-Being, between sensible and intelligible, between word and thing, is not the colourless abyss of the Nothing but the luminous spiral of the possible.[85]

From the 'crude chaotic aggregate' which troubled Kant to the 'brutish' state of nature which obsessed Thomas Hobbes, the presupposition of a terrifying 'undifferentiated' that would lie beneath a given (philosophical, political, linguistic, legal) system – thus *a posteriori* justifying its instantiation – has been a recurrent trope of Western thinking. This has been so, at least since the fault line generated by Parmenides. Emanuele Severino, who devoted his work to explore the consequences of this ancient fracture, defines as nullifying Parmenides' conception of Being as one, simple, immutable and eternal. Inserting a separation between Being and what Being is not – i.e. non-Being – the philosopher of Elea *de facto* presupposed the unspeakable evidence of nothingness, thus founding nihilism, i.e. the belief that what things come from – and go towards – is no-thing, a nihilistic becoming. This separation, Severino argues, would ultimately 'consign' beings to nothingness, that is, to a movement of be-coming *ex* and *ad nihilo*.[86]

83 Badiou, 1999.
84 Harman, 2011: 57.
85 Agamben, 1993: 250.
86 For an extensive analysis on this point see Severino, 1972. The legacy of such a separation on the philosophy to come is uncontestable. Plato who, reformulating this fracture by substituting the notion of 'non-Being' with that of 'other-than-Being', posited the relation of beings to Being as 'successive' and 'accidental' to the original fact of the 'isolation' of Being, that is, to the original separation between Being and nothing (Severino, 2009: 197–209). Even Spinoza, the philosopher of immanence par excellence, assumed the modes (beings) as depending unilaterally on the God-Substance (Being). The latter, since eternal, is ultimately posited as independent (and

The presupposition of the nihilistic becoming of beings, implies that their 'coming into existence' depends on a creation *ex nihilo*, a productive operation: a praxis. Greek thought posited a clear distinction between *poiesis* (i.e. production, creation) and *praxis* (i.e. action). As Thanos Zartaloudis observes, *poiesis* 'has nothing to do with a practical calling or a voluntary process [but rather with] the essential character of a status in presence'. Following Agamben, Zartaloudis adds that 'the Romans understood poiesis, instead, as a mode of agere, that is "an acting that puts-to-work, an operari"'. In this interpretation, *poiesis* has progressively become indistinguishable with *praxis*, that is with a conception of action directly related to an actual effect, and 'whose truth is appreciated with respect to the will that is expressed in it'. In other words, once consequentially resolved into a pre-existent intentionality, tied to a measurable result, and reduced to the realm of 'act and actuality', the 'poietic potentiality of praxis' is thus erased, an outcome already encapsulated in the Parmenidean split.[87]

It is in these terms that Western thinking has understood beings as produced by God, History, Nature, Fate, Life ... The presupposition of an original nothingness grounded the faith in the self-production of the human being through *techné*: 'the *humanitas* of the human being – Severino explains – resides in his being shaped through an art, that is, a technique able to produce a form'.[88] Thus in the book of Genesis 'man' is created by God from clay, by performing the most ancient technical operation, pottery: the archetypal reduction of (human) beings into praxis.[89] Hence the tendency in philosophy, sociology, psychology, anthropology, to assume human beings as 'creatures of lack', *homines pauperes,* constitutively and ontologically 'poor', as such condemned to 'fill' such a negativity by *producing* a 'culture'.[90] 'The subject of modernity' Colebrook writes 'suffers from this internalized, abstract, deferred and negative terror of structural negation'.[91] Heidegger's notion of 'throwness' (*geworfenheit*) is no exception. Insofar as 'thrown' into the abyss of contingency, the Da-sein is structured as an ontological poverty or, as Latour ironically put it, an original 'nakedness'.[92] There is an obvious etymological *fil rouge* connecting

thus separated) from its modes, since it will survive their becoming no-thing (Deleuze 2004[1968]: 35–6). In either cases, as in countless others in the history of philosophy, by being postulated as emanating from either nothingness, or an undifferentiated substance on which such negativity is only partially tamed, beings are deprived of their ontological status: they are made disposable, that is.

87 Zartaloudis, 2011: 147. Internal quotes from Agamben, 1999b: 69.

88 Severino, 1980: 134 (my translation).

89 *Adamah* is the Biblical Hebrew word for ground or earth (Sloterdijk, 2011).

90 Sloterdijk, 2006: 619–30.

91 Colebrook, 2009: 19–20.

92 Latour, 2009a: 140.

the terms *iactus* (thrown), *sub-iectus* (subject, literally 'thrown below') and *pro-iectus* (project, literally 'thrown forwards'). Human freedom would be implicitly understood as the freedom to 'give a positive sense to Nothingness', with troubling consequences for the philosophy to come.[93]

Let me qualify that there is no intention here to rehash yet another time a romantic, pseudo-Heideggerian critique of technology *per se.* Instrumentalism is too often prejudiced against, in the name of the special meaningfulness we would enjoy as human subjects and that would position us above instrumentality and purposes. What is problematic in this recurrent paradigm is not the trope of *techné*, but rather the implicit separation underlining it. That is, the projection of an undifferentiated substance implicitly de-coupled from politics, power, ethics: an innocent, neutral and thus manageable matter to be manipulated through the right technique. Of course, nowhere does the problem with this understanding become more evident, than when to be posited as such is life itself: that is, an a-political, bare life assumed as a ground to be manipulated and managed by human operations.[94]

It is in these terms that Benjamin Noys criticises Latour's convoluted notion of *plasma.* Latour refers to it as 'that which is not yet formatted, not yet measured, not yet socialized, not yet engaged in metrological chains and not yet covered, surveyed, mobilized or subjectified'.[95] The plasma is an undifferentiated, unformatted, 'shapeless whatever' out of which relations would mysteriously emerge. Whilst Latour intends to exclude 'negativity' in the name of a positive, vitalistic, affirmative ontology, the plasma would surreptitiously reintroduce negativity itself, Noys argues, confining it 'in a safe and ideological space', and thus leaving it 'unquestioned and unintegrated'.[96]

Again we find the core limit of relationalism, the implicit presupposition of an undifferentiated, ultimately innocent 'ground from which all relations emerge'. By seeking to immunise itself from the negativity of separation (and its 'nihilistic becoming'), relationalism ultimately reaffirms it: the linear, dichotomous logic of separation is not overcome, but more strongly and subterraneously reiterated by the flattening of its two poles into an immanent and impenetrable circularity, which merely translates the immunitary paradigm from the 'subject-object' distinction to the subject-object (or indeed object-object) relation. According to Noys,

93 Esposito mentions Günther Anders, according to whom 'exactly because he does not have *a* world, the man can be open to *the* world – is free to produce it according to his preferences'. It is the 'original lack' to ground the human possibility to 'shape the world at its own image' (Esposito, 2002: 109–10) (my translation).

94 Agamben, 1998a.

95 Latour, 2005: 244.

96 Noys, 2012: 92.

the problem lies exactly in the incapacity to fully 'traverse' and 'deal with', rather than attempt to 'evacuate', the notion of negativity. Conversely, I argue that the limit of relationalism does not lie in its willingness to eliminate negativity, but rather in the very failure of doing so or, more precisely, the failure to eliminate its unconfessed presupposition.

There is another path, one which simultaneously avoids the nihilistic presupposing of negativity, without falling yet again into an undifferentiated ground, and rather opening up to the non-relational, non-negative virtuality of the event. This is, I believe, the trajectory indicated by Deleuze, provided it is freed from the misunderstandings and plasmatic infiltrations that would otherwise neutralise its strategic potential.[97] This is what the rest of this chapter does.

3.1 Demonic is in every being, the possibility not to be.[98]

How can we unfold this notion of a 'being' shared by all entities without crystallising it into a plasmatic, Plotinian substratum out of which those entities would emanate (and that consequently would deny them any ontological status)? First, we need to explain how such a 'Being' could be defined as an inorganic 'life' in which and through which beings endure, a life which is not an all-encompassing whole, but rather a non-relational (im)potentiality that is 'structural' to every being. Second, we have to account for the ontological singularity of these simultaneously relational and non-relational beings.

The first step requires qualifying how the notion of virtual may be understood as a potentiality emancipated from the insipid status of a *possibility*, and at the same time not confounded with mere actuality. I believe aid in this sense can come from a reflection which traverses all of Agamben's work, stemming from his analysis of the famous Aristotelian distinction between *dynamis* (potentiality) and *energeia* (act), whereby the Philosopher sought to contest the thesis according to which potentiality only exists in the act, i.e. when actualised.[99] Instead, Aristotle contends that a potentiality exists, i.e. it is real, independently of its actualisation. In this sense, potentiality is essentially defined as the possibility of non-exercising the

97 In an instance Latour employs the term 'virtual' to refer to plasma, although in a rather cursory and superficial manner, and without quoting Deleuze (Latour and Hermant, 1998: 3, 63, 103). Harman follows this lead to subject Deleuze's 'virtual' and Latour's 'plasma' to essentially the same critique (Harman, 2011: 101, 129, 160). This alone is sufficient to dismiss his critique as simplistic at best, biased at worst.

98 Agamben, 2001a: 32.

99 A thesis which would imply the non-existence of potentialities as such: 'For if potentiality were always only the potential to do or to be something, we would never experience it as such; it would exist only in the actuality in which it is realised, as the Megarians maintained' (Agamben, 1993: 250) (my translation).

potentiality itself, just like the piano player has the potentiality of playing the piano insofar as she is able *not to* play the piano. Potentiality is the *form* of a non-actualised presence, an *impotentiality*. The radicalism of this theory should not be underestimated: to understand potentiality as a precise quality, already-determined by the act, is to reduce it to something amenable to control by the will (as in Harman's above example), a mere instrument or neutral form to be shaped through technique.

Instead, this notion seems to de-activate the proprietary mechanism of the I-subject, grounded as it is on the *possession* and *control* of one's will and faculties. Impotentiality sanctions the existence of a potentiality which is not *exhausted* by its actualisation:

> Contrary to the traditional idea of potentiality that is annulled in actuality, here we are confronted with a potentiality that conserves itself and saves itself in actuality. Here potentiality, so to speak, survives actuality and, in this way, *gives itself to itself*.[100]

In the terms employed so far, impotentiality appears exactly as what, in every being, is the potentiality not to be reduced to relations, to swerve away from any operation. According to Bryant, each object has 'demonic' or 'volcanic' powers in excess of any relation or local manifestation.[101] To him, this means that objects have 'the capacity to *operate*, even though they weren't operat*ing*. They [retain] the *power* of life, just not the local manifestation of life'.[102] Accordingly, the 'demonic' powers of objects are understood as 'capacities to' which an object possesses. This understanding, I believe, still maintains a relation of possession in place. More promising to think the non-relational side of the virtual seems to me Agamben's notion of impotentiality, which gestures towards a concept of 'inoperose' and non-proprietary potentiality, which as such cannot be possessed and operated but only, and necessarily commonly, *used*.

100 Agamben, 2012: 294

101 Bryant, another major promoter of OOO, integrates Harman's theory with the notion of virtual, assuming that 'all entities are absolutely concrete, but have virtual and actual dimensions' (Bryant, 2011: 122). Although I am sympathetic with Bryant's position, I disagree with his critique to the notion of the virtual according to which, he notes, the 'individual would be an effect of the virtual, not primary being itself' (Bryant, 2011: 96). There is a misunderstanding here. As Anton Schutz observes, referring to Duns Scotus: 'Individuals are not forms; it is incorrect to imagine them as formed or consolidated singular essences; if individuals doubtlessly shelter singular essences, if the singular essence of "Elena" is only found on the individual Elena, to limit individuation to the individual is, for Duns, a metaphysical blunder, an illegitimate inference from the notion of numerical oneness. The individual holds no exclusive rights' (Schütz, 2011: 195–6). Individuals are not consolidated essences. Yet, this does not mean singular essences do not exist.

102 Bryant, 2011 (my emphasis).

Differently from Bryant, whose use of the adjective appears merely aesthetic, in Agamben the term 'demonic' seems to assume a more strategic and non-rhetorical meaning: 'demonic' is 'in every being, the possibility not to be … the impotentiality'. Instead, 'evil' is one's 'fearful retreat from it [from the demonic] in order to exercise – founding ourselves in this retreat – some power to be'.[103] Differently from a naïve and 'evil' vitalism, unable to escape the proprietary paradigm of operation, I endorse a *demonic* vitalism, in which the virtual is not a mere capacity to, but rather the eventful impotency through which we live a life in 'incessant excess to its own forms and actualisations'.[104]

Agamben has beautifully expressed this quality of Deleuze's vitalism, as the simultaneous overturning of transcendence without falling into an undifferentiated immanence, in his analysis of Deleuze's very last text, *Immanence: a Life…* Deeply convinced of the strategic relevance of the title's unusual punctuation, Agamben suggests that the *colon* means 'neither a simple identity nor a simple logical connection' between the notion of 'immanence' and that of 'a life', but rather

> introduces an agencement of a special kind, something like an absolute agencement that also includes 'nonrelation' or the relation derived from nonrelation … In this sense, the colon represents the dislocation of immanence in itself, the opening to an alterity that nevertheless remains absolutely immanent.

Thus the ellipsis which follows the term 'life'

> maintains the term 'life' in relation to its pure determinability and, while carrying it into this virtual field, exclude the possibility that the indefinite article 'a' (i.e., *one*) might (as in Neoplatonism) transcend the Being that follows it.[105]

This 'inorganic life' is what allows any human and non-human being to 'persevere' in itself (in the sense of a Spinozian *conatus*, i.e. the immanent desire to persevere in one's being) by *swerving* simultaneously from a suffocating closure from relations (the cage of hyper-individualism) as well as from a hyper-active dissolution into fully actual relations (the cage of relationalism), radically exceeding and thus debunking the dualism between an undifferentiated and homogeneous 'bare life' and an already-determined 'individual life'. *Each body is a demonic double*, captured within

102 Bryant, 2011 (my emphasis).
103 Agamben, 2001c: 32.
104 Agamben, 2012: 295.
105 Agamben, 2012: 389.

two tendencies: on the one hand a movement of composition, as an opening into the spatiality of common relations; on the other, a movement of closure, as a reactionary denial of co-spatiality in the form of the immunitary self-closure of the actual individual. These are not given states, but rather the two 'indefinite extremes' between which each body is polarised.[106] *Actually* reaching one of these tendencies, as Meillassoux observes, would lead to death. This would either be a 'monadological death', in other words, an absolute closure from space and its relation, just like the cat deprived of air, the SR deprived of its thinkers; or a death 'by dissipation and progressive disappearance ... an *infinite madness* ... [becoming] a pure point of passage, a pure centre of communication of all things with all things'.[107] Death as the end of all relations (the dormant object) and death as the dissolution into all relations (the Latourian object). A body, as Deleuze would never tire of saying, is always in the middle, not simply 'in-between', but rather a fold exceeding these never fully inhabitable (since never fully separated) dimensions.[108]

To understand objects, or bodies, in this way is to understand them as double-structures, and thus never fully graspable, reducible, always situated within a relational here-and-now, and yet never actually resolved, trapped in there. Demonic vitalism avoids the chaotic condition of being 'constantly enrolled into activity' that characterises naïve vitalism, and rather affirms the ontological (reserve of) impotentiality that each being harbours. Deleuze's concept of 'a' life is not a generative ground but rather a 'detaching power', an impersonal, inhuman 'spark', as such 'counter-actualizing and anti-relational'.[109] What keeps a body 'alive' is this inoperose potency to detach, to swerve: not a capacity to do, but a capacity to undo. An inoperose potentiality that, as we are to see, by making inoperose the operational mechanism of appropriation, unleashes the excessive eventfulness of the materiality of being-together, opening up each situation to the contingency where 'a' life is put-at-stake, which is where the battleground of contemporary biopolitics lies.[110]

106 Nunes, 2010: 112.

107 Meillassoux, 2007: 107.

108 '[A]s if the object had one of its parts on the virtual and would be *immerged* in it as in an objective dimension' (Deleuze, 2004[1968]: 270).

109 Colebrook, 2014b: 29.

110 Rametta, 2006: 9–10. This goes against Thrift's observation that in Deleuze's ontology there is an excessive emphasis on the bliss of action, as if 'bodies are bodies-in-action, able to exhibit a kind of continuous intentionality, able to be constantly enrolled into activity'. Deleuze, he continues, would thus fail to account for the fact that 'the unchosen and the unforeseen exceeds the ability of the body to contain and absorb ... There is a sense of being unworthy of events ... and this is not an abnormal condition, it is a part of being as flesh' (Thrift, 2007: 10). Conversely, I believe this is exactly what Deleuze's approach permits to account for.

3.2 A representation is not true, rather, it is, it has being.[111]

Through the concept of double-structure we thus hold together both a notion of virtual as inoperose impotentiality, and the actual relationality in which it unfolds. Let us be clear: I am not implying that materiality be 'only' relational. Materiality is actual and virtual, relational and non-relational, paradoxically material and immaterial. As Ben Anderson and John Wiley suggest:

> the qualities that we consider to be immaterial are internal to matter but, importantly, do not coincide with the essential properties of a thing 'in itself' or the properties of a thing 'in relation'.[112]

That is an excess which overcomes every relation, and that the virtual allows for thinking as radically real and material, never transcendently 'beyond', or 'outside', but rather as the swerving and evental *taking place* of any entity, the unavoidable fact that each being 'must be in some place and occupy a space', its geo-sophical 'rootedness'.[113]

Beyond freezing relationalism, actual isolation or transcendent abstractions, we are thus facing a truly radical materialism based on the simple formula that *everything does matter.* This is certainly consistent with the call of 'new' materialist philosophies to re-evaluate the importance of a materiality independent from, *not for,* us: every entity equally 'matters' (although in unavoidably different ways). This is not in the sense of everything being neutral, but quite the contrary. There is no 'innocence' in matter, as there is no *actual* isolation of beings. This is the second meaning of the formula: every entity *matters* in the sense of 'mattering', by entering in relations with other bodies, affecting and being affected, never fully neutral from the power relations in which it unavoidably gets entangled.

Since everything *does* matter, everything *takes place,* and this taking place is material, ontologically productive, and as such susceptible of being explored:

> so even representations become presentations; as things and events, they enact worlds ... in their taking-place they have an expressive power as active interventions in the co-fabrication of worlds.[114]

Intangible bodies such as representations, images, ideas, are not to be assessed vis-à-vis their reference to a system of truth, but rather according

111 Doel, 1999: 5.
112 Anderson and Wylie, 2009: 331.
113 Plato, quoted in Masciandaro, 2010: 34.
114 Anderson and Harrison, 2010: 14.

to the material processes they trigger, the ontological concatenations they produce, as well as the eventful, swerving potential they harbour, as per Regis Debray's intuition:

> the capacity of an idea to put a mass in movement, to modify the balance of a field of power or to induce this or that behaviour is not dependent on its truth-value.[115]

This, to be sure, has nothing to do with the post-modern abandonment of the notion of truth. Deleuze's philosophy maintains a convinced commitment to realism, unwilling to jettison the idea of truth and yet, rather than confining it into the hyperuranion of ideas or the consensus of a community of interpretation, ties it to the notion of event 'in its eternal truth, independently of its spatio-temporal actualisation'.[116]

3.3 The event is not what occurs (occurrence), is within what occurs.[117]

Event. Something happens, something takes place, an actual state of affairs emerges, and yet: 'the event is not what occurs (occurrence), is within what occurs', an empty, mobile, differential frontier that insists on the situation without coinciding with it: not a phenomenological occurrence but an ontological event, its speculative condition of possibility. The event comes (*venire*) from outside (*ex*). It *takes place*, a formula that encapsulates at once a temporality (the occurrence), a topology (the place) and a process (eventing). According to William Sewell, there are two main misconceptions of the event. Within a 'teleological' understanding of temporality, events are reduced to mere manifestations of wider historical processes. Within an 'experimental' understanding of temporality, events are decontextualised as 'interchangeable units' for comparative analysis. An 'eventful temporality', instead, 'recognizes the power of events in history', assuming them as 'transformative' in themselves, and as such able to 'bring about historical changes'.[118] An event however, according to Deleuze and Guattari, although coexisting with and insisting in history, belongs to another temporality: 'what History grasps of the event' they write 'is its effectuation in states of affairs or lived experience, but the event in its becoming ... escapes history'.[119]

115 Debray, 1983: 116–17; Bonta and Protevi 2004: 5; Berressem, 2005.
116 Deleuze, 2004[1969]: 146.
117 Deleuze, 2004[1969]: 134.
118 Sewell, 1996: 262.
119 Deleuze and Guattari, 1994: 111.

In every occurrence, every taking-part, every entering in relation, there is an 'event', i.e. the *taking place* of these relations, what always differs from mere presence (phenomenology) and rather belongs to difference in itself, always immanently beyond the 'actual' relations, although never 'ontologically' separated from them: the empty time of an event insisting on the present without coinciding with it.[120] The event, Deleuze observes, is 'never present but always yet to come and already passed ... neutral in relation to all its temporal actualizations'.[121] An event is 'that which, in what happens, has become and will become'.[122]

In other words, events are inseparable from what becomes. They are always *eventing*, excessive vis-à-vis their situation and as such productive. From a symmetrically-opposed view, Badiou argues that the event is 'a pure break with the becoming', fundamentally rare, emerging out of the void of a (historical) situation, and as such constituting a radical rupture that cannot be incorporated within the parameters of the situation itself, thus forcing it to be radically modified.[123] Relevant, insofar as further emphasising the rupturing force of the event, Badiou's conception is less equipped to grasp its generative materiality, insofar as tending to reduce it to an 'expression of processes whose truth is best grasped by purely speculative reflection', rather than to a materiality to be explored in the contingent terrain of political practice.[124] *Pace* Badiou, events do not occur in a vacuum, but always emerge out of a dense spatiality of bodies, forces and becomings which we cannot leave unaccounted for.[125] Space is never a *tabula rasa* on which events occur, but an always thick and contingent being-together that the event does not deterministically shape, but *in* and *through* which it takes place. As Foucault clarifies,

> it is always at the level of materiality that it [the event] takes effect, that it is effect; it has its locus and it consists in the relation, the coexistence, the dispersion, the overlapping, the accumulation, and the selection of material elements.[126]

120 Deleuze, 2004.
121 Deleuze, 2004[1969]: 100.
122 Badiou, 2007.
123 Badiou, 2007.
124 Barnett, 2011a; see also Sinnerbrink, 2006.
125 Of course the complexity of Badiou's thinking warns against *trenchant* simplifications and would deserve a full analysis I cannot carry out in this context. However, his recent problematic attempt to force-fit the Arab Spring within his conception of the event shows – as many commentators demonstrated – how his approach, at the very least, runs the risk of erasing the contingent dynamics – the material taking place – of events. See Kacem, 2011.
126 Foucault, 1981: 69.

How may this be translated into a pragmatic and realistic strategy of thinking and acting within, and outside of, socio-historical contingencies?

3.4 Ce serait d'aller chercher l'expérience à sa source, ou plutôt au-dessus de ce tournant décisif où, s'infléchissant dans le sens de notre utilité, elle devient proprement l'expérience humaine.[127]

In his move from substance to correlation, Kant reoriented the axis of Western philosophy from the *transcendent*, i.e. the metaphysical domain of essences, to the *transcendental*, i.e. the conditions of possibility of experience. Kant, the archetypal phenomenologist, disarticulated phenomena from the reference to higher essences (as mere *appearances* of ideas) and assumed them as manifestations (*apparitions*), in relation to the conditions of possibility of appearing itself. Dislocating the centripetal pretence of the Cartesian *I think*, Kant described the constitution of the subject in the form of a radical passivity whereby the *me* realises (apperceives) the radical anteriority of an external *I* which affects it. That is an *I-think*, which belongs to an empty time, non-actual and non-empirical, which digs inside myself a void and that signals the external provenance of thought. *Je est un autre*, as Rimbaud wrote.[128]

Kant immunised this system from the dislocating potential of this *caesura* through the mediation of representation, and firmly locked it within the unifying principle of the transcendental subject. His solution was a typically juridical one: he argued that the I-subject was *de jure* the centre of will and proprietor of thought. We may 'agree with Kant on the *de jure* question', which the young Jean Paul Sartre observes, yet 'Kant affirms nothing about the *de facto* existence of the "I think"'.[129] Kant's 'conditions of possibility' would remain 'too large', as Deleuze lamented, that is, too generic to grasp the concreteness of what 'is within what occurs', i.e. the conditions of *real* experience.

What if the reflexive act grounding the I-subject is dependent on an irreflexive substratum, a radical anteriority denying any proprietary pretence over thought? The emersion of the 'Ego', Sartre points out, is constituted by a reflexive act of consciousness which establishes the status of the I-subject as the centre of will. Yet, this consciousness, prior to turning onto itself, i.e. to become reflexive (i.e. self-consciousness), is *irreflexive*. This is the literally unthinkable, 'irreflexive ground' of any reflection, impersonal and non-subjective. Thinking this irreflexive ground leads us to

127 Bergson, 2008[1898]: 205.
128 Deleuze, 2004.
129 Sartre, 1957: 2.

dissolve the transcendental subject into a transcendental *field*, not 'belonging' to any subject since 'purified of the I', being the latter's immanent 'condition of possibility', the *event* of its surfacing: not a shapeless whatever, but what in any body is the 'first condition and an absolute source of existence'.[130]

If on the one hand this assumption, i.e. the condition of 'being consigned to a passivity that cannot be assumed', would lead existentialism to an impasse,[131] on the other it would open the path towards emancipating thought and experience from the individual, the subjective, the phenomenological and indeed the human: that is, towards unfolding the transcendental field, or plane of immanence, as the realm of the pure appearing (taking place) of beings, of their event.[132] As Ronchi puts it, the transcendental field is a paradoxical non-relational relation or, more precisely, what actually grounds any (cor)relation:

> the constituted is the correlation I-world, the subject-object nexus. The constituent is the *event* of that correlation, which has no other place than in the correlation, yet cannot be said as correlation.[133]

If any entity can only exist by entering into relations (since there cannot be entities standing in the void), the transcendental field would be exactly

130 'This absolute consciousness, when it is purified of the I, no longer has anything of the subject. It is no longer a collection of representations. It is quite simply a first condition and an absolute source of existence' (Sartre, 1957: 106).

131 Agamben, 2000b: 100.

132 The 'plane of immanence' is a self-differentiating 'surface' where events *take place*, materially, and are joined in the machinic concatenations of concepts. A 'machinic' elaboration of the notion of Sartre's notion of transcendental field, the plane of immanence should be understood as the 'limit' of thought, or more precisely, as what allows for, without determining, the very act of thinking. It is to be emphasised that whereas the plane is 'pre-philosophical', non-presentational, pre-logical, it is nonetheless ontologically 'a [illegible] stretched over the chaos', paradoxically relational and beyond relation, ontologically coexistent with its actualisations, without ever being exhausted by them. When defining it in this way, Deleuze and Guattari imply an understanding of chaos as 'characterised less by the absence of determinations than by the infinite speed with which they take shape and vanish … chaos is not an inert or stationary state, nor it is a chance mixture' (Deleuze and Guattari, 1994: 42). Not a homogenous, external and undifferentiated chaos, but a 'chaosmos' (chaos+cosmos). In his early book on Nietzsche, Deleuze thus writes: 'chaos and cycle, becoming and eternal return have often been brought together, but as if they were opposites. Thus, for Plato, becoming is itself an unlimited becoming, a becoming insane, a becoming hubric and guilty which, in order to be made circular needs the act of a demiurge who forcibly bends it, who imposes the model of the idea on it. This is how becoming or chaos are transferred to the side of an obscure mechanical causality and the cycle is referred to a kind of finality which is imposed from the outside' (Deleuze, 1983: 28).

133 Ronchi, 2011: 11, 17 (my translation).

the impersonal 'potential' to enter in relations as well as simultaneously to swerve from being reduced to them. A relation between parts is defined by Deleuze as an assemblage, a problematic translation which we may use provided we take into account that the original term, *agencement,* indicates not only the product but also the process, not only the assemblage but also the assembling. Assemblages are the coming together of heterogeneous parts that have at least two key qualities. The first is *emergence.* The assemblage has novel properties emerging from the interaction between its parts, and can neither be reduced to phenomenological experience, nor to a simple sum of its part: its properties are contingently dependent on its internal relations. The second is *exteriority*: the parts of the assemblage are not exhausted by their relations with other parts, but retain their autonomy. As Delanda explains, assemblages are concrete, historical, individual, and yet also possess virtual tendencies and capacities, real although non-actual, as the notion of diagram or abstract machine helps understanding: 'an assemblage's diagram captures this virtuality, the structure of the possibility space associated with an assemblage's dispositions'.[134]

In the ontological, vibrating and conflictual co-immersion of being-together, machines are 'immanent ordering logics'. Let us imagine various voices singing randomly, which suddenly become tuned on a certain, common wavelength: we could say that this tune at the same time constitutes, and is constituted, by the voices themselves. An abstract machine is an 'impulse without determined goals' which 'selects', 'invents', i.e. *machines* the voices, holding them together whilst not erasing their heterogeneity.[135] Take the famous riddle of the silence – 'if you mention me, I am gone' – where what is implied is a constitutive, unspeakable absence as the groundless ground of any expression, and translate it to an affirmative notion of Being as Voice, where negation is substituted by *machination*: 'if you mention me, I am machined'.[136]

134 DeLanda, 2016: 5.

135 Amin and Thrift, 2002: 106. Accordingly, agency is not located in subjects, nor is it merely the result of the aggregation of individual action: emergence must be addressed 'both above and below the level of the subject' (Bonta and Protevi, 2004: 35).

136 This is what Deleuze achieves by assuming Being as an incorporeal absolute: incorporeal here does mean that it is only through its machination in *agencement* that its materiality unfolds: 'We must therefore maintain that *sense is a doubling up,* and that *the neutrality of sense is inseparable from its status as a double.* The fact is that the doubling up does not at all signify an evanescent and disembodied resemblance, an image without flesh – like a smile without a cat. It is rather defined by the production of surfaces, their multiplication and consolidation' (Deleuze, 2004[1969]: 125). For an insightful reflection of Deleuze's notion of being as voice see Laerke, 1999.

> The univocity of Being does not mean that there is one and the same Being; on the contrary, beings are multiple and different ... the univocity of Being signifies that Being is Voice that it is said.[137]

> ...the essential in univocity is not that Being is said in a single and same sense, but that it is said, in a single and same sense, of all its individuating differences or intrinsic modalities. Being is the same for all these modalities, but these modalities are not the same. It is 'equal' for all, but they themselves are not equal. It is said of all in a single sense, but they themselves do not have the same sense.[138]

Being and Becoming, one and all, univocity and pluralism, virtual and actual: these terms can never exist 'in separation' and are only given in a tension which cannot be dissolved into one of the two terms. Thus we move beyond the limits of post-human thinking, towards the inhuman dimension of the event.

3.5 Only the event can know what a body can do.[139]

Eventful is the ever-present potential haunting the state of affairs of a given situation, holding the possibility for it to be otherwise. In a famous passage, Deleuze sought to explain this point by differentiating between the viewpoint of a soldier within the battle, and the enigmatic 'viewpoint of the event':

> the battle hovers over its own field, being neutral in relation to all its temporal actualizations, neutral and impassive in relation to the victor and the vanquished, the coward and the brave ... Never present but always yet to come and already passed ... 'Where' is the battle? This is why the soldier flees when he flees and surges when he surges, determined to consider each temporal actualisation from the height of the eternal truth of the event which incarnates itself in it and, alas, incarnates itself in his own flesh.[140]

Keith Woodward perfectly summarises the sense of this seemingly esoteric passage:

137 Deleuze, 2004[1969]: 179.

138 Deleuze, 2004[1968]: 50.

139 Woodward, 2010: 331.

140 'Still, the soldier needs a long struggle in order to arrive at this *beyond* of courage and cowardice, to this pure grasping of the event by means of a 'volitional intuition', that is, by means of the will that the event creates in him. This intuition is distinct from all the empirical intuitions which still correspond to types of actualisations' (Deleuze, 2004[1969]: 100–1).

> the view from the event is the aggregate view, the wordly perspective, of divergent perspectives … a manifold of changing perspectives, forces and relata. The event is not simply non-representational, it is non-*presentational.*[141]

The 'viewpoint' of the event, what grounds its excess, should not be confounded with what escapes the representational cognition of a subject. It is not simply what is actually there, 'present' to the soldier, yet unperceived by him, since only affecting him pre-consciously, pre-subjectively and non-representationally. Contrary to these ultimately phenomenological simplifications, what the event's viewpoint concerns is not even 'presented'. It is a virtual multiplicity, which

> concerns an emerging situation's 'making-available' a multiplicity of viewpoints (potentially) to the bodies (humans, bits of matter, animality, languages and so on) that compose it.[142]

This is the deep sense of Spinoza's maxim: *we do not know what a body can do.* This is not simply an epistemological and 'correlational' limit (i.e. our incapacity to know), but an ontological statement (i.e. independently from *us,* a body is never exhausted by its relations): we do not know what a body can do because 'only the event can know what a body can do'.[143] Hence the non-relational status of the event: its virtual viewpoint without representation or presentation is exactly the unthinkable point of view of a world indifferent to us, that is, a world *not for us,* 'an immense spectacle without audience'.[144] Inhuman is the contingency to which the event opens the situation of its occurrence: neither in the temporal sense of an ancestral world before us (or indeed future world after us), nor in the spatial sense of something occurring billions of kilometres away from us, but rather in the 'geo-sophical' sense of a world not for us, utterly indifferent to our inescapable entanglement with it, and to which we are nonetheless open *here-and-now.* In every occurrence, every taking-part, every entering in relation, is the 'reserve of potentiality' opened by this contingent eventfulness, what is in any body the potential to swerve, and thus its ultimate irreducibility to the actuality of social, physical, biological, psychological relations.

141 Woodward, 2010: 331.
142 Woodward, 2010: 331.
143 Woodward, 2010: 331.
144 Ronchi, 2015: 110 (my translation).

3.6 Only empiricism knows how to transcend the experiential dimension of the visible without falling into Ideas, and how to track down, invoke and perhaps produce a phantom at the limit of a lengthened or unfolded experience.[145]

From this seemingly 'abstract' observation a profoundly empirical philosophy emerges. Excessive, material and processual: these dimensions of the event, expressive of its potential to produce novel normativities, drastically reconfigure practices and ways of being. The event is always, potentially, a 'liberation' from – a tearing apart of – the historical conditions and their causal chains. It is thus constitutively *excessive* to a given state of affair in which it is 'registered': an event always 'cxceed[s] its causes – and the space of an event is that which opens up by the gap that separates an effect from its causes'.[146] This is not wishful thinking of course. Virtual lines of flight are always buried in the actual and the ethico-political praxis of disentangling them so as to 'restore the connection of the actual to the virtual' (what Deleuze terms counter-effectuation) is certainly not obvious, easy, fideistic or spontaneous.[147]

The notion of virtual is indeed crucial to understand how the philosophical project of Deleuze, far from leading out of this world as hurried critics have proposed, entails an absolutely pragmatic and strategic approach, centred on the intention of locating the *real conditions of possibility* of any given situation, experience, assemblage, rather than postulating them as ideal, transcendent or, as in Derrida, only graspable *after* the event. These are concrete and real conditions of possibility of sociomaterial relations, or assemblages, concerning both their surfacing as well as the possibility for them to be re-assembled. Not actual, and yet real, these conditions lend to the investigation of any assemblage in its actual and historical unfolding and, at the same time, in the lines of flight where its virtual potential to be otherwise resides.

Thus the project of *transcendental empiricism* surfaces, as what allows one to cut through transcendental subjectivism and objective empiricism, ontologies of presence and flat ontologies of relations. In fact, 'transcendental' here is employed in reference to a field of enquiry which is 'beyond' the human, the personal, the subject/object distinction, but also, as we saw, beyond 'mere' relations. The 'ethico-methodological' proposition here (to which we are to come back extensively in the final chapter) is the injunction to be 'faithful to the event', i.e. to be faithful to a world not for us, a world never fully reducible to the relations we trace.[148]

145 Deleuze, 2004[1969]: 20.

146 Žižek, 2014: 14.

147 Patton, 2012: 27.

148 '[T]he transcendent is not the transcendental ... the transcendental field [is] defined as a pure plane of immanence, because it eludes all transcendence of the subject and of the object' (Deleuze, 2005b: 26).

Chapter 2

Atmosphere rhythm tuning

The urban is a materiality never fully totalisable into a frozen actuality, populated and constituted by *differentiating, persevering* and *swerving* bodies, simultaneously singular and in-relation, bodies that can 'be measured or registered by [their] relations, but can never be fully defined by them'.[1] The city is a surface where events *take place*, a 'state of thriving differences which do not submit to any categorisation, identification or totalisation', an agonistic field of 'free play' in which ideal distance or peaceful dialectics are chimera.[2] *Pace* Hobbes, conflict is not the denial, but rather the very fibre of the social, the ontological condition of being together. Yet the urban is never a simply chaotic or neutral, 'culturally-relative flat ontology but a tilted, power-structured surface'.[3] Order and disorder coexist and overlap in the urban space, and thus the challenge is to find a way to account consistently for how the urban is tuned, how normative orderings emerge immanently out of the common spacing of being together, without resorting to conceptual binary-traps, cumbersome dichotomies, dialectical promises. Yet, as Clive Barnett reminds us, 'just telling stories about spatially extensive networks of connection and entanglement' is not enough.[4] Simply challenging transcendent models by postulating immanent ones, where emancipatory potential would supposedly lie, is an insufficient move, indeed a dangerous one, whether it is left to itself. One must pursue this direction to its strategic consequences, not simply unfolding the immanent ontology of the urban, but actually addressing its 'mechanism of immanence'.[5]

This is the task of transcendental empiricism. More 'concrete' than social constructivism (since informed by a post-human and machinic concept of materiality), more 'abstract' than naive empiricism (since oriented towards 'the necessary [non-phenomenological] *excess* of experience: that

1 Harman, 2009: 141–2.
2 Brighenti, 2010c: 303.
3 Philippopoulos-Mihalopoulos, 2015: 3.
4 Barnett, 2011b: 252.
5 DeLanda, 2005: 88; Palmås, 2010.

which overfills any sense of immediacy'),[6] transcendental empiricism points to a strategic methodology to investigate the ordering of urban materiality by attending simultaneously to urban assemblages, by looking at their phenomenological instantiation, ecological prolongations, and eventful excess. In this chapter I propose to apply this approach to the urban through the notions of atmosphere and rhythm – and their co-imbrication in (urban) tunings.

The chapter is divided in two parts. First, I explore the intersection between assemblage theory and urban studies, especially focusing on some of the most significant critique moved to so-called 'assemblage urbanism'. Namely, an insufficient attention to the notion of affect, especially vis-à-vis the specific ways in which affects are configured in the historical contingency of contemporary neo-liberal capitalism; a somewhat static use of the concept of assemblage, also dependent, as anticipated above, on its problematic English translation of the term *agencement*; an implicit understanding of materiality as innocent, neutral and in a certain way 'beyond' power relations, which thus imply the troubling construction of a depoliticised urban ontology. Second, I challenge these critiques by introducing the notions of *atmosphere, rhythm,* and *tuning,* as a way to pursue said 'intersection' by eschewing the risks critique so aptly emphasises. I believe these concepts are able to inform a material, post-human and 'assembled' approach to the urban with a more explicit focus, respectively, on its *affective, dromological* and *normative* quality of the urban.

1.1 What is an assemblage [agencement]? It is a multiplicity which is made up of heterogeneous terms and which establishes liaisons, relations between them, across ages, sexes and reigns – different natures ... contagions, epidemics, the wind.[7]

In the last decade urban theory has come to integrate the impulses coming from new materialism, post-humanism, non-representational theory, affect studies and other radical dimension of critical geography and philosophical thinking. In an unavoidably superficial, yet useful way, these approaches are usually gathered under the label of 'assemblage urbanism' (AU), a definition that underlines the intention to overcome the human/non-human, social/material divide towards relational, post-human and ecological understandings of the urban itself. It would be mistaken to understand AU as a homogeneous ensemble. In fact, it may refer to various and heterogeneous works on urban theory that in one way or another, implicitly or explicitly, use the concept of assemblage: a variegated

6 McCormack, 2012: 721.
7 Deleuze and Parnet, 1987: 69.

ensemble of works coming from geography,[8] urban political ecology (e.g. urban metabolism, cyborg urbanism etc.),[9] urban infrastructures and infrastructural violence[10] and, of course, those that define themselves explicitly as 'assemblage urbanism'.[11]

As already explained, what characterises the concept of assemblage is a stress on notions of process and emergence, a sensibility towards the material and post-human quality of the urban, vis-à-vis its concatenated as well as excessive quality, that is, both the relations of power producing stability and continuity, and the ever-present potentials for destabilisation, and thus the emergence of the new. As Colin McFarlane argues, with respect to dialectical approaches, assemblages are characterised less by conflict and contradictions than by the lines of flight running through them, thus permitting for 'a nonlinear reading of the possible', whilst at the same time allowing for exploring 'on the ground', empirically, the way certain phenomena such as neo-liberalism are specifically instantiated in given locales.[12] In a piece seeking to systematise this variegated landscape, Anderson and McFarlane list the main characteristics of assemblage thinking: a distributed notion of agency (especially by integrating the non-human within urban theory); 'an orientation to assembling and disassembling', faithful to the Deleuzo-guattarian question: 'what holds things together?'; an attention to emergent and processual formations, rather than existent and finite forms; a certain emphasis, although not in all cases, on notions of fragility and provisionality, consistent with a firm belief in the possibility of things, relations, and agglomerations, to be otherwise.[13]

Focusing more specifically on the intersection between assemblage thinking and political economy, Brenner *et al.* individuate three levels, or degrees of penetration of the concept within urban theory.[14] First, is the *empirical* level, in which assemblages are assumed as a research object to be studied through a political-economic framework. Likewise, in their own tripartite categorisation of the use of assemblage in urban theory, Anderson and McFarlane refer to the use of assemblage as a *descriptor* for urban phenomena. This implies usually taking the most explicit, traditional meaning of the term, with the consequence of reifying it as a noun (assemblage), whilst omitting its verbal quality (assembling), and thus the

8 E.g. Massey *et al.*, 1999; Amin and Thrift, 2002; Latham and McCormack, 2004; Pile, 2005, etc.

9 E.g. Gandy, 2004; Kaika, 2005; Heynen *et al.*, 2006; Swyngedouw, 2006, etc.

10 E.g. Graham and Marvin, 2001; Graham, 2010; Gandy, 2006; McFarlane, 2008; on infrastructural violence see Farmer, 2004.

11 Farías and Bender, 2010; McFarlane, 2011a, 2011b; Smith, 2010; Smith and Doel, 2011.

12 McFarlane, 2011a.

13 Anderson and McFarlane, 2011: 125; Deleuze and Guattari, 2004[1980]: 327.

14 Brenner *et al.*, 2011.

processual and emerging aspects it connotes.[15] Second, is the *methodological* level, in which the concept is mobilised as a methodological sensibility to explore sociomaterial relations and configurations, thus allowing urban political economy to expand into new realms of inquiry. In the words of Amin, 'once urban human life in cities is seen as a hybrid of organism and machine, new aspects of social conduct immediately vie for attention'.[16] Assemblage thinking thus becomes a tool for urban studies to zoom in into aspects, relations and bodies hitherto overlooked, as well as to develop 'a certain *ethos* of engagement with the world, one that experiments with methodological and presentational practices in order to attend to a lively world of differences'.[17] Third, the *ontological* level, in which the notion of assemblage is tied to a novel, alternative ontology of the urban, one that is relational, heterogeneous, post-human. Brenner *et al.* are more than willing to take on board the first two levels as a welcome injection of higher sensibility and further methodological tools for urban theory, whilst they reject the ontological level. I am afraid, however, that a stripped-down version of assemblage theory adds very little to urban studies, and that the only way for assemblages to be significantly used is not as a prosthetic tool within already given theoretical frameworks, but rather as a fully-fledged *concept*. Whilst this implies, I believe, an ontological reassembling of the urban, such an effort requires caution. Unfortunately, so far this has been mainly carried out through ANT with the consequence of doing to the urban what ANT already did to the social: namely, providing a refreshing challenge to traditional, dichotomous, anthropocentric and structuralist ways of thinking, whilst throwing many significant babies out with the bathwater.

1.2 Behaviour can no longer be localized in individuals conceived as preformed homunculi; but has to be treated epigenetically as a function of complex material systems which cut across individual (assemblages) and which transverse phyletic lineages and organismic boundaries (rhizomes). This requires the adumbration of a distributed notion of agency.[18]

In the introduction to an edited collection titled *Urban Assemblages* and significantly subtitled *How Actor-Network Theory Changes Urban Studies*,

15 Anderson and McFarlane, 2011, refer for instance to Sassen, 2006. Similar (mis)use can be found in Haggerty and Ericson, 2000 where the notion is employed statically to refer to the way different techniques and technologies of surveillance are gathered forming a 'surveillant assemblage'.

16 Amin, 2007: 109.

17 Anderson and McFarlane, 2011: 126.

18 Pearson, 1999: 171.

Ignacio Farías qualifies this 'fervent anti-structuralist position' as grounded on an uncompromising analysis of

> space, scale and time [as being] multiply enacted and assembled at concrete local sites, where concrete actors shape time-space dynamics in various ways, producing thereby different geographies of associations...

rather than being produced by 'capital relations' or 'state strategies'.[19] As Latour once bitterly wrote, 'the social structure is a refuge of ignorance, it allows one to do without representation, or scripting, and to scorn the poor actors overwhelmed by their environment'.[20] I do not believe structures, power relations and socio-historical processes to be a problem in urban theory; unless they are employed deterministically, that is. Latour's iconoclastic urge is misplaced here. It makes little sense to understand the city as a casual emergence in the history of human (and non-human) kind, without taking into account the fact that the urban is *also* at the same time a century-old spatio-political project, and an ongoing planetary process.[21] Whether focusing on these dimensions should not prevent a careful exploration of the immanent emergence of urban assemblages, they cannot be removed from the equation either. The risk, otherwise, is that of leaving 'unaddressed important explanatory questions regarding the broader (global, national and regional) structural contexts within which actants are situated and operate'.[22] This is the critique which Brenner *et al.* move to the ontological approach to urban assemblage since, they write, it

> displacing the investigation of capitalist urban development and the core concerns of urban political economy ... the urban process is now conceived as a huge collection of human and nonhuman actants within a flat ontology devoid of scalar or territorial differentiations.[23]

This critique is appropriate to ANT, whose dogma of 'generalized symmetry' ultimately flattens the social by literally uprooting entities into a seamless relationalism.[24] Even the co-editor of *Urban Assemblages*, Thomas Bender, cautiously touches this point in his postscript, when asking tentatively whether ANT's

19 Farías, 2010: 6.
20 Latour and Hermant, 1998: 90.
21 See Cerdá, 1897; Adams, 2014; Brenner, 2009.
22 Brenner *et al.*, 2011: 233.
23 Brenner *et al.*, 2011: 232.
24 Madden, 2010. Hence Noys' piercing conclusion: 'despite Latour's claim to remove an abstract capitalism and replace it with a world of *rich concrete actualities*, his evacuation of negativity reproduces the vision of an entirely seamless capitalism that he claims to contest' (Noys, 2012: 88).

> indiscriminate absorption of elements into the actor-network had the effect of leveling the significance of all actors … this apparent leveling of responsibility in an actor-network analysis of causation worries me, for it seems to remove ethics and politics from social analysis.[25]

In fact, Bender continues, 'if Latour continues to explore the city, it is likely he will be forced to expand and enrich ANT in order to capture institutional power'.[26] Indeed. Without this attention, expansion and enrichment, assemblage urbanism ends up fetishising materiality into an innocent and neutral matter, with troubling political consequences.

1.3 Desire only exists when assembled or machined.[27]

Architect and theorist Alejandro Zaera-Polo enthusiastically endorses assemblage thinking 'as an optimal domain to explore the politicization of architecture'.[28] This understanding, he observes, allows for overcoming the subject-object separation by folding them into a spatiality in which humans and non-humans are joined in affective assemblages literally *enveloping* their being-together. Thus the possibility of a *Politics of Envelope* surfaces, that is, a politics that is no longer about ideology but rather concerns 'the most pragmatic, concrete operations', not 'politically ineffective' language, but 'the envelope's own physicality, its fabrication and materiality'.[29] Politics, in other words, becomes a matter of 'construct[ing] a hybrid world of *Things*, rather than political subjects and natural objects', so as to let emerge the 'missing link between the community of humans and the community of *things* as political entities'.[30]

We may note how a heightened sensibility towards the relational, material and affective quality of space, in this case, directly eschews any implication vis-à-vis a more sophisticated and 'material' understanding to the way structures, power asymmetries, abstractions and historical processes are actualised within sociomaterial relations. In fact, it suggests their altogether jettisoning (together with language, ideology and the likes). Echoing Latour, whose notion of *Ding-politik* (as opposed to *Realpolitik*) is a major inspiration here, Zaera-Polo calls for 'structuring the critical

25 Bender, 2010: 305.
26 Bender, 2010: 314.
27 Deleuze and Parnet, 1987: 96.
28 Zaera-Polo, 2008: 77. In the last three decades the use of this concept in architecture has become increasingly common, see for instance Eisenman, 2008. For a piercing critique of the misappropriation of this and other Deleuzian concepts, see Spencer, 2011.
29 Zaera-Polo, 2008: 88.
30 Zaera-Polo, 2008: 79.

mechanisms around spatial and material organizations rather than relying on the great revolutionary narratives and their ideological conceptions of history'.[31] Interestingly, besides the different jargon, the last affirmation perfectly mirrors current post-political rhetorics, namely: 'let us have done with ideology, left-and-right distinction and other relics of the past, and turn politics into a matter of pragmatic, technocratic and managerial praxis'. Unwittingly updating this frame to post-human and ecological height, thus Zaera-Polo affirms that overcoming the society/nature dichotomy into a relational ecology is *a* political move *per se*.[32] As Douglas Spencer caustically summarises, however, 'this does not actually politicize ecology ... but instead attempts to reframe the political as a purely *environmental* matter.'[33]

This may be a minor example, yet a quite revealing one to pinpoint what is wrong with the contemporary wedding of assemblage and the urban: simply put, the de-politicisation of urban ontology. Something emerging also from McFarlane's claim that 'the politics of assemblage thinking is to emphasise the democratic equality of *assembly* itself, of assembling commonality as an open multiplicity'.[34] Assembling, that is, is presented as a self-evidently just and emancipatory praxis, in quite the same way in which, Jodi Dean lamented, the Assembly was fetishised in the context of Occupy US. In her piercing critique of the crystallisation of the democratic process that gradually led that experience to a standstill, Dean stresses: 'occupation is not a democratic process, it is a militant, divisive tactic that expresses the fundamental division on which capitalism depends'.[35] These are fundamental divisions which result from those rifts and structures, abstractions, processes and asymmetries that assemblage urbanism appears to be often blind about.[36] Much caution is needed, it seems, if we are to avoid falling from the necessary unfolding of a materialist ontology into its moralistic fetishisation.

This is ultimately what occurs, I believe, also in one of the most influential recent contributions on the field, Jane Bennett's *Vibrant Matter*. Bennett's affirmative, relational and eventful ontology of matter is very valuable in developing a heightened sensibility to non-human actors and indeed to the vibrant and agentic quality of matter. Aware of the troubles

31 Zaera-Polo, 2008: 101; see Latour, 2004.

32 'A political ecology enables architecture to regain an active political role and overcome the division between nature and politics' (Zaera-Polo, 2008: 86).

33 Spencer, 2011: 14.

34 McFarlane, 2011a: 213.

35 Dean, 2014: 270.

36 See for instance McFarlane's definition of cosmopolitanism, his ethico-political stance of choice, as 'openness to and celebration of urban diversity and translocal connection and togetherness' (McFarlane, 2011a: 219).

of relationalism, Bennett is careful to qualify that matter is not simply relational: 'deep down everything is connected *and* irreducible to a simple substrate'.[37] Yet, whilst her approach is more than willing to allow for a notion of excess to enter the picture, a tendency to depurate matter, and thus ontology, from politics seems to surreptitiously resurface. Bennett's rather romantic call to embrace a mood of enchantment, wonder and creativity towards matter, in fact, implies that positive and emancipatory consequences will inevitably follow. Recognising the agentic capacities of matter, as well as including more and more entities, processes and 'matters of concern' within the political process, is certainly a necessary step, yet one that is far from being emancipatory *per se*. As Hannah reminds, we should not overlook

> the issue of the unavoidable selectivity of any and all particular engagements, and thus also the necessarily political issue of exactly which engagements are in fact activated.[38]

Attention, sensibility, affection, mood… under neo-liberalism, always come pre-configured within conservative politics of attention, sensoriality, affect, which we must carefully address.[39]

When introducing the *agencements*, Deleuze and Guattari emphasise the concept of desire, defined as the generative force circulating through them. Deleuze famously developed the concept of desire against its psychoanalytic entrapment within the notion of lack: that is, the missing 'thing' which would cause, and thus pre-determine, desire itself. Instead, he stressed, 'desire includes no lack, it is also not a natural given. Desire is wholly a part of a functioning heterogeneous assemblage'.[40] This means desire should not be understood as innocent, neutral, spontaneous:

> it is objected that by releasing desire from lack and law, the only thing we have left to refer to is a state of nature, a desire which would be natural and spontaneous reality. We say quite the opposite: desire only exists when assembled or machined.[41]

In the words of Juan Luis Gastaldi:

37 Bennett, 2010: xi. Likewise, 'the heterogeneous parts are not fully determined by their position within a relational configuration', write Anderson and McFarlane, 2011: 126.
38 Hannah, 2013: 239.
39 Massumi, 2009.
40 Deleuze, 2006: 130.
41 Deleuze and Parnet, 1987: 96.

> That desire, as a principle of creation is machined, means that it is not free or spontaneous, but rather determined by the situations inside which desire finds itself inextricably placed.[42]

Assemblages always harbour lines of flight which potentially open to the possibility of their reassembling. Yet, the political question here is not that of enthusiastically affirming the emergence of assemblage and their ever-present reassembling potential. Instead, we need to carefully explore how assemblages are 'determined' by the situations in which they are imbricated, so as to strategically scrutinise, dissect and follow such lines of flight, rather than optimistically waiting for them to actualise. This is also what is at stake when thinking the evental quality of matter and the situational ethics of what Bennett refers 'elemental judgements': the task of exploring the ways in which events 'are always coming *to* a particular determination', as well as constantly sought to be activated, employed and pr*event*ed, by the contemporary techno-politics of security, experience economy and the like.[43] As Bruce Braun puts it:

> contingency can never be the goal in and of itself … perhaps politics does not name the formation of publics as such, but rather the determination of incipient events, the ongoing and ever renewed work of turning contingency into necessity[44]

1.4 Thinking conceptually is no less material than building bricks.[45]

Whilst I am sympathetic with most of the critique to assemblage urbanism just exposed, I stress with Dovey that 'there are modes of assemblage thinking … broader than the ANT or network paradigm'.[46] Modes that, whilst reassembling the urban ontology in the direction of a renewed sensibility to materiality, do not necessarily imply the 'displacement' of a

42 To be sure, this does not mean determinism: 'that the machines are desiring machines means that the situations determine us only to desire and to create something new, which does not yet exist in these situations' (Gastaldi, 2009: 71, quoted in Braidotti and Pisters, 2012: 75–6).

43 Braun, 2011: 391. On the concept of 'elemental judgement', see Bennett, 2010. It is interesting that, when replying to the five reviewers of a book review forum on *Vibrant Matter* organised by *Dialogues in Human Geography*, Bennett addresses basically every point that was raised, apart from the most crucial one, namely, that attention and sensitivity to vital matter and its energetic, assembled and eventful properties appears to be already a key feature of contemporary control. See Bennett, 2011.

44 Braun, 2011: 391.

45 Latham and McCormack, 2004: 709.

46 Dovey, 2011: 348.

proper analysis of neo-liberal urbanisation, as Brenner *et al.* fear. To develop such modes, I argue, assemblage urbanism is to be duly integrated, 'below' and 'above'. 'Below', in the sense of complementing its ecological sensibility with an attention to the phenomenological here-and-now. 'Above', in the sense of complementing its horizontal ontology with an exploration of the abstract structures, apparatuses and power relations that striate and tilt this always asymmetrical surface. In order to do so, mobilising the notions of apparatus or dispositif (Foucault) and diagram or abstract machine (Deleuze and Guattari) is crucial. The latter may be understood as the virtual ordering logic of a given assemblage, that is, the intensive tendencies, blockages and lines of flight which constitute it. The former indicates the convergence between heterogeneous bodies and a concrete, historically situated strategic function, emerging at the intersection between relations of power and knowledge.[47] In other words, it is the actualisation, integration and differentiation of abstract diagrams into concrete assemblages.[48]

Later on I will employ these concepts so as to complement the 'assembled' dimension of the urban with the due attention to the abstract structures, processes and relations that characterise the current historical moment of neo-liberal capitalism. To do so, I will follow the valuable intuition of Anna Tsing Lowenhaupt, and her intention to explore the 'friction', as the 'grip of worldly encounter' in which global connections, apparatuses and structures come to life and are actualised into the world.[49] The friction indicates the ontological and phenomenological encounter between apparatuses and assemblages, and more precisely the always contingent and problematic way in which abstract structures take place in, and *tune*, the urban. This notion is extremely valuable to overcome two key oppositions in urban studies, between relational ontology and assemblages, on the one hand, and abstract structures, processes and apparatuses, on the other. Oppositions that, we just saw, are hard to die.

Whilst I will further develop and employ these notions in the fourth chapter, in the rest of this one I introduce three further conceptual tools, *atmosphere*, *rhythm*, and their entanglement into *urban tunings*, as a way to provide the approach sketched so far with more theoretical depth, terminological precision and methodological sharpness, especially vis-à-vis the *affective*, *dromological* and *normative* quality of the urban.[50] These concepts, developed at the intersection between geography and affect studies, are not meant to produce yet another 'metaphoric approach that

47 Agamben, 2009b.

48 Deleuze, 2006.

49 Tsing Lowenhaupt, 2004: 1.

50 'We might call them the "dromological" (composition of relative speeds and slownesses) and the "affective" (capacities of affecting and being affected)' (Brighenti, 2010: 304).

encourages a highly developed sense of urban complexity', as Bender observes, drastically minimising the import of assemblage urbanism.[51] Instead, they are meant to offer a way to provide assemblage theory with a useful phenomenological sensibility, whilst strategically situating it vis-à-vis the aesthetic genealogy of capitalist urbanism and, finally, providing it with a more precise attention to the intensive potentialities and lines of flight which are in the urban, real and unactualised potentials for novel assemblages to emerge.[52]

2.1 The unhistorical is like an atmosphere within which alone life can germinate and with the destruction of which it must vanish.[53]

Up until recently, the notion of atmosphere, besides metaphorical and poetic usages, was mainly employed in physics and climate science. It is perhaps no surprise that as the advent of Anthropocene has shown the extent to which the earth's atmosphere itself is a socio-political body, the concept gained increasing relevance to social theory. Explored a few decades ago by a host of German scholars,[54] and even before in Francophone works on the twin notion of *ambience*,[55] the concept has recently entered the Anglophone world where, processed through the import of affect studies, non-representational theory and new materialism, it lost some of the phenomenological orientation that framed its Franco-German interpretations.[56]

Gernot Bohme presented the atmosphere as not a subjective feeling, or an objective effect, but something in-between, a 'quasi-objective feeling ... the common reality of the perceiver and the perceived'.[57] Atmosphere is a 'potency of space', argues Martina Low, invisible and yet 'materially perceivable', and as such able to influence feelings.[58] 'What on earth moves me when I am in a particular space?', asks Peter Zumthor. The atmosphere, he replies, which emerges out of a certain composition of things, voids, sound, air, temperature, and is detected through our 'emotional sensibility'.[59] Jean-Paul Thibaud argues that the ambience shapes – or indeed 'establishes the

51 Bender, 2010: 317.
52 This approach 'allows us to take a given positive phenomenon ... and look at its actual and historical genesis *and* then look at its potentiality' (Colebrook, 2009: 13).
53 Deleuze and Guattari, 2004[1980]: 326.
54 E.g. Böhme, 1993, 1995; Löw, 2008; Sloterdijk, 2006; Schmitz, 1969.
55 E.g. Thibaud, 2011; 2012.
56 E.g. Anderson, 2009; McCormack, 2008; Borch, 2010; the special issue of *Emotion Space and Society*, on 'Staging atmospheres' (2012), etc.
57 Böhme, 1995: 16, 34.
58 Löw, 2008: 43.
59 Zumthor, 2012: 11.

terms of' – the embodied and spatial way in which we perceive and act in the world.[60] As for Bohme, Thibaud understands ambience as a *mood*, at the same time a 'quality of a situation, a sensory-motor stimulation, and a sensory background' which, as a gaseous and sensorial set of affordances, 'may increase or reduce our capacity for action'.[61] Inspired by John Dewey, Thibaud stresses the situational, contextual, pervasive and immersive quality of space that the notion of ambience helps unfolding, materialising the pragmatist dictum that 'knowledge of the experience matters less than the actual experience itself'.[62] Notwithstanding their significance, the anthropocentric and phenomenological bias of these approaches is evident. Moreover, either understood as a sensory or pre-conscious background, or as a penetrating and immersive substance, atmosphere is depicted as something external to us, separated from the individual or body on which it 'acts' or whose movements and sensations it shapes, whilst being acted and shaped by them in return. No amount of recursivity, here, would manage to displace the separation implied.[63]

A direct consequence of this 'externalism' is a somewhat instrumental reading of atmospheric engineering, for instance, as Mikkel Bille *et al.* write, as 'a practice of attuned and attuning people in space, whether that includes a focus on corporeal action, togetherness, or various degrees of sensory manipulation and orchestration'.[64] This is a reading we often encounter in texts of architecture, marketing and design, where the atmosphere (or membrane, envelope, ambience) is implicitly assumed as an innocent matter to be engineered for aesthetico-political purposes. The other side of this interpretation is a somewhat paranoid reading of atmospheric engineering as a necessarily dystopian praxis – an interpretation in which among other things obviously weights the legacy of twentieth century's political art of atmospheric orchestration, as so efficiently showed by the Nazi party.[65] In Chapters 4 and 5 we are to see in depth the extent to which atmospheric engineering has become an often explicit tool of urban planning, legislation and security policies, as well as, obviously, a key strategy in the field of experience economy. It is however important to qualify that atmospheric engineering should not be understood as simply an intentional praxis. Our urban being-together is always somehow tuned, implicitly and

60 Thibaud, 2011: 210.

61 Thibaud, 2011: 203.

62 Thibaud, 2011: 206.

63 An externalism, incidentally, non-representational theory seems unable to overcome. Even once shifted into the 'country of the half-second delay', between the effect and our conscious registering, between action and cognition, atmosphere remains unconsciously *present* and external, still penetrating the individual from the outside (e.g. Thrift, 2008: 186; Brennan, 2004: 1).

64 Bille *et al.*, 2015: 36.

65 Borch, 2012.

explicitly, in material, affective and symbolical sense. Neither optimistically assumed as an apolitical strategy for bettering urban life, nor pessimistically decried as a dystopian tool for social manipulation, atmospheric engineering is to be understood first of all as a constitutive feature of atmospheres themselves, of the way they hold together. Atmospheres are 'both emerging and engineered', as Philippopoulos-Mihalopoulos stresses.[66] This requires eschewing the externalist understanding that phenomenological interpretations carry.

Sloterdijk, as we saw, offers a potential way out. As each body is a space-creating being-in-a-sphere, atmospheres are understood as a tensegritous co-traction, co-produced by the coming together of bodies and held together by their common tension. This helps grasping the fact that atmospheres are always engineered by the bodies that constitute them. They emerge from a 'coming together of people, buildings, technologies and various forms of non-human life in particular geographical settings', as David Conradson and Adam Latham put it.[67] Thus eschewed are romantic attempts to 'escape' atmospheric manipulation into some sort of un-engineered spatiality, a bare substratum whose theoretical contradiction and political danger we already encountered. Yet, by challenging externality via relational co-construction, is the risk of falling into claustrophobic correlation avoided?

2.2

> It was always the same places in the streets, in the houses or in the parks that set off my spells. Each time I entered these spaces, the same swoon and the same vertigo overtook me. Veritable invisible snares placed here and there in town, not any different from the things that surrounded them – with ferocity they lay in wait for me to fall prey to the special atmosphere they exuded. Were I to take a step, a single step, and enter such a 'cursed space,' the spell became inevitable … The spells belonged to me and to the places where they occurred in the same measure. It's true that some of these places contained a 'personal' malevolence, but all the others were found in a trance themselves much before my coming … The doctor had prescribed quinine: another cause for amazement. I found it impossible to understand how the sick spaces, themselves, could have been cured with the quinine that I took.[68]

According to Bille *et al.* the phenomenological nuance the notion of atmosphere carries is what makes it relevant, insofar as allowing focus 'on the

66 Philippopoulos-Mihalopoulos, 2015: 122.
67 Conradson and Latham, 2007: 238.
68 Blecher, 2007[1936]: 2–9.

existential in-betweenness of subject and object', something that they see as somehow lost in more explicitly post-phenomenological tendencies such as ANT, affect studies and new materialism.[69] Atmosphere in this sense would allow to unfold that 'this-ness' of space Latham and McCormack refer to, that is, 'something tangible', simultaneously intensive and extensive, which 'exceeds the language of networks, connections and lines'.[70] I am definitively sympathetic with the intention to keep on board such a phenomenological sensibility, which is too often jettisoned by ecological accounts. However, I do not believe that an emphasis on the collective, moving, ontological and excessive quality of atmospheres would necessarily mean to 'lose their material grounding', as Bille *et al.* fear. More to the point, addressing atmosphere only through phenomenology risks overlooking what is more peculiar of their engineering, with potentially troubling consequence. As Philippopoulos-Mihalopoulos argues:

> The perfectly engineered atmosphere is one that appears spontaneous (consumerism, spaces of culture), necessary (natural reserves, airports) or even unavoidable (gated communities, prisons), and above all sensorially and emotionally responsive in that it makes bodies move in pre-specified ways. This means that atmosphere dissimulates itself as emerging and not engineered.[71]

In other words, before any seductive potential, atmospheric engineering is fundamentally grounded on the illusion of a phenomenological immediacy. Richard Grusin defines it as the fallacy of 'transparent immediacy': the perspective that 'holds that the subject's contact with the real depends upon the erasure of the medium, which correlates and thereby obscures the relationship between subject and the world'.[72] This illusion is directly tied to an understanding of freedom according to which, whether knowledge and interpretation are always reflexive and mediated, sensing and feeling are freely experienced. Transparent immediacy is the atmospheric 'trick' par excellence, that is, how atmosphere engineers its own absence: 'atmosphere dissimulates its engineering and presents itself only as an emergence'.[73]

What remains hidden, in fact, are the socio-cultural-legal saturations always traversing atmospheres and shaping the way we are immersed in them. To be sure, this is not simply in the sense of providing a background

69 Bille *et al.,* 2015: 33.

70 Latham and McCormack, 2010: 67.

71 Philippopoulos-Mihalopoulos, 2015: 129.

72 Grusin, 2015: 131. Mediation, in this sense, is not 'an intermediary to the understanding of the nonhuman world' but 'a property of the nonhuman world itself' (Grusin, 2015: 137).

73 Philippopoulos-Mihalopoulos, 2015: 145.

of enabling/disabling perceptual and performative affordances, as in Thibaud's account of ambience. More precisely, in the sense of mediating the way in which our perception, feeling and sensing unfold. As studies on attention show, the way we sense and experience our being-in-atmosphere is always already moulded by structures and institutions, knowledge and practices.[74] Overlooking this aspect opens a perilous path to vulnerable and co-optable ethical positions. A good example, from the field of art, is the well-known notion of 'relational aesthetics', coined by Nicholas Bourriaud, in which a capacity to tune oneself in the atmospheric being-together is posited as an 'embodied freedom', promising to liberate one's capacity to affect and be affected and thus to unfold micro-resistances against the dominant hegemony.[75] Here, the relations, rifts, structures and asymmetries that shape our being-together are left unaddressed, in the name of a heightened sensibility that in the end, as Matthew Poole observes, 'simply propagates the ground necessary for the more aggressive forms of subjection and subjectivation that we find in neo-liberalism'.[76] Indeed, we may ask whether the affective hyper-stimulation of neo-liberal capitalism is actually confirmed, and uncritically reproduced, by the 'privileging feeling as a source of insight into non-human reality' that characterises many post-human calls for an ethos of re-enchantment, embodiment, re-sensitivisation.[77] Paraphrasing Noys, why propose more embodiment, sensoriality, affectivity and vitalism when capitalism is able to provide them in ever-greater form?[78] Cannot this contradiction be solved only by reintroducing yet again the old rhetoric of authenticity: that is, warm feeling, genuine emotions and material affects against the cold, inhuman and immaterial atmospheric engineering of the capital?

On the one hand, a properly ontological approach is crucial to avoid the contradiction just exposed, by providing greater attention to the dissimulating work of atmospheres, and to the way this is tied to historical sedimentations, fault lines and power asymmetries. Sloterdijk's genealogical effort is very useful in this sense (see below). At the same time, atmospheric thinking is to be rescued from phenomenological reductionism *and* from the tendency of post-phenomenology and post-humanism to unfold into a flat, totalising and claustrophobic relationalism. As Philippopoulos-Mihalopoulos writes, 'atmospheres are engulfing and producing of their own inescapable immanence', and yet an atmosphere 'can never be seen as a synthetic totality because of its excess'.[79] This synthetic totality is exactly the way in which an atmosphere presents itself as a world *for* us. Through this reduction,

74 Hannah, 2013.
75 Bourriaud, 1998.
76 Poole, 2015: 208.
77 Brassier, 2015.
78 Noys, 2012: 71.
79 Philippopoulos-Mihalopoulos, 2015: 137.

atmospheres are naturalised, their immanent engineering retreating on the background. It is by thinking the excessive, eventful, inhuman quality of atmospheres, that a way out of this impasse may be found.

2.3 Gloom is not simply the anxiety that precedes doom. Gloom is atmospheric, climate as much as impression, and if people are also gloomy, this is simply the by-product of an anodyne atmosphere that only incidentally involves human beings.[80]

According to Bille *et al.*, the concept of atmosphere is particularly significant insofar as allowing 'to investigate the simultaneity of – rather than difference between – emotion and affect'.[81] This is against the tendency in affect studies to distinguish between the subjective level of feeling that the notion of *emotion* suggests, and the dimension of relations, assemblages and structures that the notion of *affect* conveys. Contrary to them, I believe this distinction is necessary, if we are to develop a properly excessive understanding of atmospheres that is different from the totalising, compulsive affections of neo-liberal atmospheres. In fact, following Spinoza, we may further distinguish affects from *affection*, i.e. the way an individual or a body affect or is affected. Whereas affection is an effect undergone by a sensing body, affects are forces independent of the bodies that undergo them. Irreducible to cognition and experience, feeling and emotion, to the human, the organic, the emotional, the non-representational and the lived: affects are 'beings whose validity lies in themselves and exceeds any lived',[82] 'as if they existed as potentialities for all time although only actualised within a specific time', affects are simultaneously affections, as well as their conditions of possibility.[83]

Accordingly, on the one hand atmospheres may be understood as interspersions of 'affect (as a pre-personal field of intensity) feeling (as that intensity registered in a sensing body) and emotion (as that felt intensity expressed in a socio-culturally recognizable form)'.[84] On the other they are traversed by an excessive potential, not simply excessive to something, but excessive in itself, insofar as being the real condition of possibility for atmospheres to emerge. Although atmospheres emerge from a coming together of bodies, they are always 'autonomous from the bodies that they emerge from, enable and perish with', always resisting a reduction to a 'totality' *for us*.[85] Affects are what remains *unlived*, unperceived, paradoxically

80 Thacker, 2012.
81 Bille *et al.*, 2015: 35.
82 Deleuze and Guattari, 1994: 164.
83 Colebrook, 2014a: 84.
84 McCormack, 2008: 426.
85 Anderson, 2009: 80.

unaffected, the virtual and unactualised (im)potentiality that any atmosphere carries, its excessive line of flight.

This radical understanding of affect can help us reorient towards an ontology or indeed cosmology of atmospheres, to be thought not simply as a co-produced, shared common, but also as a radical contingent taking place in a world that is not for us, exposed to forces that do not belong to us and cannot be appropriated, experienced or lived. In a critique of Anderson's notion of affective atmosphere, Margaret Wetherell argues that this concept seems to deprive humans of agency insofar as overlooking the way 'human participants read what is being assembled and actively position themselves within it', and thus ultimately subordinating individual action to mysterious and 'magical' atmospheric powers.[86] Yet, taking affect seriously does not imply reducing individuals to passive automatons acted upon by inscrutable forces. Quite the contrary, it means seeking to envisage

> the affectivity of atmosphere ... in ways that engage a range of more-than-human processes and relations while also remaining attentive to how these processes and relations are potentially sensed in moving bodies.[87]

This understanding opens an exploration of atmospheres that is no longer simply confined to its relational and phenomenological aspect. An example may help clarifying this point.

2.4 Tuesday, November 6th. The newspapers are black with fear, threats, and rumours. The government seems powerless. A bloody confrontation between the extremist parties appears unavoidable. Despite all this, people go to work, the rain never stops, and fear rises like vapour from the cobblestones. It can be sensed like a pungent smell. Everyone bears it like a nerve poison, a slowly working poison, felt only as a quicker or slower pulse, or as a spasm of nausea.[88]

In a compelling attempt to explore the excessive dimension of atmospheres, Derek McCormack defines it as 'a distributed field of affectivity, which, although barely and remotely sensed, can precipitate through the appearance of various materials, texts, and images'.[89] David Bissel hints at this aspect when describing the subtly tense atmosphere of UK trains, always overcrowded and 'haunted' by a 'distributed space of expectancy

86 Wetherell, 2013: 232.
87 McCormack, 2008: 414.
88 Voiceover describing the atmosphere of Berlin in the 1920s, in *The Serpent's Egg* 1977.
89 McCormack, 2008: 423–7.

existing as a diffuse field of potential', which is real and material, not actual yet always on the verge of being actualised.[90] What are they pointing at? Let us read the description of the slowly fermenting fear in Weimar Germany as narrated by the voiceover in Bergman's *The Serpent's Egg*, quoted at the beginning of this section. Is this fear simply part of that context, that era, that society? Should we understand it as an autonomous, inhuman force, which as such cannot be experienced or felt, although it can precipitate into a given historical configuration, a precise atmosphere, and as such be registered as affection?

Philippopoulos-Mihalopoulos argues that 'although firmly rooted in the *here* of the body, the affect portends to its virtual becoming, in its excess. This excess, collectively yet autonomously, is the atmosphere'.[91] Slightly otherwise, I would argue that it is the atmosphere to be firmly rooted in the here-and-now of a given situation, whilst it is the affect to be its autonomous excess. This allows us to explore contemporary ways in which affects are captured and engineered into configurations of affection, taking into account that atmospheres are always engineered in one way or another, and that affects cannot be experiences or lived 'as such', but only within a given atmosphere. At the same time, the approach here proposed yields an 'atmospheric ethics' that contrasts both the instrumental reduction of atmospheres to mere objects of post-political engineering practices, as well as romantic attempts to reclaim the bodily, the sensorial and the affective as a basis for a re-enchanted ethico-political praxis. As Colebrook effectively puts it, 'It would only be by destroying affections – the ready and easy response craved by our habituated body – that one might enable affects'.[92]

Let us come back to our example. Here, a socio-historically situated atmosphere of fear (composed by feelings, emotions and affections) emerges as an assemblage in which the *affect* of fear is captured and reduced to affection. Isolating the affect of fear in this instance, means to be able simultaneously to take into account its inhuman quality, exceeding any lived, as well as to explore the ways in which this is captured and engineered within a given socio-historical formation. Let us apply this reasoning to the climate of fear in the context of contemporary security politics. A strategy adequate to the concept of affect thus developed would entail trying to address, challenge and indeed dismantle the atmospheric engineering in which fear is captured and reproduced, for instance challenging its rhetorics, practices and oppressive configuration. At the same time, any attempt to 'get rid of' fear would be avoided. While I can arguably stop experiencing fear – i.e. be at least partially and spatio-temporally screened from the affection of fear – fear itself cannot

90 Bissel, 2010: 282–3.
91 Philippopoulos-Mihalopoulos, 2013: 8.
92 Colebrook, 2014a: 82.

disappear: it may actually vanish as a given space-time, and yet it will survive as a virtual potential. Likewise any romantic proposal to simply overcome fear by turning it into solidarity or trust would be preposterous. First this would mean shifting the onus on the individual effort to recalibrate his own affection, thus overlooking the structural and collective quality of the atmosphere that is being challenged. Second, this would imply the untenable pretence that fear would disappear once we stop paying attention to it, a rather dangerous simplification indeed. We should challenge the current politics of fear not by postulating some idyllic atmosphere in which only certain kinds of morally acceptable affections will emerge (e.g. solidarity, empathy, care). It would only be by destroying the oppressive atmospheres in which affections of fear have come to be crystallised, that we may release affects, fear included, thus seeking to reconfigure it into other, less oppressive and claustrophobic atmospheres.

Let us recap. First, bodies are not determined by atmospheres, although they are always part of them, and unthinkable outside of them. Second, bodies do not dissolve into atmospheres. Although unable to exist in vacuums, i.e. outside of the spatiality of atmospheres, each body preserves its *singular*, non-relational and swerving potential. Third, of course bodies 'feel' atmospheres. In fact, we can say that our 'sensing' of atmospheres is neither inexistent nor autonomous, neither determined (objective) nor subjective: my 'sensing' of an atmosphere is unavoidably part of this very atmosphere, constituted and constituting it. Likewise, culture, class, gender and other social 'frameworks' do not simply 'pre-structure' the perception of space and atmosphere – as Low for instance suggests – they are rather components of the atmosphere itself. Fourth, atmospheres are always engineered. Engineering atmosphere should not be understood as a *per se* dystopian praxis. Since we are space-creating beings, our urban being-together is always somehow tuned, implicitly and explicitly, in a material, affective and symbolical sense. Fifth, atmospheres are always traversed by excessive affects, which are simultaneously their virtual and real conditions of possibility, and thus their potential to be otherwise. Atmospheres are excessive insofar as they are affective. Neither deterministic nor totalising closures, it is important to finally qualify that atmospheres are not immobile either. They are instead multiple, moving and clashing. Differently from the self-enclosing tendency of structures, atmospheres are machinic, open to, communicating and most importantly conflicting with other atmospheres.[93] Conflict is both within and between atmospheres. Indeed, we could even argue that the orderings of a city emerge out of the rhythmical syncopation of these intra- and inter-atmospheric encounters

93 'The primary characteristic of the machine is the flowing of its components ... [differently from structure] which tends towards closure ... the machine ... opens up to other machines and, together with them, moves machinic assemblages' (Raunig, 2010: 31–3).

and frictions, that is, out of the excessive atmospherics of the poli-atmospheric materiality of the urban. We need to turn to the concept of rhythm to grasp more precisely this dynamism.

2.5

> Breath, you invisible poem! Pure
> Exchange unceasing between the great
> Ether and our existence. Counterweight
> In which I rhythmically occur.[94]

There is rhythm *in* atmospheres. In McCormack's terms, atmospheres are 'space[s] of affective materiality actualised through the ongoing movement of bodies'.[95] There is rhythm *between* atmospheres too. Rhythmic is the way atmospheres circulate, clash and overlap in urban space. Complementing their affective quality, the concept of rhythm provides them with a further dynamic as well as temporal nuance. Similarly to them however, in order to be applied effectively to the investigation of urban space, the material, conflictual and eventful character of rhythm must be fully unfolded. To do so, first of all rhythms must be understood as a way to overcome the unproductive dichotomy of difference and repetition which feeds the oppositional configurations into which the urban is often frozen. In other words: the opposition between the encroachment of everyday life through capitalistic and disciplinary routines, and the differential exuberance supposedly lying beneath these oppressive iterations. It is another variation of the dichotomous fixations (e.g. movement vs. staticity, order vs. disorder etc.) plaguing urban theory, that is. A way out from this impasse is to think repetition beyond merely oppressive and/or stiffening terms. Even in significant accounts, repetition is usually assumed only as a question of institutionalisation and routinisation, to indicate the way structures are embedded into material practices (Giddens) or habitus crystallises (Bourdieu). Within these terms, also the concept of rhythm tends to be referred to negatively, as an immunitary 'protection from practices which are unpredictable, other, different – in other words, protection from arhythmical practices', where 'emancipatory potential' supposedly lies.[96] Yet, this is not all. There is more to repetition than mere repetitiveness. There is more to rhythm than negation.

Already in Tarde we observed a model of sociality able to hold together imitative repetition and differential invention, thus stressing the creative potential which repetition harbours. As Derrida emphasises, the 'performative embodiment' of a norm (e.g. Bourdieu's notion of habitus as 'incorporation' of the norm) cannot be taken as merely repetitive, since it

94 Rilke, 1967: 58.
95 McCormack, 2008: 426.
96 Stavrides, 2010: 31.

is always a contingent event which every time *takes place*, and, as such, inserts a break within the supposedly smooth process of rule-internalisation.[97] There is eventfulness in repetition. This is what Deleuze stresses. Repetition is never mere 'repetition of the same', but rather of the 'singular': an always-swerving, change-triggering and space-producing taking place within the spatiality of the now-here and its overflowing no-where. The repetition, that is, is an 'ontological exception' to the dichotomy of particular and general, and as such cannot be thought in separation from, but rather as always integrated with difference, in rhythmical co-constitution: a difference-producing (differential), eventful repetition.[98] Repetitions are always contingent and it is from their differential taking place that the rhythmic syncopation that shapes the everyday life of the city emerges.[99] This is not to say that repetition necessarily generates rhythms, but rather that rhythms should be understood in the co-essentiality of repetition and difference.[100]

Elaborating on Gaston Bachelard – who was in turn inspired by the seminal, and now lost, work on rhythmanalysis by the early twentieth-century Portuguese sociologist Lucio Pinheiro dos Santos – Lefebvre's rhythmanalysis has been the most famous attempt to deal with urban rhythms, i.e. the 'music of the city', what provides tempo to its spatial overlappings:

> every rhythm implies the relation of time with a space, a localised time, or if one wishes, a temporalised place. Rhythm is always linked to such and such a place, to its place, whether it be the heart, the fluttering of the eyelids, the movement of a street, or the tempo of a waltz. This does not prevent it from being a time, that is an aspect of a moment and a becoming.[101]

As often occurs with Lefebvre, radical and innovative directions remain entangled within a dialectical framework which ultimately defuses their potential. In this investigation of the way the everyday rhythms of the city are embedded within the logics of capitalistic mode of production, the oppressive 'abstract space' and 'linear time' of the capital are discussed in

97 Butler, 1997: 100–8.
98 Deleuze, 2004[1968]: 1–28.
99 'Repetition is a prerequisite for any rhythm, but not all repetitions engender a rhythm … The existence of rhythms is contingent on the regular recurrence of pauses, silences, blanks, repetitions, and intervals … repetitions, ruptures, and surprises … In other words, rhythm is the reproduction of a process in its multiplicity and plurality. The same is not repeated mechanically but is instead subordinated to alterity, not to say alternation – that is, to difference' (Lefebvre and Regulier, 1999: 9–10).
100 Without however assuming a coincidence between the two terms: 'it is the difference that is rhythmic, not the repetition, which nevertheless produces it' (Deleuze and Guattari, 2004[1980]: 346).
101 Lefebvre, 1996: 32; see also Bachelard, 2000[1936]; Soja, 1996; Thrift and May, 2001.

opposition to a 'differential space' in which strictures and contradictions will be overcome, a dialectical sublimation whose problematic attempt to supersede (rather than face) conflict has been already criticised.[102] A residue of humanism complements this understanding, i.e. the craving for 'more humane' rhythms to be opposed to the inhuman velocities of the capital. Here we may see the evident and yet unacknowledged legacy played on Lefebvre's conception by Bachelard's and Pinheiro's rhythm-analysis, and even more perhaps the indirect influence of Leonardo Coimbra, whose *ritmontologia* was key in inspiring the latter.[103] As already mentioned, Coimbra conceived beings in oscillation between the reactive rhythm of immediate sensation and the 'rhythmical excess' where free and creative activity lies, and which would have to be reached through a typically dialectic, synthetic move. Likewise, Lefebvre stresses the relevance of the concept of rhythm as a way of recalibrating the problematic abandonment of 'the living body' by Western philosophy, centring this attempt on the human body and the related immunitary concern with restoring its unity and integrity 'as the proper yardstick of a reappropriated social space'.[104] In this way, rhythm analysis risks developing into a romantic exaltation of disorder vis-à-vis the 'oppressive routine' of the city, movement versus stability, the slower and humane rhythms of the 'local' (e.g. 'slow food') versus the schizophrenic post-industrial speed of the capital, and so on.[105] Yet, if aptly recalibrated towards a post-human, excessive, eventful and radically material understanding, this analysis can be rescued from these limitations, so as to unleash its 'schizoanalytic potential'.[106]

First, as Borch suggests in his proposition to integrate Tarde's approach with Lefebvre's rhythm analysis, we should resist the temptation to focus only on processes of stabilisation and adaptation, and also address the contingency of the rhythmic processes, the interruptions, variations and

102 According to Lefebvre, the production of abstract space by capitalism occurs through a process of fragmentation, homogenisation and hierarchisation of space: spaces are separated (in functional terms) standardised and, finally, hierarchised, so as to make them exploitable (Lefebvre, 1991[1974]: 229–92). Tied to abstract space is the production of a 'linear and quantified social rhythm', as time 'like space … divides itself onto lots and parcels', thus becoming, again, exchangeable and exploitable (Lefebvre, 2004: 74).

103 Cunha, 2008.

104 Doel, 1999: 14–15; Lefebvre develops the notion of rhythm vis-à-vis his critique of Western philosophy for having 'abandoned the living body as the store of non-formal knowledge (non-savoir) which constitutes a source of potential knowledge (connaissance)' (Lefebvre, 1996: 230).

105 This is also the case for instance of the somewhat apocalyptic stance of Virilio's *dromology*, as Chris Butler stresses in his compelling paper on rhythm. It is not entirely clear, however, whether Butler manages to avoid the Lefebvrian yearning for a post-conflictual, differential space (Butler, 2008: 484).

106 Doel, 1999: 15.

destabilisations which constantly punctuate their apparently smooth unfolding.[107] Second, if again Borch stresses the significance played by Lefebvre's focus on the relation between rhythms and materiality in the city (in this way offering a way, he adds, to complement the Tardean model), such suggestions should be complemented with a more radically machinic and post-human understanding of materiality. Not only fleshy, concrete, human and stabilising, rhythms are also abstract, post- and indeed inhuman, excessive and tumultuous. They are not only the phenomenological 'coordinates through which inhabitants and visitors frame and order the urban experience'.[108] More precisely, rhythms are machinic emergences of patterns out of urban space, 'ecologies of coexistence of heterogeneous elements', in the mutual folding and unfolding between spaces, events and bodies.[109]

Deleuze and Guattari define the notion of *ambience,* or milieu, as a vibratory 'block of space-time constituted by the periodic repetition of components', and rhythm as what coordinates these 'heterogeneous space-times'.[110] Following this inspiration, the 'folding' and 'unfolding' of overlapping and vibratory urban atmospheres can be understood as immanently and rhythmically *tuned* into given 'frequencies' in the city. This is still not enough. Coordination is only one of the modes of rhythm. This is not only to say that every rhythmical stabilisation is constantly bound to dislocation. More precisely, rhythms have an excessive potential, which prevents them from being reduced to the mere repetitiveness of institutionalisation via normative structures, as well as to simple instances of synchronisation. There is always a conflictual materiality in the rhythmic process that 'cannot be reduced to a quiet interaction order' *à la* Erwin Goffman.[111] Rhythm is conflict. Rhythm emerges out of conflict. It is not the way through which overcoming conflict and abstractions into some post-conflictual utopia, but rather the 'abstract-and-concrete' way through which conflict is experienced, traversed and lived: a 'line of flight through the chaos'.[112] Rhythms sanction the emergence of resonant syncopations between the excessive inter-atmospheric and intra-atmospheric frictions of the urban (i.e. the seismic frictions between the different scales that intersect its surface, between the bodies that populate it, between the abstractions that insist on and produce its spatiality), that is, the potential surfacing of novel urban 'tunings'. In Deleuze's words, the rhythm is 'a vital

107 Borch, 2005: 93–4.
108 Amin and Thrift, 2002: 17.
109 Brighenti, 2010a: 81; see also McCormack, 2002: 476.
110 Deleuze and Guattari, 2004[1980]: 345.
111 Borch, 2005: 93.
112 Dewsbury and Thrift, 2005: 105. 'Rhythm is the milieu's answer to chaos. what chaos and rhythm have in common is the in-between – between two milieus, rhythm-chaos or chaosmos' (Deleuze and Guattari, 2004[1980]: 345).

power that exceeds every domain and traverses them all',[113] a paradoxical refrain of urban excesses, that simultaneously joins and splays them out towards novel configurations.

The urban is tuned as result of the affective materiality of atmospheres and the dromological punctuation of intra- and inter-atmospheric rhythms. Looking at urban space through this prism allows us to focus on the affective and dromological getting-together of urban bodies in simultaneously actual and virtual terms, observing the atmo-rhythmical *tunings* emerging in the smooth and striated surface of the city, as orderings that neither determine nor pre-structure, and yet *guide* and *orient* the urban, never fully representable, and yet felt, as in the vaporous being-in-an-atmosphere or syncopated being-in-the-rhythm: an impersonal being-tuned. There is obviously a stabilising force in these atmo-rhythmical tunings. They are the way cities immanently hold together. Through the constant frictions and dislocations within and between the apparent peacefulness of urban atmospheres, the intensive potential is constantly produced by the repetitive unfolding of urban rhythms. Indeed, it could be argued that frictions and excesses are what the urban is about, eventful atmospherics of conflict more or less stably tuned into poli-atmospheric rhythms, as well as more or less effectively dislocated by novel atmo-rhythmical irruptions. Could not we argue that it is exactly on the creation and contestation of these 'tunings' that ethico-political action is grounded?

Addressing this question requires complementing the ontological effort developed in the last two chapters with a genealogical perspective. The urban is a post-human *tensegrity* joined in bubbling atmospheres, syncopated into recurrent rhythms. Yet, these tunings cannot be understood separately from the socio-historical contingency in which the urban itself comes to life. Not only an overlapping of tuned assemblages, the urban is also a long-standing spatio-political (and indeed spatio-legal) *project* as well as an all-encompassing planetary *process*. Unfolding these two dimensions is crucial if we are to provide strategic depth to the ontology just developed. I do so in the next two chapters.

113 Deleuze, 2005a: 42.

Chapter 3

Law space justice

How can we think about the material interrelation between law, space and justice? This question, encompassing the whole book, orients this chapter around two main purposes. First, the chapter builds a bridge between the recently sketched ontology of urban tuning and the forms it takes vis-à-vis the *process* of planetary urbanisation, to be dealt with in the next chapter, by providing the book with a *spatiolegal* lens. Second, it sets the stage for the overarching objective which will culminate in the final chapter, namely an ontological conceptualisation of the triptych of law, space and justice, through a material understanding of law and an elaboration of the notion of justice as its eventful excess.

First, I trace the evolution of the 'spatiolegal architecture' of modernity through a personal re-elaboration of the notion of 'state of exception'. I also provide a critical look at some sociological and legal-geographical perspectives, as well as more recent critical legal geography insights. What I find, again, is a tendency to overlook the excessive and evental quality of space, in spatiolegal terms: an unsatisfying engagement with the 'juridico-ethico-political' question of justice.

Second, I move on to one of the most compelling attempts in this direction, Derrida's ground-breaking essay *La Force de Loi.* Rather than devoting myself to a dissection of Derrida's thought, I seek to detect some fault lines within his strategy of legal deconstruction. In brief, I suggest this strategy falls short of providing a materialist account of the excessive dimension of justice. Consequently, it leaves the back door open for the problematic re-insertion of nihilism.

Third, I employ the Deleuzoguattarian dyad of *logic* and *nomic,* as well as Philippopoulos-Mihalopoulos' concept of *lawscape.* I develop a way of thinking about the materiality of the spatiolegal in both its *relational* and *eventful* dimension, beginning to sketch the contours of an alternative approach to law which, without renouncing to critical dissection, does not fall into a simplistically anti-normative position. This is only a partial and incomplete conclusion, which will have to wait until the final chapter to be complemented, and concluded.

1.1 Multiple is the polis, irreducible to one.[1]

What is the 'space' of modernity? Carlo Galli observes that the conceptualisation of pre-modern (Western) space emanates from the rift between Greeks and Barbarians, West and East, Europe and the rest. 'Pre-modern' space is conceptualised as already imbued with intrinsic qualities, inherently diverse, not simply chaotic but possessing its 'own' complexity, a space whose 'differences are qualitative, prior to be physically drawn', and 'whose logic and whose boundaries precede the work and the will of man'.[2] The earth is accordingly a space to be explored, annexed and feared, a space to be 'occupied without being counted', not a space to be represented but 'explored by legwork'.[3] Prior to modern geography, the drawing of maps was based on the account of explorers' journeys, filled with elements (rocks, fountains, trees) whose presence on the very map depends on their contingent relevance vis-à-vis the explorer's path.[4] During the classical age and throughout the Middle Ages, the idea of a space with intrinsic qualities and differences is perfectly conciliated with that of a superior harmony organising them, consistent with Plato's 'idea of a complex, organic and objective order of being'.[5] In his 'immunological' genealogy of common spaces, Sloterdijk defines the classical belief in the onto-theological unity of the cosmos as the postulation of a 'metaphysical globe', which insulates human beings within an ideally ordered and harmonious Whole, and thus immunises them from the perils of the Outside.[6]

Modernity emerges from the structural collapse of the cosmological globe, as a result of the explosion of a spatial contingency which can no longer fit inside its ordered wholeness. Luther, Copernicus and Columbus: earthquakes of enormous proportion shaking the religious, cosmological and geographical foundations of the cosmos. The project of modernity emerges as the attempt to find refuge from the radical dislocation which ensues.[7] A reaction to the metaphysical collapse and, more precisely, the explicitation of the fact that a common immunity under a unitary cosmos is no longer evidence to be assumed, but rather a *project* to be actively and technically pursued. Whereas before modernity the map is the construction of a copy of the world, subsequently it would be the world to be shaped according to the map: as Heidegger reminds us, modernity is the faith in the capacity to reduce the world to image, the faith in *re-presentation*, a cartographic revolution.[8] Now it will be politics, economy, and law, to *determine* a

1 Cacciari, 1997: 37 (my translation).
2 Galli, 2001: 19, 21 (my translation).
3 Deleuze and Guattari, 2004[1980]: 34.
4 de Certeau, 1984: 121.
5 Galli, 2001: 25 (my translation).
6 Sloterdijk, 1999.
7 It goes without saying that this is an eminently Western story.
8 Farinelli, 2003.

space which will no longer be 'occupied without being counted' and will be 'counted in order to be occupied', re-presented.[9]

It is not the intention here to locate this evolution historically and chronologically, that in any case should not to assumed in simplistically linear terms. What is more interesting is exploring its spatiolegal consequences, and precisely the role played by the logic of representation as a mechanism for articulating the (presupposed) separation between law and space in the form of a correlation, what I term the *spatiolegal state of exception.*

1.2 Each case is other.[10]

Law could be seen as the crystallisation of the infinite quest to put order on space. The history of legal thought is that of a relentless attempt to immunise law from space in order to control it, categorise it, partition it. An attempt grounded on a fundamental and never fully abandoned presupposition: i.e. the *separation* between law and space. Whereas this is evident in classic 'Natural Law' conceptions, once these naively transcendent models are overcome the separation is not abandoned. It is in fact reworked: from a taken-for-granted dichotomy into an immanent articulation. It is in Kant that this takes its most radically self-enclosed form. The separation seems to dissolve: 'judgment in general is the ability to think the particular as contained under the universal', i.e. law's intervention in the world is articulated through a logical *operation,* the subsumption of the particular into the universal.[11] Correlation, let us repeat, is 'the idea according to which we only have access to the correlation between thinking and being, and never to either term considered apart from the other'.[12] Kant applies this logic to law, by internalising 'the relationship between objects and representations *within* representation itself', and dismissing any 'legal externalism'.[13] Accordingly, 'cases do not stand externally or indifferently before a judge but appear as cases (*legal* cases, cases at law) only insofar as they have always already been subsumed by the law'.[14] Complementing this smooth gesture of subsumption is its automatic self-denial: law elevates itself onto an objective, positive, *pure* status, simultaneously depurating its operations from the conflictuality in which they occur, and instead appearing as self-evident, de-politicised, 'rational, benign and necessary'.[15]

9 Deleuze and Guattari, 2004[1980]: 399.
10 Derrida, 1990: 961.
11 Kant, 1987[1790]: 18.
12 Meillassoux, 2009: 5–6.
13 Lefebvre, 2008: 7.
14 Lefebvre, 2008: 7.
15 Blomley, 1994: 9.

However, the contingency of space lies beneath this image of purity. In fact, is not space the very 'condition of legal judgement and the limits of its reason', or perhaps more precisely, the condition of (im)possibility of any legal apparatus?[16] When Benjamin notes 'the curious and at first discouraging experience of the ultimate undecidability of all legal problems', or when Derrida observes that 'each case is other, each decision is different and requires absolute interpretation, which no existing, coded rule can or ought to guarantee completely' – are they not indirectly referring to the impossibility of law to ever tame the excessiveness of spatiality?[17] Any attempt to do so entails an uncertain leap. A performative break is implicit in every judicial interpretation. There is always an *exception* implanted at the core of any spatiolegal configuration.[18] How is law to deal with its own inescapable exceptionality?

1.3 Orthodoxy needs blasphemies, not in order to formulate its ideas but to test, maintain and exercise its social cohesion.[19]

As the popular proverb goes: *exception probat regulam in casibus non exceptis* – i.e. 'the exception proves that the rule works in non-exceptional cases', or: 'the exception proves the rule'. Behind self-evident proverbs lie deeper meanings. Whereas Sherlock Holmes's rationalism bluntly dismissed it, 'the exception disproves the rule',[20] Walter Benjamin, Carl Schmitt and Agamben have been willing to take its consequences to the extreme. Here is Schmitt: 'the rule as such lives off the exception alone'[21] and, in slightly a reworked version, Agamben: '[the exception is] the very condition of possibility of juridical rule'.[22] What this amounts to is unmasking law's direct application to the world as a *fictio juris*:

> every general rule demands a regular, everyday frame of life to which it can be factually applied and which is submitted to its regulations … a *homogeneous medium*. There exists no norm applicable to chaos.[23]

Law's application is always premised on an '*a priori* mechanism', a topological machine whereby 'the space in which the juridico-political order

16 Douzinas *et al.*, 1994: 1.
17 Benjamin, 1999: 247; Derrida, 1990: 961.
18 'Just as between the language and world, so between the norm and its application there is no internal nexus that allows one to be derived immediately from the other' (Agamben, 2005a: 53).
19 Lawton, 1993: 4.
20 Conan Doyle, 2001[1890]: 17.
21 Schmitt, 2006: 1.
22 Agamben, 1998a: 17.
23 Schmitt, 2006: 13 (my emphasis).

can operate' is created and defined.[24] Any spatiolegal intervention depends on a prior and violent 'foundational ontological gesture' whereby the *where* through which the spatiolegal is to be articulated in the form of a cartographic representation is constituted: a state, or a space of exception.[25] There is no rule – both in the sense of rule and ruling – without a space of exception, as the etymology suggests. The term 'exception' literally means to *take in* the outside (from *ex,* outside, and *capere,* to take). In fact, the mechanism of exception is the dispositive allowing us to 'take in' the chaotic, ever-escaping outside (life, world, space...) and domesticate it, that is, to simultaneously *include* space by *excluding* its conflictual, eventful and contingent materiality.

Let us take this reasoning to its logical consequences: a state of exception always *presupposes* an undifferentiated outside. This is what lies beneath the Kantian presupposition that 'cases' are always-already subsumed by the law rather than standing externally to it: an external and undifferentiated chaos (an 'absolutely disaggregated something else'), out of the encounter with which legal cases would be constituted.[26] Slavoj Žižek has suggested that Kant was 'the first to detect [the] crack in the ontological edifice of reality', the horrifying possibility that the 'empirical nature (contrary to transcendental "nature as a whole") may not be unified, coherent, and systematic but a "crude chaotic aggregate"'.[27] As it is known, it is in order to solve this potential contradiction that Kant would resort, in the *Third Critique,* to the teleological conception of an *a priori* finality, which guarantees the ontological coherence of reality and its superior purpose. A not so dissimilar problem was faced by the Christian theologians when, in order to allow for the concept of 'free will' to flourish over the cage of an ineluctable Fate, conceived God as necessarily withdrawn from the world. The co-substantiality of God with the world would have otherwise denied any possibility for human free will: everything would have been occurring according to God's will. Thus, faced with the possible heresy of a God 'separated' from the world (of a world ultimately *independent* from God), they resorted to the superior finalism of the 'divine providence'.[28] In this sense, could we not argue that the evidence of an undifferentiated, 'chaotic aggregate', rather than being the blind-spot that threatens the Kantian enterprise, is its ultimately-denied presupposition? This being the case then, Kant's

24 Agamben, 1998a: 19.

25 Minca, 2006: 389.

26 Kant posits an in-itself which is an '*absolutely disaggregated something else* seated at the limits of reason's capacity to objectivity the world', in Woodward, 2010: 324.

27 Lefebvre, 2008: 29; Žižek, 2008: 42; Lefebvre, 2008: 29.

28 According to the Gnostic heresy in fact, there exists a remote God separated from and absolutely indifferent to the material world created by the Demiurge. The world, so to speak, is *not for God,* an evident blasphemy for the Christian conception (Agamben, 2009a: 102).

'providential' immunisation from the possibility of a 'chaotic outside' would hide the fact that it is on this very presupposition (i.e. on such *negative* ground) that the subsumptive mechanism of exception of the transcendental judgement rests. In the same vein, could we not contend that the unspeakable possibility of a chaotic world ontologically separated from God is not the theological blind-spot of Christianity, but rather the actual presupposition legitimising the whole 'economy of salvation' (the 'divine techné') on which it rests?[29] Seeking to provide a definitive answer to these questions, if ever possible, would certainly lead this book astray. Yet it is important to remain within the problematic field they open. Complementing the above quote by Schmitt: not only 'there exists no norm applicable to chaos', in fact, *any transcendent norm implicitly presupposes the evidence of an external, undifferentiated and homogenous chaos which it intends to order.*

The insufficiency of the simple critique of legal abstraction *per se* – that is, of the abstract grid through which legal categories organise and freeze reality – begins to appear, whether supplemented or not, and indeed preceded, by a critique of the 'originary spatialisation that governs and makes possible every localisation and every territorialisation'.[30] The projection of any politico-legal 'geometry' first requires the *erasure* of complexity out of space, that is, the flattening of space into an undifferentiated, homogenous and empty surface or (which is exactly the same) an 'absolutely disaggregated', homogeneous chaos.[31] A spatial erasure, that is, a blank surface or *tabula rasa,* is the basic requirement of every representation, legal representations included.[32] We could obviously locate this mechanism in various instances: the colonisers flattening the aboriginal space into a *terra nullius* in order to be able to project over that their grid of property rights; Hobbes flattening the pre-social human co-existence into an undifferentiated *state of nature,* thus presupposing a chaotic *and* homogenous spatiality on which he was then able to project his statist geometry. Against romantic attempts to overcome society's mutual exclusion by postulating a more original communion, we should keep in

29 This analogy, to which we are to come back below, should not appear as a forced one: after all, it is exactly with Kant that the theological finality is finally internalised into a 'human teleology', that is, an ultimate end, the origin of which is in the human being *qua* transcendental subject. See Deleuze, 1985.

30 Agamben, 1998a: 111.

31 Galli, 2001.

32 Farinelli, 2003: 3–5. 'The constitution of modern legal space could only take place upon a prior discovery of some other space – namely, natural or physical space – and then the abandonment of that space into the background as absolute, universal space ... the insistent separation of natural or physical space did allow early modernity to visualize what, from now on, should count as pure legal space (the space of legal rules, sanctions, people and institutions) – while at the same time appearing to eliminate "impure" or "factual" natural space from its multiple, ever more probing, ever more abstract gaze' (Stramignoni, 2004: 225).

mind that every separation is grounded on the presupposition or, more precisely, the ontological production of an undifferentiated (either pessimistically *chaotic*, optimistically *common* or abstractly *absolute*) spatiality, i.e. a preliminary erasure which denies space as a differential and heterogeneous material complexity of bodies 'independent' from us. Let us reassert: the simple presupposition of a supposedly undifferentiated, uncontrollable chaos outside the law, far from being a radical destabilisation of the legal enterprise, is its *ontological presupposition*. What naively oppositional critiques of law miss, then, is exactly the *double move* grounding the spatiolegal architecture of modernity, i.e. the flattening of space *and* the geometrical projection of legal categories over it – i.e. the production of a space of exception. The originary gesture is that of positing a wedge (Geertz) between *nomos* and *physis*, norm and bare life, law and space. This is the ontological split that needs be problematised.

1.4 Positive law, Benjamin notes, is blind to the absoluteness of ends while natural law is blind to the contingency of means.[33]

Notwithstanding the latter is not a provocative conclusion, it is often left unaccounted for in spatiolegal debates, with the consequence of overlooking the preliminary *erasure* on which every legal state of exception is premised. This is not an unimportant distinction, since it leads to (rightly) criticising the alleged abstraction (i.e. de-spatialisation) performed by the formal, legal text, by (wrongly) counterpoising it to the supposedly concrete, real, spatial context, in this way neglecting the latter's as much 'artificial' character (and, conversely, the former's as much 'real' consistency). A good deal of responsibility for this outcome should be ascribed to the encounter between sociology and law.

Transversal to the dissatisfaction with the out-worldly understandings of law as divine, natural and absolute, social sciences gradually infiltrated the legal project in order to decontaminate it, we could say, from any yearning for a (divine, natural, transcendental) *beyond*. Any superior finalism was to be brought down to earth, so as to be available to the work of socio-empirical techné.[34] The socio-empirical approach would conflate 'higher principles' (be it God, morality, truth or justice) within law: justice ceases to orient law beyond itself, and rather ends up corresponding, in a circular argument, to the very deployment of the right method, that is, the correct legal procedure, to the point of becoming redundant. As Constable observes, both positivist and socio-legal approaches converge 'in affirming

33 Zartaloudis, 2011: 143.

34 If for Kant 'a Society [is] the only milieu in which the last end can be historically realized', social sciences would be the only techné through which this is to be achieved (Deleuze, 1985: 144).

that the connection between law and morality [as well as *justice*] is an empirically contingent matter of social factors'.[35] This implies a genuine 'faith that sociological enquiry or empirical knowledge of institutions and practices of society can improve law and that law can improve society'.[36] Accordingly, 'socially descriptive accounts of legal systems', whether supported by the appropriate methodology, are assumed to be able to unearth the role and functioning of this 'exclusively social' law as an 'instrument or strategy within a field of social power'.[37] The blindness of natural law for the contingency of means is replaced with a symmetrical indifference to the absoluteness of ends.[38]

Yet, this move away from higher principles is only apparent. Above, I followed Latour in criticising the sociological presupposition of the social as a 'stable and absolute third term', an all-encompassing and homogenous quality shared among social actors and framed according to laws guiding their action. This presupposition, in fact, re-enacts the double move just described: the ontological flattening of society onto a homogenous body (the social as the new centre of correlation), and the subsequent drawing of sociological categories over it, forging powerful explanatory social lenses to supposedly uncover the hidden laws of the social itself.[39] Of course, with the advent of post-colonialism, feminism, post-racism, post-structuralism and other critical movements, the sociological faith in the empirical observation and the neutrality of the social scientist has been radically shaken. Yet, critical sociology did not overcome the founding paradox of sociology: applied to law, it provided invaluable tools to contest and debunk the latter's ideological character, yet often ending up entangled within its own contradictions.[40]

Admittedly, the last two paragraphs are a rather selective and to some extent ungenerous generalisation of an extremely complex and multifaceted evolution. Many are the relevant exceptions in this narration. However, what I intended was a heuristic overview with the purpose of emphasising how the various movements reformulating legal thinking against the classical perspective of a transcendental, formal law, seem to share the same (negative) starting point, i.e. an ontological separation – and the corollary 'operational' willingness to *link* and *bridge* it – differently exposed as the supposed gap between an abstract law and a contingent reality, a formal law and a law-in-action, a formal and a material constitution, validity and efficacy, text and context, law and space, and so on. As

35 Constable, 2007: 29.
36 Constable, 2007: 10.
37 Constable, 2007: 39.
38 'Positive law, Benjamin notes, is blind to the absoluteness of ends while natural law is blind to the contingency of means' (Zartaloudis, 2011: 143).
39 Latour, 2005: 36.
40 Douzinas *et al.*, 1994: 2.

Zartaloudis reminds us, the simple shift from 'vertical' to 'horizontal' transcendentalism, rather than challenging the logic of exception, ends up reproducing its functioning.[41] Again, to be overlooked is the fact that the concrete and empirical space to which many sociological and critical thinkers propose to turn the attention to, is as much abstract as the geometrical grid that legal categories project over it. The inability to acknowledge that a 'double move' – erasure and partitioning– is at the origin of law's dealing with contingency, means that these necessary critiques mainly remain confined *within* the very opposition – i.e. law and space (law and world, law and life…) – on which the whole spatiolegal architecture of modernity is centred, and which they were supposed to debunk in the first place. It follows that the abstract/concrete dichotomy is still taken for granted, and the materiality of the spatiolegal remains unaccounted for.

1.5 Law is a force, like gravity, through which our worlds exercise an influence upon one another, a force that affects the course of these worlds through normative space.[42]

The same *aporia* founding the sociological approach to law is also to be found in the *impasse* into which legal geography has come to find itself by taking for granted a reductive understanding of space (what Alain Pottage terms a 'weak specification of contingency') and thus missing the very potentiality a proper spatial perspective would entail.[43] More than a discipline, legal geography could be understood as an interdisciplinary project aimed at developing an approach to law consistent with the 'spatial turn' in social sciences, with different degrees of intersection between the disciplines of geography and law. In a recent reader, Irus Braverman *et al.* categorise past and present works according to the profundity and complexity of such intersection.[44] First, there is the beginning of a mutual dialogue between law and geography, in which however both disciplines remain firmly within their own territory, not letting the dialogue become interdisciplinary proper. Moreover, space here is still assumed in traditional terms, failing to integrate the insights of critical human geography.[45] Second, there is a more explicitly interdisciplinary, common

41 Zartaloudis, 2002: 199.
42 Cover, 1986: 9–10.
43 Pottage, 1998: 12.
44 Braverman *et al.*, 2014. In the introduction to this edited collection a useful bibliography of these trends may be found.
45 Butler argues that this impasse will haunt legal geography for some time, as the inability to overcome the conceptual dualisms between law and space, which appears both in 'the spatial fetishism of the early "regionalist" school' and in the 'unbalanced instrumentalism' of ideological critiques. Butler, 2009: 315.

project, promoted by the movement of critical legal studies (CLS) and the work of authors such as Nicholas Blomley, Don Mitchell, David Delaney, Gordon Clark, Richard Ford, Davina Cooper, etc. Here, through the exploration of race, policing, private property, public space and jurisdiction, the spatial turn is more consistently integrated within a (spatio)legal project, officialised by the appearance at the beginning of the second millennium of three influential texts, *The Place of Law, Law and Geography* and *The Legal Geographies Reader*. These works approach law and space more explicitly in their spatiolegal conjunction, with a growing awareness of their mutual interspersion and the multiple, constructed, fluid and juxtaposed nature of the resulting spatiolegalities. Third, on accompanying these later reflections, a more explicitly trans- or post-disciplinary direction emerges in which the spatiolegal becomes a key orientation for other disciplines beyond law and geography, within a more explicitly critical and even post-critical framework, hence the emergence of critical legal geography (CLG).

CLG develops a critical and even terminological effort to integrate more radically the import of spatial, material, affective and post-human directions of contemporary critical geography within legal theory. With the notion of *splice*, for instance, Blomley indicates the crystallisations of spatiolegal dialectics, which tend to appear as a hegemonic 'order of things' and thus non-negotiable. Splices are on-going, continuously reformulated: *splicing(s)* whose role in making the world for us is crucial.[46] Braverman coins the notion of *animal mobilegalities* to explore the relation between animals and a law conceived as 'a living process that feeds on, and depends upon, dynamic human-nonhuman assemblages'.[47] Most relevant is Delaney's concept of *nomosphere*, defined as

> *the cultural-material environs that are constituted by the reciprocal materialization of 'the legal', and the legal signification of the 'socio-spatial', and the practical, performative engagement through which such constitutive moments happen and unfold* ... we ... are never outside of the nomosphere, never free of its effects, never not pragmatically engaging nomospheric traces. But, again, we are not merely *in* it. Indeed ... our very being-in-the-world, is a fundamental dynamic component *of* it.[48]

The notion of *nomosphere* covers a wider spectrum than the merely legal, encompassing rules of custom, politeness, family, religion and so forth.[49] Law is seen as a condensation of our being-together in the form of the

46 Blomley, 2002: 30–1.
47 Braverman, 2013: 105.
48 Delaney, 2010: 25.
49 Delaney, 2010: 257.

emergence of spatiolegal crystallisations (what he defines 'nomic settings' in relation to 'pervasive cultural processes and forces associated with ideological projects', that he terms 'nomoscapes') sanctioning the becoming-illegal of certain events.[50] Telling instance, Delaney notes, is the notion of 'hostile environment', in which the materiality of the nomosphere as well as its on-going juridification becomes explicit, in the way a behaviour – such as intrusively 'touching' an employee or uttering abusive comments – is re-defined from simply 'impolite' or 'annoying' to illegal, that is, an act producing a 'hostile environment', insofar as having the requisite degree of 'pervasiveness' that makes it experienced as oppressive by the victim.[51] This goes to show how signs, gestures and other elements play a material and atmospheric effect both in generating immanent and material normativities, as well as in recalibrating the scope of legal action. Significantly resonating with the discussion that is to follow, law can be said to assume an atmospheric orientation, that is, it becomes able to detect, assess and punish environmental perturbations.

Delaney's is one of the most significant attempts to pursue the aim of CLG: not simply re-materialising law but rather acknowledging its always-already materiality, at the same time avoiding the reduction of law/space's 'irreducible interpenetration' into an 'identity'. Yet, as affective, material and post-human approaches to law keep surfacing, it is important to remind ourselves that simply flattening the transcendence of law into the horizontality of post-human networks is not enough. More attention is required if we are to avoid rehashing yet another time the unproductive move from 'vertical' to 'horizontal' transcendentalism.[52]

1.6 My task is changed: not to uphold the law, or another law, but to maintain the skin that keeps law in place.[53]

In a more critical categorisation of the spatial turn in legal theory or, more precisely, of how legal theory misunderstood it, succumbing to what he terms a *fear* of space, Philippopoulos-Mihalopoulos distinguishes three main tendencies: first, the reduction of legal space to the concept of jurisdiction, that is, to a legal re-presentation, an approach thus missing space altogether; second, the idealisation of space as a fluid, dynamic

50 Delaney, 2010: 59, 100.

51 A hostile work environment is an 'intimidating, hostile or offensive working environment', that is an uncomfortable or oppressive atmosphere that 'unreasonably interfer[es] with an individual's job performance', United States *Code of Federal Regulations* (Title 29, vol. 4, chapter XIV).

52 E.g. Braverman *et al.* caution against the flattening of scale and other concepts that, even once we stop paying attention, 'continue to operate with powerful performative force, organizing legal geographies in the world' (Braverman *et al.*, 2014: 18).

53 Mieville, 2009: 373.

process, which implies 'a certain critical concept of the law as particular and embodied', overlooking the conflictual, violent and dislocating character of space, and instead reducing it to a pacific and malleable instrument: namely a neutral and innocent matter to be used as a 'panacea for social injustice';[54] third, the side-stepping of space, understood as just one among other dimensions to be added to the social, a position perfectly exemplified in the field of urban theory by Peter Marcuse's observation that 'most problems have a spatial aspect, but their origins lie in economic, social, political arenas, the spatial being a partial cause and an aggravation, but only partial'.[55] A position that misses altogether the ontological impact of the spatial turn on the politico-legal foundation of the project of modernity.[56]

Thinking about law *and* space is not a peaceful and fluid side-project for the legal enterprise – it actually entails disturbing the very assumptions of law, bringing to the fore its materiality, 'questioning its ethics' and thus gesturing towards its justice.[57] This materiality cannot be reduced to the production of inter-subjective, sociological or phenomenological performativity, since it ontologically *precedes* subject/object distinction. It cannot be approached through a simple critique of the 'immateriality' of legal representations in the name of 'an illusory desire for the "concrete"'.[58] It is not simply a question of 're-materialising' law, or 'embedding' it onto space. It is exactly in these terms that legal geographers initially approached the question, seeking refuge from the radical contingency of space either in de-spatialising representations or in the comfort of empirical, concrete, processual, pacific, performed and embedded contexts: *Ils n'ont jamais été spatiales*. As a result, the tendency has been that of oscillating between an 'abstract' or 'vertical' state of exception (where space is 'denied' through representation) and a 'concrete' or 'horizontal' state of exception (where space is 'frozen' through sociological structures and empirical method, and thus still 'excepted' from its complexity), that is, from one side to the other of the spatiolegal architecture of modernity.

Whilst recent directions of CLG, as those mentioned above, are successful in addressing most of Philippopoulos-Mihalopoulos' concerns, they still fall short from unfolding the evental dimension of materiality as discussed in the first chapter. Let us take for instance the concept of nomosphere. The latter aims to show how, Delaney explains, 'nomospheric processes are

54 Philippopoulos-Mihalopoulos, 2011a: 190–1.
55 Marcuse, 2009: 195.
56 For references to the works supposedly falling on each 'category', see Philippopoulos-Mihalopoulos, 2011a.
57 Philippopoulos-Mihalopoulos, 2011a: 195.
58 Cunningham, 2008: 466.

generative of a sense of place' through their inter-penetrating space-producing performativities, in this way emphasising 'the situated character of social life' and, against the tendency to give the law an 'other-worldly inflection', reasserting a resolutely 'sociologically and phenomenologically' inflected spatiality.[59] What seems to be missing in this otherwise compelling conceptualisation in fact, is exactly the virtual 'other-worldliness' of the spatiolegal, the eventful excess that prevents it from being reduced to a merely sociological, phenomenological and, more generally, relational construct. The failure to account for this aspect risks fetishising this newly discovered legal materiality. Legal thinking overcomes its atavistic fear of space, yet to be seized by an as much arresting fear of abstraction.

As Philippopoulos-Mihalopoulos suggests, 'by not facing its fear of abstraction, the space of the law allows whoever feels more at ease with it to manipulate its embeddedness, thereby converting it from a radical tool to a hegemonic presence'.[60] Unaccounted for, in fact, it thus remains the abstract and concrete, non-relational event of any spatiolegal correlation. Namely, the eventful excess which is the virtual and real condition of possibility of any given assemblage, splice or nomosphere, harbouring the potential for a radically alternative understanding of the spatiolegal, beyond any primacy of law in relation to a subject, a subject in relation to a law, as well as beyond any reduction of the spatiolegal itself to a phenomenological, performative, pragmatic in-between. As Colebrook observes, 'there can only be systems, differences or laws if there are virtual potentials *to differ*, to enter into relation'.[61] Without this emphasis, the nomosphere is bound to remain 'too wordly', too actual, producing a sort of hyper-positivistic, suffocating understanding of the spatiolegal as an 'immanent horizon of actuality'.[62] Notwithstanding law is made more flexible, material and atmospheric (encompassing such dimensions as the 'extra-legal and sub-legal', human and non-human, imaginary and physical, experiential and spatial), and it is still understood as a tool to pursue an ever more encompassing juridification of the world by means of penetrating and preventively neutralising the eventfulness of being-together, rather than a tool to *make space* for the emergence of its excessive potentials: its spatial justice.

A similar outcome seems to be the case with Sloterdijk's concept of *nomotop* seems to be similar, i.e. the normative architecture of co-existence or the 'moral ether' holding together society as a system of immanent tensions in permanent 'action' upon bodies.[63] If Delaney's *nomosphere*

59 Delaney, 2010: 25, 32.
60 Philippopoulos-Mihalopoulos, 2015: 33.
61 Colebrook, 2009: 13.
62 Paraphrasing Zartaloudis, 2002: 201.
63 Sloterdijk, 2006: 420.

encompasses a broader dimension than mere legality, including the wider sphere of rules, norms, customs etc., Sloterdijk's *nomotop* connects law even more radically with human and non-human materialities, as well as to a more markedly ontological, rather than merely phenomenological, dimension, assuming law as always-already imbricated in the spatiality of co-belonging in the form of an 'atmospheric tension' which exercises a permanent attraction on a collective.[64] The nomotop appears as the normative architecture of co-existence, holding together the social as a tensegritous system of immanent tensions in permanent 'action' upon bodies, made of customs, cultures, objects, rights, regulations, affects, relations of production, language games, forms of life, institutions, habitus, etc.[65] As for his more general conceptualisation however, in this 'spatiolegal' application of spherology the significant attention to the rhizomatic dynamism of the co-constituted normative 'foaming' of being-together is not accompanied by an engagement with its eventful dimension, i.e. justice. Both for *nomosphere* and *nomotop*, ultimately, 'the in-between of shared situations … is what there is and all there is'.[66] Moreover, both models betray the tendency, as Philippopoulos-Mihalopoulos stresses, to 'compartmentalis[e] the nonhuman in relation to a spatially determined human community', so that 'the human remains a central figure of perception, performance or action'.[67]

The spatiolegal however is not a merely 'human' framework, a socio-cultural construct superimposed onto an inert, external, 'natural' matter. The spatiolegal refers to a normativity that emerges immanently out of the interpenetration between bodies, structures and spaces. These approaches are valuable attempts to think the spatiolegal in ways that eschew the problematic quest for 'bridging the gap' or 'drawing a link' between law and space (and thus the implicit assumption of law/space dichotomy), which instead characterises many works in this area. This welcome and necessary move is not sufficient, however, if we are to avoid falling into the exceptional paradigm yet again. To qualify: whilst they brilliantly debunk, deconstruct and unmask the *aporias* of the *legal* side of law (law as *logos*) by showing its always-already spatial character, these 'nomospheric investigations' are yet to deal with the non-juridifiable, impersonal and inhuman event of the spatiolegal: in a word, with law's justice.

Again, we encounter the impasse of relationalism, namely the tendency, once the dichotomical categories of modernity have been debunked, to produce a frozen picture of the world that offers little hope for creation and

64 Sloterdijk, 2006: 434–43.
65 Sloterdijk, 2006: 420.
66 Thrift, 2008: 85.
67 Philippopoulos-Mihalopoulos, 2013: 3.

resistance. Producing a sophisticated account of the affective, post-human and immanent materiality of the spatiolegal, yet failing to account for its excessive dimension, risks opening to a merely instrumental understanding of law: as a result, these supposedly emancipatory theories appear to set the scene for the emergence of a 'new' spatiolegal architecture of exception whose main purpose (expressed through juridical, economic, securitarian apparatuses), is exactly that of defusing eventfulness from space. An obvious question follows: how to prevent contemporary spatiolegal speculations from reproducing an updated and post-structural form of legal hyper-positivism, i.e. an all-encompassing nomosphere, whose ontological closure only demands the necessary recalibration of socio-legal instruments (through neurological, cybernetic and other savoirs) to ensure a total juridification of the world? How is law kept 'open in possibility', thus necessarily increasing its flexibility and spatial 'awareness', yet at the same time not providing it with ever more sophisticated instruments to become all-ingesting? In other words, how can law be oriented towards the contingent fact of its taking place in a world *not for law*, without falling into the dead-ends of relativism, decisionism, nihilism?

An answer, I suggest, is to be searched for within what is missing in the above approaches, namely a satisfying engagement with the question of justice. Justice is the excessive eventfulness of the spatiolegal, and it is through justice that we can avoid producing another ultimately co-optable spatiolegal ontology. We thus face two objectives: first, providing a radical understanding of the spatiolegal as relational and eventful, and fully emancipated from 'the centrality of a human, anthropocentric and anthropomorphic subject' which the above models still seem to betray;[68] second, providing a material understanding of justice as not only 'excessive to law' (that is, not simply a juridifiable excess), but rather as law's 'non-jurifiable event'. Two objectives which almost tautologically overlap, as a tripartite configuration seem to surface, according to which the interrelation between law and space, as ontologically inseparable and yet non-coincident dimensions, must be thought of in connection with the idea of justice, i.e. the event of any spatiolegal concatenation, the always-present line of flight which provides the potential for piercing through nomospheric closures.

Fully unpacking these objectives will have to wait for the final chapter. In the next section I begin to set the stage for this effort by focusing attention on one of the most interesting attempts to think justice as a radically excessive event: Derrida's *La Force de Loi*.

68 Philippopoulos-Mihalopoulos, 2013: 3.

2.1 Beyond being and nothingness ... inhabiting until the last moment in the impotent possibility which exceeds both.[69]

How can one offer an even brief and simplistic account of the millenary philosophical, theological and political meditation on the idea of justice? The classical image of law is that of a power subordinated and delegated to the higher Good and its co-substantial notion of *dike*.[70] Justice, in this sense, is what denies law's supposed self-sufficiency, forcing it to thrust itself beyond the narrow confines of its legalistic comfort-zone, towards a higher principle to which it has to tend and depend, and with respect to which humankind's hypothetical conformity would render law itself pointless. Within this context justice is not a peaceful goal to be smoothly achieved, but an 'ontologically intractable' dimension, 'a-logical' insofar as constantly contradicting law itself, indefinitely breaking the 'harmonic rhythm of the logos, its all-encompassing and governing hubris'.[71] There is an ontological conflict at the root of the law/justice interrelation, a conflict which, at the same time, is a paradoxical necessity. Although law, 'as calculation and harmonising knowledge incessantly seeks to avoid, remove and overcome the paradox', it ontologically *needs* dike, since justice is what allows the law to 'move' and to strive 'beyond' itself, to prevent its own collapsing into the closure of a totalising juridification.[72] On the one hand, this is what the *nomos* of the polis ultimately gestures towards, i.e. the subjection of space to its rational and ordering *logos*: a spatiolegal tautology. Yet, the polis is quintessentially democratic and as such constantly swerves from any totalitarian attempt at suffocating it. An atmosphere of democracy traverses it, the breeding ground of justice, an inclination towards freedom which has the Janus-face of a *pharmakon*, i.e. to simultaneously cure and poison: As Massimo Cacciari reminds us, it is at the same time an 'indispensable remedy against the tyrannical hubris, and yet it unavoidably produces the anarchical hubris, the terrible separation between Nomos and Dike'.[73]

The necessity of keeping alive the conflictual excess of the city, however, is soon forgotten. No longer a dislocating force justice will be increasingly assumed to be a pacifying and sedating tool to 'bridge the gap' and neutralise conflict. Initially, this entails assuming a metaphysical, immaterial notion of justice as coming from above (e.g. from Nature, God, Reason,

69 Agamben, 1993: 72.
70 For the sake of our discussion it is not relevant to explore the important question of the relation between the notions of Good and Justice in Plato, which arguably tend to converge towards the end of his work (e.g. the *Republic* and the *Parmenides*) without however conflating into each other.
71 Cacciari, 1997: 49 (my translation).
72 Cacciari, 1997: 42–52 (my translation).
73 Cacciari, 1997: 25 (my translation).

Universal Rights and so on). Subsequently, the ultimate inconsistency of this impalpable justice (always mismatching the factical spatiality of beings), opens the path towards its positivist dissolution into law itself. According to a schema we already observed, either projected into some ethereal transcendence or flattened into a legal immanence, the law/justice separation remains unchallenged. Take again the locus in which this logic can be observed at its purest, i.e. Kant's elaboration of a law simultaneously emancipated from transcendent principles and empirical conditions, a law that is 'the representation of a pure form, and is independent of content or object, spheres of activity or circumstances', a pure 'form of law', where the reference to higher principles has fully folded into a circular self-reference.[74] According to Deleuze this law,

> defined by its pure form, without substance or object or any determination whatsoever, is such that no one knows nor can know what it is. It operates without making itself known. It defines a realm of transgression where one is already guilty.[75]

In other words, this is a law which preliminary defines the *where* of its application, a priori reducing the world to a *world for law*.[76] This is the paradox of a law which pretends to judge a world which has been already abstracted into a space of exception. In Agamben's terms, thus law is 'applied through its disapplication'.[77] Justice is the line of flight away from this paradoxical closure, provided it is considered beyond such nihilistic separation, in the sense of what Zartaloudis indicates as a 'non-juridical justice'.[78] This means understanding it as both immanent and excessive to the spatiolegal concatenations, inseparable from (they unavoidably belong to the same world) and yet non-coincidental with law itself, since it is utterly *not for law* (that is, non-juridifiable). Evidently, the main limitatation that the approaches just described betray, I argue, is that of missing this dimension, and thus ultimately falling short from challenging the closure of total juridification. How can we think of an excessive, eventful notion of justice, without however falling back into the nihilistic articulation of yet another separation? Could we rework the Greek schema, by conceiving a justice which would play the role of a self-subversive force inside the law, constantly dislocating it and thus preventing its self-referential closure? This is

74 Deleuze, 1991b: 83.

75 Deleuze, 1991b: 82–3.

76 'The blindness of the closure of the legal system towards the world or existence is matched by the blindness of an anarchic foundation of juridical (as well as philosophical) sense-making or "justice"' (Zartaloudis, 2011: 141).

77 Agamben, 2005a: 32–41.

78 Zartaloudis, 2011.

the path undergone by Jacques Derrida in his famous article *La Force de Loi*, where he elaborates a notion of justice as a 'sabotaging' force which constantly deconstructs law's violent foundation and its pretence to coincide with, and tame, its 'outside'.

2.2

> This is the very definition of ghostliness, as that which inhabits the clouded border between materiality and immateriality, reality and illusion, presence and absence.[79]

In his work, Derrida attacks the Western 'ontology of presence' by removing its metaphysical 'grounds', infinitely differing and deferring its dichotomical structures into a paradoxically 'groundless foundation', so that the classical categories of ontology are radically dislocated, inescapably *haunted* by a 'ghost of undecidability'. To understand how Derrida's 'hauntology' applies to law, it is useful to start from language, the breeding ground of deconstruction.

In a famous essay, Umberto Eco divides Western attempts to achieve a 'general representation of knowledge and/or the world' into two main models.[80] On the one hand, there is the *dictionary*: i.e. a static system, faithful to the Platonic presupposition of a given, stable and thus fully knowable Order of Being, reflecting the confidence vis-à-vis the possibility of drawing precise point-to-point correspondences between the text and the world. On the other hand, there is the *encyclopaedia*: i.e. a dynamic model, emerging in response to the surfacing awareness of the always incomplete, evolving and 'open' character of knowledge, and thus aware of the need for a system of knowledge to be sufficiently 'flexible', so as to be able to *take in* new discoveries as well as to always contingently provide the contextualised and finalised information required.[81] To the 'arborescent' staticity of the dictionary the encyclopaedia opposes a continuous, boundless and rhizomatic movement of hypertextual navigation, a flow which is not blocked by pre-given text-world correspondences, but rather kept in motion by flexible *rules of reasonability* which regulate the 'passage' between notions. A concern for procedures of movement, connection and circulation replaces the striving for analytical definitions of stability.[82]

Keeping in mind the heuristic value of this otherwise simplistic distinction, let us frame deconstruction in its light. Deconstruction is in the first place a strategy to debunk the 'linguistic state of exception', that is, the dictionarial presupposition of an unproblematic correspondence between signifier and signified, on which the structural stability of language

79 Mohaghegh and Golestaneh, 2011: 493.
80 Eco, 2007: 13.
81 Eco, 2007: 44.
82 Eco, 2007: 519.

supposedly rests.[83] By emphasising its lack of foundations (or the foundation being exactly a constitutive deficiency), deconstruction problematises this correspondence, unfolding the always undecidable and thus overflowing and excessive character of the sign. Derrida's famous concept of *différance* encapsulates this indefinite spatio-temporal dislocation (differing and deferring) of the signifier-signified correspondence, and thus the constitutive *impossibility* to ever tame and remove its necessary excess, its never exhausted ontological 'trace'.[84] Consequently signification, i.e. the exceptional operation of language, is bound to be endlessly displaced. In this way, Agamben observes, Derrida is able to 'call into question the primacy of presence and signification for the philosophical tradition' – yet, the Italian philosopher adds, does he 'truly call into question signification in general'?[85] According to Agamben, the answer is negative: deconstruction sanctions the constant displacement of signification by the irreducible excess of the sign and yet, whereas language is unable to find 'rest' in stable correspondences, its exceptional operation *keeps on running*, although into an infinitely disseminated motion.[86] As a result, the paradigm of operation is ultimately left unchallenged. To further elaborate this observation let us see how Derrida translates this strategy to the legal field by seeking to answer the following question: 'does deconstruction insure, permit, authorise the possibility of justice?'[87]

2.3 A decision that didn't go through the ordeal of the undecidable would not be a free decision, it would only be the programmable application or unfolding of a calculable process. It might be legal; it would not be just.[88]

First of all, the 'juridico-ethico-political' sense of justice which Derrida seeks to unfold must be framed within his conception of ethics. This is centred on the ontological (or rather, *hauntological*) condition of undecidability, before which we are paradoxically called to take the ethical responsibility to decide. A 'true' and 'just' decision can only unfold from a radical undecidability: 'a decision that didn't go through the ordeal of the undecidable would not be a free decision, it would only be the programmable application or unfolding of a calculable process. It might be legal; it

83 Namely, language's sovereign 'attempt to make sense coincide with denotation, to stabilize a zone of indistinction between the two in which language can maintain itself in relation to its denotata by abandoning them and withdrawing from them into a pure langue (the linguistic "state of exception")' (Agamben, 1998a: 22).
84 Derrida, 1976.
85 Agamben, 2005b: 103.
86 Agamben, 2005b: 103.
87 Derrida, 1990: 921.
88 Derrida, 1990: 963.

would not be just'.[89] This is a never-ending, ever-haunting ordeal: 'the undecidable remains caught, lodged, at least as a ghost – but an essential ghost – in every decision, in every event of decision'.[90] Law, Derrida explains, is always inhabited by the 'ghost of undecidability' (*la hantise de l'indécidable*), which 'exceeds and contradicts' law itself, sanctioning the instability and restlessness of every legal decision.[91] Justice appears as an impossibility, and yet also the very condition of possibility of law, its transcendental principle. In the same sense, the impossibility inserted at the core of law by its indeterminacy is also the condition of possibility for justice to emerge in the form of a necessarily unpredictable event: justice's possibility lies in 'the paradoxical necessity of performing an act [of judgement] which is actually impossible'.[92] Justice agitates the staticity of law's state of exception, forces it to *move*, producing 'a certain movement within law, a movement which may be ruptured in a new manner'.[93] Against its sociological reduction to a merely 'empirically contingent matter of social factors', the ancient meaning of *dike* resonates in Derrida, as the arrow to which law must tend and depend:

> because of this overflowing of the performative ... always excessive ... justice ... has no horizon of expectation (regulative or messianic) ... remains, is yet, to come, à venir ... the very dimension of events irreducibly to come.[94]

Rather than being a regulative idea postulating a horizon as 'the opening and the limit that defines an infinite progress or a period of waiting', justice demands urgency. It 'does not wait'. It must be done: 'the instant of decision is a madness ... [it must] defy dialectics ... [a] decision of urgency and precipitation, acting in the night of non-knowledge and non-rule'.[95] Derrida assumes the 'place' of decision as an abyssal (*abgrund*) 'groundless foundation', a non-linguistic and non-representational event occurring in the solipsistic solitude of a 'pre-ontological void'.[96] In this dark night a lightless star shines, the transcendental *to-come* of justice, paradoxically guiding the law towards the impossible possibility of its event.

89 Derrida, 1990: 963.
90 Derrida, 1990: 963–5.
91 Derrida, 1990: 962–3.
92 Gehring, 2005: 163.
93 Gehring, 2005: 158. 'It may be the very thing that keeps us moving' (Derrida, 1990: 967).
94 Derrida, 1990: 969.
95 Derrida, 1990: 963.
96 Ruedin, 2002: 243.

Yet, how can one avoid two as much doomed alternatives, i.e. a never-ending deferral of decision (seemingly implied by the very impossibility of the decision itself), or a reactive (and reactionary), self-justificatory decisionism? Aware of this risk, Derrida stresses that deconstruction is not 'a quasi-nihilistic abdication before the ethico-politico-juridical question of justice'.[97] Justice is indeed to be reached *through* and *beyond* law: 'law is not justice. Law is the element of calculation ... but justice is incalculable ... justice is an experience of the impossible.'[98] Yet every decision must 'be both regulated and without regulation', that is, the 'incalculable justice requires us to calculate', from our paradoxical position *within* the 'unstable distinction between justice and *droit*, between justice (infinite, incalculable, rebellious to rule and foreign to symmetry, heterogeneous and heterotopic) and the exercise of justice as law', as calculation.[99] Is this extremely insightful reflection ultimately able to debunk the paradigm of exception? Is it able to satisfyingly account for the materiality of law? I believe we should ultimately answer negatively to both questions. By addressing the second, an answer to the first will simultaneously emerge. Let me explain.

The attempt to reach a 'justice without law', prefiguring a 'pre-ontological' void as the 'where' from which the ethical event (of justice/responsibility) would emerge, confines the latter within a solipsistic and ultimately a-spatial vacuum, producing a fracture in the immanence of the spatiolegal which amounts to re-inserting a negativity at the very core of ontology and ethics: in this sense, as Agamben contends, '"groundless" simply means "on negative ground"'.[100] Noys criticises Derrida for ultimately failing to 'accept' and 'traverse' this 'spectral negativity', and instead of withdrawing from it, seeks to fill it with a quasi-mystical, 'transcendent superessentiality': 'deconstruction fills out spectrality as such, as a reified "positive" and irreducible moment that comes from on high'.[101] In this interpretation, in the manner of Kant facing the unspeakable possibility of nature as a 'crude chaotic aggregate', Derrida would ultimately escape the unbearable negativity to which he has opened 'thought' into a teleological refuge. I would argue instead that Derrida's ultimate failure stems from his inability to fully remove negativity from the epicentre of metaphysics in the first place: in Zartaloudis' words, his problem is that he 'may have not gone far enough'.[102] The problem is not the renunciation of 'dealing with' negativity. It is its very presupposition. Accordingly, could we not retrace in this attempt 'to fill out spectrality' a resurfacing of the

97 Derrida, 1990: 953.
98 Derrida, 1990: 947.
99 Derrida, 1990: 959, 961.
100 Agamben, 2006[1982]: xiii.
101 Noys, 2012: 45.
102 Zartaloudis, 2002: 200, n. 4.

paradigmatic urge to immunise from a presupposed nothingness? Obviously, Derrida is careful to avoid 'responding' to negativity by resorting to an immunising operation. Yet, his rather mysterious, quasi-fideistic solution can only partially eschew, and is ultimately unable to challenge the latter's paradigm. Consequently this justice, though posited as extra-legal, appears to be still thought of as within the legal system and its systemic closure of the world, that is, within the legal state of exception. Although infinitely dislocating the latter, justice seems unable to ultimately block the operational repetition of its enclosing and juridifying ontological gesture. Accordingly, justice remains confined within a *world for law*, and the 'non-relation' between law and a world *not for law* 'remains blind'.[103]

2.4 It is only by breaking open the circle ... that the dimension of sense appears for itself.[104]

According to Timothy Campbell, by assuming the 'state of exception' as the originary politico-legal relation, Agamben is unable to satisfyingly account for the radical difference introduced by the advent of contemporary biopolitics.[105] In the same vein, Kalhed Furani observes that a blind-spot haunts Agamben's framework: his notion of state of exception overlooks the threshold between the state of exception, and the 'becoming of the state of exception', that is, the fact that the 'state of exception can signal something more than a stasis. It can also signal a *techne*'.[106] Whatever their accuracy with respect to their target (which I dispute), these observations are useful in order to qualify the problem of deconstruction when applied to the spatiolegal: namely, notwithstanding its effectiveness in debunking law's 'static' state of exception, deconstruction appears as unequipped to deal with its evolution into a *dynamic* state of exception. To repeat: deconstruction conjures a powerful critique of the former, liquefying the stability of its point-to-point correspondences into a continuous dislocation. It inserts at the core of the legal system an undecidability, i.e. the impossibility for the 'operation' of law to ever 'bridge' the law/space separation, to ever tame space. By removing its grounds as well as the 'outside' against which it is supposed to erect its geometry, deconstruction debunks the transcendent structures of the spatiolegal state of exception, which now faces the ontological impossibility of its own operations. Yet, the powerful critique that 'legal deconstruction' moves to the spatiolegal architecture of modernity appears ultimately unable to dismantle its core logic.

103 '[T]he relation between law and the world remains blind ... justice as the law's self-subversive formula for transcendence is a formula for juridical transcendence, not more and not less' (Zartaloudis, 2011: 140).

104 Deleuze, 2004[1969]: 23.

105 Campbell, 2011.

106 Furani, 2014.

As Petra Gehring has observed, differently from language, contemporary legal discourse is not so naïve to assume law as a system of truth. It is instead well aware of law's paradoxes and 'schizophrenia':

> to the extent that legal discourse sees itself as a normative discourse (in contrast to metaphysics) and is capable of reflecting accordingly, it is *aware* of its own inconsistencies (as well as of its violent character) … Deconstruction was made for truth discourses, not for the … jaded normativity of legal affairs.[107]

Even more explicitly, it could be argued that deconstruction itself, by emphasising the undecidability at the core of the static state of exception, plays a key role in propelling the surfacing of such 'legal awareness'. Likewise an endlessly signifying language which, before the evidence of the utter undecidability of its signification, finds its justification exactly in the now emptied operation of signification itself, so the spatiolegal state of exception, given the impossibility of its operations (and thus the inconsistency of their by now dissolved 'purposes'), assumes the operations themselves as its own self-fulfilling and self-justifying purpose. Facing the immanent closure triggered by deconstruction (i.e. the awareness of the lack of a transcendent Outside, and thus the ontological impossibility of any attempt to tame it), the spatiolegal state of exception

> *assum[es] both this impossibility* and these techniques … [as] the final possibility of an exhausted system, which folds back onto itself in order, in a mechanical fashion, to collapse in on itself. The Outside becomes the Inside, and the Inside now has no limits.[108]

Derrida was well aware of the risks of this closure, and his notion of justice *à venir* is exactly an attempt to avoid it in the direction of a transcendental excess. Yet, this paradoxical, mysterious, irrational and mad justice appears as too impalpable, immaterial and 'empty' to really problematise the operational paradigm of exception. Notwithstanding his insistence against justice being intended as 'messianic', what seems to be ultimately produced is a sort of 'petrified messianism', i.e. a law nullified from its content and as such kept alive only in its operations.[109] Although dislocated and indefinitely disseminated by deconstruction, law continues to operate its enclosing gesture, its exceptional mechanism remaining 'intact while we await the grand and shattering arrival of the event "to come"'.[110] Criticising

107 Gehring, 2005: 168 (my emphasis).
108 Tiqqun, 2010: 116, 117.
109 Agamben, 2012: 271.
110 Noys, 2012: 45.

Derrida for placing the ethical decision within a non-linguistic, non-representational and pre-ontological void, Isaac Ruedin observes that since

> language is not a second order system of representation, but rather an originating mode of living the world, the linguistic gesture and the private act of responsibility (*pace* Derrida) are no longer incompatible; in fact, they occupy the same ontological space.[111]

Likewise, law and justice occupy the same ontological space, and there is no possibility of 'shattering' the spatiolegal situation in which we are through a solipsistic 'leap of faith' occurring in a pre-ontological vacuum.[112] Instead, the inability of deconstruction to ultimately problematise the law/space separation appears to engender an as much problematic law/justice separation, obliquely re-proposing the basic structure of Western tradition, i.e. the pseudo-dialectic of law and justice.[113] I contend that to postulate the chaotic dislocation of law via the anarchic and subversive notion of justice is not a sufficient strategy to overcome this 'great impasse'.[114] The positing of justice as 'chaos within the law' remains trapped within the operational closure of a world *for law*, i.e. an undifferentiated chaos ready to be incorporated by law as a weak, 'juridified contingency'.[115] The 'will to control' must eliminate the transcendent immutable idols, Severino reminds us, in order to be able to fully control the chaotic becoming which they deny. The transcendent idols are, so to speak, essentially anti-nomical: they ultimately prevent the spatiolegal state of exception from fully unfolding.[116] This is

111 Ruedin, 2002: 249.

112 Melissa Wright has written a compelling paper on Mexican women's struggle in Ciudad Juárez against the vicious violence, often surrounded by a cloud of impunity, to which they are subjected. In the interplay between the women's incalculable demand for justice (the impossible justice of having back their killed daughters) and their calculated, that is, specific requests to the government, she emphasises the significance played by the empathy linking their campaign to the greater public: an 'emotional connection ... crucial for assuring that the paradox of justice, as explained by Derrida, be associated with political possibility, instead of with political impossibility'. This material affectivity, sanctioning once more the fact that law and justice are in the 'same ontological space' is exactly what is 'missing from Derrida's contemplation of the paradox within the calculation of politics on behalf of an incalculable justice' (Wright, 2009: 219)

113 Zartaloudis, 2010: 280.

114 I am referring to Benjamin's observation about the 'great impasse of knowledge extending between the concepts of law and justice', in Jacobson, 2003: 167.

115 'Conventionally the law is responsive to chaos but only so through its own understanding of chaos as a juridified contingency (and a naive deconstruction of its paradoxical formation and reformation is usually a mere reconstruction of its juridical foundations)' (Zartaloudis, 2011: 142).

116 Severino, 1979: 22 (my translation).

what deconstruction ultimately misses: the fact that the state of exception always-already 'contains the seeds of its own deconstruction'.[117]

As we are to see in the next chapter, what thus emerges is a new configuration, a *dynamic* spatiolegal state of exception, no longer concerned with colonising, striating and crystallising space anymore. Once emancipated from any of these statically 'territorial' operations, as well as from any transcendent idol, what remains is only the self-referential concern with 'correct procedures of movement between connection and correlation', 'rules of passage' rather than 'true' correspondences between the text and the world: the state of exception becomes literally *encyclopaedic*, no longer static or dichotomical but moving rhizomatically at warp speed in a smooth and boundless globe.[118] The above mentioned paradox of a law which pretends to judge over a world which is however only a projection of law's state of exception, is thus transferred to the paradox of an impossible justice which ultimately becomes 'an aestheticized disinterested formula 'without engagement' ... a sterile law in itself'.[119] As a consequence, the eternally waited-for justice ultimately collapses into law, that is, blurs into due procedures, efficient know-how, problem-solving routines, social control technologies, bureaucratic apparatuses, securitarian control and all other technical and technological operations, dissolving into social policy, grounded 'in social knowledge, in cost-benefit analyses of facts and values, and in socially constructed (and constructing) procedural systems and institution of principles, rules and norms'.[120] The dichotomies that were left unchallenged within the socio legal approach (e.g. law-as-text and law-in-action, or, transcendence and immanence, general and particular, will and accident, law and its application, law and space, law and justice) are now overcome, only to blur in a functional correlation.

In words I am to qualify in a few pages, it could be said that law's vibrating dislocation is no longer abstracted into an a-spatial frame of reference (i.e. an *abstract* state of exception) nor sought to be contextualised and frozen through socio-empirical means (i.e. a *concrete* state of exception): the dislocated, 'pragmatic and impersonal' mechanism of exception keeps on running, absolutely deterritorialised and dislocated, since it is this very movement and its constant lubrication to become law's

117 de Sutter, 2011: 56 (my translation).

118 Deleuze and Guattari (2004[1980]: 411) contend that 'within the legal model, one is constantly reterritorialising around a point of view, on a domain, according to a set of constant relations; but with an ambulant model, the process of deterritorialization constitutes and extends the territory itself'. Yet, it is with the 'ambulant' side of law which today we need to confront.

119 Zartaloudis, 2011: 142.

120 Constable, 2007: 40.

self-referential purpose.[121] What is produced is a sort of immobile movement, akin to the frozen dynamic of a *jet d'eau*, whose smooth circularity constantly defuses the potentiality for the emergence of events, since it is exactly this *event*uality (the contingent opening of a non-juridifiable world that justice prefigures) that the centripetal movement of the legal operation neutralises: swept into this idle movement, justice is unable to 'break open the circle', can only observe it from outside, can only offer its endorsement, ultimately becoming a sort of 'critical apology', a justification for the legal system itself: 'justice is identified with the administration of justice'.[122] In other words: *justice is reduced to mere techné.*

Deconstruction always arrives late, always preceded by the self-deconstruction of the spatiolegal system itself.[123] By failing to provide this ghostly justice with the ontological materiality it deserves, and ultimately presupposing a negativity at the core of ontology, justice risks being ultimately consigned to the machinations of contemporary biopolitics. Justice is not an impossible *à venir*, but rather an excessive potentiality which *is* here-and-now, an absolutely material, virtual and excessive event:

> not some abstract and undifferentiated, or unknowable beyond that we can only approach negatively and critically ... not as some structural condition that we only know after the event, but the virtual as the real potentiality from which actuality unfolds.[124]

Thus the emergence of spatiolegal assemblages is no longer posited as something that occurs (Kantianly) beyond our capacity to know, but rather something whose potentials we can enquire. Hence we 'put the material into the Derridean ghost of the undecidable', by simultaneously asserting the inescapability of every situation, as well as the cosmic contingency to which, through which, every situation is opened, strategically, to the

121 In order to appreciate the difference between a sociological model still anchored on what I term a 'static' *concrete state of exception*, and the biopolitical model of control, enacted by a dynamic state of exception, it is necessary to introduce Deleuze's notion of control. This is done in the next chapter.

122 *Enkiklos*, the root of the term encyclopaedia, is the Greek world for circle.

123 A limit which will become particularly evident especially in those applications of the strategy of deconstruction to the legal field, that lack the complexity and sophistication of Derrida's. As this critical endeavour would succeed in forcing us to re-think the role of law (e.g. vis-à-vis gender, race, colonialism etc.), it would however fail to provide strategic counter-points (besides the already-criticised, simplistic calls for a 'turn to the concrete' against the legal ideology) and instead surrendering to a relativistic 'obsession with indeterminacy and indecision', which is arguably the quicksand in which for instance the movement of Critical Legal Studies ultimately ended (Zartaloudis, 2011, p. 139).

124 Colebrook, 2009: 13.

intensive, non-juridifiable potential of an inhuman, impersonal, and yet absolutely material justice.[125]

3.1 The periods in which nothing happens don't fall between two events, they're in the events themselves, giving events their depth.[126]

Law, Deleuze and Guattari stress, is first of all the law of the State, of logos and striation. Law of the logos is violence and order at the same time, *despot* and *legislator*. Law's state of exception is grounded on this violent installation, i.e. the 'flattening' of the ontological multiplicity of space and the projection of an ordered politico-legal geometry. This is only a part of the story, however. An 'other' law is to be taken into account, the law of the nomos. Although nomos is the Greek word designating the law itself, what Deleuze and Guattari wish to turn their attention to is the more original and *nomadic* etymology of the term, which indicates a meaning in direct 'opposition to the law of the polis', i.e. a 'scattering' rather than a partitioning, 'distribution' rather than allocation: in fact, a 'special kind of distribution, one without division into shares, in a space without borders or enclosure'.[127] The nomadic law of smoothness is always 'exceptional' vis-à-vis the logic law of striation, that is, exceptional vis-à-vis the latter's state of exception, and thus vis-à-vis law's attempt to transcend itself – just as the smooth space is always exceptional, i.e. irreducible, to any striation, never fully colonisable. This is not to say that two laws are in place. Smooth space and striated space 'exist only in mixture'; likewise, *nomic* and *logic* law cannot exist independently of each other. There is no smoothness without emersion of striation, and no strata without secretion of smoothness, but rather degrees of smoothness and striation: these are the two 'characters' of the spatiolegal, its logic and nomic qualities, only formally but not ontologically distinguishable.[128]

Let us qualify that the nomic is not the violence of law. As Benjamin famously stressed, violence is inscribed in law since its very inception: the ontological gesture of law, its flattening and partitioning of space, is constitutively violent.[129] There is, we saw it, a structural relation within law, between its violent installation and the purified ordering it produces, between the two poles of violence and order: a structural couple held together by the *logic* of exception. Yet, the nomic is foreign to this coupling.

125 Philippopoulos-Mihalopoulos, 2011b: 14.
126 Deleuze, 1989: 160.
127 Deleuze and Guattari, 2004[1980]: 420, 621 n. 51.
128 Deleuze and Guattari, 2004[1980]: 524. From now on I use the term 'nomic' in order to distinguish it from the classical use of *nomos* as law.
129 Benjamin, 1999.

When discussing the State as the quintessential representation of the logos, Deleuze and Guattari define the nomic in terms of a radical exteriority to the state apparatus (a 'war machine' opposed to the 'state'), as the constitutive blind-spot (the 'obscure nomos') of the state's structural correlation between the two poles of the despotic and the legislating.[130] In other words, the nomadic law is what dislocates the two Janus-faces of the law of the logos: the 'structural relation' between the two poles of the logic (i.e. the state of exception) should not be confused with its 'dynamic tension' with the nomic. The nomic always puts the structural relation out-of-joint, constantly de-territorialising the exceptional territorialisations of law:

> there is a great danger of identifying the structural relation between the two poles of political sovereignty, and the dynamic interrelation of these two poles, with the power [puissance] of war.[131]

The spatiolegal emerges out of 'coexistence and competition, in [the] perpetual field of interaction' of nomic and logic, smooth and striated: the nomic and the logic are inseparable and yet non-coincident, the two irreducible sides of the spatiolegal.[132]

Although the nomic of law is always irreducible to its logic structuration, at the same time it is necessary for law to move, and thus to swerve so as to prevent law from coinciding with space – i.e. from becoming a totalitarian tautology. This prefigures a moving spatiolegal materiality, never coincident with the comfortable regularity of the Kantian subsumption from particular to universal, nor with a merely fluid and processual understanding of legal spatiality, never peacefully dialectical, but rather a syncopated, complex rhythm of territorialisation and de-territorialisation.[133] What has been defined as law's state of exception – either as a transcendental abstraction, or empirically grounded through sociological approaches to law, or more critically translated onto hidden structures of power relations – should thus be seen as a constant attempt of the law of the logos to naturalise, domesticate and tame its own 'opaque core', this non-representational force always already distributing bodies onto space, exceeding and dislocating the logos itself, since *a-logical*. There is a constitutive impossibility for the law of logos, for both its 'abstract' and 'concrete' states of exception, to ever conquer, domesticate, tame and expel its nomic normativity, thereby fulfilling its 'all-ingesting' dream – and the reason should begin to surface: any attempt to 'tame' such a nomic spatiality presupposes a separation between the logic and the nomic, which is what I am denying.

130 Deleuze and Guattari, 2004[1980]: 387–468.
131 Deleuze and Guattari, 2004[1980]: 391.
132 Deleuze and Guattari, 2004[1980]: 398.
133 Brighenti, 2006b.

To be sure, when assuming the nomic as what utterly dislocates the law as well as simultaneously keeps it 'alive', in 'movement', I hasten to stress that I do not intend to conflate it with the notion of justice. Were this the case, that would amount to simply 'materialise' Derrida's ghost without, however, fully challenging its core flaw, namely the fact of postulating a subverting dislocation *inside law*, that is, an excess *de facto* produced by law itself through its differing and deferring operation, that is, an ultimately juridifiable justice. A corollary trouble with conflating the nomic with justice, moreover, is to assume such nomic dislocation as emancipatory and 'just' *per se*. This is, as will be discussed at length, a dangerous ethico-political strategy. Here, Deleuze and Guattari's often forgotten reminder should be reasserted: 'never believe that a smooth space will suffice to save us'.[134]

Therefore, in order to qualify, the spatiolegal materiality is neither only a structural relation between the two poles of the logos, nor only a dynamic relation between a logic ordering and a nomic dislocation. It is also an event. Every spatiolegal concatenation, in its deterritorialisation and reterritorialisation, *takes place*. This taking place is simultaneously what sanctions the inescapable as well as the dislocated belonging of law to a situation (the impossibility to transcend space), as well as the non-relational, 'evental viewpoint' insisting in every situation, that opens the spatiolegal to the cosmic contingency of a world *not for law*. This is not a regulative ideal, nor an indefinite to-come, but the virtual and *real* conditions of possibility of a given situation, a potential to produce new relations and thus to allow for emergence and change. Above, following Woodward, I termed it the impersonal 'making-available' of the virtual potentialities which every situation harbours, its radical irreducibility to the spatiolegal closure.

We may thus appreciate the crucial strategic import of Deleuze's notions of virtual and event, which allows us not only to *think* a transcendental line of flight able to overcome the given situation (as in Derrida's impalpable justice), but to recalibrate the attention towards a model in which the transcendental becomes empirical and such lines of flight are no longer Kantianly postulated as regulative conditions of possibility, but are rather explored in their intensive potentialities as the *real* conditions of possibility of a given situation. This is encapsulated in the concept of spatial justice I will develop in the final chapter. A notion of justice, that is, that neither coincides with the logic nor the nomic of the spatiolegal, but is rather 'between' the two or, more precisely, their eventful excess, perforating their texture by folding them back to their geo-legal rootedness. It is not a force subverting or sabotaging law, nor law's paradox or impossibility and not an indefinite *à venir*. Justice is not the nomic of law. Justice is what allows law to be *used*, that is, what allows its intensive potentials to emerge as a material and concrete possibility, able to open any legal situation to the

134 Deleuze and Guattari, 2004[1980]: 551.

geo-philosophical potential of a world not for law (i.e. beyond the legal and as such non-juridifiable), which is nonetheless here-and-now.

3.2 Méfiez-vous du rêve de l'autre, parce que si vous êtes pris dans le rêve de l'autre, vous êtes foutu.[135]

Philippopoulos-Mihalopoulos proposes to explore the inseparable and non-coincident form of the spatiolegal by translating it into the interrelation between the law and the city, through the notion of *lawscape*, namely 'the ever-receding horizon of prior invitation by the one (the law/the city) to be conditioned by the other (the city/the law).'[136] This concept is congenial to my attempt to think the spatiolegal in itself, i.e. without presupposing one of the two terms (law/space) as already given, whilst simultaneously not suggesting their identity: lawscape is an ontological continuum simultaneously traversed and agitated by a difference which prevents its collapsing into a mere tautology.[137] This allows for thinking the logic/nomic dyad not only as a one-way relation between an ordering and a disordering force, but as a recursive process, within an explicitly urban dimension. Accordingly, between the law and the city there is a turbulent relation of reciprocal invisibilisation, each side 'needing' the other to project its own 'dream', and simultaneously to prevent this dream from being *actually* fulfilled: the law seeks to invisibilise the city since it fears its nomic spatiality, and yet necessarily '"relies" on the city, "acknowledges" its continuum, constructs a rigidity between them that resists the surrounding liquidity'.[138] On the other hand, the city seeks to invisibilise law by projecting its deterritorialised space of joyful and pacific and differential disorder.[139] The two extremes to which each side of the lawscape tends are never pre-given, as well as never reachable 'self-perpetuating myths', constitutively utopian, that is, without place: a 'holy city of justice perpetually floating in a post-conflict space', and 'a law without a city [i.e.] a law without materiality, an abstract, universal, immutable law that trammels the globe'.[140] The vanishing point in which

135 Deleuze, 2012[1987].

136 Philippopoulos-Mihalopoulos, 2007b: 10.

137 The 'palpitating boundary between continuum (and the subsequent fear of tautology) and difference' (Philippopoulos-Mihalopoulos, 2007b: 8).

138 Philippopoulos-Mihalopoulos, 2007a: 87.

139 Simultaneously, both 'law's obsession with naming, categorising, organising and 'tidying up' is revealed in the city's working order (semblance or reality, depending on the city) both socially and spatially [and] the city's multipolarity and social differentiation (again, to a city-dependent degree) helps visualise the 'material' side of the law, namely its relation to violence in the sense of its force of perception/application, its attempt to control power struggles, and of course its role in the process of capital production and consumption' (Philippopoulos-Mihalopoulos, 2007b: 8).

140 Philippopoulos-Mihalopoulos, 2013: 2.

these two utopian tendencies mutually fold, I contend in the next chapter, is the 'abstract form' that the spatiolegal takes in contemporary neo-liberal societies, what I define as the *spatiolegal architecture of control.*

Exploring law through these lenses requires a shift from its traditional understanding as a set of rules we rationally, cognitively and pragmatically decide to follow, or as a merely 'social' pressure, as the classic sociological approach would pretend.[141] Law is only *partially* so. Whereas law is a *project* aimed at manipulating, governing and channelling the urban into precise categories, boundaries and definitions, it is at the same time a *process* emerging out of the intermingling of human and non-human, tangible and intangible bodies, as such inseparable from this continuum.[142] Evidently, this is not a merely 'human' framework, a socio-cultural construct superimposed onto an inert, external, 'natural' matter. The spatiolegal refers to a normativity that emerges immanently out of the interpenetration between bodies, structures and spaces. A configuration resulting from socio-natural interpenetration, where the hyphen between social and natural does not indicate an *a posteriori* link but an *a priori* inseparability.

Let us take the tensegrity of the urban space of London, where the incoming darkness of the night merges with the appearance of a black, hooded boy, connected with the affective pressure of anti-social behaviour legislation: a normative tuning has emerged. Let us imagine the post-human normativities produced by foxes in the city nightlife, generating a climate of fearful attentiveness in other small animals, and exploiting the connection with the waste legislation, as well as the normative routines, which inform the practice of leaving bags of rubbish outside the door, in the street. As Braverman puts it,

> the law is not a static narrative that produces monophonic meaning, but a living process that feeds on, and depends upon, dynamic human-nonhuman assemblages ... [law] is bounded – defined, even – by the very materialities that it seeks to rule.[143]

'Not merely operating "through normative space"', law 'is normative space and normative body and normative movement.'[144] The concept of Anthropocene helps visualising this point, showing explicitly that the law is not a socio-cultural construct that is superimposed over an inert world, but

141 Both positivist and socio-legal models, most famously Hart's notion of 'social pressure', frame law only with reference to social power and/or mutual communication and conformity to pre-agreed rules by subjects – thereby missing the role played by its immanent and material normativity in 'tuning' the social (Hart, 1997: 84).

142 The distinction between *project* and *process* is inspired by its use by Moore vis-à-vis capitalism (Moore, 2015).

143 Braverman, 2014: 105, 108.

144 Philippopoulos-Mihalopoulos, 2015: 69.

rather a normativity made of flesh and stones, thought and water streams, cosmic and everyday interaction, human and non-human sensing. This does not mean that there are no norms. It certainly means, however, that normativity can no longer be discussed through the common frame of humanity. Law is not a socio-cultural construct but rather a way in which the world is organised.

3.3 Do everything, but don't worry. Worrying binds.[145]

Let us recap. First, since law can never be out of space, it is ontologically *powerless* vis-à-vis transcending its 'situation': whatever its attempts, law would never be able to 'step back' so as to gain the clear distance which would allow for its unilateral action, since this would mean stepping back from itself.[146] Second, law is never 'alone' but always part of a spatiolegal assemblage of human and non-human bodies, and thus is to 'be observed in the framework of an immediate continuity of heterogeneous elements, not all of which reducible to a rational-normative scheme, acting in the social field'.[147] Third, the spatiolegal is always concatenated *and* dislocated, as well as excessively eventful. The materiality of spatiolegal concatenations is not frozen into mere actuality: law is always-already material both in the actual situation *and* in the 'virtual field of expectancy' in which it wafts as a virtual (although always on the brink of being actualised) materiality. There is always a virtual multiplicity haunting the 'actual' manifestation of law itself into given things, signs, norms, performances, thus overflowing the interpenetration of bodies, their mere being embedded, embodied, performed or networked into a nomospheric spatiality. Fourth, by thinking the spatiolegal not only as a structural relation between the two poles of the logos (violence and order), but also as a dynamic relation between a logic ordering and a nomic dislocation, this conception allows us to overcome the one-sided, negative-only understandings of law, in the direction of an affirmative normativity.

Not only more than human, normativity is not simply about numbing effervescence and stabilising tensions. Both presuppositions derive directly from the immunitary paradigm of the legal state of exception, and the already explored presupposition of the human condition as being constitutively one of disorder, disequilibrium and poverty. The original lack would explain the emergence of the legal apparatus accordingly: 'to be human means to be entrapped by norms', that is, to systematically repress the chaotic being-together into the 'functional separation' of normative,

145 Meher Baba, quoted in Masciandaro, 2013.

146 As Moore puts it, 'law attempts to take a "step back" so as to address its own grounds. However, in so doing, law merely displaces its grounds, leaving the final "step back" always another step away' (Moore, 2007a: 459).

147 Brighenti, 2006a: 50, 62.

co-immunitary systems.[148] If life, as Esposito observes, is what 'by definition tends to escape its own place', then this would mean that 'from this turbulence the law must immunise life: from its irresistible tendency to overcome itself ... law must sacrifice the intensity of life for the necessity of its conservation'.[149] Contrary to this understanding, the conception here exposed points to a

> normativity [which] has become dynamic and creative, transforming reality always according to hidden intensities which are not limitless, but which, in going beyond the human and organic organization of the world, present the ethical norm of finding new ways of how we might inhabit the earth.[150]

There is no relation of oppression/suppression vs. proliferation/escape, but rather a spatiolegal surface on which material law (law folding into space) and legal materialities (spaces folding into law) are reciprocally affected, and on which surface each fold pursues its own mythology of origin, meaning, direction, teleology. This understanding opens up a rather more complex reflection on how the spatiolegal assemblage could unfold, accepting and yet moving beyond the unavoidable discrepancy between the de-spatialising project of law and the material process of legal emergence. The abstraction of law should be understood as not simply an illusionary veil to be removed, but as generative *qua* abstraction of ways of being and inhabiting the world. Legal abstractions operate in the world shaping ontologically and phenomenologically the way it is lived.

For instance, one can provide an impression of 'freedom' and 'liberation' to the enjoyment of certain sensorial excesses whilst masking their being part of a complex web of relations. Let us take the relation between law and the senses. Paraphrasing what has been written above, we may argue that law is a *project* aimed at manipulating, governing and channelling senses into precise categories, boundaries and definitions; at the same time, it is a *process* emerging out of the sensorial intermingling of human and non-human, tangible and intangible bodies, as such inseparable from this continuum. On the one hand law appears to construct the socio-cultural parameters of 'good taste', commonsense and sensibility out of which law's dealing with senses supposedly emerges. On the other, in this way law manages to dissimulate the fact that senses are blended or anaesthetised by something other than the individual. This is its atmospheric dissimulation: law maintains an illusion of phenomenological immediate perception and evaluation of senses, while building socio-political and cultural repositories

148 Esposito, 2002: 112–13, quoting Plessner (my translation).
149 Esposito, 2002: 35, 37 (my translation).
150 Braidotti and Pisters, 2012: 8.

of sensorial taste construction that dissimulate the role of law itself in orchestrating both senses and its very own apparent absence of involvement.[151] The phenomenology of senses is thus elevated to a quintessential corollary of personal freedom, as the freedom to taste, smell, hear… Law allows us to think that we own our senses in full phenomenological immersion, whilst hiding the fact that it is within the socio-legal structuration of the very socio-cultural-legal atmosphere in which we are immersed, that senses come to be perceived as individually owned.

The fundamental misunderstanding about this complex mechanism of dissimulation and emergence entraps various anti-normative strands of contemporary critical theory in contradictory, unproductive and indeed co-optable positions. Thus immanence as collective self-creation is posited against the entrapment of norms (e.g. Michael Hardt and Toni Negri), or the primacy of the body's neuro-phenomenological embeddedness in the world against the abstractness of law (e.g. António Damasio).[152] Whatever their complexity, ultimately these approaches differently reproduce, under different guises, the classic dichotomy of law vs. non-law, thus missing the complex abstract-and-concrete imbrications of the spatiolegal, with consequences which will become apparent in the next section. Two examples will be helpful in clarifying this point.

3.4 We need to witness our own limits transgressed, and some life pasturing freely where we never wonder.[153]

Roberto Esposito has elaborated a compelling way to integrate a positive understanding of the spatiolegal within a vitalistic approach, in the direction of an affirmative biopolitics where the emphasis lies in the immanent normativity of life. In order to provide an alternative to a merely negative understanding of the legal mechanism, Esposito neither seeks to unfold a dimension opposed to and thus separated from the law (e.g. space, life, freedom), nor resort to transcendental principles supposedly dislocating or sabotaging it. Instead, he underlines the 'generalised diffused normativity that characterises life, what Spinoza has called "rules for living"'.[154] Elaborating on Canguilhem's conception of 'normality', he defines a 'positive' and 'affirmative' understanding of norm, which is not derived from the exclusionary and static presupposition of a given 'normal state' (of exception) with respect to which variations would be defined (and sanctioned) as deviations. Norm is not something external (and transcendentally imposed by law) to living beings, i.e. a systematic abstraction

151 I am paraphrasing what I co-wrote in Mandic *et al.*, 2013.
152 Colebrook, 2014b.
153 Thoreau, 1962: 255.
154 Philippopoulos-Mihalopoulos, 2013: 2.

from life. It is instead 'biological' and 'biopolitical', that is, 'intrinsic and immanent' to the living, always-already belonging to the materiality of life: a norm-of-life: 'differently from law, this norm is not situated at the border of *separation,* but rather at the point of *tangency* between life and the living', in the 'middle' where life germinates.[155] If Benjamin once observed that behind law's self-presentation as transcendent there is no other than immanence, Esposito provides such legal immanence with a fully positive and vitalist dimension.

Accordingly, the generative and differential repetition of the norm-of-life is opposed to the 'false' and exceptional repetition of the juridical norm: whilst the latter is based on the reduction of each singularity to a particular which is recognisable into a generality, the norm-of-life is a living normativity emerging out of contingent and singular encounters. Opposed to the immunitary paradigm of 'conservation', what counts for this norm-of-life is the capacity to integrate rather than deny variations. This is not a matter of producing 'ontological interruptions' to the flow of life through mad decisions, but rather a capacity to adapt to this becoming by entering into ever new relations. Following Deleuze, Esposito observes that the risk for life is not dislocation, disorder and chaos, but rather the atrophying of one's capacity for integration, transformation and adaptation. What should concern us then is not the weakening of life's immunitary capacity for conservation, but rather the surfacing of an 'excess of conservation', i.e. the rigidification that life undergoes by becoming increasingly 'incapable of facing new risks', to produce new problems. Consequently, the ethico-political task to 'preserve' life is not a negative matter of building spatiolegal apparatuses of compensation, immunity and re-equilibrium but rather, in the Nietzschean sense, it means preserving the vital power to produce new norms, keeping life open in possibility: to exist is to endure in *agencements,* to be able to *adapt, cope with* and engage in different relations, to live in variation.[156]

3.5 You don't reach the BwO, and its plane of consistency, by wildly de-stratifying.[157]

Laurent de Sutter somewhat echoes these observations when proposing to 'get rid of legal theory' and developing a purely immanent 'practice of

155 Esposito, 2002: 171 (my translation and emphasis).

156 Esposito, 2002 134–73 (my translation). If politico-legal apparatuses systematically neutralise and defuse the potentials of problems and the intensity of events into the immunitary consensus for a common *doxa,* leaving societies into what Deleuze calls the 'puerile' subjection to the search for solutions to already-presupposed 'problems', it is a *right to problems* that he (as well as Esposito) endorses, i.e. a right to participate in and manage the creation and production of problems.

157 Deleuze and Guattari, 2004[1980]: 178.

right', i.e. an 'art of creating new relations', producing assemblages in extensive and corrective forms and thus 'providing juridical operations with a becoming', a practice of association and chance which only knows concrete singularities and is indifferent to law, politics and economics.[158] Sutter observes that legal critique in its different forms always subordinates law to something beyond: the Kantian critique to a higher Judgment; the deconstructive critique to a transcendental Justice; the 'denouncing critique' of the ideology to some deeper truth.[159] In this way, it always remains trapped within the pseudo-dialectic of law and justice traversing Western thought. Following Deleuze, Sutter and Kyle McGee argue for the need to complement the *critique* of law with a *clinique* of law, that is, from the (necessary but not sufficient) step of deconstructing notions such as legal rational subject and sovereign self, to the productive dimension of jurisprudence as a practice of investing new connections and creating new norms.[160] What follows is a radical pragmatism, purely effectual and explicitly relational. As Sutter observes, 'there is no ontology in [law's] declarations of imputation. There is no content. There is only the effect of words that allow things and people to stick together'.[161] In the style of Deleuze's famous injunction 'to have done with judgement', and resonating with Esposito's reflection on a non-conservative, non-immunitary law, Sutter exclaims with iconoclastic optimism:

> law does not adapt itself to social change; law *is* the language of social change … is revolution – everyday revolution … the lawyers should never trust what *is*. Instead, they should trust what *becomes*.[162]

Indifferent to justice and laws, jurisprudence thus only 'gives account to life, jurisprudence is life'.[163] Deleuze's call for a 'right to problems' and a 'right to metamorphosis' thus becomes the cornerstone around which a 'practice of right' should be organised.[164]

It should be pointed out that Sutter's use of the term 'jurisprudence' concerns its French rather than English meaning. Jurisprudence is the pragmatic and productive casuistic practice of right (*droit*), as opposed to the dogmatic image of the Law (*loi*). Although Deleuze was notably dismissive of the latter, he was extremely fond of the former, which he defined as the veritable 'philosophy of law', a strategy of pragmatic creation of

158 de Sutter, 2011: 76, 83, 85 (my translation).
159 de Sutter, 2011: 47 (my translation).
160 de Sutter and McGee, 2012.
161 de Sutter, 2005: 42
162 de Sutter, 2005: 47.
163 de Sutter, 2011: 101 (my translation).
164 Deleuze, 2006[1986]: 87.

norms from which, he argued, philosophy itself should learn.[165] Deleuze, with Guattari understood thinking as the creative production of new compositions or 'problematic fields' in response to an encounter (event). Producing problems, that is, actualising the potentialities that emerge out of the contingent engagement with the materialities of living, Philosophy has to do with the creation of concepts as emerging out of, and in response to, such problematic fields. The fundamental task of this philosophy, Sutter and McGee sum up, is 'wedding concepts to singularity', by crafting them around the singular event so as to make them universal.[166] In fact, the 'philosophical exercise of tailoring concepts to events as they emerge' is something that law routinely does in its casuistic practice when answering to the singularity of the events it encounters, and this is exactly what fascinated Deleuze about the practice of *droit*.[167]

3.6 I'm not interested in how people move, but what moves them.[168]

With Sutter and Esposito we face two different and equally compelling ways of developing a 'dynamic and creative' understanding of normativity: 'laws and institutions are positive tools; rather than being limiting or organizing, they spread like rhizomes'.[169] This is consistent with Latour's proposal, against any attempt 'to define law by means of rules', to

> begin law at the beginning, that is to say, at the stamps, elastic bands, paperclips and other office paraphernalia which are the indispensable tools of cases. Jurists always speak of texts, but rarely of their materiality. It is to this materiality that we must apply ourselves.[170]

Such urge to get rid of concepts, meanings and forms, however, runs the risk of fetishising materiality itself. Is it enough to challenge the spatiolegal operation of exception? Is the latter only a cumbersome apparatus that denies variation and prevents the production of new relations into a static rigidity, that is, a comfortable illusion belonging to the 'lawyer's sense of law', which as such we must get rid of, as Pottage argues?[171] Or instead, does not the post-sovereign folding of the state of exception of contemporary neo-liberal societies prefigure a flexible, dynamic and immanent configuration whose peculiarity exactly rests in the capacity to adapt, cope with

165 Deleuze and Parnet, 1987.
166 de Sutter and McGee, 2012: 205.
167 de Sutter and McGee, 2012: 206.
168 Pina Bausch, speech held on the occasion of the Kyoto Prize award ceremony in 2007, available at www.pinabausch.org/en/pina/what-moves-me
169 Boundas, 2011a.
170 Latour, 2009b: 72.
171 Pottage, 2012, 170.

and adhere to the pulsating spatiality of life without pretending to re-allocate it into a given order? 'Why proclaim the need for a right to difference, variation, and metamorphosis, – Noys asks – if capitalism will supply them in far more radical, a-subjective, and inhuman forms than any mutated subject?'[172] Above, I criticised deconstruction for its insufficiency vis-à-vis the spatiolegal state of exception. Yet, does not the call to 'get rid of law' – optimistically and uncritically endorsing the tumultuous and rhizomatic production of relation and association of an imminent practice of right – risk equally mirroring the becoming dynamic of the state of exception, becoming indistinguishable from its uneventful, liquid and accelerated circulation? Whether in the last chapter doubts were raised about the unquestionably positive value McFarlane granted to the practices of *assembling* and *commoning* the urban, here we might ask, are the variation, movement, and metamorphosis, 'free and savage creation' of *droit*, emancipatory *per se*?

There is no smoothness without striation. Creation is never free and savage, just as there is no life as a generative principle beyond diagrams. Life or desire is not a romantic substance outside the logic of the norm (which is only a way to reactively confirming it), but rather an inhuman and impersonal potential for relations to emerge. Life, or desire, are always machined, hence the need to explore the real conditions of possibility which simultaneously close and open the smooth paths of creation, rather than simply chanting the glory of transgression. As Constantin Boundas proposes, we need to keep into account 'the constraints inscribed in the rhythms and articulations of the real' that always coexist with the emergence of any assemblage, so as to explore the questions of validation and confirmation vis-à-vis law, instead of following the idea of creativity into an uncritical celebration of 'associative bricolage and normative anarchy'.[173] The spatiolegal is no flat and smooth surface in which free-flowing rhizomatic creation may occur, but a materiality striated by socio-historical contingencies, as well as traversed by impersonal, virtual potentialities. Legal concepts, meanings, forms and abstractions won't simply go away once we stop taking them seriously.

It is therefore necessary to intersect the ontological plane with the historical one, that is, to offer a clear explanation of what is the risk these approaches face vis-à-vis the contemporary historical contingency. This requires to account for what I term the spatiolegal architecture of control, both in its theoretical foundations, as well as in the legal, securitarian and economical operations through which it shapes the space. This is the *real*

172 Noys, 2012: 71.
173 Boundas, 2011b.

'state of exception in which we live' (Benjamin), that is, the abstract form that the spatiolegal takes in the context of neo-liberal capitalism: an immanent, impersonal, unauthorised and self-regulating configuration of power whose functioning logic does not entail blocking the variation and metamorphosis of life (as naïve vitalism would pretend), but rather adhering to the machinic, post-human and vibrating movement of being-together, by neutralising its eventful potential into a smooth variation within an uneventful horizon.

Chapter 4

Control urban event

I take up this challenge through three steps. First, I explore the relation between biopolitics and the demonically vitalist ontology I proposed in the first chapter. The notion of *control*, as developed by Deleuze, will offer a way to push biopolitics beyond Foucault and to make it consistent with the biopower of contemporary 'control societies'. Second, I account for the fate undergone by the spectacular and glorious aura of sovereignty in post-sovereign societies of control. I believe it is simplistic to assume that a crude shift from spectacle to biopower, representation to 'production', 'glory' to management, would supposedly characterise the post-ideological ethos of contemporary control societies. More precisely, the two poles of sovereignty fold into each other forming an abstract-and-concrete spatiolegal architecture whose *bipolar* character does not disappear, but rather takes a new shape, which is what we need to address. I develop this point through Kant's notion of *achtung*, Marx's 'real abstraction' and Cerdà's urbanisation, emphasising the fundamentally urban quality of the relation between law, space and control in the capitalist age. Third, elaborating on Sloterdijk's notion of *interiorisation*, I introduce the concept of *brandscaping*, as an attempt to apply the concept of spatiolegal architecture of control (or more simply, as I will often refer to it: control)[1] in more explicitly material terms to the urban and its tuning, Although in certain context they are used as exchangeable terms brandscaping is meant to provide control with a more explicitly spatial as well as phenomenological dimension, which is often lacking from a certain account of 'control society' that depicts control as a configuration that simply dissolves the thickness of space into deterritorialised flows.[2] Brandscaping is a way to investigate how control rhizomatically ramifies in such a spatial thickness, both as a certain 'form

1 The notion of 'spatiolegal architecture of control', I believe, integrates Deleuze's concept of control by providing it with a proper 'spatiolegal' dimension and allowing it to be framed within the evolution of the state of exception described in the second chapter. Therefore, unless contextualised otherwise, my use of the term 'control' is to be assumed as the abbreviation for 'spatiolegal architecture of control'.

2 This is the case for instance of Maurizio Lazzarato's otherwise compelling work.

of urban experience' as well as in its concrete realisation into urban assemblages of consumption and immunity. At a more pragmatic level, if control, as we are to see, can be assumed as an impersonal and unauthorised emergence of an immanent configuration of power, brandscaping is a tool flexible enough to allow for exploring its unfolding through more explicit and context-specific attempts to 'steer' and 'retune' the urban by generating commodified experiences of safety and safe experiences of consumption in the city, in the sense suggested by Ball and Wood, according to whom 'brandscaping can be viewed as a more or less successful institutional attempt to inscribe spaces and their inhabitants in their own terms'.[3] This implies, finally, that brandscaping can be also employed as a very useful methodological tool to explore urban control empirically, as I demonstrate in the following chapter.

1.1 Actually, it is evident that monuments inspire social wisdom and arouse a veritable awe. The storming of the Bastille is symbolic of this state of affairs: it is difficult to explain such a crowd movement, except by taking into account the animosity of a people against those monuments who are their real masters.[4,5]

According to the Holy Scriptures, 'glory' is the attribute of God, who as such attracts the incessant glorification of his creatures. Yet, what if God is not the *cause* but rather the *effect*, that is, not simply glorified but ontologically *produced* by glorification itself? In political theory, a well-known formula expresses this theorem: the king is the king as long as the people believe him so. A void lies at the core of divine, monarchic and legal sovereignty. This is the 'secret' that public ceremonies and all the other spectacular instances of 'public display of power' are meant to conceal: public recognition, acclamation and glorification are not the consequence of sovereign glory, but what constitutes it. Who could be more appropriate than Hegel to capture the dialectical nuance of this circularity? The master is the master insofar as the slave recognises him *qua* master. Recognition is the operation whereby the slave literally constitutes the master. At the same time, recognition is the operation which defines the slave, who is a slave insofar as he recognises the master *qua* master. The operation of recognition, therefore, is the vanishing point of the master/slave dichotomy, the circularity in which they fold.

The definition of human beings as 'operators', that is, those who produce and whose 'doing' is a *praxis* – i.e. the 'manifestation of a will which produces a concrete effect' through a precise art (techné) – has

3 Ball and Wood, 2008.
4 Bataille, 1929.
5 Deleuze, 2004[1968]: 75.

been shown as depending on the preliminary postulation of nothingness: the theologico-politico-legal paradigm of techné always emerges *ex nihilo*. It is a sovereign-producing techné, that is, the constant filling of the void at the core of sovereignty (God, king, Law...), and thus the productive concealing of the latter's unspeakable impotence. Within the perspective of nihilism, what the humans produce is nothing other than their own subjection to a sovereign power. More precisely, they ontologically coincide with this operation: 'the creature is essentially the glorification of glory'.[6]

At first it appears that the possibility for a sovereign to hold its power rests on a capacity to deny and conceal this 'secret', i.e. to 'administer the mystery' in the sense of articulating the presupposed gap between the king and its people. Yet, more precisely, it is the paradigm of operation (i.e. the reduction of being to praxis) to ground the sovereign state of exception. For this reason, whereas the apparent unmasking of the 'secret' propels the crisis of sovereignty, this by no means leads to the collapse of its mechanism, but rather its reformulation, no longer as concealment from, but rather as direct management of, life: biopolitics.

1.2 In its virtual truth, law has already disappeared from the Earth. What remains of 'law' is a dissolving complex of relics from political sociality, nostalgic media-driven theatre, and pre-automatised commodification protocols.[7]

Biopolitics: the management of life, or the 'vitalism' of the spatiolegal exception. Framed in biopolitical terms, the spatiolegal 'exceptional' double-move appears as the *erasure* and *partitioning* of life, i.e. the insertion of a fracture between a (presupposed as) homogenous, flat, 'bare life', and a 'qualified' life, to be then differently dressed with various categories (e.g. the individual, subject of right, member of a society).[8] Besides the countless interpretation to which it has been subjected, what is particularly significant with the notion of bare life is the biopolitical separation it expresses, namely the necessity for law to deny (to immunise from) the *singularity* of beings, by plunging them into a homogeneous and bare substratum where it is able to operate on them: as observed above, law cannot act on space without *a priori* projecting the where in which it is to be applied.[9] On this

6 Agamben, 2009a: 221, 236 (my translation).

7 Land, 2011: 259–60.

8 Agamben, 1998a: 128.

9 Law has 'no power over the living beyond what the law supposes as their bare life'; Zartaloudis interprets this point in temporal terms: 'Mythical violence is, in this sense, chronogenetic in that it presupposes its capacity (its trigger) to judge and to take life as lying in the very legally supposed, but timeless, bare life of those of whose life it takes. The law cancels the time in which it acts to presuppose bare life in order to ensure the timelessness with which it is taken and abandoned' (Zartaloudis, 2011: 145).

split between life and the living reverberates the basic scission of Western metaphysics (soul/body). It is a bionomical *caesura* that posits human beings as self-owning subjects, endowed with (moral) conscience and free will to perform their own actions, whilst tied to the burden of a bare life they need to manage, hence the ethico-moral-political question of the soul's 'management' of the body, i.e. the necessity for the subject to govern and conduct its *own* body (i.e. bare life) towards a higher, divine or profane good. The ontological core of this ethics is the *ought,* not the *being*: humans are assessed regarding the operations they perform and the result they achieve.[10] A 'reduction of being into praxis', whose ethico-political consequence is implanting a constitutive guilt within every being: is not, in fact, the task of governing and managing oneself according to a divine or profane (legal) virtue a constitutively unfinished one, i.e. a constant approximation to principles which, by definition, cannot ever be matched? Does not this configure an infinite duty, and thus an infinite debt, forcing humans (and non-humans alike), 'to bear the burden of law's own groundlessness, of law's 'own' guilt'?[11]

If such a bionomical split is the exceptional dispositif for 'making beings governable', the crisis of sovereignty is the crisis of this mechanism of capture. The folding of the state of exception that follows could then be reframed as a shift in the configuration of power, from the *presumed* capture of beings within the spectacular transcendence of the sovereign glory, to the *actual* capture of beings through the immanent techniques and technologies of biopower. In Foucault's formula,

> what generalizes the power to punish, then, is not the universal consciousness of the law in each juridical subject; it is the regular extension, the infinitely minute web of panoptic technique.[12]

10 Agamben recently explored this point focusing on the scholastic doctrine of virtue, according to which to be good (Christianly so) does not concern *being* in a certain way, but rather *acting,* that is, *operating* the potentialities which God has provided us, so as to fully actualise the divine providence. Through the definite setting aside of Aristotle's notion of impotentiality (see Chapter 1) within this school the Aristotelic prioritisation of the *act* over the *potentia* (according to which a 'good virtue' was defined as that which orients the potentiality towards its perfection, i.e. its full actualisation) reached its climax (Agamben, 2013: 65–87).

11 Zartaloudis, 2011: 144. See also Agamben, 1998b: 120–1; and Agamben, 2008. Other recent compelling explorations of the concept in relation to contemporary neoliberalism are Lazzarato, 2012; Graeber, 2012.

12 Foucault, 1995: 224.

> **1.3** What is to be assaulted is not law as an idea 'in general' but the juridical paradigm of law's relation to violence as the performing art of determining guilt and taking life through a supposedly paramount, higher, ever deferred order of Last Judgement.[13]

In the thought of Michel Foucault we find one of the most radical attempts to account for the reconfiguration of systems of power as result of the crisis of sovereignty. His well-known theory of the emergence of disciplinary societies investigates a logic of government which no longer seeks to capture its own subjects within the glory of public spectacles, and rather shifts the attention from thc soul to the body of the individual, a body to be disciplined through an 'infinitely minute web of panoptic technique'. The shift from *ancient regimes* to disciplinary societies is famously framed through Bentham's notorious architectural project, the panopticon. Thinking through the latter, Foucault is able to define the immanent logic of what he famously terms the 'disciplinary society', i.e. *panopticism*, namely 'the pure function of imposing a particular taste or conduct on a multiplicity of particular individuals, provided that the multiplicity is small in number and the space limited and confined'.[14] The concept is not to be understood in a metaphorical, but rather an *analogical* sense: instead of merely being a 'signifier' employed to refer to heterogeneous phenomena, the panopticon is paradigmatic insofar as it is a singular case that, by means of being isolated from its context, exposes a certain functioning, i.e. the *canon* it shares with the other phenomena to which it is paradigmatically related.[15] The panopticon, a singular case, expresses panopticism, the 'diagram of a mechanism of power reduced to its ideal form'.[16] This is what Foucault implies when referring to panopticism as simultaneously a formal function as well as a precise, historically situated political technology developed in eighteenth century not only in prisons, but also in schools, factories and in the society in general.

Every society has its diagrams, Deleuze reminds us. With the surfacing of a 'generalised crisis in relation to all the environments of enclosure', from the family to the school to the state, the configuration of power would undergo a gradual modification, along the path leading from the ancient regime to contemporary societies.[17] Thus surfaces a different logic of management, in response to a novel problem: the need '[for] administering and controlling life in a particular multiplicity, provided the multiplicity is large (a population) and the space is spread out or open'.[18]

13 Zartaloudis, 2011: 144.
14 Deleuze, 2006[1986]: 60–1.
15 Agamben, 2009b.
16 Foucault, 1995: 205.17 Deleuze, 1992: 3–4.
18 Deleuze, 2006[1986]: 60–1.

The name of this diagram is *governmentality*. No longer dependent on authoritarian rule, this power strategy is adapted to the context of liberal democracies, responding to the need to manage a 'free' and moving population, so as to mould it into a docile and productive force. Deep knowledge of the population is thus required. Whilst in former times people were conceived as a uniform mass to be subdued, exploited and occasionally aroused through public displays of power, they now become a population to be analysed in detail through systematic observation and data collection.[19] Co-constitutive to this evolution is the surfacing of a new series of savoirs constructing an image of society as a homogeneous body, whose patterns of behaviour are to be discerned by collecting and correlating data (hence the rising of disciplines such as demography, statistics, etc.). Governmentality sanctions the beginning of the shift from transcendent models of governance based on a dichotomous, top-down subjection, to immanent ones, aimed at the self-regulation of the whole,

> to establish an equilibrium, maintain an average, establish a sort of homeostasis, and compensate for variations within this general population and its aleatory field ... Unlike discipline, which is addressed to bodies, the new nondisciplinary powers applied not to man-as-body but to the living man, to man-as-living-being; ultimately, if you like, to man-as-species.[20]

Enter security. Foucault's classic epidemiological parallel is perhaps schematic, yet remains the most suggestive account of this three-step evolution. First, *leprosy*: its management based on the systematic exclusion of the infected outside of the city, whose walls must be sealed, waiting for the contagion to end. Second, *plague*: the characteristics of which do not allow clear exclusion, so that management needs to be articulated through a capillary set of norms regulating the conduct of the sick persons within the city, such as curfews and so on, a disciplinary system. Third, *smallpox*: this is no longer an anomaly but a normality that cannot be excluded or isolated, so therefore needs to be managed differently, involving the universal screening, for the internal protection of the entire social body, hence the praxis of vaccination, the culmination of a gradual shift from *exiling* outside, or *channelling* inside, to a concern with *regulating* systemic and endemic matters.[21]

Evidently, techniques and technologies such as ubiquitous data-gathering practices and extensive surveillance are not anomalies vis-à-vis liberal regimes: they are necessary and constitutive to them, in order to

19 Foucault, 1979; 1997: 73–9.

20 Foucault, 2003: 242.

21 Foucault, 2009.

guarantee the security of freedom, and thus the freedom *in* security: '*security mechanisms* have to be installed around the random element inherent in a population of living beings so as to optimize a state of life': biopolitics.[22] As a deeply realistic paradigm, security neither atomises individuals nor erects authoritarian spaces of control, but rather addresses a population to be managed in the open. It is concerned with a milieu, a territory, a city in which people, objects and spaces are in constant circulation. The problem

> is no longer that of fixing and demarcating the territory, but of allowing circulations to take place, of controlling them, shifting the good and the bad, ensuring that things are always in movement, constantly moving around, continually going from one point to another, but in such a way that the inherent dangers of this circulation are cancelled out.[23]

The chaotic disorder of the social is no longer spectacularly denied, nor simply confined to enclosures, but fully accepted and directly targeted as such: if 'discipline wants to produce order, security wants to regulate disorder'.[24] Again, beneath this 'acceptance' lies the convenient (preliminary) framing of disorder as homogenous and undifferentiated, 'bare' and manageable.

1.4

> In its extreme form, the capitalist religion realizes the pure form of separation, to the point that there is nothing left to separate.[25]

A further configuration is on the way. This is what Deleuze hints at in his short and hugely influential *Postscript on the Societies of Control.* William Burroughs defined control as the repressing power of language, and more precisely of the 'word', understood as a virus which systematically '*prevents* expansion of consciousness' by 'controlling thought feeling and apparent sensory impressions of the human host'.[26] To Burroughs the word 'entraps' thought within the 'dimensions' of language (designation, manifestation and signification), in this way preventing the expression – the event – of

22 Foucault, 2003: 242.
23 Foucault, 2009: 65.
24 Agamben, 2001a. 'Freedom is something which is constantly produced. Liberalism is not acceptance of freedom; it proposes to manufacture it constantly, to arouse it and produce it, with, of course, the system of constraints and the problems of cost raised by this production' (Foucault, 1997: 65).
25 Agamben, 2007: 81.
26 Burroughs, 1961 (my emphasis).

sense.[27] Inspired by the American writer, Deleuze develops an understanding of control as viral and parasitic, not frontal, transcendental or '"outside" of that for which it would "legislate" (as an absent centre)', but always 'internal' and immanent, a 'field of forces which pretend to control and dominate the world without collocating it within an immutable order'.[28]

Control does not deal with 'individuals' or 'subjects' and their position with respect to a mass, but with 'dividuals, and masses, samples, data, markets'.[29] Neither the exercise of power over a body, nor social subjection or individuation, control refers to an immanent and emergent configuration of power 'acting' on the 'pre-individual, pre-verbal, pre-social dimension', i.e. the 'machinic components rather than the human component', constantly rearranging and *enslaving* them into legal, securitarian and economical apparatuses.[30] Evidently, this is not a configuration that seeks to block, but encourages circulation, metamorphosis, translatability, movement and variation. Keeping the movement alive, and yet in the frozen form of an immobile movement, this is a flow which does not become decontaminated from 'inherent dangers', the events.

With the notion of control, a different diagram of power emerges, in response to a novel problem: no longer that of disciplining bodies in enclosures (panopticism), or managing the life of a population (governmentality). To repeat, Foucault's notion of governmental biopolitics emerges as a response to the problematic milieu produced by a novel understanding of the population as a multiplicity which could not 'be broken down' and should instead 'be treated as a single living being (hence, biopolitics)'.[31] Understanding the novelty of control in this regard requires referring back to the definition of life provided in the first chapter. 'A' life, I argued, may be understood as the impersonal event virtually insisting on every situation, the inoperose (im)potentiality that every being harbours, to swerve away from actualisation, from being exhausted into the relationality of 'organisms', 'subjects', 'personae', 'organisations'. As Paolo Virno explains, this is what Karl Marx intended in

27 Moore, 2007a; 2007b.

28 Moore, 2007a: 460.

29 Deleuze, 1992: 5–6.

30 Deleuze and Guattari, 2004[1980]: 543. 'Machinic enslavement consists in mobilizing and modulating the pre-individual, pre-cognitive and pre-verbal components of subjectivity, causing affects, perceptions and sensations as yet unindividuated or unassigned to a subject, etc. to function like the cogs and components in a machine ... Machinic enslavement is therefore not the same thing as social subjection. If the latter appeals to the molar, individuated dimension of a subjectivity, the former activates its molecular, pre-individual, pre-verbal, pre-social dimension' (Lazzarato, 2006a).

31 Brighenti, 2010b: 10.

the *Grundrisse* when observing that the labour-power capitalism exploits is the worker's potential to produce, its potentiality (*dynamis*).[32] What grounds capitalism is the reduction of beings to (productive) relations, and thus the systematic denial and suppression of their unactualised (im)potentiality. Describing it vis-à-vis the field of language, Moore explains that control has not to do with discipline and co-ordination, but is rather concerned

> to access and regulate their [the propositions] virtual dimension: the breakage wrought by sense itself. In other words, control seeks to control the very creation of propositions, striking pre-emptively in the attempt to determine what it will be possible to think and say.[33]

Control does not refer to 'regulation' (the management of an actual multiplicity), but more precisely to 'modulation' of life in its inoperose, virtual potential.[34] If on the one hand it refers to the management of flows, relations and circulations, it most importantly concerns the neutralisation of its demonic potential, *praeventio.* In Tiqqun's terms, what it

> must circumscribe and put a stop to does not exist at the level of the actual *but at the level of the possible.* The discretionary power here is called *prevention* ... the enemy ... is within. The enemy is the event.[35]

Control entails the modulation of the virtual in order to produce 'fully actual' relations, freeing any actualisation, i.e. any *taking place,* from its excessive and eventful swerving.[36] This is the truly biopolitical quality of control, in the sense of targeting the inoperose potency of life, debilitating and atrophying each body's capacity to swerve, and thus to resist, escape and disrupt a given state of affairs: an art of defusing contingency. Whereas Deleuze, following Spinoza, maintains that oppressive forces separate us from our power to act, the sense of control is more precisely captured by Agamben's observation that today's 'democratic powers' separate us from our power not to act, from what we can 'not do' or, more precisely, undo: from our impotentiality.[37]

32 Virno, 2004.
33 Moore, 2007a: 441.
34 'Enclosures are *molds,* distinct castings, but controls are a *modulation*' (Deleuze, 1992: 4).
35 Tiqqun, 2010: 152–3.
36 As Lazzarato, 2004a, has explained, control must be understood as a modulation of the virtual, or more precisely, of the 'actualisation' of virtual potentialities into actual relation, which it seeks to neutralise from its excessive swerving.
37 Agamben, 2007: 81.

This is the point missed by naive vitalism which, holding the conception of life as an 'inherently positive, primal propulsive force that opposes domination and control',[38] assumes the ethico-political task of *liberating* life from the subjugation of control. Deleuze himself, after all, argued that systems of power do not constitute, but rather emerge out of the social and its concatenations of bodies, whose vibrating desire or life they then seek to capture and striate, 'crush or plug'.[39] Is not freeing such a vibrating life, desire or matter the ethico-political task par excellence? We should reply negatively. This deduction fails to understand that the notion of an uncontaminated and undifferentiated bare life, or innocent matter, 'far from being a subtraction from bio-power, is the latter's product and structural effect'.[40] Control is both the abstraction which *presupposes* and *posits* the non-evental closure of relationalism, as well as the concrete form of its modulations, the apparatuses organising its tunings. Failing to unpack this point leads to contradictory outcomes also sophisticated attempts, such as Esposito's quest to unfold a life in a 'zone not yet occupied by diagrams of power'.[41]

Let us repeat: it is not possible, insofar as contradictory, to postulate the possibility of *actually* achieving a mode of life free from power, such as the life beyond politics that Marx envisages in his Communist Manifesto. As discussed in the first chapter, in every action, every 'entering into relation', there lies an impotentiality, the 'inoperosity internal to the operation itself', where the potential for developing an ethico-political model alternative to the exceptional paradigm of operation resides.[42] There is no authentically pure life beyond power. This is a dangerous illusion produced within systems of power themselves. If systems of power 'crush and plug' life, then the question is not that of 'liberating' some sort of neutral life in a world beyond power relations, but rather that of 'deactivating' and 'unplugging' these systems, and thus reorienting their residual power to build alternative configurations.[43] It is in this dimension, at the threshold of the actualisation of impotentiality into a 'productive' actuality, where the eventful potential of life lies, that the question of the 'bio' of biopolitical control is to be explored.[44]

38 Hall *et al.*, 2010: 42.
39 Deleuze, 1997.
40 Rametta, 2006: 10 (my translation).
41 Esposito, 2007: 171 (my translation).
42 Agamben, 2009a: 268–76.
43 Weizman, 2010.
44 Thacker, 2013. 'The passage from disciplinary societies to the societies of control cannot be understood by starting out from the trans-formations of capitalism. We must begin instead from the power of the multiplicity' (Lazzarato, 2006b: 172).

> **1.5** Enclosures are molds, distinct castings, but controls are a modulation, like a self-deforming cast that will continuously change from one moment to the other, or like a sieve whose mesh will transmute from point to point.[45]

Control is an unauthorised and impersonal emergence, an immanent configuration of power tied to the historically-specific convergence of different theoretical, scientific, technological, socio-cultural evolutions. Every diagram, Deleuze observes, is both abstract (a 'pure function' or 'logic of ordering') as well as immanent to a series of given techniques, technologies and savoirs through which it gains ontological reality. The two planes are not necessarily contemporaneous in history. It is the *degree of consistency* that these different elements achieve with respect to a diagram of power to sanction, or not, its immanent surfacing. For instance, whereas prisons were obviously in place well before the surfacing of the 'disciplinary society', it will be only within the latter that they would become a central technology, that is, that the panopticon would mutate into panopticism:

> if the techniques – in the narrow sense of the word – are caught within the assemblage [*agencement*], this is because the assemblages [*agencements*] themselves, with their techniques, are selected by the diagrams.[46]

As Deleuze makes clear, 'machines don't explain anything, you have to analyse the collective arrangements of which the machines are just one component.'[47] Through the immanent coming together of different components, selected, invented and machined into the given diagram (or abstract machine) of a certain epoch, certain techniques or technologies would become central, allowing one to 'cross the [socio]technical threshold' and thus to actualise the diagram itself into a socio-historical configuration.[48] This understanding does not imply technological determinism, but rather points to the surfacing of a machinic consistency (*apparatus*) between different components at a given socio-historical space time, whereby the diagram of control is actualised within neo-liberal societies. For instance, Moore observes that control differs from governmentality

> by distinctive technological apparatuses: control can only develop once an 'electronic revolution' has occurred, enabling it to not only pursue its aims more extensively and vigorously, but which also (and most

45 Deleuze, 1992: 4.
46 Deleuze, 2006[1986]: 34–5.
47 Deleuze and Negri, 1990.
48 Deleuze, 2006[1986]: 35, referring to Foucault, 1995.

> importantly) transforms those aims through a logic developed in and through the technology itself.[49]

In fact, we may suggest cybernetics is both the technology *and* the actual logic of control: it makes explicit its principles (self-regulation, feedback and continuous movement), and 'entails a transformation from static to dynamic, from linear to circular models', that is a *folding* of the spatiolegal state of exception into an immanent and dynamic form, both presupposing and ontologically producing the totalising, relational 'closure' of the world which subtends the iterative and self-referential manipulation characterising the reality of control in contemporary society.[50]

To repeat, whilst the 'static' mechanism of exception is based on the bionomical extraction/abstraction of individuals from the spatiality of being together, a different nuance is implied by the abstraction that the dynamic logic of control introduces. It is no longer the static separation of a bare life from a life worth living, but rather the reduction of the whole life to a bare life, the whole space to a bare space. Separation sublimates into the flatness of a seamless and uneventful relationalism. Abstract flattening and concrete manipulation are no longer distinguishable: 'bare life is free only insofar as it is manipulated, and it is manipulated only if it is let "naturally" be'.[51] Thus we may better appreciate direct correspondence between the 'liberated' life of neo-liberal credo and its being always-already re-captured into the uneventful movement of control. 'The man of control is undulatory, in orbit, in a continuous network', writes Deleuze. He is meant to negotiate its way through multiple lifestyle choices, whose empowering flexibility – the apparent liberation of the post-modern *nomad* – hides the constant injunction to 'keep on moving', never sit back, always strive for something:

> in the disciplinary societies one was always starting again (from school to the barracks, from the barracks to the factory), while in the societies of control one is never finished with anything.[52]

49 Moore, 2007a: 446.

50 Teixeira Pinto, 2013. The word 'cybernetics' derives from the Greek *kybernetes*, i.e. steersman, which in Latin is translated as *gubernator:* the verb *to govern* initially developed from the field of navigation, and *cybernétique* in French means exactly 'the art of governing'. As Guattari explained, 'enslavement' is used by him and Deleuze 'in a sense akin to that used in cybernetics: in other words, remote control, feedback and opening up to new lines of possibles' (quoted in Lazzarato, 2006a).

51 Tuppini, 2010: 23–32 (my translation).

52 '[J]ust as the corporation replaces the factory, "perpetual training" tends to replace the "school", and continuous control to replace the examination' (Deleuze, 1992: 5).

This, in a nutshell, is the amphetaminic ethos of neo-liberalism, where flexibility becomes 'forced', turning into precariousness, in the constant exposure to values of meritocracy and competition, constant learning, fixed-term jobs, uncertainty and perpetual examination. Indeed, this is a truly egalitarian perspective, since it *actually* realises the absolute 'equality' of life enshrined in the juridical notion of the liberal individual: accordingly, every relation becomes an equally manipulatable resource to be consumed and capitalised, as social media marketing perfectly shows. *Everything is possible* is the slogan of this era, akin to both new-age spiritualism and corporate marketing, a formula which underscores at once the liberating call of capitalism, the empowering undertone of human rights and the traumatising warnings of security.

Let us pause. Although Deleuze's short text offers important and prescient insights into the evolution of contemporary neo-capitalist societies, we should resist the temptation to apply it in a simplistic, unsophisticated and apocalyptic manner. This would risk providing an over-simplified, rigidifying, deterministic as well an as over-paranoid account of contemporary society, succumbing to a revelatory hubris, which is simply another declension of the paradigmatic 'will to know' that propels control itself. This, in a nutshell, is the most significant of the critiques moved to the 'control society' thesis.[53] A valuable reminder against its simplistic application, what this critique misses however is that the concept of control fundamentally reformulates the language of sovereignty. It thus cannot be framed within the latter's coordinates, namely as a repressive, intentional and centralised form of power.[54] If this were done, then the control society thesis would certainly appear as ridden with shortcomings.

First, it would assume a simplistically linear evolution (the shift from one model of sovereign power to another, and the taking-for-granted dichotomies this entails: discipline vs. control, factory vs. corporation etc.). Second, it would provide a paranoid and conspiratorial reading of contemporary forms of power, conspiratorial, since such concept of ubiquitous control would be assumed as related, directly or indirectly, to some entity orchestrating it: the language of sovereignty, as Peter Goodrich reminds, 'helps to maintain the mystery of an ineffable and ungraspable center of power';[55] and paranoid, since this all-encompassing characterisation would appear as rather inadequate to take into account the failures and opacities that characterise the reality of power: the language of sovereignty assumes power as necessarily implying transparency, certainty and infallibility.

53 E.g. Birchall *et al.*, 2010.

54 This is 'the defining component of sovereignty as a political code … a claim to occupy a privileged position of observation and intervention' (Pottage, 1998: 13).

55 Goodrich, 2012: 65.

Third, the thesis would betray a structuralist rigidity (since understood as implying a re-structuration of the sovereign power, rather than the removal of its substantial principle) as well as a techno-deterministic bias. Fourth, it would depend on an economy of truth and revelation, insofar as assuming a sort of

> hidden logic, a structure of control underpinning diverse collective arrangements that *can* be 'exposed', a riddle that can be deciphered, a thread that can be traced, or a conspiracy that can be unmasked beneath totalising environments of control.[56]

If the basic mechanism of sovereignty is the 'secret', then the basic mechanism of the critique of sovereignty is the 'revelation'.

Let me qualify then: the complexity of contemporary society warns against simplistic and linear accounts. Apocalyptic scenarios of oppressive and ubiquitous control appear to reside more in the minds of whoever described them, than on the tentative, opaque and fragmented reality in which they live. I agree with Birchall *et al.*, that these theories often tell us more about 'the will to power and knowledge of their authors', than the actual functioning of the society they are describing.[57] Yet, if many simplistic applications of the control society thesis are undeniably vulnerable to the critiques, the latter tend to misfire if applied to the notion of control I am elaborating in these pages.

Control, let me reassert, has to do with a contingent emergence of an unauthorised and immanent configuration of impersonal power with no conspirators or all-encompassing intentionality behind. It is not an emanation from a *substantial* centre. It signals a simultaneously abstract and real, formal and historical shift.[58] As we are to see soon, there is no transparency, infallibility, secrecy, determinism or linear evolutionary logic in this concept. Failure, opacities, mistakes, uncertainty and unpredictability are fully assumed as self-justifying rationales. Instead of transcendent notions of repression and subjection, ideology and domination, concealment and revelation, control is to be grasped through such notions as coping, flexibility, adaptation, that do not refer to an imposed but an *emergent* configuration, not to 'subjects', 'individuals', 'bodies', but rather to machinic compositions, decoded flows, circumstances, relations, tunings, events. It is most importantly in this sense that control moves further with respect to the notion of governmentality, which remains still too entangled with the

56 Bissell *et al.*, 2012: 704.

57 Birchall *et al.*, 2010.

58 A shift between 'two attitudes to contingency, one which avoids or absorbs contingency (substance), and another which pre-supposes, and thrives on, contingency (emergence)' (Pottage, 1998: 9).

notions of subject and human, state and population, to fully address the post-human, planetary and impersonal dimension of control.[59] Moreover, control vis-à-vis governmentality signals the crossing of a key 'socio-technical threshold': not only the digital revolution, but more generally what Sloterdijk terms the spatio-affective *explicitation* of the materiality of being together, which I shall discuss at length below. Finally, whilst crucial in raising the question of the managerial dimension of power, governmentality overlooks the spectacular dimension (which Foucault relocates in the 'society of spectacle' of pre-disciplinary era), as well as the generative power of the abstractions through which control thrives.

To be sure, to abandon the language of sovereignty does not mean to get rid of the concept of sovereignty as an obsolete veneer no longer of theoretical use. More significantly, it entails demanding what form the spectacular and glorious catafalque of sovereignty will take, once it folds into the spatiolegal architecture of control. Answering to this question avoids assuming a linear shift from sovereignty to control, spectacle to biopower, representation to production, from 'the sovereign language of law to the biopolitical language of norm';[60] but rather as the subtle folding together of the two terms into a circular, immanent configuration, which nowhere as in the contemporary city, and more precisely in the planetary process of urbanisation, finds its explanation.

2.1 The true problem, the core arcanum of politics is not sovereignty, but government, not God, but the angel, not the King, but the ministers, not the law, but the police – that is, the governmental machine which they produce and keep in movement.[61]

Let us recall the above-quoted passage by Foucault:

> what generalizes the power to punish … is not the universal consciousness of the law in each juridical subject; it is the regular extension, the infinitely minute web of panoptic technique.[62]

Beneath the glorious abstraction of law lies the 'apparatus of capture' of legal operations: the 'decisive act of power', as Canetti put it, is 'seizure'.[63] The configuration of the spatiolegal state of exception rotates around two

59 'The shift from governmentality to control involves the subsuming of the state within broader processes of "globalization"' (Moore, 2007a: 448).
60 Esposito, 2002: 65 (my translation).
61 Agamben, 2009a: 303.
62 Foucault, 1995: 224.
63 Canetti, 1994: 247; see also Brighenti, 2009.

poles. On the one hand, there is law's pretence 'to possess the capacity to realise the harmony' between law and justice, between violence and equality, between its always traumatic application to the world and its self-description as neutral, objective and necessary.[64] A self-description which, evidently, is also a self-justification, namely law's attempt to evacuate the political nature of its own operation. On the other hand, there is the 'machinery of non-legal governance', i.e. the bureaucratic, securitarian, economical ramifications into which law blurs and through which law 'entangles' its subjects beneath the façade of their acceptance as free-willed individuals.[65] Kafka of course comes to mind: on one side, a law which only nominally functions as a transcendent power, immutable and inflexible, whose glorious aura keeps K. 'entrapped' in his doomed attempt to seek justice; on the other, the capillary bureaucratic, psychological, securitarian, panoptical operations which gradually and inescapably 'capture' him.[66] What remains outside of the exceptional *project* of law, of course, is its immanent *process*, the diffuse normativity resulting from the frictional coming together between legal abstractions, socio-technical apparatus and the contingency of space.

As for K., the glorious spectacle of law threatens to divert the efforts of the legal thinker, either by proposing itself as a positive ideal to follow (i.e. fostering the belief in the intrinsic value of law itself as a solution or counter-balance for socio-economical contradictions, political violence etc.), or as a hypnotising illusion to be unmasked through the revelatory work of critique. The idealistic search for legal solutions ironically overlaps with the critical work of legal deconstruction, both blinded by the glorious light of law, both losing sight of its 'real operations'.[67] Should we thus ignore the spectacular façade of law and concentrate on the capillary apparatus of management into which it proliferates, the angels, the ministers, the police? The answer is affirmative, and yet requires a qualification. To focus on the material concatenations in which law unfolds does not entail simply ignoring (or unmasking, denouncing, deconstructing) the abstraction of law as an illusionary veil behind which more concrete reality would supposedly reside. The legal abstraction cannot be dealt with from a merely epistemological point of view: it must be addressed directly in its ontological reality.

64 Cacciari, 1997: 51.
65 Goodrich, 2012: 48.
66 Deleuze and Guattari, 1986.
67 '[G]lory is nothing other than the splendour emanating from that void' (Agamben, 2009a: 233).

2.2 Law weighs with all its might, even before its object is known, and without ever its object becoming exactly known.[68]

Kant offers perhaps the most effective configuration of law's apparatus of capture through the mechanism of legal subjection. In Kant the concept of guilt and the *sense of duty* implied by a norm, that is, the *ought* to which I am required to comply by the norm itself, are emancipated from any reference to an external power (most notably God) and instead internalised into a purely abstract *form of law*: the immanent and self-generated 'moral law inside me'. As Kant put it, 'duty is the necessity of an action done out of respect for the law'.[69] Accordingly, the sense of duty is self-referentially conceived as a 'necessity to act for the pure respect of the law'.[70] *Respect* (*achtung*) is the operator of such subjection. It is conceived as a 'feeling' that 'the reason produces by itself' and that every subject experiences before the law. Simultaneously objective (an obligation) and subjective (an impulse which affects me), the *achtung* does not imply a mere obedience to a norm, but rather a respect and reverence to the law *qua* law: respect is the reflexive self-consciousness of knowing oneself as 'subject', and thus one's always-already being 'captured' within the apparatus of exception.[71] It is, in other words, the form of law *qua* subjection. One complies with the law not for the mere fact of being obliged (as well as threatened) by an external entity, but more precisely for the inner *sense of duty* which derives from one's self-recognition as being constituted as subject of law by the law itself.[72]

Agamben has noted that what lies hidden at the core of this scheme is that the norm is structurally constituted by the imperative form, i.e. the command: to materially ground the subjection to a norm is the simple fact that the norm is *commanded*, that is, that it *must* be complied with.[73] The sense of duty, in other words, does not depend on the subjective, threats-and-opportunities evaluation of a subject vis-à-vis the consequences of complying or not with the law. Instead, it is a material and affective *seizing* which exceeds any characterisation of the norm according to normative, rational and cognitive schemes. Brighenti, elaborating Popitz, offers a compelling way to grasp this material and affective quality of law, its

68 Deleuze, 2004[1969]: 59.

69 Kant, 2012[1785]: 55.

70 Kant, quoted in Agamben, 2013: 130.

71 The concept of 'respect' (*achtung*) is the 'dispositif making operative' this self-capture; it 'simply expresses the consciousness of the subordination of my will to the law' (Agamben, 2013: 131).

72 There is obviously a paradox, also evident in the unconvincing (and to some extent unconvinced) way in which Kant deals with the concept: respect in fact must be at the same time an objective (obligation) and subjective (impulse) that is, simultaneously something that we *must* do as well as that we *want* to do.

73 Agamben, 2013: 133.

simultaneous normative (you ought) and imperative (you must) functioning, by means of looking at the atmosphere of threat that underlines and supports the very structure of the norm:

> Although we usually think that menace consists of a clear linkage between a specific behaviour of the menaced and a specific negative sanction, we could in fact be surprised by the fact that very often the negative sanction is widely indeterminate, and that such indeterminacy actually serves the effectiveness of the menace. What really counts in menace, therefore, is not the specific link between behaviour and sanction, but primarily the redefinition of the situation of the menaced, what we might call the 'menace mood'.[74]

This 'redefinition of the situation', simultaneously rational and affective, abstract and concrete, is the core functioning of law's mechanism of exception or, in other terms, the space of exception on which the legal application to the world rests. Here we may appreciate the material and affective force that the abstract mechanism of law exerts on the social, as a 'virtual' menace that, independently from the 'actual' reaction of bodies, is already affecting them. The menace mood is the materialised description of the Kantian *sense of duty*. Whilst in Kant this is posited as fundamentally 'subjective', internal, representational and self-reflexive, we may force this interpretation to unfold its affective and machinic character, that is, the 'non-contractual' and 'non-binary' materiality of the legal norm, a 'pure tension without subject, without object and without interpretant' that overflows the *logic* correspondence between action and sanction, and is *felt* in bodies with all its weighting force.[75] Such a material 'indeterminacy', I stress, should be understood as the 'ontological product' of the bionomical abstraction of law. In other words, this ontological noise (i.e. indeterminacy) is the *reality* of the abstract guilt (and thus, of the endless striving to 'repay' a debt that is constitutively infinite) that law implants in every being. Let us re-read Deleuze's statement: 'law ... defines [i.e. ontologically produces] a realm of transgression where one is already guilty'.[76] This is what is missed by the simple critique of legal abstraction *per se*: namely, the fact that the voiding of legal abstractions that the critique achieves via the removal of their reference to transcendent and sovereign scaffoldings, leaves untouched the ontological reality that such abstractions produce, as well as their immanent articulation into the contingent, historically specific conditions and concatenations of a given epoch. Abstractions might have been unmasked, yet their ontological effects do not disappear.

74 Brighenti, 2006a: 54 (n. 18).
75 Brighenti, 2006a: 61; Deleuze, 2004[1969]: 59.
76 Deleuze, 1991b: 83.

In control societies, the contradictory gap between law's necessity to spectacularly communicate itself as neutral and objective, and the reality of the apparatuses through which it applies to the world, is no longer presupposed as 'contradictory' (and thus denied) but rather assumed as the real content of law's relation to the world, a gap which is to be operationally 'coordinated and managed'.[77] Accordingly, there is no shift from the 'spectacular' to the 'managerial', but rather a folding of both poles into an impersonal and glorious techné. Yet, there is a further aspect. Above, I observed that the spatiolegal architecture of control sanctions the assumption of the chaotic, noisy and turbulent status of reality that the sovereign apparatus denied. In the light of what has just been written, it can be argued that control does not simply imply the direct attempt at managing such a chaotic outside. It sanctions, more profoundly, the awareness of the need to ontologically produce such a reality. In this sense control can be defined as the internalisation and reproduction of the crisis of sovereignty onto the social, an indeterminacy which is nothing but the reality of the crisis on which it thrives. This constant reproduction is in fact 'necessary' – Schütz observes – in order to circumvent interpretation and deconstruction and to assert the imperative of 'coping' and 'attention', adaptation, vigilance, flexibility, that characterise its smooth movement.[78] Here lies the ontological shift the spatiolegal architecture of control inaugurates: both the spectacular production of 'crisis' *and* the simultaneous deployment of the pragmatic operations through which it is to be managed.

Evidently, critique risks remaining entrapped within this circularity, hypnotised by the abstractions of law and caught within the glory of techné. A strategic shift is required, one that would allow to address the ontological reality produced by this spectacular abstraction, as well as the eminently

77 The mismatch between the two poles (the spectacular and the managerial) of control is overcome 'in their mutual exposure and in the redrawing of their constant (if constantly suppressed or marginalised) co-ordination' (Schütz, 2009: 242). Philippopoulos-Mihalopoulos (2007a: [illegible]) maintains that the 'lawscape is law and city brought together in a circular continuum, and kept separate in a distance of différance that feeds into the paradox'. This circularity implies a *gap*, the void of the circle's interior, which sanctions the unavoidable proliferation of blind spots that continuously frustrate law's 'panoptical' attempt at producing a perfectly visible 'city saturated with *control*' (Philippopulos-Mihalopoulos and FitzGerald, 2008: 442). Yet the post-sovereign configuration of control is not frustrated, but rather propelled by the acknowledgement of the inevitability of the continuous production of blind spots. In fact, control refers to a system in which the *gap* is no longer sought to be bridged, but is rather articulated. As Moore (2007a: 448) puts it, 'this gap is the zone where law, in all of its technical and historical modes, unfolds … it is not the case that this gap does not exist under regimes of sovereignty, but that there it exists only negatively, or even unconsciously', with control that becomes 'explicit is the gap between validity and efficacy, a gap that it is the function of the police to coordinate and manage'.

78 Schütz, 2009: 235.

anti-evental character of this configuration. In order to do so, the concept of abstraction must be rescued from its reduction to a merely intellectualist 'extraction' (from *abstrahere*, 'to extract') from a concrete reality. That is, the commonly held view of a separation between the abstract and the concrete must be radically put in question.

2.3 What creates an inauthentic totality is, technically speaking, the split of the nexus of action and being.[79]

To address the ontological reality of abstraction requires reversing the persistent tendency of critical thought to assume it as an illusionary veneer to be stripped away by the work of critique. Nurturing this tendency is what Peter Osborne terms the 'reproach of abstraction', according to which abstraction is charged with *reducing* 'the rich heterogeneity of the lived', *withdrawing* from the world, *distancing* 'from bodily and affective influences', *universalising* particular positions, *alienating* from warm and authentic forms of life.[80] Such simplistic critique of abstraction *per se* is doubly problematic: first, because it takes for granted the opposition between the abstract and the concrete and second, since by assuming abstraction as functioning only in the negative mode, misses its 'positive' function, i.e. generative role in creating and giving consistency to relations, spaces and worlds.[81]

Marx's notion of real abstraction provides a key insight into understanding abstraction as not merely 'abstract', 'a mere mask, fantasy, or diversion, but as a force operative in the world'.[82] It does so by challenging simultaneously two main assumptions about abstraction: its opposition to 'lived experience' and its confinement into the 'individual mind'. In this way, Marx opposes Ludwig Feuerbach's prioritisation of the sensible over thought, without however falling into Hegel's altogether dismissal of the sensible as a mere shadow of the all-ingesting self-referentiality of thought itself.[83] For Marx abstract concepts are *concrete,* insofar as being 'the point of origin of perception and imagination', in the sense that 'the sensible and the empirical appear as a final *achievement* rather than a presupposition-less starting point'.[84] This radical reformulation of the relation between thought and experience marks a significant difference vis-à-vis the phenomenological tradition and its prioritisation of lived experience *over* abstraction, alimenting a line of thinking going from Whitehead all the way to Deleuze.

79 Schütz, 2009: 238.
80 McCormack, 2012: 717–8; Osborne, 2004: 21.
81 McCormack, 2012.
82 Toscano, 2008: 274.
83 Virno, 2001: 170.
84 Toscano, 2008: 274.

Marx develops his second key intuition in the *Grundrisse*, where the notion of *General Intellect* points to the transindividual, socio-historical and collective character of abstraction.[85] This is crucial. A radically materialist approach to the reality of abstraction must not concede 'to idealism that reality possesses *irreducible* conceptual form', and instead needs to explore, as Brassier suggests, the 'conceptual form as generated by social practices'.[86] With an important caveat. Abstraction is not to be dissolved into an empirical account of its socio-historical conditions of emergence. We already saw the limits of such a sociological reductionism vis-à-vis law. Virno moves a similar critique to sociologists of knowledge for failing to grasp that the distinction between 'theory' and 'life' is not a theoretical illusion, but rather 'the *material* result of *material* conditions'.[87] In other words, it is exactly insofar as being abstract, that abstract categories have a constitutive effect on the social. It is not by 'looking for the dirty laundry that lies behind the categories of theory', that we are able to account for their ontological force, but rather by exploring the 'abstract connections ... that pervade society and make it cohere'.[88] There is no secret behind. The secret is a paradoxically open one: 'not the content hidden by the form ... but, on the contrary, the "secret of this form itself"', its 'reality'.[89]

The ethico-political consequence of this understanding is evident. Contradictory would be any escapist attempt at liberation from control via joyful deterritorialisation or ascetic purification. Any strategy willing to challenge this configuration will have to deal with the reality of its abstraction, and thus with the patient task of dismantling its exceptional operations.

Control should be accordingly addressed as regards the 'abstract form' of material relations it produces, as well as simultaneously vis-à-vis the specific socio-technical and historico-material configuration in which this 'reduction' is actually realised and, finally, with respect to the capillary biopolitical modulation of these relations in conditions of uncertainty, through the various strategies, techniques, practices, technologies and expertise – converging on the twin requirements of consumption and immunity – that characterise it. To do so, we need to come back to the spatiolegal constitution of the urban, because it is there that control unfolds in the current neo-liberal condition.

85 Virno, 2004: 37–8.
86 Brassier, 2014.
87 Virno, 2001: 167–9.
88 Virno, 2001: 167–9.
89 Žižek, 1989: 11.

2.4 I pray that Stasis, insatiable of evil, shall not thunder in the polis.[90]

As we saw, Philippopoulos-Mihalopoulos' notion of lawscape expresses the contradictory spatiolegal coexistence of law and the city. On the one hand, the law hopes to transcend the city by becoming 'a law without a city [i.e.] a law without materiality, an abstract, universal, immutable law that trammels the globe'.[91] On the other, still intoxicated by the dream of the polis, the city opens to transcend the law into a differential space of joyful difference and healthy political confrontation, becoming a 'holy city of justice perpetually floating in a post-conflict space'.[92] Yet, law requires the city to prevent its utopia from turning into a totalitarian tautology, as much as the city requires law to prevent its romantic dream from turning into a nightmare. The city reminds law of its materiality. The law reminds the city of its conflictuality. The lawscape is the assemblage that 'swings' between its two limits: territorialised closure and deterritorialised madness,[93] each side simultaneously propelling the other towards its limit and each side restraining the other from *actually* reaching it. The urban is a foamy tensegrity, and like any foam is in perpetual oscillation between a stability which, if too rigid, would make it so inflexible to burst at the minimal perturbation, and a flexibility which, if too loose, would make it so inconsistent to dissolve.

In Greek thinking the law had the purpose of preventing the delirium of the polis (*de-lirare*, going beyond the *lira*, i.e. the furrow or boundary). Emerging out of human relationships, which naturally tend to proliferate and grow without limits, the polis is the 'insatiable' (*Aeschylus*), *nomic* figure of the city, which constantly swerves away from closure: the natural 'thrust toward limitlessness' which is countered by the *logic* figure of the law, which avoids its delirium from becoming pathological by setting its limits, outside (the city wall) and inside (oikos/polis).[94]

Whereas the polis is physically, politically and ethnically enclosed, the Roman *civitas* emerges out of the 'coming together of extremely different (ethnicities, religions, etc.) people whose common accord is granted exclusively through law'.[95] If the polis, as Plato and Aristotle told us, finds it difficult to 'maintain its spatially-controllable character', Rome is by definition the *civitas augescens* (city that grows), constitutively expanding,

90 Aeschylus.
91 Philippopoulos-Mihalopoulos, 2013: 2.
92 Philippopoulos-Mihalopoulos, 2013: 2.
93 'Assemblages swing between a territorial closure that tends to restratify them and a deterritorialising movement that on the contrary connects them with the Cosmos … These are "the two limits of any possible assemblage"' (Deleuze and Guattari, 2004[1980]: 337).
94 Arendt, 2007: 183–7 .
95 Cacciari, 2009: 9 (my translation).

mobile, delirious, an infinite empire (*imperio sine fine*) open to ingesting more and more citizens and territories in its movement without end towards the spatiolegal Romanisation of the world.[96] Given the indissoluble connection in Rome between the notion of politics and an expansive, colonising and universalising project, the Roman *lex* would not be conceived as a containing bulwark, but rather as the primary instrument of limitless expansion. Rome, as Virgil wrote, *totum sub leges mitteret orbem* (has to put the whole world under its law).[97]

Yet, beneath the *civitas* lies the *urbs*. As Pier Vittorio Aureli explains, if the *civitas* is the political space of the city as a coming together of citizens under a common law, the *urbs* is its material constitution, a space that fully transcends the political: the *urbs* refers to the city as a structure of cohabitation, a material process of aggregation which is thus generic, universal, replicable and expandable. The *urbs* is the infrastructure of the *civitas*, the in-between (*infra*) 'space of connection and integration' that assures its smooth functioning.[98]

2.5

> [Urbanization] led him to the state of society; it taught him culture; it civilised him. In a word, to the urbanization which was born with him, and grew with him, man owes everything he is, everything he can be in this world.[99]

This is the meaning that in 1867 Ildefons Cerdà exhumed in order to coin the notion of urbanisation. As the industrial revolution and widespread political turmoil were plunging it into a seemingly irreversible crisis, Cerdà maintained the problem of the city to be the city itself. Urbanisation, to him, is a natural, transhistorical and universal process, 'an essential category of humankind', immanent to the coming together of human beings and coessential with civilisation.[100] The city, instead, is a historically contingent concept, one that by Cerdà's time had become corrupt and anachronistic to the point of preventing urbanisation itself from unfolding. Rather than the human being a political animal, in this conception, it is the political to be posited as a fundamental disruption to the realisation of humankind. Accordingly, the city would have to be reduced 'to its bare, physical immanence of cohabitation and movement, dismissing the political form which had come to "obstruct" it'.[101] Cerdà's project was to

96 Cacciari, 2009: 9–17 (my translation).

97 Virgil, *Aeneid*, book iv: 231.

98 Aureli, 2011: 7.

99 Cerdà, quoted in Adams, 2014: 18.

100 'Civilization cannot be attributed to the artificiality of political form, but rather it emerges in the natural, immanent fact of human cohabitation' (Adams, 2014: 18).

101 'The political, as it were, is displaced by the material fact of an assemblage of buildings and the infrastructure connecting them' (Adams, 2014: 19).

return to the simple principle of the *urbs*, that is, to the material constitution of the city and its functional integration, a necessary generic and universal question of organisation depurated from political and spatio-temporal contingencies, and implemented through a novel normative science: urbanism.

The *pure function* Cerdà's diagram of urbanisation expresses is circulation (*vialidad*), a concept directly tied to the contemporaneous becoming-urban of the capital. In fact, as the city is to become the productive machine of the capital, then it is paramount for the circulation of people, services and goods, to be functionally smooth, whilst at the same time making sure that, as Foucault writes, the 'inherent dangers of this circulation be cancelled out'. Hence there is the need to immunise circulation from disease, dissent and other potentially disruptive events, through regulation, surveillance and security. Thus conceived, the urban appears as a post-political, a-spatial apparatus or, as Ross Adams suggests, a

> meta-apparatus … an abstract, universal matrix of circulation … apolitical, and *generic* … a scaleless diagram for ordering life which both produces and coordinates a vast array of apparatuses which themselves circulate.[102]

The paradigmatic reduction of beings into praxis finds here its urban dimension: whereas the paradigm of operation rests on the assumption that 'action has no foundation in being' but rather on the self-producing operation itself, the parallel paradigm of urbanisation rests on the assumption that the urban has no foundation in the city, but rather on the self-producing process of urbanisation itself.

2.6 City is everywhere, ergo city is nowhere.[103]

In his short essay *The Metropolis and Mental Life*, George Simmel drew a parallel between the *blasé attitude* of the urban dweller, systematically indifferent 'towards the distinctions between things', and the 'money economy', which 'hollows out the core of things', reducing everything to a comparable and measurable quantity,[104] a 'hollowing out' that Lefebvre, as mentioned above, exposed as the systematic fragmentation, homogenisation and hierarchisation of the urban space generated by the capital's production of 'abstract space' and 'linear rhythm'. As we implied above, it is this very universal, transhistorical indeterminacy or, more precisely, 'absence of determination', to characterise the reality of the capital

102 Adams, 2014: 16.
103 Cacciari, 2009: 50.
104 Simmel, 2002[1903]: 14.

abstraction: the 'void at the heart of the Capital' around which the concrete, spatio-historical relations in which it is every time and everywhere actualised, revolve.[105] In stating the intention to update urban theory to the twenty-first century, Brenner emphasises the extent to which today 'the urban appears to have become a quintessential floating signifier', no longer graspable with the categories of traditional urban theory.[106] Indeed, more than an epistemological limit, the emptying out of meaning from the urban appears to be the unavoidable consequence of its progressive abstraction into the planetary process of urbanisation.

On the one hand, in Cerdà's notion lies encapsulated the constitutively urban form of the capital as a precise spatio-political project. On the other, this form gains full ontological reality in the current historical condition only by overcoming a certain socio-technical threshold: namely after the emergence of the economic-industrial machine of the *metropolis*, emancipated from space and ideally connected to a smooth global space of networks and flows of which the city is but a node.[107]

> If it is the modern State that gives capitalism its models of realization, what is thus realized is an independent, worldwide axiomatic that is like a single City, megalopolis, or 'megamachine' of which the states are parts, or neighborhoods.[108]

The 'metropolis', in David Cunningham's words, is 'the manifestation of a distinctively modern spatial-productive logic … which unites a differential whole in which every particular "place" is rendered *"equi-valent"* in a universal circulation and exchange'.[109] This single city, so placeless to render redundant any nostalgic musing on non-places, is the urban diagram of capital, the abstract-and-concrete locus of the convergence between the economic and the juridical, the (no)where in which the self-perpetuating myth of the city merges with the self-perpetuating myth of the law, finally pacifying the contradictory and conflictual tension at the core of the lawscape: no longer two arrows projected on opposite ends but a smooth embrace in which both ends meet, a universal (international) law, a universal (global) city.[110]

105 Toscano, 2008: 176; Cunningham, 2005: 19.
106 Brenner, 2013: 90.
107 Cunningham, 2008: 455–6.
108 Deleuze and Guattari, 2004[1980]: 480.
109 Cunningham, 2008: 156–7.
110 Just as the factory is arguably the diagram of 'classical' capitalism, see Toscano, 2004.

2.7 Le véritable vécu c'est absolument de l'abstrait. L'abstrait c'est le vécu. Je dirais presque que dès que vous atteignez au vécu, vous atteignez au plus vivant de l'abstrait.[111]

Taking abstractions seriously does not mean to fetishise them, however. If it is absolutely necessary to grasp the core logic of abstraction in which the capital converges with the urban into a process of planetary urbanisation, at the same time it is crucial not to overlook the fact that abstractions, to paraphrase Anna Tsing Lowenhaupt, always 'come to life in "friction", the grip of worldly encounter'.[112] This is not simply to say that there is always a below that challenge and dislocates an above, multiple and 'insurgent' *urbanisations* that challenge, resist, oppose and traverse *urbanisation*.[113] The latter consideration is certainly a healthy reminder against structuralist myopia, and yet runs the risk of confining the field yet again into an unproductive binary, not to mention falling into the temptation to somewhat overemphasise these 'insurgent' moments well beyond their capacity to actually fracture the hegemonic process of urbanisation. The urban, Brenner observes, is a

> 'concrete abstraction' in which the contradictory sociospatial relations of capitalism (commodification, capital circulation, capital accumulation, and associated forms of political regulation/contestation) are at once territorialized (embedded within concrete contexts and thus fragmented) and generalized (extended across place, territory, and scale and thus universalized).[114]

This simultaneous territorialisation and deterritorialisation, however, is always problematic, turbulent and sketchy. Abstractions are always actualised in the contingency of a given locale: they take place in the turbulent singularity of everyday life, which always resists being fully translated into them.[115] The local, Sloterdijk reminds us, is not a particular opposed to a universal but rather a singular, asymmetrical uncompressible that 'can neither be reduced true to scale nor expanded beyond a certain degree'.[116] If this is not necessarily reason to be jubilant (the capital can do with a degree of imperfection), it certainly is an injunction to recalibrate our attention to the fact that there always must be an 'actual immanent moment, and an actual site wherein the apparatus' efforts precipitate or insist', a turbulent and problematic event of actualisation that always

111 Deleuze, 1978.
112 Tsing Lowenhaupt, 2004: 1.
113 E.g. Holston, 1998; Miraftab, 2009.
114 Brenner, 2013: 95.
115 Tsing Lowenhaupt, 2012.
116 Sloterdijk, 2013: 257.

requires to be investigated, rather than simply presupposed.[117] Whereas it is not possible to understand a place without taking into account the extent to which it is constantly pulled away by de-territorialising forces seeking to reconnect it to the rhythms and diagrams of the capital, at the same time ethnographically *going* to these places is as much necessary in order to explore how the urban vibrates on the effect of these tensions: 'friction still requires a specific, almost literal, way of being there', as Federico Rahola continues, a key methodological suggestion we are to mobilise in the next chapter.[118]

Notwithstanding at times succumbing to the temptation of apocalyptic descriptions, post-political theorists have described efficaciously the current neo-liberal condition, as the systematic colonisation and neutralisation of the *political* (assumed as the space of agonistic encounter, contestation and dissensus) by means of technocratic and consensual mechanisms of governance. The 'post-political' city is accordingly depicted as a post-conflictual, consensual and uneventful space of socio-economic transactions where conflict, dissensus and risks are (sought to be) neutralised or removed.[119] Understanding control as a real abstraction allows us to implement this theoretical insight by not drawing apocalyptic scenarios or yearning for post-apocalyptic nostalgias, not only by stressing how urban deterritorialisations are always re-routed by the inescapable fact of its taking place but more precisely, by taking into account that the diagram of control always emerges from, as well as contributes to produce, the rhythms and the atmospheres of the urban itself. In this configuration, the event appears to be the battleground where the preventive ethos of control clashes with the contingent taking place of the urban, and where the risk of oppression and the potential for emancipation are constantly played out.

3.1 [The Crystal Palace is] perhaps the only building in the world in which the atmosphere is perceptible.[120]

In the Crystal Palace erected in London's Hyde Park for the Great Exhibition of 1851, Sloterdijk sees the paradigm of a process he calls *interiorisation.* Before, the epoch of *expansion* was exemplified by the unilateral movement towards the unknown of missionaries, conquerors, explorers. As the world's edges were reached, however, the expansionist hubris was gradually recalibrated into the task of arranging our being together within

117 Rahola, 2014: 384.
118 Rahola, 2014: 391; Brighenti and Mattiucci, 2014.
119 E.g. Rancière, 2001; Žižek, 2000; Swyngedouw, 2011.
120 Merrifield, 1851: 2.

a dense and limited space: from a vertical aspiration to a horizontal project: the ontological question of cohabitation.[121] In this futuristic steel-and-glass architecture, built a few years before Cerdà was to coin the concept of urbanisation, the concept of interiorisation appears to be materialised, as the historical process of integration of social life into a series of technological, normative, affective and physical enclosures, as a result of which everyday life will be increasingly moulded within safe, comforting, commodified and entertaining spaces, relations and practices, from which any event must be expunged. Enter the society of comfort.

A novel 'aesthetic of immersion' would thus surface, as result of what Sloterdijk terms *explicitation*, that is, a shared awareness about the common spaces on which life depends. To become gradually explicit, he explains, is our essence as space-creating being, always 'inhabiting the outside' through a 'praxis of world-making', co-producing tangible and intangible 'interiors' whereby we guarantee our physical and affective immunity.[122] Although this awareness does not only belong to our epoch, here it reaches a significant degree of consistency: from chemical warfare to the ever-rising environmental concerns, from the fascination with collective containers such as shopping malls and stadia to the surfacing of experience economy, from phenomenological thinking to installation art. Since the end of the nineteenth century, different ideas, disciplines and practices progressively converged in turning urban atmospheres, hitherto intangible, implicit and invisible, into a tangible and explicit field of mission, centred on the question of *how to organise*, materially, emotionally and symbolically, our common spaces. A novel awareness for the co-constitutive spatiality of coexistence means a renewed attention to our 'co-fragile' condition, and thus the surfacing of a new immunitary ethos: in Sloterdijk's efficacious image, the passage from a theological to an immunological paradigm.[123]

Whatever its limits and unavoidable simplifications, the significance of this narrative rests in offering a resolutely spatial lens to capture the convergence between immunity and consumption in the space of the neo-liberal city, that is, the convergence of strategies and discourses of planning, security, marketing, law, etc. on the common objective of producing commodified experiences of safety and safe experiences of consumption in the city.

121 Sloterdijk, 2013: 171.

122 '[T]o inhabit always means to build spheres' (Sloterdijk, 2009: 82) (my translation).

123 Sloterdijk, 2006: 477.

> **3.2** New York restaurants now have a new thing – they don't sell their food, they sell their atmosphere … they caught on that what people really care about is changing their atmosphere for a couple of hours. That's why they can get away with selling their atmosphere with a minimum amount of actual food.[124]

Mark Andrejević made a compelling synopsis of the historical process which saw the industry pursuing a twofold symmetrical activity of surveillance and data gathering for the sake of efficiency, to optimise both production and consumption phases.[125] The history of marketing is the history of the developments of techniques to collect, gather and analyse data about potential consumers so as to narrow down wide patterns of (purchasing) behaviour from an indistinct mass to ever smaller groups. Initially absorbed into CRM practices, these premises soon spilled over into policing institutions, willing to employ data-gathering practices in order to profile people and predict criminal behaviour. With the gradual shift from the factory to the metropolis as the new diagrammatic locus of power, the technical, technological and strategic convergence of security, surveillance and marketing is increasingly 'spatialised'.

Key in this sense would be the surfacing of the experience economy, a marketing strategy concerned with organising and manipulating the contextual and contingent modality of *fruition* of a commodity, that is, the actual encounter between consumer and product and thus, more precisely, the relational spatiality of the experience of consumption itself.[126] In this context appears the notion of *brandscape*, a concept as well as a strategy that spatialises the *brand* into the landscape of everyday life. First introduced by anthropologist John Sherry, in marketing literature, brandscape indicates the convergence of brand and space in branding strategies, i.e. the convergence between the promotion of a certain image (informed by a certain narrative, symbolic imaginary, atmosphere (young, cool, serious etc.) and so on) and a place-making activity.[127] The branded-landscape, brandscape, is the 'social, economical and cultural landscape where brands are produced and consumed',[128] both the projection of an institutional discourse as well as 'a material and symbolic environment that consumers build with marketplace products, images, and messages'.[129] The brandscape is

> not merely a landscape filled with logotypes and images, but rather a culture where consumption and commodities are given meaning … a

124 Warhol, 2007: 159.

125 Andrejević, 2007: 56–81.

126 Pine and Gilmore, 1999.

127 The term was introduced by Sherry at the 1986 conference of the Association for Consumer Research, in Toronto, Canada; quoted in Klingmann, 2007: 86.

128 Salzer-Mörling and Strannegård, 2007: 412.

129 Sherry, 1998: 312.

> landscape where norms and values are produced and consumed … a field of relationships where consumers' experiences are ideologically infused.[130]

In the brandscape notions of performance, event, seduction and affectivity complement those of functionality and rationality in producing 'atmospherically enriched experiences' in which the figure of the producer and the consumer are no longer distinguishable.[131] If instances such as Disneyworld and Starbucks are by now textbook examples, today this practice expands beyond the private and the commercial sector, encompassing urban renewal projects, mega events, whole neighbourhoods, as part of a 'concerted attempt to re-engineer the *experience* of cities'[132] by making them increasingly interactive, omnisensorial, adaptive and event-generating, i.e. 'to create a new set of "experience" commodities which are, in effect, the spaces themselves'.[133]

3.3 So when he first announced it, he said, 'Muslim ban.' He [Donald Trump] called me up. He said, 'Put a commission together. Show me the right way to do it legally.' … We focused on, instead of religion, danger – the areas of the world that create danger for us. Which is a factual basis, not a religious basis.[134]

Social control had been deeply, if slowly, influenced by this novel spatial consciousness. With the so-called turn from 'transformative' to a 'managerial' paradigm, criminological concern shifted from law-abiding citizens to efficient users. Moving away from rehabilitative and structuralist frameworks, and thus discarding the search for the social, moral and psychological roots of crime, this approach focuses on the analytic calculation of risk and opportunities made by a deviant, yet rational actor, engaging in purely utilitarian decisions and assessments.[135] As crime is demoralised and thus normalised as an unavoidable occurrence ingrained within everyday routines, the question becomes that of preventing it, by designing space accordingly.[136] Quoting Foucault yet again,

130 Salzer-Mörling and Strannegård, 2007: 413.
131 Klingmann, 2007: 6.
132 Amin and Thrift, 2002: 124.
133 Amin and Thrift, 2002: 125
134 Retrieved from www.politifact.com/wisconsin/article/2017/feb/03/donald-trumps-executive-order-muslim-ban/
135 Garland, 2001; Lianos, 2003.
136 Garland, 1996.

> the field is left open to fluctuating practices, in which [a] minority of individuals and practices are tolerated, in which action is brought to bear on the rules of the game rather than on the player, and finally in which there is an environmental type of intervention instead of the internal subjugation of individuals.[137]

This would be evident in the surfacing, from the 1960s, of various 'environmental' approaches to crime prevention, most (in)famously Wilson and Kellig's *broken windows,* enthusiastically applied by Rudolph Giuliani in his zero tolerance campaign in New York.[138] To be sure however, for all their renewed attention to contextual contingency, at the centre of these approaches persists the causal presupposition of a rational and individual agent. 'Space' as we know it had not entered the picture yet. At the same time, as Giuliani's New York showed best, the pragmatic realism of environmental crime prevention models increasingly coexisted with a seemingly incompatible discourse of security. The unwillingness to openly define crime as post-moral and contextual – as per the rationale of the very crime models they were implementing – since this would have meant publicly admitting the impossibility of actually eradicating it, would lead to conceal this very impossibility behind a façade of *decisionismo* and zero-tolerance populism.[139] According to David Garland this was a 'hysterical' contradiction, or more precisely a conscious attempt, as Loïc Wacquant observes, to include within the concern of security other social aspects that would normally be alien to it. After all, this is the key to the famous Foucaldian quip on the advent of biopolitics as sanctioning the shift from the sovereign who 'lets live and makes die' to the government that 'makes live and lets die'. If the birth of biopolitics means that every aspect of life becomes the concern of government, it is through the lenses of security that this integration is to be performed. Accordingly, Wacquant argues, zero tolerance populism is perfectly consistent with an intention to expand the penal treatment of poverty, the symptom of a slipping into a judiciary and carceral management of the poor.[140]

Foucault already provided a precise explanation for the apparent contradiction between the biopolitical task to improve the life of the population and the sovereign right to kill: *racism,* according to him, was the dispositif that would allow to simultaneously foster the population through welfare measures, whilst at the same time killing (or discriminating, excluding etc.) all the *others* who were perceived as a threat to the social body. If racism

137 Foucault, 1997: 260.

138 E.g. 'Situational Crime Prevention' (Clarke, 1983); 'Defensible Spaces' (Newman, 1973); 'Environmental Design' (Jeffery, 1971), etc.

139 Garland, 1996.

140 Wacquant, 2000: Ch. 2, para. V.

today can no longer be overtly mobilised, in theory at least, the notion of danger, with the corollary of fear, proves extremely useful in solving the 'conundrum of discrimination'. Lianos and Douglas define *dangerization* as the tendency 'to perceive and analyse the world through categories of menace' – a self-constitutive tendency, that is, insofar as it does not detect danger, but rather perceives discrepancies vis-à-vis *normalcy* as dangerous. In other words, it produces normality via the constant redefinition of the abnormal, and thus dangerous, allowing for *de facto* discrimination whilst escaping its *de jure* the accusation.[141] It is again Rudolph Giuliani, quoted at the beginning of this section when candidly speaking in the midst of the actualisation of Trump's 'Muslim ban', to offer us the best example.

3.4 The whole point of power is its ability to change not only the rules midstream, but the aesthetic of flows and rhythms.[142]

Giuliani notwithstanding, risk seems a more accurate concept than danger to describe the peculiar short-circuit between the managerial and the spectacular we are observing today. Although closely connected, there is a significant conceptual distinction between risk and danger. While danger may be described as the inherent potential for harm, adversity or injury in some person, event or thing, risk is a *measure* of that potential's likelihood and consequences/impact.[143] Uncertainty is accordingly a crucial variable affecting risk. As we saw, the spectacular discourse of security does not rely on a narrative of risk management – according to which the existence of risk and thus uncertainty is deemed inevitable and thus sought to be realistically minimised – but of risk control, according to which risk is not something ultimately unavoidable and whose eventuality must be to some extent accepted, but rather an anomaly which must be prevented, avoided and erased (whatever the consequences).[144] Terrorism is obviously the most explicit context in which this strategy, and its psycho-social consequences, can be observed at their contradictory best. Simply put, the absolutisation of safety that the risk control model entails is inevitably tied to an increase in the feeling of vulnerability.[145] Enter the 'safety-paradox': the more the society is sought to be purified into a given normality, the more 'variations' from the norm will be singled out as impure, and dangerous.[146]

As a consequence, the perception of security becomes its central concern. John Stuart Mill once famously argued that 'the only purpose for

141 Lianos and Douglas, 2000: 267–8.

142 Taussig, 2013: 150.

143 Garland, 2003: 50.

144 Clear and Cadora, 2001.

145 Enter the 'safety-paradox': the more the society is controlled and normalised, the more 'variations' from the norm are singled out as dangerous. Lianos and Douglas, 2001.

146 Lianos, 2003.

which power can be rightfully exercised over any member of a civilized community, against his will, is to prevent harm to others.'[147] Supplementing this libertarian understanding and its rigid demarcation of private and public sphere, Douglas Husak proposed the notion of 'public wrongs', according to which the State has a legitimate interest to punish only wrongs which are done not only to individual victims but also to shared values and interests of communities, i.e. wrongs that are public.[148] Yet, far from being clearly defined, 'harm' and 'public wrong' are vague, floating signifiers, to which many 'things' can be attached. In fact, what happens when floating affects such as fear, anxiety, unease and discomfort become perceived as a public wrong *per se*?[149]

It happens that social control strategies undergo yet another qualitative shift. To become the target now are no longer the individual and his/her situational cost-opportunities evaluation, but rather such impersonal, collective, intangible affects. Not simply a question of discouraging crime through spatial arrangement, security now becomes a matter of tuning, and thus '*generating engagement* through the manipulation of mood ... generating the same wavelength'.[150] In other words, overflowing the concern with preventing crime and violence (or, to use the cumbersome jargon of the field, with 'objective security'), security becomes an atmospheric endeavour, with the task of producing reassurance, or the conditions of being at ease, in 'peace of mind' and 'absence of fear' (namely: 'subjective security').[151] Prior to dwelling on the aesthetic-phenomenological outcomes of this evolution, we should mention the role law plays in it, dissolving into these affective atmospheres, whilst inoculating them with the quintessential liberal abstraction, *the right to be left alone,* affectively reworked into a *right to be free from fear.*

3.5 The society that moulds all its surroundings has developed its special technology for shaping the concrete basis of this ensemble of tasks: its own territory. Urbanism is that taking possession of the natural and human environment by capitalism that, developing logically into absolute domination, now can and must remake the totality of space as its own setting.[152]

In the light of what has been said so far, to Mitchener-Nissen's observation that security seems increasingly to target 'harms that are not crimes' (i.e.

147 Mill, 1869: 22.
148 Husak, 2008: 135.
149 Ramsay, 2010.
150 Thrift, 2007: 245.
151 Baldwin, 1997: 14.
152 Debord, 1983: gloss 169.

'fear of crime, feelings of safety' etc.), we should reply that, more profoundly, security reconfigures those very harms as crimes.[153] Nowhere can this be better observed than in UK Anti-Social Behaviour Orders (ASBOs), which define anti-social behaviour as 'conduct which caused or was likely *to* cause harm, harassment, alarm or distress'.[154] In this context, Peter Ramsay observes,

> it is not the offensiveness of the conduct which causes 'harassment, alarm or distress' that is the problem, even where the conduct concerned is offensive, but rather it is the underlying threat to others' sense of security'.[155]

To be criminalised, in other words, is a conduct 'which, without necessarily being a criminal offence, can by its cumulative effect generate a *climate* of tension and insecurity'.[156]

In classic situational crime prevention models the individual is responsibilised in two senses. On the one hand, obviously, s/he is responsible vis-à-vis committing crime (although the environment may be assumed, at least indirectly, as an extenuating circumstance). On the other hand, the individual is also responsible for not providing a favourable environment for crime itself. In a post-holistic world, Francisco Klauser reminds us as follows,

> immunity and integrity are not to be gained from the submission to a larger whole, but must be achieved as the outcome of a personal effort of seclusion.[157]

Do not become a crime victim, is a common sign on the London Underground. Mitchell Dean termed it 'new prudentialism', that is, 'the multiple "responsibilization' of individuals, families, households, and communities for their own risks".[158] A responsibilisation that, let us not forget, is always coupled by delegation, that is, the constant outsourcing of the responsibility to act in line with socio-technological legal protocols: texts, strategies and technologies which produce an architecture of delegation prompting the pervasive potential for de-responsibilisation or, to put it otherwise, immunising anyone from the risk of being 'held responsible'.[159]

153 Mitchener-Nissen, 2014: 76.
154 *UK Crime and Disorder Act 1998*, s1(1).
155 Ramsay, 2008: 9; see also ICHRP, 2010.
156 COM, 2000: 6 (my emphasis).
157 Klauser, 2010: 338.
158 Dean, 1999: 162; Hay, 2006.
159 Brighenti and Pavoni, 2017.

There is more though. Ramsay observes that

> the key to the ASB that renders a person liable to the imposition of an ASBO is that the disposition of contempt or indifference, made manifest by the defendant's conduct, *fails to reassure* others with respect to their security in the future.[160]

Remarkably, this 'reverses the onus of proof in respect not of accusations about the past, but of *fears about the future*'.[161] What is more, it removes agency from the individual, since control over one's capacity to produce fear is obviously dependent on various socio-cultural, historical, contextual, more-than-human factors. It seems law finally managed to perform its own relational and post-human turn, with little reason to celebrate, however. Fear, as we saw in Chapter 2, cannot be contained within the confines of the individual, the rational, the body. It is an impersonal affect traversing and electrifying urban atmospheres, as well expressed for instance in the US Terror Alert System (a warning system tailored around colours or words which indicate an increase or decrease in the level of a given threat). In Brian Massumi's brilliant analysis, this system is shown as affectively modulating the *socius*, not in a deterministic sense (evidently not everybody would act in the same way once the terror alert is shifted to, say, orange), but more precisely insofar as producing a state of common attunement, by activating direct bodily responses (e.g. anxiety, fear, uneasiness) depending on given levels.[162] Whether, as Ian Hacking observes, risk could be understood as a modulator of the relationship between fear and harm, once fear becomes a harm in itself this configuration collapses into a self-referential circularity.[163] Once it becomes pervasive, in fact, threat is radically deterritorialised, true to its nature:

> A threat is only a threat if it retains an indeterminacy. If it has a form, it is not a substantial form, but a time form: a futurity. The threat as such is nothing yet – just a looming. It is a form of futurity yet has the capacity to fill the present without presenting itself. Its future looming casts a present shadow, and that shadow is fear. Threat is the future cause of a change in the present.[164]

Fear is present. Risk is future. They are the two sides of the same event: one does not exist without the other, although the former is actual and

160 Ramsay, 2008: 8.
161 Ramsay, 2008: 12 (my emphasis).
162 Massumi, 2005.
163 Hacking, 2003.
164 Massumi, 2005: 35.

affective, the second virtual and speculative.[165] Once it is understood as a virtual event, always real even when non-actual, risk becomes an ever-present occurrence whose very potentiality has to be constantly defused and neutralised and yet, because of its radically de-bounded character, is bound to constantly re-produce fear in the present.[166]

It is easy to see, incidentally, how this very activation, i.e. the production of an atmosphere of pervasive alertness, undermines security in the first place. As Massumi punctually observes, in fact, this signals the entrance of pure indeterminacy within political calculation: now, *everything is possible.*[167] McKenzie Wark quips: 'what secures security? Its absence. Insecurity secures the necessity for security'.[168] Yet it is not simply insecurity that secures security but, more precisely, the very surfacing of a right to be free from fear, turning insecurity into a rightfully intolerable occurrence, not only in the borderline field of terrorism, but also in the everyday exceptionality of urban life.

The legal abstraction of the (neo)liberal subject's negative freedom from harm, once materialised into atmospheric regulations, thus becomes a self-fulfilling prophecy, producing more and more noise that justifies their ever-increasing deployment for the preventive pacification of the urban.[169] According to Wolfgang Sutzl, when addressing security we have to take into account the extent to which the deployment of its apparatus (in disciplinary, situational and socio-economical sense) is sustained by a symbolic dimension that justifies and legitimises its deployment.[170] There is more. Between the hidden work of extensive surveillance and the deafening rhetoric of zero tolerance populism, the relentless production of an indeterminate risk in the future and the pervasive diffusion of fear in the present, the urban space is increasingly shaped around comfort-oriented tunings. It is within the latter, it seems, that the contradiction of liberalism – namely the simultaneous quest for autonomy *and* protection, the libertarian strive for the unconstrained realisation of one's own interests, and the interconnected demand for the protection of these interests – finds its (partial) solution. The comfort bubble

165 Massumi, 2005.

166 Boyle and Haggerty, 2009; Beck, 2002.

167 '[W]ith affect, perceptually addressed, chance becomes politically operational' (Massumi, 2005: 35).

168 Wark, 2005.

169 See for instance *Deneys Reitz* v. *SA Commercial Catering and Allied Workers Union 1991*, when a workers' protest was forbidden on the grounds that it was infringing the 'right to peace and quietness' of the residents; in Van der Walt, 2007.

170 Sützl, 2009.

> becomes the place where the individuals follow their vocation to the accomplishment of pure immanence. The realisation of oneself is a disguised definition of the consumption of oneself.[171]

3.6

> The capitalistic economy of the present day is an immense cosmos into which the individual is born, and which presents itself to him, at least as an individual, as an unalterable order of things in which he must live.[172]

The awareness of the affective materiality of being together thus becomes explicit in the production of spectacular urban installations, wherein different institutions, technologies and practices converge into the common objective of producing commodified experiences of safety and safe experiences of consumption in the city: in other words, simultaneously secured and enticing spaces, defused from their eventfulness and stabilised by legal injunctions so as to be safe, consumable and capitalisable. Thrift, after Sterling, has termed it the *security-entertainment complex*: i.e. 'a complex made up of two particular linked assemblages which have gained increasing purchase by feeding off each other',[173] not a context-based, but a context-generating strategy, not simply seeking to manipulate a context (as in 'broken windows' theory for instance), but actually producing it: a *worlding*.[174]

Following Ball and Wood, I propose to use the notion of *brandscaping* to define the way the post-conflictual logic of neo-liberalism is materially actualised into the city. Ball and Wood define *brandscapes of control* as

> the apex of late capitalism, of hyper-consumption, personalisation, niche-marketing, lifestyle ... It is the seamless combination of surveillance, marketing, and sociospatial construction, where the timespace of the subject becomes ineluctably aligned with the techno-social protocols, tools and ideology of particular institutions.[175]

John Allen called it a logic of seduction, in which power works 'through the experience of the space itself, through its ambient qualities', by tailoring various sensuous regimes to foster inclusion within an atmosphere that is

171 Sloterdijk, 2006: 498 (my translation).
172 Weber, 2003[1905]: 54.
173 Thrift, 2011: 7.
174 The corporations 'produce a world ... its world, its objectivity, its reality, merges with the relationships enterprises, workers and consumers have with each other' (Lazzarato, 2004b: 188).
175 Ball and Wood, 2008, 2013.
176 Allen, 2006: 442; Degen, 2008.

meant to be comfortable, consensual, shared, convivial.[176] These brandscapes of comfort may indeed be seen as the aesthetic-phenomenological apex of the 'domesticization of the city' envisaged by Cerdà 150 years ago.[177] Take for instance the case of security policies in Gothenburg, Sweden. Here the public space is semantically privatised by the public campaign THINK: 'we want to create a feeling of being "at home" by making everyone seeing the city as our "common living room"'.[178] In this attempt to 'make the city safer, beautiful, and comfortable', security and entertainment, safety and aesthetics, converge onto the concept of comfort, here exemplified in the Swedish term *trivsam,* indicating something simultaneously comfortable and attractive. As Thörn punctually notes, what is primarily problematic in this account is the very understanding of public space and city that remains hidden, beneath the apparently sensible intention to make the urban more beautiful, comfortable, and safe. For one, the fact that there is a specific category, the homeless, that is being surreptitiously designed out by making sure (through legal regulations and obstructive design) it won't be 'feeling at home'. As the empirical investigation of the next chapter will show, the quest to immunise space from unease, discomfort or fear always intersects with the socio-economical asymmetries of the urban, that is, it is bound to exclude those unable to afford or unwilling to enter such a 'comfort-animated artificial continent', which will keep floating 'in the ocean of poverty'.[179]

What is of interest here, however, is not only its exclusionary consequences but the eminently preventive ethos of brandscaping. As already discussed, Deleuze refers to control as 'modulation' in order to emphasise that control does not imply the shaping of what is to be thought, but rather the modulation of what *could* be thought. Control, in other words, has to do with generating the space of the thinkable, that is, an *environment of thinking,* whilst neutralising it from the event of sense. I employ the notion of brandscaping as a way to translate this concept into the urban. Brandscaping accordingly is not to do with disciplining bodies into acting in a certain way but rather with phenomenologically modulating the space of the experienceable, the 'environment of experiencing': i.e. the urban. Brandscaping may be seen as a strategy for simultaneously arousing *and* pacifying the 'experience' of being-in-the-city, through a frenetic production of spaces and happenings which strive to make 'you feel vibrant, alive', and which at the same time are constantly neutralised from their potentially disrupting eventfulness, so as not to compromise their

177 'If the "city" had been delineated by spaces specific to politics, to the market, and to the household, the urbe would propose a single, domestic expanse in which all of these would intermingle in a single, universal space of nondistinction: the domestic sphere. Urbanization, most succinctly put, is the domesticization of the city' (Adams, 2014: 22).

178 Thörn, 2011: 989, 997.

179 Sloterdijk, 2013: 195.

commodifiable and consensual potential.[180] Mike Fisher writes about the all-encompassing boredom seizing contemporary hyper-stimulated students, in their increasing incapacity to affect and be affected in the face of an over-production of affects.[181] The paradoxical coexistence of hyper-stimulation and sensorial deprivation is indeed a key facet of neo-liberalism. In the urban space, Philippopoulos-Mihalopoulos notes, this may be observed as 'urban hyperesthesia goes hand in hand with a punctilious attempt at separating the senses' into 'sanitised' atmospheric insulations, such as museums.[182] In fact, brandscaping seems to point beyond a compartmentalisation, rather actualising the co-presence of hyper-stimulation and sensorial deprivation in the production of 'hyper-experiences' simultaneously neutralised from their eventfulness.

3.7

> [Dracula] can also control the meaner things of life: the bat, the rodent, the wolf. He can appear as mist, as vapour, as fog, and vanish at will.[183]

Let us pause for a moment. It is legitimate at this point to ask whether in the last section I indeed succumbed to the 'all too tempting gesture of revealing the relations of power at the heart of affective modulations', offering a 'paranoid reading of the systematic and instrumental "engineering" and "manipulation" of affect by the powerful' and reducing 'affect to a diagnosis of our times of late capitalism and the like, as exemplified in the affective modulations of the security society'.[184] What is wrong with the latter stance should be evident. Simply put, the reduction of affects to a merely manipulatable and engineerable instrument of the powerful is a position which is twice wrong: first, since assuming a substantial rather than an emergential understanding of power, still implicitly referred to one or more sovereigns able to wield it and second, since denying the excessiveness of affects, and thus the always uncertain and fallible character of any spatial 'manipulation'. By focusing on some practices of micro-resistance such as humour and seduction, Bissel *et al.* show that affective atmospheres are always excessive, open and unpredictable, thus escaping the rigid depiction of those theories that instead assume them as always-already captured within the hidden logics of power.[185] However, I do not think this

180 Foster Wallace, 1998: 264; see Sloterdijk, 2006: 458–63.

181 Fisher, 2009.

182 Philippopoulos-Mihalopoulos, 2013: 3.

183 in *Dracula*, 1992.

184 Bissel *et al.*, 2012: 706.

185 Bissel *et al.*, 2012: 705. Bissel *et al.* focus on an airline 'safety demonstration' and the way humour and seduction offer ways to dislocate the preferred disciplining outcome. Whilst acknowledging that play, entertainment and lightness are certainly part of contemporary capitalist strategies, the authors are willing to resist 'the fashion of "mass-

argument runs counter to the configuration of control so far described which, to paraphrase Thrift, is 'naturally experimental ... aspires to be all-encompassing but it must perforce retain an openendedness'.[186] Let me qualify then: with the notion of brandscaping I aim to explore urban control by looking more explicitly at material and context-specific attempts to retune the city, through a direct convergence between institutions, practices and technologies of security and entertainment, enacted and stabilised by the legal scaffolding. However, in this way I am not inferring that brandscaping is to be understood as an oppressive model of manipulation. The function this configuration of power exposes not the blanket-elimination of resistance and transgression, whose intensive potential in fact it needs absolutely. Opacities, failures and blind-spots are all constitutive parts of the reality of control, which by means of being flexible is able to internalise transgression and resistance, rather than rigidly opposing them.

Instead, the function that brandscaping expresses is exactly one of preventive de-potentiation of the intensity of urban life, exploiting its potential and simultaneously (and of course, always tentatively) defusing it from its conflictual and eventful charge, into a comforting atmosphere which 'tolerates transgressions, provided they remain soft ... [keeping] the lowest possible minimum of intensity... to make sure that the confrontation *does not take place*.'[187]

Nowhere is this evident as in the current proliferation of multiple scale 'urban events', in whose proliferation in the urban space we may locate a key contradiction at the core of brandscaping, namely a frenetic production of post-political spaces of generalised consensus, whose eventful potential needs to be simultaneously aroused and neutralised. Event-generation and event-neutralisation in fact co-exist in the paradoxical challenge to 'employ the event in order to enmesh the event itself'.[188] Incidentally, as I will expand in the next chapter, this also means that urban events, and especially mega events, play a significant methodological relevance for urban research, since they express and perform (and thus offer a compelling chance to investigate) the very essence of brandscaping, a logic which can be encapsulated within this oxymoronic formula: *the pre-emptive production of events*, or the production of always-already neutralised events.

diagnosing" the enrolment of affect in the capitalist management of life', and thus the denigration of these affects 'as yet another sinister form of aeromobile governance', and instead propose to understand 'seduction as a form of play that operates at the surface, eschewing the temptation to discover latent content beneath the manifest ... emphasis[ing], rather, the unpredictability built into the logic of seduction by virtue of its superficiality' (2012: 705–7).

186 Thrift, 2011: 7.

187 Tiqqun, 2010: 170.

188 Severino, 1979: 42.

Therefore, if we assume that brandscaping concerns the prevention of events from becoming intense, then we may have an argument to counteract the otherwise insightful point made by Bissel *et al.* Could not we argue that their admittedly 'capricious examples' of micro-resistance to control strategies occur exactly insofar as 'capricious', as they put it, that is, low-intensity occurrences that fall short of threatening to disrupt the internal consistency of the brandscaping in which they occur?[189] This is not to say that humour and seduction, together with other instances of everyday resistance, are irrelevant. Everyday life is full of these moments of liberation, which are important in themselves, and unaccountable only by referring to some supra-structure into which they would be already subsumed. Freedom and resistance are not only to be understood as 'heroic escape[s] from a totalising logic', decisive acts of revelation of hidden logics of oppression.[190] I certainly agree with Deleuze's more modest and strategically consistent observation that 'our ability to resist control, or our submission to it, has to be assessed at the level of our every move'.[191] Yet, it is also important to eschew the problematic romanticisation of these 'liberating moments', an attitude that too many accounts of everyday life and its 'revolutionary' potentials betray. In this sense it may be useful to conclude the chapter by coming back to Sloterdijk, since his approach, although more than aware of the limits of such romanticisation, ultimately seems to end up in a deadlock which we should better take into account for the pages to come.

3.8

> We are, we move and we thus live in the work of man! We are grasped and controlled (maîtrisés) within the proportions he has chosen. We cannot escape ... being inside the work of man as fishes are in the sea, being entirely immersed in it, living in it, and belonging to it.[192]

As already observed, Sloterdijk offers a radically materialistic account of the contemporary immunological condition, avoiding the optimism of libertarian vitalism as well as any conservative techno-phobia, rather emphasising the need to develop an 'atmospheric ethics' based on the common immunological attempt to synchronise our being-together according to an ecological and constructivist praxis of world-making. Awareness of co-immersion is awareness of co-fragility, hence the need to synchronise, to develop 'a new ethics of techné' so as to envisage new ways to build the 'global work of installation art' in which we live.[193] This is, first, an insightful and helpful way to deal with the abstract-and-concrete installations of the

189 Bissel *et al.*, 2012: 706.
190 Bissel *et al.*, 2012: 706.
191 Deleuze, 1995: 176.
192 Thus claims Socrates in Valéry, 1944: 41.
193 van Tuinen, 2009: 17.

social, resisting to the tendency to resort to paranoid approaches to techné. Second, it is a healthy reminder of the inconsistency of merely oppositional and 'ideological' approaches to (juridical, economic etc.) abstractions, and especially of the temptation to find some more 'authentic' dimensions behind them, e.g. in the creative praxis of multitudes, the post-human relationalism of networks, the propulsive force of naive vitalism, the enchanting vibrancy of matter, and so on. Without falling into simple reformism, this approach expresses a valuable counterpoint to the fascination with deterritorialisation and flows, also avoiding easy escapism. Yet, his prioritisation of praxis of synchronisation over the eventful frictions and excesses which constantly splay them out, is symptomatic of Sloterdijk's underestimation of the significance that events play in the urban, and more precisely of the centrality their prevention assumes for the apparatus of control.

In this sense, it could be argued that Sloterdijk overlooks a *second* aspect of the explicitation he describes. The fact that he explains the historical shift in collective perception through the notion of spatial explicitation, whilst disclosing the 'common spatiality' of being together, at the same time forecloses its virtual, excessive, inhuman event, by neutralising it within a common meaningful plane of cohabitation, in this way making it socially, politically and economically exploitable. Accordingly Sloterdijk, whilst rightly avoiding any demonisation *per se* of techné, and rightly criticising any prejudicial understanding of strategies and tactics of spatial manipulation, at the same time overlooks that what is at stake with control is not simply manipulation but, first of all, the neutralisation of the urban from its excessive eventfulness.

Let me qualify. I am not suggesting that Sloterdijk's spherology implies a rigid conceptualisation of the social. The German philosopher proposes an immanent and tensegritous notion of immunity which is not static, stable and pre-given (as the liberal 'individual sphere') but rather results from battles, interventions and on-going adaptations. His concept avoids the rigidity of liberal immunity, at the same time eschewing the accelerated vulnerability of naive vitalism and its deterritorialised complicity with control. Yet, there is an unresolved tension that traverses his work. As Borch emphasises, although Sloterdijk's theory preserves an emphatic 'vitalist impetus' which differentiates him from the systemic self-organisation of a Luhmann, a problematic oscillation remains between the celebration of (foam) vitalism and the need to synchronise and immunise.[194] Is there not a risk, of such a tension being internalised as just another variation of the liberal call to 'strike a balance' between vitalism and management, autonomy and protection, freedom and security? In this sense, is not the search for a 'new ethics of techné' bound to be ingested and modulated by the impersonal techné of control? Does not the quest for synchronisation risk

194 Borch, 2010: 230; 2008: 565.

being entrapped into the post-dogmatic dogma of *efficiency, usefulness, correct procedures*, defusing every situation from its evental potentiality, accepting the space as it is, and thus reducing political action to the search for ways to cope with the conservative and claustrophobic task of living-together? Indeed, does not this entail falling yet again into a neutralisation of matter as innocent?

It is evident that the problem with synchronisation is not that of being somewhat oppressive vis-à-vis some sort of un-synchronisable vitalism or joyful disorder. It is more profoundly, the fact that such synchronisation is prefigured within the closed ontological horizon of control. It is for this reason that an alternative and properly emancipatory (for lack of a better term) ethico-political stance should not entail the celebration of vitalism as opposed to the need to synchronise. It is exactly that unresolved tension that must be debunked. At the end of his *In the World Interior of Capital*, Sloterdijk stresses the need to rethink the value of the local, not in opposition to the global, but rather as a way to re-emphasise the asymmetrical, uncompressible, extended quality of being there, the dimension in which we reside and that unavoidably resists in the face of 'the progress of de-contextualization, compression, mapping and the neutralization of space'.[195] This uncompressible (the uncompressible body and place in which we are, the uncompressible time of reading or learning, for instance) 'can neither be reduced true to scale nor expanded beyond a certain degree' and signals 'the resilience of the asymmetry we call life'.[196] Sloterdijk does not clarify completely where this return to the local will lead us, leaving it more as a hopeful ending to his book than a strategic commitment. Indeed, as just observed, the untranslatability of any locale prompts us, at least methodologically, to take care of the frictional way in which it resists and splays out the deterritorialising and reterritorialising forces of the capital. This praise of the asymmetry is thus necessary, as that of the phenomenological, in the face of the excessive iconoclasm of certain theoretical and political tendencies.

Yet, we should remember Siegfried Kracauer's dictum about capitalism, that it 'rationalises not too much, but too little'. It is true, he noted, that capitalist abstraction 'is incapable of grasping the actual substance of life', yet this objection is absolutely inadequate when 'raised in favour of that false mythological concreteness whose aim is organism and form', i.e. in favour of the 'ebb and flow of life' that would supposedly lie beneath: 'a return to this sort of concreteness … would sacrifice the already acquired capacity for abstraction, but without overcoming abstractness'.[197] Kracauer precisely diagnosed the humanistic mythology which underlines any critique of abstraction that aims to overcome or cure its 'alienation'. As Philippopoulos-Mihalopoulos puts it, following Cunningham, 'only on

195 Sloterdijk, 2013: 255.
196 Sloterdijk, 2013: 259.
197 Kracauer, 1995: 83.

their level of abstraction can despatialising mythologies be fought'.[198] Both methodologically and politically, and consistent with the discussion developed so far, this entails seeking to rescue our capacity for abstraction from its entanglement into given structures of power, rather than obliterate it in the name of a more corporeal, sensuous, libidinal and affective, uncompressible reality. In fact, such obliteration seems to be more akin to the mode of functioning of capitalist experience economy than to a critically emancipatory mode of resistance. Opposing abstraction by praising the irreducible concreteness of the uncompressible locale may be uplifting, and yet does not lead us far away, since overlooking the extent to which such multiple 'uncompressibles' actually obstruct the capitalistic machine, or simply fall unnoticed beneath its process. Instead of keeping fighting alienation *qua* abstraction, or opposing abstract compression with the irreducible locale, could not a more promising task be, as Matteo Pasquinelli suggests, that of 'recovering the alienated power of abstraction' itself?[199]

I believe the notion of brandscaping has different advantages, by allowing for: first, addressing the material consequences of the increasing atmorhythmical convergence of security and marketing, i.e. the spacing of the security-entertainment complex; second, accounting for the folding of spectacle and biopower, materially understood as a simultaneous generation-and-manipulation of 'inhabitable maps' 'based on exceptional topologies rather than sovereignty as such and founded in protocols of resonance';[200] third, providing the notion of control with a more explicitly material lens, as well as an attention for both its ecological and phenomenological unfolding; fourth, offering a useful concept to explore the unfolding of control in more direct, explicit and context-specific instances; fifth, and for all these reasons, providing a methodological tool to explore control in the urban, as the next chapter shows through an empirical investigation of an urban mega event. In this context, the normally fragmented and scattered reality of urban brandscaping reaches rare levels of intensity, expansion and syncretism of its multi-faceted operations in an urban-wide extent, unfolding in what I term the 'mega event brandscaping', an urban-wide installation that exposes to a paradigmatic extent both the abstract form of the spatiolegal architecture of control and the reality of its modulating tunings. It follows that mega events cannot be simply reduced to a compelling object of study in themselves. More significantly, they are one of the privileged contexts for exploring urban control. For this reason, the next chapter takes us to Johannesburg, and to the 2010 FIFA Football World Cup.

198 Philippopoulos-Mihalopoulos, 2015: 30.
199 Pasquinelli, 2014.
200 Thrift, 2011: 13.

Chapter 5

Tuning the city

This chapter explores some of the theoretical issues defined so far by looking at the city of Johannesburg, South Africa, in the context of the 2010 FIFA Football World Cup. A key consideration orients the chapter and justifies its chosen subject: mega events (such as the World Cup or the Olympics) are not to be seen as exceptions, but rather *explicitations* of emergent configurations of control in the city. They are thus relevant both as an object of study in themselves, as well as a methodological tool to explore the urban more in general, provided they are approached through a radically material and 'situated' perspective that avoids 'explaining away' the event by referring to pre-given theoretical structures, and instead proposes to investigate the encounter between the mega event and the city in its contingent unfolding. Mega events do not occur on flat surfaces, but in urban spaces that are already normatively tuned in unique ways: they are always tentative processes of *re-tuning*. The chapter thus offers an opportunity both to test the spatial framework proposed in the first two chapters – by applying the notion of urban tuning to the city of Johannesburg – and the spatiolegal framework developed in the following two. It is organised in four parts:

In the first I introduce my understanding the a mega event (ME), as a public ritual thrown onto the urban space and accelerated to a maximum socio-cultural, economic, symbolic and political significance. The ME may be seen as an urban-wide 'air-conditioning' installation, to be explored in both its abstract form and concrete spatialisations. In the second part I deal with some pressing methodological questions, seeking to understand how to address empirically the urban ontology so far described, doing justice to the antagonism of the city without defusing it into a pacifying account. In the third part I filter the ethnographic experience through my theoretical lenses in order to define the *Joburg Tune*, i.e. the immanent getting together of bodies, spaces and laws that normatively tune one's being-in-Johannesburg. In the fourth part I finally investigate the 2010 FIFA World Cup, looking at its brandscaping of security, entertainment and law, and most importantly how it encountered, interacted and clashed with the Joburg Tune.[1]

1.1 Capitalism ... 'concretely and deliberately' organises environments and events in order to depotentiate life.[2]

From flash mobs to neighbourhood festivals, from mass demonstrations to international fairs, multiple scale events increasingly syncopate the rhythm of contemporary urban life. Events have always been part of everyday life in the cities (parades, saints' days, carnivals). Yet, the 'use' of events as a precise strategy of urban branding and development is a rather more recent affair. As Greg Richards states in a book aptly titled *Eventful Cities*, cities increasingly 'need to be eventful', because it is through events that the 'most precious of modern commodities – symbolic capital' is generated.[3] Today, the 'festivalisation' of urban politics theorised by Harmut Haussermann and Walter Siebel more than two decades ago explicitly unfolds as the city becomes an eventful space of deterritorialised happenings, instrumentally employed for political action (manifestations, marches, protests), commodified entertainment, urban planning (e.g. event-led regeneration), and so on.

Doreen Jacob has coined the notion of *eventification* to refer to the 'process in which urban space, itself, is represented as a spectacle and transformed into an aesthetised place of consumption'.[4] In a similar vein, John Pløger distinguishes between 'serial events' – equating to 'consuming the city, rather than living it' – and 'presence-events' such as impromptu 'reclaim the street' parties and other extemporaneous and spontaneous re-appropriation of urban space, that are 'shaped by the will to create a moment of present presence'.[5] Since they potentially allow for the 'rupture of conventions not to be repeated', Pløger assumes presence-events as instances of what he calls *eventalisation,* insofar as bearing the potential for unleashing the 'political content' of the event (cf. Jacques Rancière) into the space of the city. The distinction between *eventification* and *eventalisation* is useful to critically capture the 'eventful turn' of contemporary urbanism. However, it should not be assumed as a way to categorise urban events along an oppositional axis (e.g. planned vs. spontaneous, one-off vs. serial, commercial vs. free, artificial vs. authentic), but rather as a tool to explore their always twofold quality.

Every event, even a highly planned one such as the Olympics, is a 'controlled decontrolling', an attempt to spectacularly manage into a 'normalised' exceptionality the contradictory task of simultaneously

1 Part of this chapter has been published as Pavoni, 2011.
2 Agamben, 1996: 64 (my translation).
3 Richards, 2010: 12.
4 Jacob, 2013: 3.
5 Pløger, 2010: 849–50.

generating *and* regulating enthusiasm.[6] Public rituals have always played this dual role. On the one hand, there is the need to stimulate, reinforce and confirm the common, affective and material getting-together of bodies that constitute any community: the ritual as a strategy to rendering more 'tangible' and effective the urban being together, 'mobilising people, publics and crowds in order to transform them'.[7] On the other, there is the necessity for the collective to self-immunise, through a series of codified and performative procedures, against the excess of this very common.[8] Likewise in contemporary public events, whilst the affective quality of the event is key to neo-liberal urbanisation, its disruptive and conflictual potential is most feared. The 'resonant fusion' of the crowd is at the same time the dream and the nightmare of event organisers, who rely on this 'fusional instant that *produces the event*', but at the same time are aware of the danger of this 'explosive mixture'.[9]

It is by focusing on the spatial quality of this paradoxical intersection between event *production* and *prevention*, that promising insights may be gained. In particular, this may entail turning attention to what Rahola indicates as

> the violent and open-ended encounters between capital apparatuses and logics of translation into scalable inventories and the unreproducible, subjective and nonscalable experience of urban forms of life and labor.[10]

Nowhere as during the quintessential urban event of our times, the mega event, is such a 'violent encounter' manifested, sublimated and magnified.

1.2 Life within communities tends first and foremost to obliterate any consciousness of our participation in the cosmic course. The role of history, even in its most murderous epochs, is to reassure, to force us to live, to provide a counterbalance to the fear of the stars.[11]

In his classic work, Maurice Roche observes: 'to understand mega-events better is to understand something more broadly about the nature and fate of human agency and social structure, and of continuity and change, in

6 Elias and Dunning, 1971: 31; Iles, 2009.
7 Boullier, 2010: 93 (my translation).
8 Esposito, 2002; Nancy, 1991; Derrida, 2005.
9 Boullier, 2011.
10 Rahola, 2014: 395.
11 Trost, 1953 (passage translated by Catherine Hansen at www.mitpressjournals.org/doi/pdf/10.1162/ARTM_a_00025)

modernity',[12] and, we may add, something more deeply about 'the relation between modern existence and its forms'.[13]

The ME is in fact a paradigmatic locus in which the process of neo-liberal urbanisation is simultaneously reproduced *and* problematised. We may understand it as an abstract form in at least three senses, first, in the sense of incorporating the concretely abstract ideal of *publicness* that public rituals convey: simultaneously a transcending feeling of common belonging, as well as the situated, actual resonance contingently produced between bodies; second, as a form (as well as a 'format') of urban control in which every place is rendered equivalent; and third, as an explicit instance of the erasure-and-partitioning through which, as we saw, the spatiolegal state of exception is instantiated. Let us explain.

First, MEs directly exploit the 'social cement', enthusiasm, effervescence and cohesion that qualify public rituals. Durkheim famously described public rituals as symbolical processes through which the cohesion and continuity of society is reaffirmed and reinforced by producing a sense of collective identity and solidarity among the individuals.[14] This is made explicit in the resonant and carnivalistic effervescence of being together which urban- and nationwide celebrations always trigger, and which is crucial to foster the de-politicised consensus which MEs enjoy among various strata of society, an essential lubricant for easing its process of urban (re)tuning. In André Jansson's precise words,

> the social power of public spectacles ... stems from their capacity to: create, reinforce and circulate a public sense of fatefulness; and, promote a (superficial) solution to the very same fateful moment.[15]

Second, the standardised format of the ME makes it one of the most efficient generators of capitalistic deterritorialisation. Through their spectacular, affective, normative and material apparatus, MEs trigger an efficient and accelerated deterritorialisation of the urban, reterritorialising it into a global circulation of bodies, services and commodities. Acting as a transnational operator of neo-liberal capitalism, the ME is an efficient mediator between the different scales of the urban, that is, between the specific, local instances of the 'neo-liberal city' and its global, generalised form. This is a function well testified by MEs' ever-increasing diffusion in so-called 'emerging states' – see for instance the numerous MEs taking place in the recent past and future in BRICS (Brazil, Russia, India, China and South Africa) countries.[16]

12 Roche, 2000: 235.
13 Cacciari, 1995: 3.
14 Durkheim, 2008[1912].
15 Jansson, 2005: 1672.
16 Grix and Lee, 2013.

Third, the existence of a ME (i.e. its legitimation and justification) is always premised on a void, simultaneously posited and naturalised, with respect to which the ME itself emerges as a 'fulfilling solution'. As their urban footprint becomes increasingly vast, increasingly explicit becomes the dispositif of 'hopefulness' on which ME narratives rest: there is always a 'present lack' – e.g. the lack of global recognition (China), the image of a crime-ridden country (South Africa), the 'need to regenerate' a 'degenerate' neighbourhood (London) –, to be connected to a future 'non-yet', which the ME will supposedly create.[17]

1.3 Marketing has preserved the idea of a certain relationship between the concept and the event. But here the concept has become the set of product displays (historical, scientific, artistic, sexual, pragmatic), and the event has become the exhibition that sets up various displays and the 'exchange of ideas' it is supposed to promote. The only events are exhibitions, and the only concepts are products that can be sold.[18]

Many interesting works analysing MEs vis-à-vis the social cohesion they may or may not generate share with their archetypal precursor, Durkheim, the same reliance on a homogenous and transcendent, all-explaining notion of society. Even insightful contributions such as those of Salomé Marivoet, and C.R. Pramod, for instance take these affirmations as self-evident.[19] It is more effective, I believe, to employ the work of Durkheim's contemporaries such as Tarde or Arnold Van Gennep, whose approaches do not take for granted the effects of the public rituals, but rather investigate their actual, performative and pragmatic enactment.[20] See for instance the work of Vida Bajc who, focusing on George Bush's 2005 presidential inauguration, explores the role of security practices immunising the ritual from the uncertain liminality caused by its *taking place.* Security functions as a 'meta-ritual', she explains, through a set of bureaucratic, securitarian and legal procedures aimed at assuring the practical and logistical as well as meaningful tuning of the ritual itself.[21] Not only does this entail policing the preferred narrative to be produced, but also instils certain normativities as regards the ritual's functioning which then spill out on to everyday life: the 'bringing about

17 Anderson and Holden, 2008.

18 Deleuze and Guattari, 1994: 10.

19 Marivoet, 2006, and Pramod, 2008, differently emphasise the role played by ever-controversial tendency to build grand works (most notably, stadia) in producing a 'special atmosphere' as well as crystallising the symbolical charge of the ME, in the context of the Euro 2004 football competition in Portugal, and the 2008 Beijing Olympics, respectively.

20 Van Gennep, 1960[1909].

21 Bajc, 2007.

public security through a meta-ritual legitimates surveillance practices of the state security apparatus and normalizes the social order it creates', generating a pedagogy of security and de-sensitisation to over-control.[22]

Focusing more specifically on proper 'mega' events (e.g. the FIFA World Cup and the Olympics), Philip Boyle and Kevin Haggerty emphasise the interplay between the operational 'nuts and bolts' of security provision and the management of the 'representational elements of those efforts', that is, the increasing convergence between the managerial and the spectacular in ME-related security strategies: a 'spectacular security', that is, increasingly concerned with 'communicating' safety, even regardless of logical relation with actual dangers.[23] If this is consistent with the seductive logic of security described above, what is of interest is the extent this process reaches in the context of MEs. Whether brandscaping, Ball and Wood argue, is a 'more or less successful institutional attempt to inscribe spaces and their inhabitants in their own terms', nowhere as in this context can this be observed.[24] Moreover, although brandscaping is a fragmented process, always reworked and displaced in its urban unfolding, it is during MEs that it gains an unmatched level of intensity and extension, as a result of the extensive convergence between technical, tactical and symbolic operations of security and entertainment, complementing each other as different instances and inclinations of the same event-neutralising, and thus capitalising effort: i.e. the operational production of a spectacular consensus, a city-wide brandscaping enacted and held together through an exceptional tuning. This occurs in highly concentrated form, both institutional and spatio-temporal. The ME in fact occurs in precisely delimited space-times (demarcated by legal, securitarian, aesthetic and physical boundaries), and is enacted by a limited amount of institutional actors (the governing body, the local government/municipality, the sponsors).

Ad hoc regulations (by-laws) and extensive deployment of security (allowed by the interplay between elevated amounts of funding and the weakening of both legal as well as socio-cultural counter-weights to measures which would normally be perceived as excessive and/or oppressive) patrol and secure the physical and representational space of the ME, exemplifying its role as preferred tool for the 'shock and awe' mechanism through which neo-liberal politics proliferate in the urban setting by neutralising political, legal and financial constraints.[25] This scaffolding supports, contains and channels the atmospheric engineering of the ME brandscaping, whose affective intensity is made explicit, and measured, in various ways. In London 2012, for instance, the Mood-o-Meter recorded daily the level of

22 Bajc, 2007: 1671; Boyle and Haggerty, 2009; Adey, 2009.

23 Boyle and Haggerty, 2009.

24 Ball and Wood, 2008. On the notion of Olympic brandscaping, see Pavoni, 2010a; Osborn and Smith, 2016.

25 Horne, 2011.

emotions of the Games according to a range of levels, an interesting joyful version of the terror alert system.[26]

Evidently, such a complex, abstract and concrete apparatus appears as a perfect instance of the preventive logic of control, understood as an attempt to immunise the urban from the turbulence of its own spatiality, allowing for movement and circulation, whilst neutralising the potential for actual events to occur. The ME brandscaping aims to keep the urban flow alive, producing atmospheres of pervasive entertainment and frenetic festival rhythms whose effervescence must be constantly kept at a low, consensual and politically uncontroversial intensity: *the 'mega' event is meant to be the un-eventful event par excellence.* In this sense the ME is not simply an exceptional moment (of capitalistic exploitation, legal suspension, securitarian siege), as many inconsistent copy-and-paste applications of the 'state of exception' theory suggest, but rather an accelerated, concentrated and sublimated *explicitation* of the abstract form of neo-liberal urbanisation. The 'single city' of the capital appears to be actualised by the ME-led urbanisation in a smoother, quicker and more effective – yet by no means unproblematic – way. It is a process in which a crucial role is played by the discourse of *legacy*, whose surfacing in the last two to three decades, as the overarching angle through which MEs are justified, implemented and evaluated, has been paramount in deeply entangling MEs within processes of urbanisation, dramatically intensifying their urban impact.[27]

1.4 The legacy of a mega sporting event is all that remains and may be considered as consequences of the event in its environment.[28]

From its very 'advent', the moment in which the 'bid' is won by the host and the ME is officialised, a 'topologically complex space-time of the non-yet' is opened up, releasing a cloud of worries and expectations which require fine-tuning into preferred narratives, procedures and practices.[29] The discourse of legacy is the dispositif through which this fine-tuning occurs. According to some, legacy allows for inserting evaluation and accountability within the ME process, thus countering the tendency of MEs to be just 'footloose industries' that 'come to a place with a need for resources and then disappear'.[30] To others, it is a 'consistent justificatory apparatus' that builds consensus around an event by neutralising its controversies into the vague promise of future reaps.[31] However, either seen as positively

26 'How was it for you?,' *The Sunday Times*, 19 August 2012, www.thesundaytimes.co.uk/sto/Magazine/Features/article1104115.ece
27 Part of the next section is an elaboration from Pavoni, 2015a.
28 Chappellet 2012: 77.
29 Anderson and Holden, 2008: 155.
30 Preuss, 2013: 3852.
31 Costa, 2014: 114.

encouraging a more sustainable impact, or negatively concealing its damaging effects, legacy is still understood as external to the urban dimension of the ME. I propose to zoom in instead, understanding it as internal, and thus directly constitutive of the relation between the ME and the city.

Of course MEs, especially the Olympics, have always been supposed to be more than just a festival. Up to the mid-1970s this has been mostly translated into general rhetorics of pacifism, multiculturalism, healthy competition and the like, with very few, 'vague and fleeting' references to the role the event may have played vis-à-vis the city that was hosting it.[32] As their politico-economical relevance, as well as scale, grew, the focus shifted on their social and territorial impact. In the Olympic bid documents, the word legacy first appears in Melbourne 1956, but it is only with Los Angeles 1984 and most importantly Barcelona 1992, that the Olympics begin to be properly understood as a vehicle of urban development.[33] In the 2000s the process is officialised, becoming compulsory since the bid stage. In 2003, the International Olympic Committee (IOC) includes in the Olympic Charter the mission: 'to promote a positive legacy from the Olympic Games to the host cities and host countries'. Likewise, in 2005 FIFA adds among its missions 'to build a better future through the power of the game'.[34] Since then, legacy would cement the link between the ME and the city, providing the 'environment of sense' for the articulation of this relation.

Burroughs' notion of the word as control is absolutely appropriate here. Let us remind: the word is a virus that, by entrapping thought within the dimensions of language (designation, manifestation and signification), systematically 'prevents expansion of consciousness', and thus the event of sense, from occurring (see above). In fact, as more and more attempts to define and measure legacy through ever-refined instruments and classifications surface, the viral quality of the word usually remains unspoken.[35] As a result, the legacy discourse becomes professionalised – in an increasingly blurred distinction between academia, think-tanks and the 'event industry' – and de-politicised. For instance, it is reduced to economic parameters, as Iain Macrury and Gary Poynter emphasise by showing the reduction of London 2012's social legacy discourse to a 'commodity mode', where the meaning of 'sustainability' is conflated with 'non-expensive' and, in John and Maragaret Gold's words, 'short-term needs take precedence over long-term outcomes'.[36] Caught in the gap between aspiration and affordability, the hopeful potential of the ME is thus frozen: nothing can be hoped for anymore unless it is within the budget.[37] More generally, the

32 McIntosh, 2003: 451.
33 Moragas *et al.*, 2003.
34 Retrieved from www.fifa.com/about-fifa/
35 E.g. Cashman, 2003; Preuss, 2007; Costa, 2014.
36 Macrury and Poynter, 2008; Gold and Gold, 2009: 194.
37 Mules and Faulkner, 1996; Girginov and Hills, 2008.

de-politicisation of legacy (or, more precisely, the viral de-politicisation of the ME engendered by the discourse of legacy) reduces the debate to technical matters of *hows* (i.e. how a given problem is to be solved) leaving unaddressed the *whys* (i.e. the parameters of such a pre-emptive problematisation). Hence legacy becomes a self-fulfilling prophecy: the more it is defined, assessed and measured, the more the very framework that provides legacy with meaning and legitimacy is taken for granted.

Arguably, many critical works rightly denouncing the negative legacies of MEs eventually remain confined within the horizon of legacy itself, unable or unwilling to address its consequentialist presuppositions. Consequentialism is an ethical position that evaluates the rightfulness or wrongfulness of an action according to its consequences. This approach assumes intentional and rational control over individual and social agency, and takes for granted the possibility to visualise, measure and assess the consequences of action. Challenging this understanding requires rethinking legacy by dismantling its environment of sense and the official categories of visibility and measurement producing it, thereby gesturing towards a notion of legacy that would emerge against the brandscaping of the ME or, more precisely, out of the frictions unleashed.

Indeed, paradoxically it is the very discourse of legacy that seems to have had the (unintentional) consequence to intensify, and gradually make explicit, MEs' contradictory status as sites in which the capitalist production of space is simultaneously accelerated and problematised. As a result, Kevin Gotham suggests, 'rather than viewing mega events and other spectacles as instruments of hegemonic power', we may understand them as 'destabilising events that display inequalities and social problems, provoke intense conflict and engender collective struggles',[38] or 'moments of discontinuity [that] effectively reveal … the dynamics and tensions of globalisation processes' – 'disputed places' whose ideological narratives always enter a field of contestation and struggle, re-appropriation and re-interpretation.[39] Incidentally, this is especially the case since the rise of social media that, by allowing invisible narratives and counter-hegemonic readings to come to the fore, provide countless opportunities for 'digital deterritorialisation', creative disruption and semiotic 'occupation' of the official ME brandscaping.[40]

1.5 Instead of 'feeding the planet' we'll feed the conflict.[41]

The contemporary wave of ME protests (especially from Vancouver 2010

38 Gotham, 2011: 200.

39 Dansero *et al.*, 2011: 196.

40 Frew and McGillivray, 2014.

41 Comitato no Expo, 2012 (my translation). Here the (polemical) reference is to the title of the Milan '15 Expo: *feeding the planet, energy for life.*

onwards) seems to support the assumption that it is not so much their 'sportive', symbolic or otherwise character, but rather the extent to which today MEs have become entrenched, abstractly and concretely, in the process of urbanisation, that turned them into 'frictious sites' in which the paradigm of neo-liberal urbanisation is simultaneously reproduced and problematised.[42] It also provides a promising ground to explore empirically how such frictions may be manifested, as well as their potential impact and legacy on the urban fabric. In fact we may speculate whether this is a partial explanation for the reason why resistance to Los Angeles 1984, Atlanta 1996 and (the road to) Salt Lake City 2002, as Matthew Burbank *et al.* observe, did not succeed in coalescing into proper 'antigrowth movements', but rather only produced scattered instances of 'piecemeal resistance'.[43] This is a similar fate to what Enrico Dansero *et al.* observed vis-à-vis Turin 2006, where opposition ultimately failed 'to generate a public environmental consciousness'.[44] On the contrary, recent instances of protests in Vancouver 2010, London 2012, Brazil 2014 and 2016 and, to a minor but still remarkable extent the Milan 2015 Expo, appeared as more organised, locally and transnationally coordinated, as well as informed by a 'motivation to shift development policy away from exchange value toward use value', rather than simply 'deflect or mitigate the negative consequences of a particular development project'.[45]

A minor and yet instructive example comes from London 2012, where the East End area, in which the Olympic Park was built, had been repeatedly framed as a 'wasteland', a 'void', an 'emptiness', a 'dead space', thus grounding *a priori* the necessity of its event-led regeneration. Before any consideration of the positive or negative impact of the ME, the viral effect of legacy had already reshaped the urban regimes of visibility, condemning to invisibility those spaces and communities that remained undetectable to the Olympic gaze.[46] Here the most brilliant critiques of the 2012 Games have been those coming from artists whose work was not simply focused on socio-technical speculations on the potential negative effects of the Games (speculations which can always be countered by narratives of positive effects: namely the legacy itself), but rather on contesting the preliminary erasure which supported the whole narrative of the 'regeneration games'. Just like their colonising ancestors, the LOCOG presupposed the evidence of a *terra nullius* in Hackney. Instead of playing

42 This view deviates in this sense from Sadd, 2013, or Harvey *et al.*, 2013. On the notion of 'frictious site', see Rahola, 2014.

43 Burbank *et al.*, 2000.

44 Dansero *et al.*, 2011: 214.

45 Respectively, what characterises 'antigrowth movement' and 'piecemeal resistance', according to Burbank *et al.*, 2000: 39.

46 On the characterisation of the East End as 'dead space', see Raco and Tunney, 2010: 2082.

within this already-closed horizon ('What is the best way to regenerate this wasteland?'), and thus entering the debate as already-weakened actors, these artists exposed the already-existent tunings of the pre-Olympics space, i.e. spaces, bodies and practices that that were irreducible from being translated into the Olympic brandscaping.[47] Their 'resistance' was not only reduced to (rightfully) questioning the actual, socio-legal-economical consequences of the ME but, by emphasising the frictions produced by the ME's re-tuning, gestured towards other forms of abstractions and normative tunings not already recuperated within this operational paradigm. Hence the particular significance of their critiques, insofar as embodying a protest which, if on the one hand acting directly on the concrete space of the urban with artistic, ironical, demonstrative and sabotaging guerrilla-like initiatives of opposition to the brandscaping of the ME, was at the same time directed towards its abstract form. This was not simply an attempt at re-imagining space, but an ontological challenge to the reality of the Olympian abstraction, piercing through its immanent closure by means of letting emerge those very frictions that its smooth planning sought to defuse. It was the unquestioned consensus for its glorious operation (the self-fulfilling claim to have a solution in the form of a legacy, whereby urban space is *de facto* eliminated into a self-justificatory temporal horizon) that these initiatives indeed questioned, emphasising that beneath debate on the *hows* lies the question of the *whys*. This is after all what the famous Lefebvrian definition of the right to the city points to, that is, 'the *right to the oeuvre*, to participation and appropriation (clearly distinct from the right to property)': the right to political and fully material involvement in the urban-making process, that is, the 'right to create problems' by defining the questions at stake in urban space.[48]

The Rio de Janeiro 2016 Olympics offered another compelling instance. Here, in a situation deeply influenced by the turbulent political climate (the decision over the impeachment of the president Dilma Roussef would be ratified only few days after the end of the Olympic Games, and before the start of the Paralympic Games), artists, researchers, activists and local communities gathered in different initiatives – on the trail of the nation-wide 2014 FIFA World Cup protests – directly aimed at challenging the Olympic brandscaping. As I explained elsewhere,[49] an important role was played in this context by the local *Comitê Popular para a Copa do Mundo e a Olimpiada*, in which various instances of civil society (social movements, NGOs, associations, etc.) were gathered and loosely coordinated in a com-

47 For a comprehensive review of these works, see Powell and Marrero-Guillamón, 2012; see also the film project *Swandown*, by film-maker Andrew Kotting and geographer Iain Sinclair, whose critical potential is explored by Stephens, 2015.

48 Lefebvre, 1996: 174.

49 Burocco and Pavoni, 2016.

pelling tripartite strategy:[50] first, *research* – a far-reaching activity of investigation, producing reports, organising debates and exhibitions, engaging with social and mass media, and generally seeking to uncover, explain and communicate the various issues tied to the Olympic process, thus constantly challenging the official narrative; second, *support* – personal, legal, emotional support to the various communities displaced, contaminated or in other ways negatively affected by the Olympic process; third, *testimony* – that is, giving voice to local communities themselves, by organising encounters and providing space for them to express their claims and narrate their plight. In this way the Olympic brandscape was challenged not simply through critique, but also by showing the multiplicity that survived buried beneath. This tripartite strategy allowed them to simplify and communicate effectively, locally and globally, research results and counter-narratives, developing an effective counter-narrative through the strategic use of existing and new media, thus fracturing the atmosphere of celebratory optimism the discourse of legacy conveyed, and plunging popular support for the ME to a historic low. The various activities culminated in the organisation of the five-day event the *Jogos da Exclusão* (Exclusion Games), that took place in the centre of Rio from 1–5 August, the day of the opening of the Olympics.[51] The event, held in the occupied building of the Faculty of Social Science and Philosophy of the Federal University of Rio de Janeiro, attracted more than 100 organisations, local communities, artists, researchers, activists, journalists and passers-by, providing a common space to communicate information, make claims, denounce and testify one's plight.[52] This was obviously small given the low budget and the deafening Olympic apparatus, yet it effectively functioned as a counter-event, attracting and magnifying the scattered instances of anti-Olympic protest in the city into an effective assemblage which provided a perhaps tiny, and yet by no means insignificant breach of the smoothness of the Olympic brandscaping. The materialisation of an atmosphere of dissent, evidently not only dependent on the campaign but strongly shaped by it, had important effects. At the local level, the protest managed to build a solid legacy of resistance that would reverberate in Rio in the years to come.[53] At the global level, this was even more impressive, as

50 The Comitês Populares para a Copa do Mundo, Popular Committees for the World Cup, emerged in Brazil since 2009, on the eve of the 2014 FIFA World Cup. Gathering various instances of the civil society, they were organised in a national network, ANCOP. All committees were dissolved after the World Cup apart from Rio de Janeiro's, that morphed into the *Comitê Popular para a Copa do Mundo e a Olimpíada*, keeping the important work also vis-à-vis the Olympic process. See http://rio.portalpopulardacopa.org.br/

51 The title Exclusion Games is a direct response to IOC president Thomas Bach's declaration about Rio 2016 being the 'most inclusive' Games in history.

52 CPCORJ, 2015.

53 E.g. Zirin and Boycoff, 2016. For an account of a 'resistant legacy' in Vancouver, see Boycoff, 2011: 53, 77.

the three years of protests in Brazil have been key to reverting the Olympic consensus worldwide, as is evident in the various cracks represented by cities like Hamburg, Boston, Olso, Stockholm and Kracow, which had to withdraw their Olympic bid for lack of popular support.

In fact, we may argue that, on a level, regardless of 'visible' and 'tangible' outcomes and context-specific claims, for the very fact of embodying an ontological refusal to enter the 'festival atmosphere' of the event, the protest challenges the very 'operation and scope' of its politics.[54] In this sense ME protests do not simply oppose local to global, concrete to abstract, but rather *their* local to the localisation of capital, *their* abstraction to the abstraction of capital. In fact, it is the very form of the ME that paradoxically fuels them further. The local and concrete dimension of ME protests, exactly insofar as they are local and spatially-embedded within the material contradictions of urban development, becomes global and universal. The abstract and global form of the ME, exactly insofar as it is deterritorialised and transnational, prolongs the protest beyond its local boundaries, 'bringing the local terrain of struggle to a national and international scale', as an activist puts it.[55] Thus the claustrophobic traps of localism, nimbyism and piecemeal resistance may be turned into the collective production of 'large backyards', as another activist adds.[56] In fact, it is exactly the possibility of such a simultaneous localisation of global struggles and globalisation of local opposition – what Smith defined as *scale bending* – that the telluric shock of the ME potentially brings about.[57] A different narrative thus emerges, from the oppositional ones usually polarising the debate on MEs between, on the one hand, the hegemonic spectacle of the event and its productive planning and, on the other, the resistance and its reactive and transgressive re-appropriations: *strategies* versus *tactics*. The atmospheric engineering performed by ME brand-scaping is to be traversed as a transversal and emergent, complex and multifaceted process, rather than a simplistically top-down projection.

1.6 The practical productive possibilities of the metropolitan system of connectivity are not exhausted, in advance, by their abstract structuring by the conditions of capital accumulation.[58]

The eventful potentialities of the urban do not surface, as either romantic or grand political positions suggest, only in spontaneous, unpredictable

54 Douzinas, 2014: 159.

55 In Boycoff, 2011: 54.

56 In della Porta, 2008: 42.

57 Smith, 2004. In a similar vein McGillivray observes that the digital acceleration provided by new media 'shifts the power of scale, demonstrating the active mobilisation of citizens' (McGillivray, 2014: 108).

58 Cunningham, 2005: 22.

and/or politically explicit occurrences such as 'retake the street' parties, clandestine raves, mass demonstrations or indeed revolutions, but can also occur in the accurately pre-planned context of a ME. The urban always harbours unactualised potentialities, hence the significance of exploring their contingent, conflictual and frictional taking place. Whereas the 'shock' of MEs on the urban is certainly instrumental to the 'creative destruction' of neo-liberal capitalism, at the same time its attrition provokes wider and uncontrollable telluric shocks in the material, affective and normative fabric of the city, whose impact is never fully predictable, preventable or controllable, and may exhume deeply entrenched contradictions, threatening to burst the gaseous consensus produced by its brandscaping. The 'abstract structuring' of the ME never exhausts the 'productive possibilities' of the urban. In fact, it multiplies them. Their actualisation is always materially and historically situated into a specific tuning, the 'where' in which its deterritorialising hubris always gets 'dirty', diffracted and problematised.

This is certainly not a call for a romantic endorsement of the ME as an instance of social cohesion. Quite the contrary, it is an eminently strategic position, which assumes the tunings of the urban, their creation and contestation, as the locus of ethico-political actions. By acting upon these tunings and their potentials, on the frictions they produce with abstract forms of control, the possibilities are unleashed for producing 'particular way[s] of occupying, taking up, space-time, or inventing new space-times', for the good and for the bad.[59] It is therefore a suggestion to study the mega event vis-à-vis both the lines of flight it opens by the very fact of taking place in the urban, *and* the tentative, controversial and conflictual attempts that are put in place to manage and cope with this turbulence.

This not only implies that greater attention is to be given to explicit and (more or less) organised instances of resistance to the ME. At the same time, it gestures towards the exploration of other, less evident aspects, those forms of being together 'emerg[ing] in the space between invisible resistance and normative hegemony', that is, the space in which the urban and the ME brandscaping encounter and clash, and which are *alternative* in both concrete and abstract sense, not merely in opposition, to the securitised and capitalised brandscaping of the ME itself.[60] This is not to underestimate the ME brandscaping or to downplay the value of ME-protest, but rather to complement this observation with an attention to the more subtle and ambivalent dimensions of this process; those dimensions pertaining to the everyday tuning of the urban experience or, to put it with Kracauer, the 'tiny catastrophes that make up daily life'.[61]

59 Deleuze, 1995: 176.
60 Brighenti, 2010d: 40.
61 Kracauer, 1995[1963]: 252.

A valuable example in this sense comes from Angharad Closs Stephens' analysis of the 'affective atmosphere of nationalism' that surrounded the London 2012 Olympics. Stephens develops a transversal approach, by emphasising the role played by 'little experiences' of 'shared banalities' in allowing for a certain atmosphere to emerge and take hold. Describing the atmosphere emerging around and through the London Olympics torch relay, he presents it as an assemblage produced by the coming-together of a series of bodies, affectively modulated by media, enacted by (in my terms) the Olympic brandscaping, and yet absolutely not reducible to 'a state engineered affect', but rather taking 'hold through affective forces which resonated in excess of attempts at engineering feelings'.[62] Following this path, I signal the need to keep an eye on less evident, unintentional, and less explicitly political outcomes of the encounter between capitalist apparatuses and everyday life, in whose frictions promising opportunities for ethnographic research emerge. This is what is done below, by exploring the emergence of a ME brandscaping in Johannesburg, South Africa, during the 2010 FIFA World Cup, and its impact on the everyday tuning of the city.

1.7 What happens between bodies during a demonstration is far more interesting than the demonstration itself.[63]

In event research, notwithstanding the 'predominance of the case study approach and descriptive level of much events research published in academic journals', attention to this ambivalent, we may say, atmospheric dimension, is rather scarce.[64] An ever-growing body of critical works, whilst being relevant in documenting/denouncing ME-related abuses, often succumb to taking certain ideological frameworks for granted, and uncritically copy-pasting them into the context of MEs, thus assumed as Trojan horses fostering neo-liberal politics of hyper-commercialisation and hyper-securitisation.[65] Among those, particularly numerous are contributions looking at security strategies, practices and technologies implemented in the context of MEs, mostly through descriptive applications of existent theories of security and control, which implicitly take for granted a correspondence between increase in security and decrease in freedom.[66] This is certainly not to downplay the pernicious effects of ME-related hyper-securitisation and neither, more generally, to overlook highly problematic questions surrounding MEs, such as income polarisation, urban

62 Stephens, 2015: 188.
63 Tiqqun, 2010: 211.
64 Page and Connell, 2012: 9.
65 E.g. Eick, 2011; Broudehoux, 2007; Boycoff and Fussey, 2014; Olds, 1998; Newman, 1999; Waitt, 2003.
66 E.g. Samatas, 2007; Richards *et al.*, 2011; Boyle and Haggerty, 2009; Atkinson and Young, 2005; Giulianotti and Klauser, 2009; Klauser, 2009.

propaganda, social exclusion, violence, evictions, corruption, excessive expenditure, environmental pollution, gentrification, real estate speculation and so on. There are obviously critical aspects that cannot be overlooked in any ME analysis, and yet they should not be understood as supra-structural shortcuts to simplistic binary oppositions between the ideological smokescreen of an Olympic narrative and the reality of exploitation.[67]

In methodological terms, such tendency is often reflected in the way MEs are temporally split, and either addressed *a priori,* through their preparatory phase, e.g. organisation routines, practices, programs etc., or *a posteriori,* through outcomes, impacts and legacy. Symptomatic for instance is the scarcity of studies which deal with MEs' securitisation (and more generally with the ME-related implementation of the security-entertainment complex) *during* its spatio-temporal occurrence, besides analyses of pre-ME security strategies, planning and abuses (displacements, evictions etc.), or post-ME legacies of legal, social and technological over-securitisation. Likewise, there is an often insufficient attention to materiality in empirical research on events, which means their unfolding and implications are considered separately from the material settings and overall spatial conditions in which they take place.[68] Even when notions of space, materiality and context are emphasised, this is generally done from a managerial understanding of the context of the event, considering uniquely the official framing of events – i.e. their 'desired effects' rather than 'emerging effects' – with respect to which its 'success' or 'failure' is assessed, whilst ignoring the complexity of its non-linear, contingent taking place.[69]

Ian Lamond and Karl Spracklen have recently proposed to critically problematise the notion of 'event' in event studies, so as to disentangle it from the neo-liberal parameters to which the dominant event-management approach often reduces it.[70] An interesting suggestion in this sense comes from the field of social movement studies, from Mastaneh Shah-Shuja's exploration of the immanently generative quality of protest, to Donatella della Porta's suggestion to look not only 'at what produces protest but at the "byproduct" of protest itself'. Rather than analysing the protest as an instrumental and 'dependent variable', 'explained on the basis of political opportunities and organizational resources', the suggestion is to address it as an always 'eventful protest', as such to be explored in the contingency of its occurrence and in the immanence of its effect.[71] This is the direction the present approach wishes to take into the field of MEs, with the intention of

67 E.g. Shaw, 1993.
68 Hall and Page, 2012: 150.
69 Sharpley and Stone, 2012: 352.
70 Lamond and Spracklen, 2014.
71 della Porta, 2008: 27–30; Shah-Shuja, 2008.

looking at the most organised, controlled and 'neo-liberal' of urban events, through a sensitivity to its eventful and conflictual nature. This leads to a more pragmatic methodological question: how to explore such a conflictual dimension, which is abstract and concrete, visible and invisible, atmospheric, and contingent?

2.1

> Something else orders and locates, gathers and situates, binds and distinguishes, sets the pace and the rhythm, but that something no longer has the shape of a Society and must be followed, step by step, by other methods.[72]

Gregory Fieldman has suggested that, given the increasingly dislocated and dislocating 'world of apparatuses' in which we live, the methodological value of the bodily and sensorial 'being-there' of traditional participant observation begins to wane: 'the nonlocal character of the apparatus needs a nonlocal ethnographic methodology'.[73] This is a useful reminder against the tendency to fetishise the here-and-now in ethnographic practice. Yet, it should not lead to altogether abandon it, thus running the risk of 'explain[ing] away the eventfulness of events by referring them back to a set of conditions that structure and, ultimately, determine them'.[74] Clive Barnett provides a revealing example in this sense by criticising the way several (Western) political thinkers interpreted the 'events' of the Arab Spring, in other words, by force-fitting them within their own theoretical frameworks. Neither being present, nor listening to the voices of those who were there, these thinkers provided analyses which, as many local commentators lamented, were notable for their de-contextualised myopia vis-à-vis the contingent dynamics and complexity of what was actually going on.[75]

Answering to Fieldman's proposal, Rahola notes that, notwithstanding the abstract and non-local character of apparatuses, they are always actualised into a contingent spatio-temporality.[76] There is 'something tangible about collective events', Latham and McCormack observe, a 'phenomenological this-ness' that cannot be deterministically explained or written away.[77] As Pløger explains,

> the social effect of an event is that it is experienced as a particular situation because the effect relies on a 'drift, an unplanned result of

72 Latour and Hermant, 1998: 5.
73 Fieldman, 2011: 390.
74 Anderson and Holden, 2008: 143.
75 Barnett, 2011a.
76 Rahola, 2014: 384.
77 Latham and McCormack, 2010: 67.

> the cumulation of adjacent interactions', that includes the intensification of people's sensed and lived experiences.[78]

The lack of such a sensibility explains why, in the field of ME security, the tendency of transnational analyses has usually been that of transferring patterns of ME-securitisation from one context to another, an even more problematic practice when this occurs along the 'North-South' axis.[79] A 'more detailed insight into the ways in which people experience and cope with the splintering urban spheres of security on an everyday level' is required, Klauser reminds us.[80]

Studying the event requires a sensibility simultaneously attuned to its territorialisation and deterritorialisation, that is, to both its contingent occurrence in the here-and-now as well as its prolongation into other space-times. Attuning to the excessive and situated quality of the event requires focusing on this conflictual *encounter* between the event and the city. In fact, since events always take place, ethnographically going to these places is indeed necessary in order to explore how the urban vibrates due to the effect of this turbulent occurrence.

2.2 ...produire le miracle de cet instant fusionnel qui, seul, fera. événement.[81]

Generally we can observe insufficient empirical methodologies in the study of MEs, usually relying on classical humanist sociological practice over less conventional post-humanist ones. Ethnographic accounts are lately emerging, but they are still scarce, moreover with widespread recourse to techniques – such as questionnaires – which provide empirical evidence problematically separated from its spatio-temporal contingency.[82] Atmospheres, rhythms and tunings, I believe, are closer to the messiness of socio-material connections, and focusing on them appears more effective 'to the task of apprehending the affective and processual logics of the space-times in which moving bodies are generative participants', and thus the way the ME interacts with, shapes and is shaped by urban tunings.[83]

It is not surprising that attention to the material, dynamic and contingent dimensions of the event emerges in those studies that are exploratively and critically focused on their explicitly conflictual aspects. This is for instance the case of Giulianotti's study of the Premier League as

78 Pløger, 2010: 859; internal quote from Linstead and Thanem.

79 There are of course many relevant exceptions, as for instance the work of Philip Boyle, Kevin Haggerty, Francisco Klauser, Pete Fussey, etc.

80 Klauser, 2010: 338.

81 Boullier, 2011: 10.

82 E.g. Stadler *et al.*, 2013.

83 McCormack, 2013: 11.

providing diffuse sport mega events, where the focus on the 'disquiet, transgression and resistance' emerging in this context allows to highlight the opaque link between commercialisation and securitisation in the transformative processes affecting stadia.[84] The same goes for Edensor's compelling analysis of the modulation of intensities and staging of atmospheres in football stadia.[85] Boullier's work on urban events likewise underlines their capacity to overflow pre-given spatio-temporal boundaries.[86] Duffy *et al.* compellingly explore the role of bodily coordination and rhythmic synchronisation, showing how the material unfolding of the event, the conflictual interaction that its taking place engenders, is the key dimension through which it takes shape as well as, we add, the locus of its 'political' potential.[87] Frey and Macgilliray, Schreiber and Adang, and Millward, differently focus on the way events are enacted through promotional and securitarian means, how this impacts on fans' perceptions and actions, and the way 'security and entertainment' institutions deal with them.[88] Besides the already mentioned work of Stephens on the atmosphere of London 2012, it is also worth mentioning works such as those of Porter *et al.* on the emotional impact of ME-related displacement, and Raco and Tunney on the process of invisibilisation that Olympic discourse entails.[89] These are *all* significant contributions insofar as showing a particular sensibility towards the frictional space in which the ME encounters the city – a sensibility that I wish to carry within my approach.

2.3

> When we define the Commune … we will not leave the other aspects of the events: we will forget neither its antecedent and circumstances, not the relations between people and groups and the ideas that took part in action, not finally the demand of analysis and historical accounts. But we intend to show how Paris experienced its revolutionary passion.[90]

My methodology, consistent with the reflections so far developed, avoids ontological distinctions (and the related prioritisations) between social representations and individual practices, narratives, affects, rationalities, regulations, human and non-human objects. Accounting for the 'tuning' of the city means observing the way in which all the bodies of the urban get together in the performative, ongoing, open-ended dimension of everyday

84 Richard Giulianotti, 2011: 3304.
85 Tim Edensor, 2015.
86 Dominique Boullier, 2010.
87 Michelle Duffy *et al.*, 2011.
88 Matt Frew and David McGillivray, 2008; Martina Schreiber and Otto Adang, 2010; Peter Millward, 2009.
89 Libby Porter, *et al.*, 2009; Mike Raco and Emma Tunney, 2010.
90 Lefebvre, 1965.

life. In his insightful book on 'post-methodology', John Law convincingly challenges some methodological premises of social sciences from a radical actor-network perspective. Principally, he contests the taken-for-granted assumption of an independent, definite, singular, anterior (to the observer) and constant reality. Instead, he observes that realities are continuously produced by a set of assumptions, practices, arrangements, an assemblage which is necessarily ontologically incomplete, vague, indefinite, contingent:

> if things seem solid, prior, independent, definite and single then perhaps this is because they are being enacted, and re-enacted, in practices. Practices that continue. And practices that are also multiple.[91]

This does not lead to a post-modern abdication of research in the face of the absolute relativism of flows. Solidity, whilst not dependent on an anterior and external reality, is not an illusion of the observer, but rather is the result of the crystallisation of heterogeneous elements into given assemblages, that is, of a sedimentation produced by habits and routines which efface the co-constructed nature of assemblages, but for this very fact always contains lines of escape, points of rupture and reformulation.[92]

I am extremely sympathetic with Law's approach although, for the reason explained above, I am sceptical with the ontological presupposition that animates it. His radical relationalism ultimately risks depriving external things of their own reality. Their 'solidity' is taken only as the result of a more or less stable crystallisation behind which, however, lies the nothingness of their purely 'relational substance' (i.e. an oxymoronic reality). As shown above, this is a problematic presupposition. The reduction of bodies to their relations exposes them to potential categorisation, appropriation, capitalisation. It prefigures the possibility to define, control and indeed 'produce' them through the modulation of relations – and as such it is ethically problematic. To be sure, Law vehemently opposes any of these outcomes, and his book is indeed a passionate attack on the 'will to know' that permeates social sciences, a desire which is systematically pitted against the complexity of events exceeding our capacity to know them.[93] Yet, this is not enough. The ontological role that relationalism plays vis-à-vis control should not be overlooked. Arguably it is on this basis that the unwitting complicity between the post-structural academy and sophisticated forms of control rests, and it is especially on the methodological ground that it is to be challenged.

This means that my endorsement of Law's approach as well as my use of some of his methodological suggestions is attuned by a different

91 Law, 2004: 56.
92 Law, 2004: 32, 39.
93 Law, 2004: 9.

orientation, probably difficult to appreciate vis-à-vis the practical unfolding of the ethnographic fieldwork presented here, and yet significant with respect to the ethical attitude that nurtures it. Our incapacity to know reality, I contend, is not simply due to its plasmatic fluidity, but to the ultimate fact that whilst bodies are always involved in some sort of relation, they are never fully defined by them, and certainly not by our relation to them. The ethical attitude behind such endeavour, therefore, is not the iconoclastic optimism of 'relational' approaches, looking for solidities perennially hanging on the void which their fully relational structures implicitly presuppose, but instead a sort of 'methodological pessimism', fully aware of the impossibility of extrapolating the singularity of reality into whatever methodological template. Here pessimism is, as in Giacomo Leopardi's famous definition, truly *cosmic*, in the sense of being radically open to one's situatedness in a world that is never reducible to our relations to it, absolutely not for us. This is not a negative denial but rather the unavoidable acceptance of the materiality of our taking place. As Masciandaro writes, after Cioran:

> The real significance of cosmic pessimism lies less in doctrine than in its conscious disowning of the comprehensiveness of knowledge in the name of an ineradicable gap between science and its event, between knowing and the capacity *to* know … showing, outside the parameters of formal proof, the non-philosophizability of the universe.[94]

Although I will develop the ethico-political nuance of this orientation in the next chapter, here I assume it is a call for a *method* which does not 'pursue or follow after' something (*meta-hodos*), does not analyse the city as a closed system in which to apply the 'right technique' of knowing, but rather strives to 'make space' for the eventful contingency of the urban, i.e. what always escapes its relational closure.

2.4 To capture a rhythm one needs to have been captured by it.[95]

Ethnography is almost a necessity if we are to consistently explore the immersive and tuned materiality of the urban. Taking for granted the need to avoid the transcendent yearning of certain methodological presuppositions, such ethnography should avoid explaining away the field into supra-structures as well as losing touch with the phenomenological 'thisness' of the urban, whilst at the same time eschewing any temptation towards the exaltation of the field per se, i.e. its fetishisation (the holy grail of the here-and-now). Thus, an ethnography focused simultaneously on the

94 Masciandaro, 2012a.
95 Lefebvre, 1996: 219.

different 'scales' of the urban, the excessive frictions that constantly problematise both structures and relations.[96] What matters is not really *knowing* a substantial, abstract or relational reality, but rather letting the contradiction, frictions and eventfulness of such reality emerge, thus making space for the conflictual coming-together of urban bodies, for the frictions between the different tunings traversing the urban. As Doel emphatically suggests, this is 'our duty as geographers ... simply to make space for the deforming force of alterity'.[97]

In this case, this has meant immersion within the tuning of Johannesburg, through the web of overlapping official and unofficial advice, coming from the street and institutions, from every class, race and profession, from the policeman to the academics to the squatter, the 'safety tips', the foreign and national media, the special legislation, the geographical, architectural and infrastructural elements, the changes of light and density of human and non-human objects etc., all intersecting, contrasting and somewhat *held together* into the consistent normativity of a 'tune'. The impossibility for the ethnographer to claim any neutrality was self-evident: this was no ethnography to be conducted from the 'Cartesian window' Lefebvre writes about, but rather an immersive stance, understanding myself as a body among other bodies, willing to intervene, touch, provoke and breach in the manner of Garfinkel, experimenting with the potentialities of the urban rather than merely 'glancing intently at' them from above.[98] Yet, this was no 'just glancing around' either.[99]

As any other inhabitant, my being-in-the-city neither consists in determined 'reactions and adjustments', nor in 'intentional and teleological acts', but rather in contingent responses to the spatiality of the city, to its tunings.[100] Researching the urban certainly cannot be reduced to simple spontaneity and exaltation of immediacy. This would mean merely shifting from the untenable externality of the objective observer to the overwhelming proximity of the urban stroller.[101] Immersed into, and exposed to the urban, I could not simply get carried away like a *flaneur*. Another sort of passivity was required, not understood in opposition to 'activity', but rather in the sense of a 'passability': making oneself traversable (passable) by the tuning of the city, developing an 'affectivity to a number of external

96 Tsing Lowenhaupt, 2004.
97 Doel, 1999: 198.
98 Lefebvre, 1996: 224.
99 Casey, 2007: 91.
100 Lingis, 1998: 4.
101 This is the risk of the otherwise compelling methods such as the 'liquid' or 'drifting' ethnography proposed by Jeff Ferrell. See for instance Ferrell and Weide, 2010; and Ferrell, 2009.

fluxes'.[102] Just like a surfer, the ethnographic researcher is willing to attune to the tune, to the waves of the city, but also aims to respond to and ride those waves, to stand on them skilfully and critically.[103] Law suggests that developing an ethnographic method is akin to building a 'radio receiver' tuned to the frequencies of the urban.[104] Likewise, in this context we may need to build a 'seismographer', a method able to detect and investigate the telluric waves generated by the encounter between the ME and the city.[105]

However, how can one express this attunement into an empirical account? How can one write this 'chaotic experience' without at the same time pacifying it, that is, depriving it of its frictions, conflictuality, eventfulness? Perhaps it is useful to understand this process as the drawing of a sort of 'commentary' of the urban. A commentary to an implicit text, that is. In his geo-philosophical elaboration of the genre, Masciandaro explains that a true commentary never attempts to go beyond, behind or below the text in order to find hidden meanings. It rather '*stays* within its text'.[106] This is what geo-philosophy means: neither to flee, nor to ascend, but rather to stay within the urban, to remain, since

> staying with the earth is the means of not remaining stuck on it … staying within the encounter of the crux and passing through its difficulty (*ex-per-ientia,* coming out of and going through) … the geophilosopher is one who experiences rather than flees the earth, who passes through by remaining with it.[107]

This affirmation of immanence as literally *in-manere* (to stay within, to remain) is the affirmation of a method that wishes to 'stay with the urban without "getting stuck" in it, thus avoiding the result-obsessed tendency of academic methodology without falling into a mere wandering for its own sake, that is, beyond presumptuous and arbitrary attempts to structure the world, as well as naive and/or lazy renunciations to understand it. The task is 'to maintain oneself on the outside, but to hold oneself close, thus to some degree closed, and thus to discipline into writing a chaotic experience.'[108] Kathleen Stewart usefully terms this task an attempt to produce a

102 'This is why becoming – and particularly active becoming – must be thought as essentially *passive*; must be thought, even, as an increase of the passivity of the living being, of its "passability", a way for it to register an increased affectivity to a number of external fluxes' (Meillassoux, 2007: 101).

103 Following Tim Ingold, Adey *et al.* (2013: 303) similarly propose for 'the ambiance researcher … the disposition of the "wayfarer", actively threading a way through and adapting to the environments being researched.'

104 Law, 2004: 117.

105 Citroni and Pavoni, 2016.

106 Masciandaro, 2010: 51.

107 Masciandaro, 2010: 28.

108 Meillassoux, 2007: 107.

'writing and theorising that tries to stick with something becoming atmospheric … approaching the thing that is happening by attuning to it'.[109] Making space for these tunings to emerge, means to constantly challenge one's own personal 'state of exception', i.e. one's own subject position, tentatively reasserting the evental viewpoint of one's own situatedness: not as a subject in the city, but a body among other bodies. This is what a commentary applied to the urban should be, paraphrasing again Masciandaro: a practice which 'materializes the movement, the flow of the [urban] that makes it more than itself … [thereby holding] open the event of the [urban]' without simply succumbing to a drifting *per se* or to Joycean soliloquy, but rather generating 'more and more perceptual enclosures, spaces within which the unrepresentable is brought into presence'.[110]

Hence this is the style of my commentary, accounting at the same time for my own singular experiencing of the city, as well as expressing its real abstract forms, oscillating between the unavoidable singularity and partiality of my situatedness, and the tunings traversing me. The point, to conclude, is not that of emancipating methodology from order, rigour and structures, but more precisely from any obsession with them, which too often suffocates *a priori* the eventful potential of the urban into neutralising accounts.[111]

2.5 Knowing the city is dependent on attunement to a particular wavelength, a process involving the adoption of an attitude of lyrical expectancy and availability to experience.[112]

In the specific, as a means of exploring, recording and reflecting I employed memory, notebooks, pictures and videos, not simply to 'record data' but more precisely

> to produce a disposition which encourages sensitivity to events through equipment, movement and collaborative experiences emerging throughout the spaces of the site, both as and after they happened.[113]

To complement these outputs, I carried out about 50 'vox pop' interviews with randomly selected people (from fans to security guards). With respect to in-depth interviews, this seemed the most appropriate technique, as Frew and McGillivray suggest, in order to capture the fleeting 'festival

109 Stewart, 2011: 444, 450.
110 Masciandaro, 2010: 30. In the quoted passage I substituted the term 'text' with the word 'urban'.
111 '[N]ot without, but freeing itself from result, from anxious care about what does not belong to us' (Masciandaro, 2010: 52).
112 Sheringham, quoted in Thrift, 2007: 145.
113 Adey *et al.*, 2013: 303.

atmosphere' of the city and the way it overlaps with the practices and perceptions of security.[114] Furthermore, I analysed various documents (online and offline safety tips, fan guides, media reports, promotional, informative and legal material, etc.), selected through a 'convenience sampling approach', i.e. according to their relevance to the research, forming the assemblage of official and unofficial, public and private texts through which the normative tuning of the city is produced.[115] Special attention has been given to the immunising character of the tuning, due to the crucial significance it assumes in the context of Johannesburg.

My purpose was not simply to understand how people 'think and experience' the city, but rather to explore 'how meaning is produced and sustained in-the-moment',[116] out of the getting-together of different bodies in atmo-rhythmical tunings, by means of attuning to 'the latent potentiality in a situation'.[117] For this reason, rather than subjecting those texts to exhaustive content analysis, I joined them in a 'method assemblage' constituted by the various research outputs – observations, notes, pictures, interpretations, documents, interviews – constantly re-shuffled in a feedback-loop between personal account, self-introspection and analytical interpretation.[118]

Finally, a last remark. I am aware, how could I not be, of the different ways in which blacks and whites, Western tourists and African migrants, gated communities and township dwellers attune to and are tuned by the urban tune. It would be extremely imprecise and naive to pretend to extrapolate my ethnography from the fact of me being a foreigner, in the country only for a limited amount of time, and lacking an in-depth knowledge of its intricate social and historical evolution. Any pretence of exhaustiveness, completeness or generalisation would be highly untenable. Yet, my situation also provided some advantages. Sloterdijk suggests that the condition of a foreign visitor to a city, characterised by increased vulnerability, heightened attentiveness and little entanglement with the urban routines, is in a privileged position to experience its normative tension: the latter, if often imperceptible to the local, is materially felt by the foreigner.[119] In this sense, the way in which I could experience my own immersion into a web of advice, tricks, suggestions and regulations, as well as fragmented imaginaries, concatenated into the tuning of Johannesburg,

114 Frew and McGilliray, 2008: 188.
115 Atkinson and Young, 2005: 58.
116 Duffy *et al.*, 2011; 17–24: 19.
117 Thrift, 2011: 19.
118 Law, 2004: 84.
119 Sloterdijk, 2006: 420 (my translation). Of course this does not imply a privilege for the foreigner, but at least gives some credit to his/her point of view.

could be said to have some empirical value, at least. Prior to moving to the 2010 World Cup, a brief introduction to Johannesburg is required.

China Miéville's novel *The City and the City* is set in two overlapping cities, Beszel and UlQoma. Although there are 'total' areas, belonging 'only' to Beszel or UlQoma, for the most part the cities are 'crosshatched', sharing the same overlapping buildings, streets, parks. Seeing the other city however, is illegal: the citizens have learned to unsee the other city's human and non-human bodies, and violations are promptly addressed by a policing entity called *Breach*. Visitors, as we may imagine, have a hard time. Visa procedures are long and tough, and include a mandatory training as well as an exam with theoretical and practical role-play parts to check the degree of one's attunement. This assures that visitors 'would know, at least in outline, key signifiers of architecture, clothing, alphabet and manner, outlaw colours and gestures, obligatory details … distinguishing Beszel and UlQoma, and their citizens'.[120] Although they would be unable, after such a short course, to 'have metabolized the deep prediscoursive instinct for our borders that Besz and UlQomans have, to have picked up the real rudiments of unseeing', they would be supposed to act as they had, expected to comply with the tuning of the city, and pretending not to see and experience, though unable to actually unsee and un-experience, the other, 'crosshatched' city.[121]

3.1 Johannesburg loses its original contours, is reduced to an empty set, or, paradoxically, gains depth. By forcing the city to open up, this process of deframing and enframing has set different repertoires of spatial imaginations and practices into collision.[122]

After Apartheid, Johannesburg confronted a dramatic spatial crisis: with the dissolution of the former state (of exception), the multiple spatialities of the country, hitherto frozen by the Apartheid regime, literally exploded opening an unstable limbo of 'weakened immunity'.[123] The ensuing deterritorialisation of the urban was only partially, patchily reterritorialised by the

120 Mieville, 2009: 76.

121 Masciandaro, 2010: 93.

122 'The space inherited from the apartheid city is either drawn out and stretched, or the links of each part of the city with what used to be the whole are interrupted or saturated.… The architecture of hysteria in contemporary South Africa is the result of a painful, shocking encounter with a radical alterity set loose by the collapse of the racial city' (Mbembé, 2004: 399–402).

123 Mbembé, 2001.

tentative constitutional, securitarian and urban planning efforts that ensued. Whilst spectacularly re-established in the form of a monumental constitution, the legal sovereignty faced an unavoidable erosion of legitimacy and national cohesion, failing for a long time to crystallise into standardised patterns of application, and having each time to precariously and tentatively *take place* in the uncertain and contingent multiplicity of the city. In this destabilised post-Apartheid space, increasingly fragmented and privatised through economical, legal and securitarian devices, unauthorised normativities began to emerge. Not a direct result of top-down interventions, these *exceptional tunings* are explicitations of the 'immanent ordering logic' of the city, post-sovereign configurations of an immanent and impersonal power 'whose role is no longer one of authorising or authoring imperatives, but of internally discovering and communicating information in view of "common survival"'.[124]

How to does one account for them? If in the introduction I referred to the necessity of overcoming urban studies' 'fixation with the binary',[125] this is an even more pressing need when dealing with a city like Johannesburg, which by definition escapes stereotypical academic modes of thinking usually framed according to the Western image of the city. Let us for instance see how Michael Watts, criticising a piece by Sarah Nuttall and Achille Mbembé, describes it:

> a particular sort of hybrid of urban involution … weak citizenship, and limited governmentality [to] the extent to which a Foucauldian reading of Johannesburg – a rendering of the city and its subjects visible and regulated – is inadequate even within the circumference of Africa's most modern metropolis.[126]

What here is taken for granted is an equivalence between the notions of order and regulation and those of institutionalisation and formality, with the corollary of finding only disorder, precariousness and unpredictability where a strong institutional presence – in the form of law, policing, social state and so on – appears to be lacking.[127] Contrary to that, I stress that visibilities, regulations and orderings emerge out of the urban fabric as a result of heterogeneous concatenations of different bodies organised in tunings in which the direct role, or even presence, of institutions is not to be taken for granted. In this sense, Matshikiza's claim that 'no one has really

124 Schütz, 2009: 235.

125 Pieterse, 2006: 300.

126 Watts, 2005: 190; Nuttall and Mbembé, 2004.

127 Hence the neat counter-critique of Nuttall and Mbembé (2004: 195–6), according to whom Watts 'takes the metropolitan form as something that can be organised in advance and whose complexities can be settled or decided by the application of more or less mechanical ideological beliefs onto a reality that is fundamentally elusive'.

been able to wrestle Johannesburg into any kind of civilised order',[128] should be only accepted if we link the formula 'civilised order' to its Western origin: that Johannesburg has never achieved – and probably never will – such an order is true. However, that does not imply that Johannesburg is just a 'disorderly city'.[129] In the city order and disorder intersect in specific tunings, which cannot be evaluated through an urban evolutionary chart going from sheer chaos to 'civilised' order, according to the usual 'trope of copy/unique' around which, McFarlane underlines, Southern cities are routinely measured.[130]

Alan Smart suggests that 'we need to pay more attention to areas in which control seems to be conspicuously absent, where neglect is more apparent than surveillance'.[131] To which Watts adds: 'neglect, but also incapacity, incompetence, and inability'.[132] This is not the point, I believe. Smart's observation should be instead assumed as a call for developing 'ways of seeing and engaging urban spaces that are characterized simultaneously by regularity and provisionality', that is, ways of attuning to and accounting for the immanent and unauthorised normativity of the city.[133] Take for instance AbdouMaliq Simone's analysis of Johannesburg's inner city, where regularities appear to emerge out of multiple negotiations with the environment, from a capacity to interpret and improvise rather than a strict compliance to institutional rules. Surely open and flexible, these are orderings nonetheless, rhythmically organising the urban experience. Let us quote him fully:

> it is important to emphasize that these flexible configurations are pursued not in some essential contrast to non-African urban priorities or values but as specific routes to a kind of stability and regularity that non-African cities have historically attempted to realize … a conjunction of heterogeneous activities … capable of generating social compositions across a range of singular capacities and needs (both enacted and virtual) and which attempts to derive maximal outcomes from a minimal set of elements.[134]

This approach is even more important whether we refer to issues of social control and security. In fact, in (usually paranoid) accounts of urban securitisation, the opposition between panoptical surveillance and institutional control and, on the other hand, 'disordered and chaotic' everyday life, is

128 Matshikiza, 2008: 222.
129 Murray, 2008.
130 McFarlane, 2008: 342.
131 Smart, 2001: 31.
132 Watts, 2005: 185.
133 Simone, 2004: 408; see also Robinson, 2006.
134 Simone, 2004: 410–11.

often taken for granted. The corollary is a narrative of over-securitisation according to which the increase of institutional control unavoidably leads to freedom-reduction, as if freedom would only reside in disorder, informality would necessarily lack of order, or indeed security and freedom would be mutually excluding. This narrative misses the fact that formal and informal practices intersect and re-configure the way the city is experienced in different, often unexpected ways. Security and liberty, freedom and self-regulation, order and disorder are in constant interplay, enacted and re-enacted in contingent assemblages that static dichotomies cannot account for. Topical is the case of mega events, where the increase in social control and spatial securitisation tends to be always framed as unavoidably oppressive for the citizens. To be sure, this could often be the case. However, and especially vis-à-vis the urban South, a blind transposition of worn-out equivalences – as the usual presupposition that any technological, legal and sociological 'security legacies' of a ME are necessarily negative – should be avoided. What if, for instance, 'enduring legacies' of ME-securitisation would not produce an oppressive increase in self-regulatory behaviour, but rather allow for its relaxation?

The challenge is to find a way to observe how these contradictory tendencies unfold immanently in the city. This is what the notion of urban tuning may allow. In the next section, I explore the 'immunological' tuning emerging out of the 'weakened immunity' of Johannesburg.

3.2 Back in my country everybody was telling me I was crazy to come here, I would have been killed.[135]

Going to Johannesburg is to become attuned to an atmosphere of alertness where one already dwells before touching South African soil. Affective flows of panic and danger, media-ted and anecdotal reports of violence, statistical evidence, all these together form an assemblage of crime-ridden South Africa which is not simply 'representational' or 'meta-discursive', but 'carries an affective charge'. Following McCormack, this is 'not only an imagined space [but] also a space of affective materiality actualised through the ongoing movement of bodies', that is, a 'distributed space of expectancy existing as a diffuse field of potential'.[136] The country's most notorious town already awaits its visitors as a 'menacing monster', its atmosphere of real even if non-actual danger constantly haunting one's being-in-Johannesburg.[137] Like a visitor of Beszel, attuning to the syncopated rhythm of the city means to undergo a 'training', through the tide of overlapping

135 Visitor from Singapore interviewed by the author, 17 June 2010.

136 McCormack 2008: 423, 426.

137 As in Mpe's novel, where well before arriving the protagonist, for the stories he heard, 'already knew that Hillbrow [a notorious neighbourhood] was a menacing monster' (Mpe, 2002: 3).

narratives, practices, advices, official and unofficial 'safety tips', rules of seeing and unseeing.

A qualification is needed. Although these features (safety tips, etc.) are common to many other countries, as a quick visit on official embassy websites around the world would show, the amount and the prominence they have in South Africa and most notably in Johannesburg is peculiar, as is the level of awareness by both citizens and visitors about them – virtually every visitor I talked to knew and to some extent complied with them. Therefore, their significant contribution to the tuning of the city is incontestable. Moreover, as my observation confirmed, remarkable is the correspondence between official and unofficial safety tips, and the word-of-mouth advice coming, often unprompted, from any social and racial background. What is lacking, in other words, is the usual discrepancy between over-paranoid advices appearing in official sources and the counter-balancing reassurance coming from the street: in Johannesburg there is a quasi-literal correspondence between the two sets of advices, formal and informal, official and unofficial, oral and written, narratives and practices, the different levels overlapping and reinforcing each other onto a peculiar tuning.

What I call the Joburg Tune (JT) is an atmo-rhythm of attention, interpretation, anxiety and syncopation, a wavelength shaping without determining the way the city is experienced and lived. It is simultaneously affective and dromological, phenomenological and ecological: socio-cultural representations, density of people, historical memories, changes of light, buildings, fear, suspicion, walls, global flows, ways of saying and seeing, urban interventions, commodification, the way of feeling and walking the city. It is a coming-together of bodies, practices and affectivities that intersect, overlap and crystallise in constituting the JT, to which our being-in-the-city soon becomes attuned and unstably immunised. To be sure, the JT should not be understood as a meta-discursive frame filtering out subject's perception, or as a hidden logic the inhabitants unconsciously follow. It is instead an atmo-rhythm where sensing and sensed, conscious and unconscious blur. There is more than a Goffmanesque interaction-order at work here: neither only a set of rules we rationally decide to follow, nor simply subjects pragmatically choosing to interact in a certain way, but a pervasive 'menace mood' holding bodies in the tension of an effervescent state of alertness from which we cannot simply opt out.[138] Like a diver in the water, we have to inhabit the tune by attuning to it, by responding, complying with or swerving from its impersonal imperatives of coping and attention, care and vigilance, showing confidence and being suspicious.

The attentive reader could note that in the description that follows the pre-eminence given to the web of advice, tips, etc., through which a visitor

138 I agree with Mbembé and Nuttal (2004: 354) that the public space of Johannesburg should not be too stereotyped as an anxious space of fear. Nonetheless, it is often perceived and materially felt as such by its inhabitants.

'attunes' to the ordering of the city, apparently sidelines the role of law in producing the tune. Yet, as just suggested, it is important not to reduce the analysis of law only to its texts and formal legal apparatuses, but rather to look at the way normativity emerges in less obvious ways. In the weakened immunity of Johannesburg, this 'web of advice, etc.' appears as the very way in which the immunological ordering of the city *operationally* unfolds, the way in which bodies immanently attune to the city's nomotopic tensions. In this sense, rather than sidelining the legal discourse, the Joburg Tune is an attempt to investigate it more deeply, in its material and affective sense. Notwithstanding the unavoidable differences in which this normative materiality is dealt with in the city, I propose to describe it through three overlapping 'keys'.[139]

3.3 A. [alertness]

> Develop an awareness of what people in the street around you are doing.[140]

Since from the start, 'be particularly aware at airports and transport hubs: you'll be most vulnerable when you first arrive'.[141] A 'constant state of preparedness' is produced by the constellation of formal and informal advice, warnings, clues, tips.[142] Advice to develop 'an awareness of what people in the street around you are doing' is complemented by discouraging interaction with, and trust for, others: 'be aware of your surroundings' pairs with 'don't let strangers get too close to you – especially people in groups'.[143] Therefore, 'don't walk alone' and 'beware of anyone asking you for help'.[144]

> It may sound harsh, but ignore anyone stopping you in the street and asking you to, say, sponsor them for a scholarship or other such good cause, and never give cash to anyone begging.[145]

139 Although the tune must be understood as emerging out of a getting together of different bodies, perceptions, representations, affectivities, practices, technologies and so on, the 'entry point' has been the individual perception of fear/safety, which I explored both ethnographically and auto-ethnographically. I qualify that I employ individual perception as a way to investigate a phenomenon, and thus a tool for the exploration, rather than simply its end-point, in the sense Hannah gestures towards when proposing to 'a phenomenological path to a critical awareness of inhumane aspects of life in capitalist societies' (Hannah, 2013: 239).

140 McCrea *et al.*, 2002: 82.

141 FSF, 2010: 22.

142 Simone, 2004: 424.

143 FIFA, 2010.

144 COJ, 2010b.

145 FSF, 2010: 23.

Attuning to this minatory mood means to be an attentive interpreter, scanning the space for menace and trickery.[146] This is a position incidentally shared along socio-economical lines: the constant awareness of the visitors scanning the environment for trouble is somewhat mirrored by the African migrants' 'need for maintaining hyperawareness of their surroundings ... constantly on the lookout for police officers'.[147] The key condition here is *alertness*. In if-you-see-you-report Western societies we have become accustomed to slightly dystopian depictions of a sociality characterised by ubiquitous dangerisation. If in many metropolises of the North such an atmosphere is often to be found only in the paranoid depictions of academics and activists, its density and pervasiveness in Johannesburg is incontestable, where it weighs over bodies as a set of potential, always on the brink of being actualised, dangers that carry 'an affective charge, heightening their expectancy and mobilising affects of fear'.[148]

B. [confidence]

You have to rhythmise yourself.

In the urban spatiality sensibilities and materialities overlap in a continual, resonating movement out of which a tune emerges and through which certain 'subjectivities' crystallise: how is one supposed to act, to be actor in the city? The key condition is *confidence*, as obsessively reminded by everyone and most eloquently put by a police officer: 'never look disorientated, always look confident ... you don't have to seem that you don't know where to go ... you have to rhythmise yourself'.[149] 'Try not to look like a tourist', as every guide suggests. The synoptical presentation of oneself as 'confident' overlaps with the panoptical scanning of the environment to decrypt potential threat: an attentive going with the flow in which can be recognised as a proper post-modern way to live the city in the age of uncertainty.

146 'Watch out for staged mishaps – like someone bumping into you or spilling a drink – this could be a ploy to divert your attention and steal your bag and passport' (Department of Tourism, 2010: 92).

147 'Many foreign Africans cite the need for maintaining hyperawareness of their surroundings. They are constantly on the lookout for police officers... When interviewing migrants, one notices their constant wariness about whom they can safely talk to and in what contexts' (Simone, 2004: 416).

148 The quote is from Bissel who is discussing the affectivity of alertness on UK train stations: 'Reports of such atrocious events as people being pushed onto railway tracks in response to confronting so-called "antisocial behaviour" loom large in the public consciousness.... The circulation of such discourses therefore carries an affective charge, heightening their expectancy and mobilizing affects of fear' (Bissel, 2010: 281).

149 Policeman interviewed by the author, 14 June 2010.

C. [pre-planning]

Wherever you go, don't go to Bree.[150]

As in every other town, official and unofficial narratives produce an imagined geography that gains reality by producing concatenations with the physical one. Fear and safety play an important role in this process. Every city has its own notorious areas. Yet it is the pervasiveness of this mapping that characterises the peculiarity of Johannesburg. This is not simply, of course, a matter of standard advice against going to the dangerous suburb or the deprived slum. Here, the whole city becomes a map of 'potential curfews'. As one could expect, different people do different mappings, often dependent on their socio-economical, racial as well as experiential background. A street which is an utter danger for one, can become perfectly safe for another. Yet everybody experiences dangerous spaces whose categorisation as safe or unsafe may shift depending on day and night, the density of people and so on. Nobody seems to ultimately contest the geography of danger of Johannesburg: the different mappings never remove, but simply shift the spatial threshold along the city's topography.

What is the rhythm such mappings 'force' on the movement of bodies? The logic is: 'plan your route in advance'. This is no city for *flâneurs*. Walking in the city is supposed to be a highly structured, pre-arranged experience, a point-to-point endeavour to be performed quickly and self-confidently, zigzagging through no-go and better-not-go areas: pre-planning, no asking no phoning no map-checking: 'Do not stop to ask for directions'.[151] As Ivan Vladislavic reminds us in his intimate portrait of Johannesburg, 'asking for direction, city people … declare their vulnerability'.[152] Walking itself is deemed a sort of enterprise – 'get advice from your hotel prior to *embarking* on foot' – to be avoided if possible.[153] Likewise public transport, particularly the notorious old Toyota 13-seater taxis, is usually not recommended, especially at night. Moving in the city has a pre-planned, motorised and privatised rhythm centred on cars, whose movement is as much tuned to a state of alertness: drive smoothly through

150 Young Afrikaner living in a gated community interviewed by the author, 12 June 2010. Bree Street is one of the longest and busiest streets in Johannesburg's CBD (Central Business District).

151 Therefore, 'plan your route in advance … Do not stop to ask for directions or check your map on the street' (Gauteng Tourism Authority); and do not 'walk around talking on your phone in the street' (Department of Tourism, 2010: 92).

152 Vladislavic, 2009: 11.

153 Department of Community Safety and Liaison (KwaZulu-Natal), 2010 (my emphasis); 'Most social activity … tends to be done at malls around town, reached by car or taxi … most city centres – or Central Business Districts – are deserted after business hours, aren't really worth seeing, and can be dangerous' (FSF, 2010: 22).

the city, 'fasten your seatbelt, lock your door and only leave your window open about 5 cm ... Be aware of your surroundings when you stop at a robot or stop street'.[154] The key condition here is *pre-planning*: 'everyone becomes a route planner in the dense traffic of crime and disorder'.[155]

3.4 Day after day I begin to understand the imposed rhythm of Joburg, its written and unwritten code mapping the city according to light and darkness, density and emptiness, speed and slowness, danger and safety.[156]

As in Teresa Caldeira's São Paulo – where crime and violence are everyday dealt with through

> 'narratives and practices [which] impose partitions, build up walls, delineate and enclose spaces, establish distances, segregate, differentiate, impose prohibitions, multiply rules of avoidance and exclusion, and restrict movement ... simplify and enclose the world'[157]

the JT appears as the ordering of a 'disorderly city', generating, modulating, fixating atmo-rhythmical patterns which simultaneously lubricate and immunise everyday life.

In the city's post-Apartheid patchwork of malls and townships, gated communities and business districts, insufficient transport systems and huge highways, the JT surfaces as an affective mood sensible to changes of light, police uniforms, the increasing or decreasing density of people, as well as a syncopated rhythm of point-to-point movement, speeds and slownesses, moving fast, minimising the stops, then relaxing in atmospherically sealed interiors, a rhythm of cars and malls and cautious, attentive walking. As a result, the urban atmosphere is shaped into a 'dual tone' made of two subsequently alternating states: *being at ease*, and *being alarmed*, a condition famously encapsulated by Goffman at the outset of his analysis of 'normal appearances':

> Individuals, whether in human or animal form, exhibit two basic modes of activity. They go about their business grazing, gazing, mothering, digesting, building, resting, playing, placidly attending to easily managed matters at hand. Or, fully mobilized, a fury of intent, alarmed, they get ready to attack or to stalk or to flee.[158]

154 Department of Community Safety and Liaison (KwaZulu-Natal), 2010. 'Robot' is South African slang for traffic lights.
155 Hentschel, 2010: 181.
156 Fieldwork note, 14 June 2010.
157 Caldeira, 2001: 20.
158 Goffman, 1971: 238.

Nick Prior distinguishes a similar dual tone in London between the 'turbulent rhythm of the metropolis' and the 'quiet rhythm of civic humanism ... and professional control' of the National Gallery.[159] In Johannesburg, this syncopation is taken to a new level. The JT entails a modality of inhabiting-the-city by 'generating redundancy', extracting flows from the multiplicity of the city, dynamically shaping them into certain rhythmic and atmospheric patterns, tuning the urban experience into a shared frequency which works to eliminate the risk of chance. Its 'different timings and spacings *produc[e] the ordinary*', differentiating it from – as well as constituting – the unusual, the extraordinary, the dangerous: the routinised experience of being-in-the-city increasingly takes the form of a 'bubbled experience', screening from, as well as propelling the perception of danger.[160] According to an already-observed mechanism, the reduction of noise is bound to its simultaneous re-production in the form of insecurity, fear and thus vulnerability. Reactive attempts to escape the unstable 'outside' into the insulated comforts of gated suburbs, shopping malls and other armoured bubbles, beneath the temporary relaxation and escape from its oppressing *mood* they seemingly offer, only reinforce the JT itself by confirming its dual tone.

From the 'immunological' perspective provided by Sloterdijk, the JT appears as perfectly consistent with the immanent, exceptional tunings in which the contemporary metropolis is ordered. In the post-holistic world 'immunity and integrity are not to be gained from the submission to a larger whole, but must be achieved as the outcome of a personal effort of seclusion', that is, through an eminently individual way to immunisation tied to neo-liberal logics and grounded on the individual ability to develop the skills and obtain the tools of private defence.[161] In this context flexibility becomes precariousness, as the neo-liberal responsibilisation for security generates 'self-perpetuating cycles of activity which make 'security' less a stable condition of well-being and more a state of endless striving'.[162] Ever more evident this appears in the 'weakened immunity' of Johannesburg, traversed by private bubbles moving through a public space whose socio-economical disparities are mirrored by the unequal degree of immunity available, a different ability (and possibility) to surf the noisy urbanity of the city. Whether Apartheid as a juridico-political system had crumbled, an invisible Apartheid is still looming over the psycho-geography of the city in the form of an exceptional tuning in which consumption and immunity strictly overlap.[163] Walking in some areas of the CBD (Central Business

159 Prior, 2011: 209.

160 Amin and Thrift, 2002: 103.

161 Klauser, 2010: 12.

162 Loader, 2009: 152.

163 In fact, a good deal of life away from home occurs in places of safe consumption *par excellence*: the malls.

District) means having to constantly negotiate between the contingency of here-and-now – with all its encounters, details and occurrences – and the ever-present potentiality of a violence which, when occurring, may even be assumed as 'deserved'. Here lies the 'weight' of the JT: not simply the result of the anxiety it generates but more importantly the layer of responsibility and guilt it secretes. Failing to attune, being out-of-sync, is perceived as an unacceptable irresponsibility almost to the point of 'deserving' the crime. As the individual of neo-liberal globalisation is supposed to be always motivated, learning, optimistic and responsible, with meritocracy surging as quintessential value, the individual of this state of crisis must always be on alert, concerned about his own immunity and under constant moral self-examination: 'do not become a crime victim'.

I should qualify that I do not wish to suggest an excessively totalising, deterministic or pacifying understanding of the JT. Certainly the JT provides a stabilising frequency around which the city organises itself; its syncopated rhythm continuously traverses, constituting – and being constituted by – the atmospheres of alertness and scanning, suspicion and mistrust overlapping in Johannesburg. Yet, at the same time it is constantly overflown by the excessiveness of urban itself. The conflictuality of the city can only be traversed but never actually sedated by the tune, constantly punctuated and dislocated by frictions and always potentially open to contestation. In fact, transgressing the *tune* equates to performing a 'breach' (as in Miéville's book) which often triggers a *response* from the city itself.

From an impersonal and machinic perspective, this way to responding to transgressions can be understood as amounting to actualising dangers (anecdotal and statistical evidence of violence are everywhere) as well as preventing them through a sort of *caring response* whereby the out-of-sync individual is 're-immunised' – a caring response, of course, which is again strongly influenced by class and racial belonging, thus reinforcing the invisible Apartheid referred to above.[164] In my surely privileged condition of white, male European visitor, I experienced this caring response in the form of unsolicited help by random passers-by, taxi drivers, volunteers, all willing to help me by informing, advising and even escorting me whether my actions appeared as out of tune, or my presence in a certain area was out-of-place, and thus potentially in danger. Interestingly, this modality of transgression had a neatly different meaning during Apartheid, when, 'because of the logic of segmentarity and overlapping divisions, *crossing* boundaries, transgressing them, or eluding them became the main modality of action for blacks in the city'.[165] If transgressing the spatiality of Apartheid was a common act of political resistance, transgressing the

164 I am here reworking the ubiquitous *'24h armed response'* sign which hangs on many gates in Johannesburg's residential districts.

165 Mbembé, 2004: 398.

invisible Apartheid of the JT is reduced to a private matter of irresponsibility.

In this context, rhetorical affirmation such as the following – 'this event [the World Cup] provides us with a chance to reinforce the sense of nationhood. We will have an opportunity to mobilise our people to create a sense of belonging'[166] – should not be simply dismissed as a smokescreen concealing a reality of capitalistic exploitation. If this cynicism has clearly more than a point, that is not all. Could we not read such a 'sense of belonging' as a willing attempt to challenge the private precariousness of insecurity instituted by the tune, towards a way of being together in which antagonism is not eschewed privately but dealt with commonly? Or instead is this just a call for a denial of the tune itself, a doomed attempt to conceal its oppressive and discriminating logic onto the narcosis of consensus? Certainly, in order to address this question it is necessary to understand how the WC-brandscaping encountered and clashed with the JT. It is by looking at this complex and contingent encounter that the next section progresses, first by introducing the general meaning of the 2010 World Cup vis-à-vis South Africa, and then seeking to define in what way the brandscaping enacted by the World Cup as a city-wide effort of affective modulation and atmospheric engineering, impacted and coped with the immanent normativities of the city. How a certain atmosphere of safety and enthusiasm was sought to be implemented (through legal, promotional, technological and spatial means), and what did actually emerge from the specific assemblages of human, non-human and discursive bodies, in the performative and contagious contingency of the ME.

Well before touching South African soil international media helped me visualise the potential nightmare I was heading for. Under the reassuring headline 'Why Going to South Africa for the World Cup Terrifies Me', Louise Taylor was briefly summarising that 'Statistics, anecdotes and research suggest that touring the Rainbow nation as a fan next summer could be a dangerous option'.[167] If security is an unavoidable issue in a country with worrying crime rates and a deeply entrenched culture of violence produced by a turbulent past joined by huge levels of socio-economical disparities, war-zone-like descriptions were perhaps a step too far. A few weeks before the event, the security firm G4S decided to withdraw from taking part at the event. Its CEO, Nick Buckles, stated 'we are not

166 Gauteng MEC for Community Safety, Mr Firoz Cachalia addressing the *Gauteng Provincial Safety and Security Summit on 2010 World Cup* [link no longer available].

167 Taylor, 2009.

going to be involved because we don't think the security is going to be that good – they are not that well organised yet', adding that 'for G4S, South Africa was the most dangerous country in the world to work in – ahead of Iraq and Afghanistan – with around two staff fatalities every month.'[168] *The Telegraph* was pretty discouraging as well, with an article apocalyptically titled: 'World Cup 2010: England fans "virtually certain" to die in South Africa'.[169] Another security firm, Baysecur, was adding to the global paranoia by suggesting that 'the possibility for the players of moving outside of the hotel boundaries should be kept to a minimum. Otherwise there must be a full escort; armed security guards and bullet-proof vests for the players'.[170] In fact, the same firm was also the protagonist of the surreal marketing-campaign for bullet-proof jackets for tourists.[171] In the months preceding the event we were also bombarded with information about the huge effort of the SA police in taking on new personnel (during the World Cup the police officer-foreign tourists ratio would approximately be 1-to-10)[172] and new equipment ('R665-million worth of new equipment. This includes six new helicopters, 10 mobile command vehicles, 100 high-performance vehicles, unmanned aerial vehicles, body armour and water cannons', as well as a brand new CCTV system in Johanneburg),[173] for what was assuming the contours of a war-like build-up. Perhaps it was the apt preparation for what Altbeker cynically describes as 'a country at war with itself'.[174]

4.1 Without security guarantees there cannot be a successful Olympic Games, and without security guarantees the national image will be lost.[175]

The words opening this section, by the Chinese president Hu Jintao, testify for the unquestionable relevance played by security in today's MEs. According to Michael Atkinson and Kevin Young, it was most notably in the 2002 Salt Lake City Winter Olympics, the first post-9/11 one, that Olympic *humanism* was extensively joined by the need for a pervasive and reassuring showcasing of security: America's new war-on-terror ideology was to be translated at the international level, as a global affirmation of the American

168 Retrieved from www.reuters.com/article/idUSLK4638820090520
169 Berger, 2009.
170 Alexander, 2009.
171 'Bullet-proof vests for 2010?' *sport24*, 21 October 2009, available at www.sport24.co.za/Soccer/WorldCup/Bulletproof-vests-for-2010-20091021
172 Gadebe, 2007.
173 'South African police "raising their game"', 24 February 2010, *SouthAfrica.Info*. Available at: www.southafrica.info/2010/police-240210.htm
174 Altbeker, 2007.
175 Chinese President Hu Jintao, quoted in Richards *et al.*, 2011: 103.

(and generally Western) capacity to guarantee security in the face of the terror.[176] According to a consistent, if reversed logic, the 2010 World Cup was immediately framed as the stage for South Africa to finally demonstrate that it had embodied Western standards, most notably in the sense of being capable of providing security, not simply in the face of terror, but more precisely vis-à-vis its own devastating crime reputation. ME-securitisation usually appears as a question of immunisation vis-à-vis dangerous others, event-specific threats triggering event-specific responses (e.g. terrorism in London 2012, hooliganism in Germany 2006, political protests in Beijing 2008 and Brazil 2014). Instead, in the case of South Africa the source of trouble is an absolutely internal and ordinary issue, crime. More than spectacular anti-terrorism measures, implementing security at the 2010 World Cup first of all meant dealing with an everyday problem in an extraordinary spatio-temporal context: securing the World Cup would be not simply a matter of possible disruption to the event, but its main narrative. Much more than elsewhere, here the effort to assure and communicate security does neither sit uncomfortably with the 'festive atmosphere' of the event, or risks over-militarising it, since it is meant to be a constitutive part of the World Cup atmosphere, not a safe atmosphere, but an atmosphere of safety. In this context security explicitly becomes both what allows for an event to unfold *and* the event itself. The 'legacy of safety' in South Africa is not feared as a potentially Orwellian outcome as in other ME narratives, but generally auspicated as a chance to breach the everyday experience of violence in the city (i.e. to relax from the oppressive JT), as well as the crime-ridden international image of the country, towards a 'new-found sense of safety'.[177]

Whether a World Cup could fit this ambitious purpose is another matter. Whilst the radical potential of urban events lies in shaking existent tunings

176 Atkinson and Young, 2005: 67.

177 As Craig Urquhart put it, 'perhaps crime-weary South Africans can look forward to a new-found sense of safety. It's one of the most important legacies the World Cup is likely to leave with us' (Urquhart, 2008). See the difference with what the Head of London 2012 security Tarique Ghaffur contends: 'This is a celebration of what London is about and of the Olympics … it's not about security or safety. Making the games as accessible as we can without security being obtrusive, is the trick we have to pull off' (cited in Culf, 2007). As regards 'reassuring' uses of Orwellian mythologies: 'Gerrie Gerneke, a director of licensing, prosecutions, municipal courts and special projects in the metro police department believes that the public should feel safer in the inner city, because "Big Brother" is watching over them' in "Big Brother Watches over Joburg", available at www.joburg.org.za/index2.php?option=com_content&task=emailform&id=2112&itemid=208. In fact, a project manager of the Jo'burg City Safety Programme (JCSP) confirmed to me that the new state-of-the-art CCTV system implanted in Johannesburg for the World Cup could be seen, together with the renovation of transport system, as the most important technical legacy of the World Cup (Personal Communication).

by potentially generating new cartographies that challenge the status quo, a socio-economically, politically and symbolical successful brandscaping requires the capacity to control the uncontrollable, i.e. to normalise the turbulence of the (mega) event, capturing the immanent *desires* it unleashes within a temporal continuity and spatial coherence which would allow for control, predictability and capitalisation. It is in the delicate balance between international visibility and internal matters, social and economical concerns, national and FIFA interests, that this recalibration occurs. As for the JT, I analyse the World Cup Brandscaping (WCB) through three main 'keys'.

4.2 A. [caring for you]

> In this time, we need good South Africans. Let them just for four weeks be good. Just for four weeks ... Let us forget our own problems for a moment and make other people at home in our country.[178]

If welcoming the visitors was intended as a patriotic mission for every South African, for the thousands of World Cup volunteers it was an official duty, corresponding to a clear ME-strategy to 'mobilise' people, generating public acceptance and a 'friendly' atmosphere.[179] The role of the various 'city ambassadors', 'information officers', 'goodwill tourist ambassadors', 'match-day marshals' and so on was 'to give advice to spectators, point them in the right direction, hand out information leaflets, such as "Safety Tips to Prevent Crime" and generally to be a friendly welcoming presence in the streets of host cities and at airports and other points-of-arrival'.[180] Besides giving information, they complemented the police's role in producing symbolical security by providing actual security – i.e. orienting people, calming tensions, etc.[181] Briefly, their role was that of promptly re-tuning those who appeared 'out-of-sync' vis-à-vis the WCB. Besides observing many instances of this practice, I also experimented with it myself, purposively experimenting *à la* Garfinkel to 'breach' the tune: whether I would be standing isolated from the crowd, perplexed, disorientated and unsure about where to go, it would be matter of minutes to be approached by a volunteer's kind 'you seem lost, where do you need to go?' When instead I

178 South African President Jacob Zuma, retrieved from www.iol.co.za/index.php?set_id=1&click_id=13&art_id=nw20100609075959168C211965. In the same article, tellingly titled 'Government urges SA to behave during Cup', the government spokesman Themba Maseko added: 'All football fans have a responsibility to ensure a safe and secure World Cup tournament for everyone'.

179 Hagemann, 2010: 728.

180 Minnaar and Van Jaarsveld, 2010.

181 Shearing and Stenning, 1984.

would insist in seeking off-key activities such as walking out of fan parks alone at night, I would be either discouraged or even sometimes escorted to my destination. If these are of course normal, if slightly over-zealous practices of ME-volunteering, what was peculiar in Johannesburg, and significantly different from Cape Town for instance, was the eminently securitarian nuance they assumed, and thus their explicit role in reinforcing the immunising normativity of the JT.[182]

On the one hand, volunteers did challenge the atmosphere of suspicion (i.e. 'do not trust anyone', 'ignore anyone'), by showing a friendly and trustworthy readiness to help. On the other, however, by constantly stressing their 'official' trustworthiness, sanctioned by their uniform, vis-à-vis unofficial people whose help they encouraged to mistrust, they were a constant reminder of their own exceptionality vis-à-vis 'normal people' – and thus, of the exceptionality of the World Cup atmosphere vis-à-vis the everyday alertness demanded by the city.[183] Likewise, whilst the volunteer's *caring response* somewhat rarefied the atmospheric weight of the JT, decreasing the individual need to be responsible for one's own security, on the other hand, by systematically re-synchronising bodies within the tune as well as through their constant reassertion of the necessity for everyone to comply with their advice to 'avoid troubles', they implicitly confirmed and indeed magnified the urban dangers looming outside of their protective caring. Besides 'providing the human face for what otherwise might seem as overly policed city',[184] the volunteers ultimately reasserted its normative tuning, functioning as a visible, uniformed and institutionalised caring response.[185]

182 According to volunteers in Johannesburg, their function was 'to provide a safe and secure experience to the fans' (volunteer interviewed by the author, 15 June 2010). In Cape Town (as well as in Durban), as a volunteer told me: 'our role? It is helping people, giving them information, guiding them out' (volunteer interviewed by the author, 22 June 2010).

183 In Cape Town, where their uniform was not sparkling yellow and immediately evident as in Johannesburg, I had an interesting exchange in this sense: 'we are here to inform people because tourist are not … they don't know Cape Town, they don't know where to go, so we try to help them, but we are also retreating from them' *what do you mean*? 'yes, because we don't have to look aggressive to them … because when they see us, the tourists sometimes are scared, they think we want to ask them something, beg money … we told the supervisors, it happens all the time, so now we sit here and wait for tourists to come, and we offer them information in a friendly and convenient way' (volunteer interviewed by the author, 22 June 2010).

184 Roberts, 2010: 1493.

185 Although of course volunteers exhibited a different motivation from similar instances of Johannesburg's caring response, as in the case of those Hentschel calls 'instant mercenaries', i.e. for instance the improvised parking guardians, ubiquitous in Johannesburg, who according to her exhibit 'money-driven commitments as crime fighters' (Hentschel, 2010: 199).

B. [police visibility]

> The police system is not simply an unseen seeing eye; it also exercises an exemplary visibility through its own visibility [employing] uniforms to create and stabilise a certain definition of contextual situations.[186]

Johannesburg was indeed an over-policed city during the World Cup, with security personnel of every kind, local, metropolitan, national, custom police, private guards, the army. Yet, it would be too easy to draw a direct equivalence between an elevated police presence and an oppressive over-militarisation. To this rather automatic and abstracting reading I oppose a situated attention to the atmosphere actually produced by the police, and their interplay with the JT. In fact, as far as my observation was concerned, rarely did this over-policing appear as threatening and oppressive. Quite the contrary, it was almost unanimously praised by both visitors and locals for its capacity to immunise public space, allowing for usually avoided behaviours and producing spaces in which the urban 'brushing of shoulders' between strangers could occur. Although my sample of interviewees was far from being statistically exhaustive, it proved to be at least atmospherically indicative: even if unprompted, people would always express their immediate approval and indeed enthusiasm for the police presence, independently of their nationality, age, racial or class background. From squatters in the deprived areas of Hillbrow and Joubert Park to inhabitants of the rich suburbs of Sandton and Rosebank, everybody was eager to emphasise how important the quantity as well as the quality of policing was. Normally criticised for being corrupt, incompetent and brutal, the police were now praised for their newly focused and 'vigilant' attitude, not only for relieving people from their 'need to be alert' but also fostering an unusual hopefulness, in relation to the potential 'legacy' that the event could foster in terms of a renewed approach to policing the city.[187] In fact, the police's 'soft approach' was generally acknowledged as usually polite, non-threatening and laid-back, to the point of being criticised as 'too bland' by some Western observers.[188]

Of course, on the one hand this fitted in somewhat well with the soft logic of the security-entertainment complex, according to which security becomes 'increasingly implicit, soft, and embedded' with entertainment,[189]

186 Brighenti, 2010a: 154.

187 To be sure, these were not only random impressions from the streets. For instance a manager working on the Johannesburg City Safety Programme (JCSP), I had the chance to interview, emphasised the role the World Cup played in compelling different police departments to act together and in coordination, thus stimulating tactical, as well as technical and technological improvement (interviewed by the author).

188 E.g. Crary, 2010.

an affective policing focused on 'acting within a festive context' and thus both aimed to guarantee safety as well as avoiding any disruption to the 'World Cup atmosphere'.[190] On the other hand, however, the self-fulfilling presuppositions of 'revelatory' approaches should be eschewed, and the encounter between the WCB and the JT should not be consigned to pre-given templates. Instead, policing strategies and the concatenations they generate are to be situated in the material contingency of their taking place, by observing and accounting for their encounter and friction with the city itself. In this sense it is undeniable that this affective policing functioned to ease the weight of the spatiolegal normativity of the urban, by providing people with a newly-found ability to go out of tune, allowing for crossing, if only temporarily, some invisible barriers and thus to challenge the supra-geography of the JT. Could this approach prove relevant to generating an enduring 'mood of safety' even after the event, i.e. a 'legacy' of safety?

Arguably, it is dubious how extraordinary measures of security, besides guaranteeing short-term safety, could actually turn into a legacy able to challenge, rather than reinforce and further institutionalise, the JT. Indeed, how can the potential unleashed by the 'weakening' of the oppressive alertness of the tune be kept open? As the event-related over-policing disappears, also the event-related 'sense of safety' seems destined to wane, unless an effort to capitalise on both the short-term increase in urban safety and police reputation – a result of the strategic coupling of higher police visibility *and* 'soft' approach – is pursued. Promisingly, this seemed to be the official intention, as stressed in a post-event report on the 'possible legacies' of the event, where the emphasis is on the need to 'build on the good reputation that JMPD (Johannesburg Metropolitan Police Department) has achieved during the event with respect to public perceptions of Joburg as being a safe city. This requires that JMPD enhance visibility, especially in the Inner City and at night.'[191] Only accurate and long-term post-WC researches could possibly provide an answer in this sense.

At the same time however, avoiding the bias of revelatory approaches must not lead to naivety. Repeating the critique mentioned above to Bissel *et al.*, let us recall that contemporary forms of urban control are not characterised by simple 'manipulation', but are more precisely to do with the prevention of events from becoming 'too intense': that is, with an art of defusing contingency by keeping urban potential alive as long as it is below

189 Hentschel, 2010: 143.

190 Schreiber and Adang (2010: 471) here refer to the low-key approach of Portuguese police during the UEFA Euro 2004, as opposed to the aggressive and highly-criticised 'hooligan-oriented' approach of 2006 World Cup's German police. In South Africa the modest hooligan concern (due to the country's geographical position) together with the complementary role of volunteers was certainly conducive to a smoother policing.

191 COJ, 2010a: 91.

certain thresholds of intensity. This should warn against uncritical emphasis on the supposedly 'liberating potential' that volunteers and police alike did play vis-à-vis the JT. I do not wish to cynically dismiss the latter, yet framing policing within the seductive logic of brandscaping means especially to take into account the reaction and recalibration implemented in response to surges of intensity: in other words, the way in which the frictions and excesses produced by the WCB were sought to be managed. The idyllic picture of soft and enthusiastically praised policing is thus recalibrated, whether we observe the police's swift reactions vis-à-vis the events that threatened to 'poison' the atmosphere of consumption and immunity and thus to disrupt the smooth flowing and coherence of the WCB. Most notably, those acts and initiatives either challenged the de-politicised consensus for the event by inserting a political conflictuality within, or threatened the legal immunisation of economic privileges by breaching 'ambush-marketing' protections and the like. The heavy-handed, *armed response* of police to the security-guards' strikes, with documented use of teargas and rubber bullets, is a compelling case in point.[192] In this sense, such reactions should not be understood as 'exceptional' vis-à-vis the spatiolegality of the WCB, but rather as fully consistent with its event-defusing mechanism. Below, I will offer further examples to support this observation.

C. [fan zoning]

> Unless they are in the stadium, no other event during the FIFA World Cup™ will allow South Africans to experience the authentic FIFA World Cup™ atmosphere other than the FIFA Fan Fests™.[193]

Fan zoning refers to the direct, material projection of the WCB onto the city through an immersive spatiolegal cartography, in which the gate-keeping and flow-regulating presence of security and volunteering personnel was complemented by a disembedded network of micro-geographies (venues, team hotels, road networks, fan parks, etc.) officially defined as *Controlled Access Sites*.[194] In this way, the WCB was given a physical, legal and atmospheric (the FIFA 'look and feel' of safety and entertainment) consistency onto the urban. Among those spaces, especially relevant are the Public Viewing Areas (PVAs).

192 E.g. 'World Cup embraces triumph and disaster', *Mail and Guardian*, 19 June 2010, available at www.mg.co.za/article/2010-06-19-world-cup-embraces-triumph-and-disaster

193 FIFA, Fan Fest FAQs for the 2010 FIFA World Cup South Africa.

194 *Controlled Access Sites* are stadium, official events locations, media and accreditation centres, FIFA Fan Parks, official hotels and 'any other area designated or demarcated by the Municipality as a Controlled Access Site and shall include private property located therein' (2010 FIFA World Cup South Africa by-laws (from 1.1.21.1 to 1.1.21.10)).

Briefly, these are zones (usually squares or parks) provided with giant screens, where fans gather to watch the games during the event. Although watching the World Cup match of the national team in the city's main square is a tradition in many countries, this became very popular during the Korea and Japan 2002 World Cup, where many spontaneous PVEs (Public Viewing Events) were set up, with no FIFA involvement and no particular legal, security and copyright restriction. These events were very successful and convinced FIFA to officialise them from the Germany 2006 World Cup onwards. Since then, FIFA has the monopoly of PVAs during the event (officially named *fan fests*, *fan zones* or *fan parks*) and although unofficial PVAs can be organised, they nonetheless depend on FIFA granting the licence, and must comply with the same branding restrictions.[195] Although entrance is free, fan zones are surrounded by high fences and patrolled by security personnel (both private and public) regulating the access at the gates through search and seizure procedures, not only for weapons and the likes, but also for food, drinks as well as any branded product not matching with the official sponsors. In fact, fan zones are strictly branded spaces where only official sponsors are accepted, with minor exceptions made for 'informal areas', i.e. zones dedicated to local food-sellers, provided their products are not direct competitors of the official brands (which have their own food-and-merchandising stalls within the premises). Special by-laws, allowing hitherto-forbidden behaviours (e.g. drinking alcohol in a public square) and forbidding hitherto-allowed ones (e.g. wearing a Pepsi t-shirt to a Coca-Cola-led event), further reinforce the normative re-tuning produced by the fan zoning.[196]

Anke Hagemann contends that fan zones are part of the process of festivalisation of city politics according to global capitalism's standards:

> her 'main thesis is that the stadium has become a spatial prototype for the temporary and long-term changes observable in urban spaces, projecting its functional, economic, social and regulatory conditions into public spaces.'[197]

In fact fan zones, together with demarcated, more or less secured and branded 'Fan Walks', may be seen as strategic spatial apparatuses 'that

195 Although non-commercial PVAs (where there is no direct/indirect entry fee) have their licence automatically granted, commercial PVAs require formal FIFA approval, see FIFA, *World Cup South Africa™ Regulation for Public Viewing Exhibition*. A particularly byzantine provision stated in the '2010 Soccer World Cup Liquor Policy' obliged bars and pubs wanting to show the matches as well as sell alcohol to purchase a separate licence. For this reason many pubs and bars, either unwilling to pay or unable to get the licence in time, were not able to show the match, thus losing significant amounts of money.

196 Klauser, 2009: 70.

197 Hagemann, 2010: 725.

translate the nonscalable into the scalable', that is, the singular contingency of the urban space into the form of the ME, channelling the flow of high numbers of ticketless fans into a tightly-controlled, securitised and branded geography.[198] They respond simultaneously to the ME-related needs of immunity and consumption: first, by minimising the risk of overcrowding around stadia, as well as the common problem of potentially troublesome fans roaming around the city;[199] second, by addressing the main economical shortcoming of the ME, namely the need to channel the consumption of visitors towards the official sponsors, thus guaranteeing the sponsors themselves the 'symbolical monopoly' of the city-branding; third, by allowing for a more concentrated, intensive and controlled acclimatisation of urban space according to the tune of the ME.

In the official documents the blurring of security and entertainment, spectacle and biopower, is expressed in explicitly atmospheric vocabulary. For instance, in Johannesburg's *Transport Operation Plan*, it is stated that

> 'planning for a limited number of large exhibition sites would have the appeal of concentrating activities such as security, big screen transmissions and assist in promoting a *carnival atmosphere*'.[200]

That is, what FIFA terms an 'authentic FIFA World Cup Atmosphere [with a distinctive] FIFA look and feel'.[201] Whether the ME is defined as a 'democratic spectacle', the fan zones are accordingly 'communal gatherings [that] reinforce the game's power to unite',[202] or a 'cultural melting pot', providing a

> safe, recognised and exciting environment for visitors who have limited comparable alternatives ... Hospitality, tolerance and mutual understanding must have absolute priority ... what is more, in a friendly, peaceful environment even violent fans behave more peaceful, and join in the relaxed, cheerful atmosphere.[203]

198 Rahola, 2014: 386. Fan Walks or Fan Miles are branded, unfenced walks connecting the Fan Park to the stadium. For the notion of 'disembedded' and 'fortified' networks, see Rodgers, 2004.

199 See Minnaar and Jaarsveld, 2010; and Burger, 2007. In the context of Germany 2006, Police Director Juergen Mathies observed that 'We must make the public viewing sites as safe as the stadiums', retrieved from www.paktribune.com/news/print.php?id=114608

200 COJ, 2008: 26.

201 FIFA Fan Fest FAQs and Official Info Pack. As the 2010 Director Operations for Cape Town Lesley de Reuck observed, fan fests are 'a safe, convenient and convivial alternative to being at the stadium [where ticketless fans] get to experience the excitement and thrill of being caught up in the roar of the crowd', quoted in Pedroncelli, 2010.

202 'People power reigns at Fan Fests', 3 July 2010, available at www.fifa.com/worldcup/news/newsid=1266969/

203 Organisation Committee of Germany 2006, quoted in Frew and McGilliray, 2008: 187.

Fan zones, recently adopted also in the context of the Olympics (in both London and Rio de Janeiro) as 'live sites', thus form a flexible semiotic, material and affective assemblage, in which the logics of security, branding and entertainment blur, an overlapping perfectly summarised in their definition as 'safe, recognised and exciting'.

The WCB is an assemblage of bodies, (security personnel, volunteers, performers, athletes, fans, fences, CCTVs, slogans, signs, discourses, media), practices and affectivities, tuning the city through three main overlapping keys (volunteers *caring*, police *visibility*, fan *zoning*). In its simultaneously panoptical and synoptical character, it corresponds fittingly to the description of brandscaping as a bipolar configuration (spectacular and managerial) that tunes the urban without simply blocking the movement – as in the disciplinary enclosure of stadia – but rather keeping it alive whilst defused from its (whatever positive or negative) eventfulness, turning the potential *desire* unleashed by the advent of the ME into a controllable, consensual and capitalisable *pleasure* (i.e. de-politicised enjoyment).[204]

As Frew and McGilliray explain,

> the sport fan becomes more central to the experiential representation of the spectacle, therein. In their desire to sustain spectacular and memorable events organisers are increasingly turning to the spectator to create event 'content'.[205]

Nowhere is this more evident than in the fan zones, as the atmospheric management unfolds through a systematic attempt to produce 'celebration', 'enjoyment', 'party', through rhythmical syncopation and atmospheric stimulation. A series of security-entertainment repetitions (from the searches at the gates to the waving of the flag) generating an atmo-rhythm which is multi-sensorially pervasive and involves individuals in a set of practices typical of the stadium and, to some extent, of staged spectacle.[206] As the speaker at Cape Town Fan Fest summarised: 'it doesn't

204 Incidentally, one could argue that fan parks, with their fences, are more consistent with the old disciplinary model of enclosures than with the logic of control. Yet this is not the case: they are porous and open, fitting more evidently with a logic aimed at managing flows rather than secluding 'individuals'. This does not mean that evident exclusionary practices are not present. In Durban, I saw three youths being denied entrance to the Fan Fest because, as a policeman explained, 'they are street kids, they are dirty, they come here to steal, to make trouble' (interviewed by the author, 7 July 2010). Incidentally, this confirmed what a 13-year-old boy in Durban told *The Times* in the months preceding the World Cup: 'They tell us we must go back where we came from. They say Durban is dirty because of us' (quoted in Khumalo, 2010).

205 Frew and McGilliray, 2008: 182.

206 For instance, the repeated 'initiations' at the gates (body and bag searches, seizure of food, drink and unwanted brands etc.), followed by relaxation inside the fenced,

matter the result, here it's all about celebration, it's all about fun, it's all about entertainment'.[207] Entertainment, that is, carefully channelled within the flow of consumption, as in the overlapping between crowd incitement and marketing promotion that was explicit, for instance, in the speakers' continuous prompting to shout the term 'ayoba': a term meaning 'cool', 'great' in South African slang, but at the same time the key word of the mobile company MTN's World Cup marketing campaign.

If law seems to disappear in this 'mixture of control through surveillance and distraction through entertainment', it is merely dissimulated, in fact playing the central role of enacting and sustaining the WCB.[208]

4.3 Any hooligans or criminals who try their luck during the World Cup will also feel something – the red card of the law.[209]

The legal scaffolding of the WCB is centred on special, spatiotemporally delimited FIFA *by-laws*, defined as

> an addition to the Municipality's existing by-laws ... if any, and to the extent that conflicts may arise between the Municipality's existing by-laws relating to Advertising; Controlled Access Sites, Public Open Spaces and City Beautification; Public Roads and Traffic Guidance and Street Trading, if any, and these By-laws, the provisions of these By-laws [the World Cup by laws] shall prevail.[210]

FIFA by-laws deal with various issues (advertising, controlled access sites, beautification of public space, roads and traffic, street trading) so as to satisfy the main requirements of the WCB, i.e. the securitisation, commercialisation and 'beautification' of public space. They allow for stabilising the WCB and its 'look and feel' by protecting it from tangible incursions (e.g. crime) and intangible, atmospheric poisoning to its value and reputation, preventing ambush marketing as well as any expression of 'racist, xenophobic cause, charity or ideological concerns', forbidding ugly scaffolding, unwanted sounds, 'protected' words, unpleasant smells, unofficial events: the whole city is meant to be 'free and clear' from any disruption, airspace included.[211] This capillary acclimatisation of the urban is also given financial

securitised and CCTV-monitored areas, where other sets of choreographed repetitions (blowing the vuvuzela, waving the flag, cheering when prompted by the speaker etc.) intersected with commercial transactions (food, drinks, gadgets etc.).

207 Heard by the author in Cape Town Fan Fest, 27 July 2010.

208 Thrift, 2011: 11.

209 Deputy Justice Minister Andries Nel, in Naidoo, 2010.

210 2010 FIFA World Cup South Africa By-Laws 1.2.3.211. FIFA Host City Agreement. Incidentally, FIFA's eventification is total: during the ME, no other substantial cultural events other than those approved by FIFA shall be organised (FIFA Host City Agreement: 4.13.7 (iii)).

protection, through the constitution of 'tax bubbles' around stadia, fan parks and other controlled access sites, *de facto* 'making any income earned off goods sold within them exempt from taxation'.[212]

The setting up of such an inhabitable space of exception within the city produces unavoidable exclusionary effects, weighing more explicitly on those lacking the resources to 'participate' in the WCB, and/or prevented from taking advantage of it. For instance, begging in public spaces and roads is explicitly forbidden,[213] and street trading is subjected to oppressive limitations. Atlanta, during the 1996 Olympics, was famously called a 'street bazaar', a nightmare for the event organisers as the 'uncontrolled' street trading seriously compromised the value of the Olympic brand, that is, the immunity of its brandscaping.[214] Since then, the protection of sponsors' monopoly over consumption has been heightened to a remarkable extent, making it increasingly difficult for street traders to capitalise on the enormous flux of fans triggered by the event. Even more controversially in South Africa, where it is a widespread and well-established activity, street trading has been systematically excluded from actively taking part in the World Cup, through high costs for authorisations, strict controls, exclusionary zoning and draconian by-laws, and by chasing street traders away from the 'designated areas' and, when present, failing to provide them with promotional and logistical facilities to compete with the sponsors.[215]

Not only special laws but also special 'World Cup Courts' have been established during the event. Paralleling the aforementioned support for the quantity and quality of policing during the World Cup, this judicial accelerationism also gained praise for constituting a potential antidote to the impunity vis-à-vis crime which allegedly characterises South Africa. Johan Berger, of the Pretoria-based Institute for Security Studies (ISS), noted that 'there is no bigger deterrent [to crime] than a successful prosecutorial system', hoping that 'special courts' would stay after the World Cup.[216] Some were less enthusiastic, observing that faster sentences

212 FIFA Host City Agreement: 8.8; 'The Act creates a "tax-free bubble" around FIFA-designated sites so that profits on consumable and semi-durable goods sold within these areas will not be subject to income tax; neither will VAT be applied' (*Revenue Laws Amendment Act* (20 of 2006), available at www.polity.org.za/article/revenue-laws-amendment-act-no-20-of-2006-2006-01-01). 'The Host City hereby waives any and all claims of liability against the LOC, FIFA, any FIFA subsidiaries and their officers, directors, members, agents, representatives or employees, for any loss or damage to the city whether or not such loss or damage may have been caused by or resulted from the[ir] negligence' (*FIFA Host City Agreement*: 9.5 (i)).

213 2010 FIFA World Cup South Africa By-Laws: 4.2.13, 5.1.1.10.

214 In Girginov and Parry, 2004: 89.

215 The 2010 FIFA World Cup South Africa By-Laws widen powers of search and seizure as regards street trading (7.5.1.1), to the point that *any place* (private property included) can be declared restricted to street trading during the Term (6.4.1).

216 Byrne, 2010.

are not necessarily fairer sentences, and rather increase concerns about the lack of basic guarantees for the accused (sentences such a five-year term for a stolen mobile phone seems to prove this point).[217] Others criticised the special courts for being simply a means for FIFA to have the national judicial apparatus working on its behalf.[218]

Very controversial in fact were the restrictions as regards advertising, and not only for the broad and thus highly discretionary definition of the latter, i.e. 'visual representation [of different forms and element] ... or any combination of such elements with the *object of transferring information*',[219] but also, for the explicit urban-wide ambition (i.e. beyond the designated spaces of the ME) of the legislation, making it illegal to 'affix, place, arrange or create any Advertisement of whatever nature anywhere within a Public Open Space'.[220] Such a vague and discretionary style, through which law is sublimated into a vaporous, atmospherically sealing device, also characterises other provisions which, besides their explicit public-order concerns, have an implicit role in acclimatising the space by protecting and de-politicising the WCB. An example is the prohibition on bringing into the stadium 'objects which could compromise public safety and/or harm the reputation of the Event as assessed at the sole discretion of the FIFA World Cup Authorities'.[221] Another is the restriction on the 'use of abusive or otherwise objectionable language or behave in an abusive, objectionable or disorderly manner'[222] as well as the explicit request (in stadia as well as fan parks) not to

> engage in conduct which expresses racist, xenophobic cause, charity or ideological concern related materials, including but not limited to banners, signs, symbols and leaflets, objects or clothing, which could *impair the enjoyment* of the Event by other spectators, or detract from the sporting focus of the Event[223]

Local activists have observed the absurdity of such legal provisions, pre-emptively defusing any potential for the ME to act as a global platform for publicising political matters to global media and visitors.[224] De Vos stresses their blatant unconstitutionality, since banning 'both commercial advertising and any form of political expression in and around the stadiums as

217 Smith, 2010.
218 E.g. Nkepile, 2010; Hyde, 2010.
219 2010 FIFA World Cup South Africa By-Laws 1.1.3.
220 2010 FIFA World Cup South Africa By-Laws 4.6.2.
221 FIFA Stadium Code of Conduct, 4.r.
222 2010 FIFA World Cup South Africa By-Laws 3.5.5, 4.2.2.
223 FIFA Stadium Code of Conduct 4.e, 5.6.e (my emphasis).
224 E.g. Pillay, 2010.

well as the fan parks – which are situated on public property'.[225] Alice Thomson, of the Durban Social Forum was arrested for distributing anti-FIFA pamphlets at the Durban Fan Fest,[226] and a similar fate was reserved, according to what I have seen, for activists leafleting on behalf of an evidently less controversial subject (an anti-xenophobic rally) according to a rather loose interpretation of the FIFA 'Stadium Code of Conduct'.[227] Evidently, these behaviours were not targeted for their 'illegality', but for their disruptive, poisonous role vis-à-vis 'festive atmosphere' of the WCB.

It would be compelling to frame the spatiolegal installation of the World Cup vis-à-vis the way in which the relation between sporting events and political protest is being rearticulated as part of the general surfacing of preventive brandscaping strategies in the security-entertainment field, in other words, towards the systematic disempowerment of the political potential from sport events.[228] The designation of specific areas for political protest (and, of course, for capillary monitoring and categorisation of protesters) in Beijing 2008 is only the more explicit instance. Although there is no space here to pursue this avenue, the example of the treatment of hooliganism at EU level is worth mentioning, insofar as mirroring in at least three aspects the spatiolegal apparatus of the ME: namely, the urban-wide scope (that is, beyond the event-venues), the vague, discretionary and atmospheric legal language, the de-politicising, event-defusing strategy. As Tsoukala observes, the EU approach to hooliganism has been oriented by a gradual extension of control beyond the enclosures of stadia, as well as by

225 '[A]ny person from distributing any pamphlets near or in stadiums or fan parks without the prior written approval of the Municipality. A person who nevertheless distributes any pamphlets could be convicted and fined up to R10,000 or six months' imprisonment. This provision seems to impose quite a drastic limit on the freedom of expression of everyone in South Africa. In effect it bans both commercial advertising and any form of political expression in and around the stadiums as well as the fan parks' (de Vos, 2010).

226 Pillay, 2010.

227 FIFA Stadium Code of Conduct, art. 1(e), 8.0.c. Accused of ambush marketing and incitement for promoting an anti-xenophobic rally, filmmaker Giuliano Martiniello, research student Samantha Spencer-Mura and director of the Centre for Civil Society (CCS) Patrick Bond were detained at the Durban FIFA Fan Fest. Policemen told Patrick Bond, according to his reconstruction: 'No distribution of pamphlets, especially which mention xenophobia.' Bond continues: 'The reason the pamphlet was banned was not just procedural – it was political. The policeman thus continued, Bond reports: 'You are reminding [people] of xenophobia. Even myself I had forgot about that thing, but now you write it down' (Bond, 2010).

228 Greenfield and Osborn (1997: 381) discuss for instance the political significance of sport through an account of the anti-South Africa protests at cricket matches during Apartheid, comparing it with the increasingly restricting legislation enacted by the *UK Criminal Justice Act*, a veritable counter-move to decontaminate sport from its political nuance, so as 'the right of sport fans to demonstrate in "traditional" ways have been grievously undermined'.

an increasingly wide and blurred definition of its target population, from 'known troublemakers' to all 'potential troublemakers and people under the influence of alcohol or drugs', allowing for increasing restrictions on fan behaviour in general.[229] Interestingly, this evolution involved a significant shift in framing the issue, from the legal notion of 'offence' to the political one of 'conflict', defined as 'any act that is contrary to the general public's perception of normality or which adversely affects their quality of life',[230] a very fitting example of the sublimation of the urban spatiolegal state of exception into a preventive and conflict-defusing installation of comfort: brandscaping.

In his nostalgic book *Sport, Space and the City,* John Bale narrates an involutionary parable of football as a collective gathering, from a game being played in pitches with blurred edges and attendants surrounding the fields, without a neat distinction between players and spectators, to one played simultaneously in the detached mediation of televised games as well as in the segregating territorialisation of hyper-securitised and commodified stadia. The will to control and capitalise on the separation between the game and the spectators, he observes, has gradually eroded the eventful potential that the taking place of 'football' as collective gathering possessed. In 1992, during the European Championship Final between Germany and Denmark (in Sweden), several Danish supporters gathered on a spontaneous PVA set up in Copenhagen.[231] Excessive to the logic of consumption and immunity expressed by both stadia and television, this was according to Bale the paradigmatic opening of a 'third space', 'exemplify[ing] a tension between the apparently logical need for a predictable environment and the place-making potential of fandom'.[232]

This compelling account is marred by a soothing nostalgia, which risks slipping into unproductive rhetorics of authenticity. Processes of spatial commodification, securitisation and juridification are not to be read in opposition to some sort of more genuine and 'authentic', phenomenological and immediate urban space: the urban is always-already 'saturated with mediations and prolongations'.[233] Nonetheless, Bale's account provides some interesting inspiration. According to Brighenti, 'the public appears when a certain urban site is turned into a venue of "public address"'.[234] Accordingly 'publicness' is to be understood as alternative, although not merely in opposition, to the securitised and capitalised brand-

229 Tsoukala, 2006: 8.
230 Council of Europe, 1985.
231 The screen was set up in Fælled, a locus of 'significance to Danes, being the "home" of their footballing traditions' (Bale, 1988).
232 Bale, 1988.
233 Brighenti, 2010d: 38.
234 Brighenti, 2010d: 39; the notion of 'public address' is elaborated from Iveson, 2007.

scaping of the ME, 'emerg[ing] in the space between invisible resistance and normative hegemony', that is, in the space in which the urban tuning and the ME re-tuning meet and clash.[235] Publicness is always frictional, conflictual, kept alive by the eventfulness of its taking place. Beyond facile romanticism, the space referred by Bale can be certainly assumed as an instance of such an eruption of 'publicness', as the unleashing of the intensive potential of the football event away from its defusion into the logics of consumption and immunity. Beyond facile pessimism, it is evident that the evolution of spontaneous PVAs into today's fan zones is a parable consistent with what Jean Baudrillard in typically apocalyptic fashion maintains:

> spectators may cease to be spectators and slip into the role of victims or murderers ... sport may cease to be sport and be transformed into terrorism: that is why *the public must simply be eliminated*.[236]

ME brandscaping can be seen as a strategy for dealing directly with these 'third' or frictional spaces, not by simply denying them into synoptical or panoptical confinements but directly adapting and coping with their 'place-making potentials', seeking to re-capture and exploit these affective flows within the controllable and capitalisable passivity of a 'trained fandom'.[237] Accordingly, the WCB is more than the 'culmination of a long process of segregation, standardisation and commercialisation of fandom'.[238] More precisely, it is the 'concrete realisation' of the empty form of the ME onto the urban space through an immunising strategy aimed at stimulating, arousing and propelling the turbulence of urban being together and at the same time working as a mechanism of coping with a city-wide enthusiasm by defusing it from any radical, dangerous or non-commercially exploitable outcomes.[239] This is done by channelling the affective 'effervescence' of the city within an atmospherically-enclosed, bubbled-up spatialisation, enforced by technologies (from fences to CCTVs), regulated and policed by private and public guards as well as volunteers, 'protected' by by-laws, as well as infused by a *de rigueur* rhetoric of multiculturalism.

235 Brighenti, 2010d: 40.

236 Baudrillard, 2009: 79 (my emphasis). See also Deleuze, 1986.

237 'By being "coached" and "cared for" [people] would be less likely to engage in deviant behaviour' (Frew and McGilliray, 2008: 191–2).

238 Bale, 2001.

239 Even in the sense of defusing the 'agonistic' conflictuality of the football matches themselves, not simply diluted into the Olympian 'it-is-important-to-take-part', but in the more market-friendly 'it-is-important-to-have-fun', as the fan park speakers relentlessly reminded their customers.

Mattias Kärrholm proposes to understand the rhythmic logic of consumption in the city as a process of 'isorhythmia', whereby different flows and mobilities are not homogenised in a single order, but rather kept separated and yet tuned on a given wavelength, the rhythm of consumption.[240] The WCB functions in a similar way, superimposing a palimpsestic heterogeneity of different space-times tuned according to a common refrain.[241] An event-defusing machine, that is, deterritorialising the urban from its materiality and reterritorialising into the global circulation of capital, an explicit allegory of which is *Global Fan Fest* project, an addition to the South African fan fests which consisted of six contemporaneous 'global' fan fests set in Berlin, Mexico City, Paris, Rio de Janeiro, Rome and Sydney, a veritable 'superterrestrial topography' of ME brandscaping.[242] Whilst the by then FIFA President Joseph S. Blatter claimed that 'The FIFA Fan Fest will continue to be a fundamental part of future editions of the FIFA World Cup', adding that the 'decision was taken a long time ago, by the fans themselves', it is tempting to read this sentence in reverse, that is, understanding the Fan Fest as a gradual attempt to close the *unauthorised public space* that the 'fans themselves, long time ago' had opened within the spacing of the ME.[243]

4.4 The thing is, now we park the car very far away from here … now we're quite afraid of going back to the car because there's no light, we haven't thought about that, but we'll have to go … security is a problem in this World Cup, definitely.[244]

It is hard to deny that 'FIFA's attempt to implement a security and surveillance assemblage is to be understood as a means to enhance profit'.[245] Moreover, I am perfectly aware of the notorious role played by mega events in displacing people, cleaning up public spaces of 'undesirables', curbing local business by advantaging aggressive corporation branding, increasing and legalising hitherto illegal social control measures through special

240 '[R]educing complexity not primarily by turning orders into a singular order (as in the modernistic tendency of spatial homogenisation) but by inscribing different orders in a system guided by a common denominator (the rhythms of consumption)' (Kärrholm, 2009: 435).

241 Thus the 'threat' (i.e. the reduction of complexity from public space, the defusion of the potential for events to occur) does not lie in synchronisation *per se* (linear time, repetition etc.) but rather in the capacity to gather different activities, events, transgressions that, if from a narrow perspective might seem to introduce complexity, from a wider urban-wide perspective appear to re-tune space according to an event-defusing, controllable and capitalisable logic (Kärrholm, 2009).

242 Paraphrasing from Seabrock, 1996: 211.

243 Retrieved from www.fifa.com/worldcup/news/newsid=1576927/index.html

244 Uruguay fan interviewed by the author, Johannesburg, 18 June 2010.

245 Eick, 2011: 88.

legislation, and generally smoothing the process of privatisation, commodification and securitisation of public space. Many witnesses, activists, papers and books have been doing outstanding work in denouncing these issues, some of which I briefly touched upon, and they seem to leave little room for both 'alternative' and non-naive perspectives on the overwhelming role FIFA plays in bullying the host nations into *de facto* allowing for extraordinary and undemocratic measures to be put in place. I acknowledge these works and their worries. Yet, this is not all.

Notwithstanding the attempt to 'neutralise' the eventful potential of the urban via the capillary production of an atmosphere of secured consumption where fandom can be 'freely' expressed according to pre-ordered modalities tied to commercial interests, the resonance produced by the spatio-temporal syncope of the ME can never be completely channelled into the modulation of brandscaping and its relentless attempt to *tame* and *theme* the city. The ('non-capitalist' and non-immunitary) potentialities of being together are stimulated by the taking place of the ME and never truly re-captured by its brandscaping machine. Thus for instance, whether the routine of the JT arguably decreases 'the capacity of the body to experience more positive affects', then the disruption of such a routine promises to unleash it with uncontrollable results.[246] We do not know what bodies can do.

Fan parks reproduce the logic of the enclosure of malls and gated communities, but at the same time they are much more open and less disciplined, offering an opportunity for the emergence of unusual urban assemblages. According to some the 'place-making potential' of fan parks, whether employed 'as a network of critical intervention(s) within the urban fabric', could be conducive to reinsert a dimension of publicness into an urban space weakened by low levels of security, mutual attachment and shared responsibility.[247] Non-FIFA fan parks, for instance, offer opportunities to get together in contexts where the discipline, control and branding of the security-entertainment ethos of FIFA fan parks function in a less 'aggressive' and much more fragmented way.[248] Probably, the potential of 'unofficial' fan parks should be taken into account for future mega-event strategies and analyses, especially in the sense of deactivating

246 Bissel, 2010: 277.

247 Haferburg *et al.*, 2009: 194.

248 With respect to the meticulous set up of the bio-spectacular brandscaping of FIFA fan parks (heavily fenced with big FIFA banners, with spiked tops to prevent physical trespassing and colourful logos preventing 'visual' trespassing; characterised by theme-park-like grand gates suggesting the entrance to a different level of atmo-rhythmical spatiality; with strict searching procedures and a constant, proactive attempt by performers to involve people in celebration and entertainment), the unofficial fan parks were a rather more 'low key' matter. The principal one in Johannesburg, in Mary Fitzgerald Square, had a metallic-wire fence and thus no visual protection from the

outside. Controls were very relaxed, often turning a blind eye to the odd bottle of water or sandwich sneaked through, as well as generally allowing the admittance of 'vagrants' and 'street kids', who were often stopped in FIFA fan parks. Inside, the atmosphere is more akin to a place for people to enjoy the game and relax, without being 'forced' to 'rhythmise' themselves to the brandscaping as it occurs more invasively in the official fan parks, either by being persuaded to buy stuff or through the experiential involvement into the 'celebratory and festive' FIFA atmosphere. It is interesting in this sense to briefly mention some of the peculiarities of Johannesburg's fan zoning with respect to Germany 2006. As Frew and McGillivray (2008: 190) observe, in Germany fans were channelled in an orderly way through the city by fan zoning: 'Watching fans assimilate the prominent Fan Park signage and move in line towards the Olympic Stadium metro-stop emphasised the rational, planned approach employed to direct incoming visitors to the officially-sanctioned public viewing spaces'. Completely different was the setting in Johannesburg, where huge highways and a notorious township (Alexandra) surrounded the main fan park (Innes Free Park). Reaching the place by walking meant negotiating one's way through traffic and pollution. At night, this was strongly discouraged. Buses, taxies or private cars were used to reach the park instead. In the Central Business District the central fan park was connected to the Ellis Park stadium by a 'fan walk' passing through notorious neighbourhoods such as Joubert Park and Hillbrow. Yet, also due to some communication problems, it never worked. Without the fences providing an added experiential value of safety, there was no effective enough 'break' from the 'dangerous' surrounding area. Consequently, the fans mainly avoided it. The officials did not bother to give them too much information either, perhaps sensing that the risk was too high. In Germany, Frew and McGilliray note, the main purpose was that of controlling, smoothing and sedating the potential for dangerous behaviour, according to the 'continuing governmental concern with a hyper-masculine football culture and the deviant spectre of hooliganism', and at the same time offering a platform for attracting 'accepted' agencies as preferred 'fan behaviour' (2008: 191–2). In Johannesburg this logic worked in reversed fashion. Instead of seeking to protect the city from the fans by enclosing them in fan parks, the concern here was to protect the fans from what the 'city' could do to them. We could thus appreciate better the difference in policing between a proactive, invasive and panoptical stance (Germany) and a protective, sheltering and synoptical one (Johannesburg), not a matter of containing potentially troublesome flows of people, but of offering them a shelter, a safety bubble to separate the fan from the inhospitable outside. Here lies the key 'experiential value' of security. Johannesburg's fan parks were less hyper-experiences of enjoyment providing 'micro-level resistance to the everyday banality of work' (Germany) than rather more mundane experiences of 'liberation' from the urban *alertness*, that is, sort of micro-level resistance to the everyday anxiety of the Joburg Tune: what resulted was a joyful atmosphere of safety, that is, mirroring the role shopping malls play in South Africa as places in where, as Fred de Vries notes, 'you can walk around without any worries ... an antidote to Apartheid, a place where people blend and can forget about the past and current anxieties' (2008: 302). In fact, similar atmo-rhythmical configurations to the 'hyper-experiences' of fandom described by Frew and McGilliray in Germany could be observed in the smaller fan parks set up in Johannerburg's big shopping malls such as Rosebank, Melrose Arch, Montecassino. Arguably, shopping malls are sterile, securitised and disciplined spaces of consumption. Within these spaces, the fan parks did not function as bubbles of safety amidst a space of danger, but rather as bubbles of hyper-enjoyment within a commodified space of control. In other words, within what I referred to above as the 'slowed-down' rhythm of malls, the fan park produced a re-acceleration of the tempo directly conducive to a 'carnival' atmosphere, insofar as in direct opposition (i.e. nurtured for the fact of being opposed) to the disciplined environment in which it was taking place. Different authors

the spatiolegal apparatus of exception of the ME in order to open it up to the potential of its contingent eventfulness – a concept I explore in the following chapter. Likewise, in Johannesburg the multifaceted policing of the city allowed many people for the first time to walk into zones they would normally never venture into (let alone by *walking*), thereby partially challenging the taken-for-granted psycho-geographical assumptions of the JT, and thus producing (temporary) publicness into usually neglected areas. Could not the dimples in the smoothness of the JT generated by these occurrences be employed to propel strategies of public space reformulation?

Regardless of the different answers that one can provide, the point I want to make here is that we should avoid instrumental readings of ME brandscaping as a pacific application of pre-given sets of narratives, strategies and practices into a passive and flat urban surface. The outcome of a ME is always the turbulent and situated result of its encounter with the complexity of the urban, always bound to produce frictions and excesses, whose singularity requires situated analyses, radically material perspectives and consistent methodologies.

That being said, my tentative conclusion is that the clash between the JT and the WCB ultimately left the JT unchallenged. The strategic operations of *caring*, *policing* and *fan zoning* allowed certain agencies, otherwise 'restricted', to be expressed. The JT's mood of alertness, anxiety and distrust was sought to be defused through spectacular narratives of multicultural joy (the Rainbow Nation), police high-visibility and great effort in 'welcoming' the visitors. This, however, rested on a hyper-immunological spatialisation consisting in the production of atmospherically enclosed areas through physical, legal and techno-securitarian boundaries, which confirmed and indeed reinforced the slow-tempo of shopping malls onto a wider urban space: by producing, enclosing and patrolling an atmosphere of fun and safety, the WCB ended up reinforcing the syncopated rhythm of bubble-to-

have noted the role shopping malls play in contexts such as the United States or South Africa, where with the parallel privatisation of public space they are increasingly taking the role of marketplace or city square (e.g. Wakefield, 2003), that is, the place where people hang out, meet and carry out their social life. This also means that a ban from a shopping mall in certain contexts could play the same significance of being banned from a public square. Moreover, being privately owned, malls and other privatised former public places are characterised by higher behavioural expectation (e.g. the prohibition of alcohol) and far wider and discretionary powers of surveillance, control and exclusion (Gray and Gray, 1999; Kempa *et al.*, 2004). In this context PVAs opened up spaces of 'chaotic enjoyment' free from the discipline of the mall, breaking its strict rules (no-drinking, no-smoking, no-shouting etc.) and allowing people to 'act unruly', for instance drinking beer, smoking and blowing vuvuzelas, thus spatio-temporally reconfiguring the place. By functioning as a 'bubble within the bubble', the fan parks thus produced tunings much closer to the ones observed in Germany.

bubble movement ('ensure that you walk along the demarcated pedestrian routes') and fragmented atmospheres characterising the key tonalities of the Joburg Tune: *alertness* and *immunity*. Acting as a vaccine, the WCB inoculated a 'low level of transgression' to the JT's rhythm of alertness, mistrust and exceptional mapping, yet without addressing the conflictual antagonism of the city, but spectacularly denying it in the de-potentiating strategy of consensus, as well as practically confining it, through securitarian, legal and commercial operations, outside the World Cup zoning and its smooth, secured and capitalised circulation. Ultimately, we may say that the WCB *institutionalised* the JT, adapting to its pulsating immanence by recalibrating its frequency to the securitarian and commercial needs of the FIFA 'look and feel', through the *caring response* of volunteers, the *therapeutic* security of visible policing, and the physical, legal and branded boundaries of the *fan zoning*. It will not be impossible therefore, but certainly difficult to offer an affirmative reply to Christopher McMichael's rhetorical question:

> [will] turning our cities into heavily patrolled corporate theme parks make life safer and more secure [and generally, improved] for ordinary South Africans after the tourists and cameras have gone home?[249]

It was the night of the elimination game between the last African team remaining in the competition, Ghana versus the USA. The atmosphere was electric. Doctor Cape, Cape Town's notorious ocean wind, was blowing furiously. The giant screen in the fan park oscillated worryingly. Too much. The fan park was to be closed. People moved to the various pubs, restaurants and cafes in the central avenue, Long Street. Sheltered from the wind in fragmented micro-spaces of fandom, they watched the emphatic last-minute victory of Ghana. After the match, pan-African enthusiasm could no longer be contained by fences. The party now spilled over into the street, a celebratory affectivity disruptive to both the traffic and the controlled and securitised flow of the event: no fences, no guards, no channelled consumption practices, no spectacular production of entertainment. Affects, bodies and wind conjured together in allowing the eventfulness of the ME to escape the brandscaping modulation, a friction too intense to be contained. You never know how objects can get together, what configuration they may take. The intensive charge of the moment resonated for hours in the city centre. This was celebration, and yet no peaceful one. There were shouts, dancing, hugging, and also some fights.

249 McMichael, 2010.

The assemblage of bodies, affects and wind de-activated the operational mechanism of the ME, its immunitary, event-defusing brandscaping, and yet kept in place its eventful resonance, transforming the city centre into an open-air festival, for some time irreducible to the spectacle of the ME.

It is easy to romanticise this instance as a sort of more 'true' and 'authentic' dimension of being together. Instead, I propose to take it as a partial and uncertain instance of a temporary de-activation of the operational mechanism of the ME, not a critical deconstruction, but a direct dismantling of the operation of the WCB, that is, of its twin strategy of immunity and consumption, through the immanent, unauthorised, impersonal emergence of a configuration of bodies, affects, wind. 'Atmosphere is a field of virtual movement' writes McCormack 'from which certain bodies, including wind, are always in the process of actualizing'.[250]

To assume it as an instance of emancipatory urban politics would be quite naive, if not utterly ridiculous. Yet, beyond the easy fascinations, this example is helpful in offering some inspiration, from the methodological issue of how to observe and account for these fleeting moments of friction, to the political question of how to 'use' the potentialities that these frictions produce, how to 'keep open' the space they generate, the lines of flight they potentially trigger. Precise strategic questions follow: how can the intensity of urban life be allowed to emerge, beyond the immediate spontaneity that the just-narrated example suggests? How can the immunising attempt to reduce it into predictable, controllable and capitalisable tunings be deactivated, whilst avoiding the dangerous outcomes of 'liberationist' tendencies? How can the spatiolegal mechanism of exception be dismantled, without pretending to eliminate it, and instead opening it to different uses? How can the urban be open to the contingent potential of its justice?

250 McCormack, 2008: 417–8.

Chapter 6

Law profanation justice

This chapter goes back to its principal vectors – events and justice – and projects them towards a common vanishing point: spatial justice. This entails a two-step strategy: first, to contextually dismantle the exceptional tuning of control, opening the situation to the eventful contingency of spatial justice; second, to *use* the potential thus freed to retune the situation into alternative configurations. The politics of Walter Benjamin, according to Ari Hirvonen, is

> neither a politics of great revolutionary programmes, ends, events and heroes, nor an infinite gesture of waiting for an always yet-to-come justice and democracy or revolutionary moment. Instead, we must read this as an interruptive and ruptural politics which recognizes in every instant a 'small gateway' in the continuum of global capitalism and its legal systems and which aims to exploit these in order to bring about liberation, equality and justice.[1]

The paradoxically modest messianism of this programme is inspiring, and yet to some may appear both too little, as a praxis that never challenges the continuum but limits itself to exploit its cracks; and too ambitious, if it pretends these cracks would lead anywhere else than to temporary autonomous zones to be soon re-ingested within the said continuum. Aware of these potential limits, this chapter argues for a stance that rather than contenting itself with the task of exploiting the small gateways to justice, seeks actively to produce them through a praxis of dismantling and retuning. There is no messianic fantasy of liberation, equality and justice here, but rather the simultaneously modest and strategic task of unplugging power relations and reorienting their residual power into potentially emancipatory tunings. Spatial justice responds to such a task. The chapter is articulated in three parts.

1 Hirvonen, 2011: 115–16.

First, I provide a brief overview of some significant attempts to think the notion of justice. Individuating some fault lines within this milieu, as well as drawing a link to the reflections developed in the third chapter, I am able to provide a more accurate indication of the concept of justice I am envisaging. This exploration is unavoidably limited to few relevant instances, chosen because they are exemplificative enough to allow delineating the problematic field in response to which the concept of spatial justice emerges. Second, I employ the notion of surfing as a conceptual figure allowing the delineation of a notion of ethico-political action emancipated from the unproductive dichotomy between active and passive, the grand hubris of revolution and the innocuous self-contentment of temporary autonomous zones. At the same time, I clarify my position vis-à-vis the danger of being re-internalised within the ethos of control, through a brief detour to ancient China. Third, I relate this interventionism to the spatiolegal reflections developed so far, suggesting a strategy that moves beyond the false alternative between a 'justice within law' and 'justice without law', and rather envisages the potential of an *inoperose* use of law, by means of disorienting law itself, deactivating its exceptional apparatus and thus forcing it to reorient towards the event of its (spatial) justice. The oscillation between 'abstract' speculation and pragmatic strategy that characterises this chapter should not appear contradictory. In fact, one implies the other. At times, the narration is interrupted by parentheses that provide ways of thinking about this strategy as applied in specific projects, approaches or situations.

1.1

> The declaration of the Rights of Man should be reformulated in topological terms to express the idea that all men are not only born free and equal but that they're condemned to look after the space in which they live.[2]

Most of the early attempts to think justice in connection with space come from the field of geography. Mustafa Dikeç retraces them to Bleddyn Davies' notion of 'territorial justice' (in the book *Social Needs and Resources in Local Services*), a normative concept 'designed to assess the distribution of local services with respect to the needs of designated service areas'.[3] Other similar attempts to reduce the encounter between space and justice to the question of distribution would follow, implicitly premised on the assumption of space as a pre-existent 'platform upon which social processes and relations unfold and a container for social practice, rather than as a social structure arising out of extant power relations'.[4]

2 Sloterdijk, 2005: 230.
3 Dikeç, 2001: 1786.
4 Stanley, 2009: 1000.

In her influential account, Iris Marion Young challenged the conflation of justice with distribution, emphasising the questions of domination and oppression, and claiming a politics of difference that would acknowledge individual disparities and work towards overcoming them.[5] Acknowledging difference is not enough, however, whether differences are taken for granted, and individualities assumed as givens. Whether the relational and eventful quality of difference is unaccounted for, then the concept surreptitiously becomes a vehicle for identity politics, a post-political ally for the multiculturalist disavowal of conflict, accordingly (un)seen as either inexistent or as an anomaly to be eradicated through *just* solutions.[6] Although in principle it seeks to eschew these positions, this is where Susan Fainstein's notion of *just city* eventually lands.

This is perhaps unsurprising to our point of view, given the Habermasian influence on notions of participation, communication and deliberation that Fainstein, in her attempt to think justice, space and the city together, mobilises. The result is a strikingly restrained proposal, content, as she puts it, to provide an 'analysis of the possibility for attaining a better quality of human life within the context of a global capitalist political economy'.[7] Justice thus appears as a teleological solution to be reached via a shared agreement on a moral (read: de-spatialised) framework, to be carved within the horizon of capital. The resulting intention of 'restructuring capitalism into a more humane system' is in the end hardly distinguishable from the well-intentioned declaration of any 'social-capitalist' CEO.[8]

Already in his early attempt to merge justice and space by developing the concept of 'territorial social justice', in conjunction with Davies' work, David Harvey was conscious of the need to subordinate the question of distribution that of the (capitalist) production of social injustices.[9] It is not surprising that he would criticise Fainstein's approach insofar as limiting it to 'mitigating the worst outcomes at the margins of an unjust system'. 'The freedom of the city' Harvey argues 'is far more than a right of access to what already exists: it is a right to change it'.[10] This is what Lefebvre's notion of right to the city points to. In Harvey's words, the 'right *to* change ourselves by changing the city' or, in Lefebvre's original definition, 'the *right to the oeuvre*, to participation and appropriation (clearly distinct from the right to property)', and thus to political and fully material involvement in the urban-making process.[11]

5 Young, 1990.
6 Sharma, 2006.
7 Fainstein, 2011: 470.
8 Fainstein, 2011: 6.
9 Harvey, 1973.
10 Harvey and Potter, 2009: 45.
11 Harvey, 2008; Lefebvre, 2006: 174.

An eternal promise of radical urban politics, the right to the city has the potential to embody Sloterdijk's proposal to 'reformulate human right in topological terms'.[12] Its mounting resonance, both as a concept and a strategic claim, in an increasingly urbanised world has been officialised in the *World Charter on the Right to the City* (2004), and testified by the significance increasingly played in various initiatives around the world.[13] Yet, going mainstream also exposed the concept to the risk of co-optation, a fate already encountered by notions such as participation, sustainability, social capital and many other 'radical' concepts gradually converted, in Brenner *et al.*'s words,

> into a basis for legitimating existing, only weakly participatory forms of urban governance, or for exaggerating the systemic implications of newly introduced forms of citizen participation in municipal affairs.[14]

Within this context, the concept of spatial justice reclaims significance.

1.2

> The prefix geo does not signify a specialized branch of philosophy; it signals, rather, the topos, or the nowhere, of philosophical inquiry in place of a transcendental metaphysics that believes itself above being placeable, abstractly nowhere and universally everywhere.[15]

In his 1983 paper 'On Spatial Justice', Gordon Pirie sought to develop the concept, however failing to account for how it would differ from another way of addressing 'social justice in space'.[16] Almost 30 years later, in a book explicitly titled *Seeking Spatial Justice*, Ed Soja pointed to the value the concept would harbour, to eschew the totalising universality of the concept 'just city', as well as the lack of critical edge betrayed by notions such as territorial justice.[17] In particular, Soja was interested in its potential as a strategic tool in the hand of local communities and social movements, a tool to *re-spatialise* political debate and social struggle, that is, gathering and polarising different interests in resistance movements, and advocating for a geographically equitable distribution of resources, services, and access. It is undoubtedly a valuable conceptualisation, and yet somewhat insufficient to make a case for the autonomous relevance of the concept: spatial justice, again, appears as a way to insert the 'spatial' into the logic of social justice.

12 Sloterdijk, 2005: 230.
13 For a relatively recent state-of-the-art of the Right to the City Movement around the world, see Sugranyes and Mathivet, 2010; and Brenner *et al.*, 2012.
14 Brenner *et al.*, 2012: 6.
15 Chisholm, 2007.
16 Pirie, 1983: 471.
17 Soja, 2010.

This would be even more explicit, for instance, in Peter Marcuse, who interpreted spatial justice as an aspect of 'broader injustices', thus spectacularly failing to grasp the key intuition this concept gestures toward: that *any* injustice has an ontologically spatial dimension.[18]

With these premises, we may understand Harvey's logical conclusion: spatial justice, he bluntly noted a few years ago in London at a 'Spatial Justice Workshop', in the end is not a useful concept at all.[19] This should not be surprising. Notwithstanding being routinely indicated as the key reference on spatial justice, Harvey never used this concept. Likewise, in his compelling conceptualisation of the relation between space and justice, he always kept in place an implicit separation between tangible (physical) space and intangible space (supra-structures), subordinating the former to the latter,[20] a position which is incompatible vis-à-vis the task of developing a properly *spatial* notion of justice. As Philippopoulos-Mihalopoulos summarises, again, Harvey's should not be understood as 'a conceptualisation of spatial justice, but a spatial perspective on social justice'.[21]

There are obviously more interpretations of the concept, yet these are by far the most influential, as well as extremely useful to emphasise what is missing from the contemporary debate. In a nutshell, a willingness to pursue the promises of the spatial turn to their radical consequences. The result is a generally 'weak' interpretation of spatial justice so that, in the face of its increasing application, what remains is a persistent incapacity to indicate what in this concept would be really novel and indeed 'radical', and why we should actually use it in place of more conventional notions such as social justice and the likes.[22] Although some would frown upon this definitional attempt, perhaps they should not. If concepts are not ethereal emblems distracting us from real problems, but rather strategic tools created in response to emerging problematic fields, then crafting them adequately is a necessity.

The first step is to avoid redundancy: if the matter at stake is simply that of providing justice with a spatial nuance, then there is no need to add yet another word to already congested academic political jargon. The second step is to avoid co-optation: weakly-crafted concepts easily become

18 '[T]he spatial injustice which Harlem represents is part of a pattern of discrimination against African Americans that goes back centuries in United States history, starting with the importation of slaves from Africa, white legal privilege, political power, and economic exploitation, visible in all aspects of life. The spatial injustices of segregation and resource distribution are derivative of these broader injustices' (Marcuse, 2009: 195).

19 A brief account of that London workshop, in parallel with Soja's book launch, can be found as Pavoni, 2010b.

20 E.g. Harvey, 1996; 2009. For a piercing critique of Harvey on this point see the introduction to Doel, 1999.

21 Philippopoulos-Mihalopoulos, 2015: 180.

22 For other conceptualisations and applications of the term see in particular the journal *Justice Spatiale | Spatial Justice*, at www.jssj.org

dangerous weapons to foster consensus for conservative politics. The third step is to avoid occupying a space in which more valuable and strategically useful concepts may emerge.[23] Clearly, this is a possibility not so remote for spatial justice itself, a notion already in the process of being diluted within the technocratic rhetorics of the EU Research and Innovation programme *Horizon 2020*, where it is presented as a simple relation between space, as the locus of discrimination and inequalities, and justice, as the normative framework allow evaluation of them.[24] It is urgent, it seems, to rescue spatial justice from its ongoing neutralisation into a pacific and uncontroversial solution to urban problem.

Spatial justice does not only belong to the domain of critique, and neither can it be simply reduced to a mere 'aspect' of social justice. Instead, it is meant to wrest the social away from justice, by asserting justice's always-already spatial and material character. Understanding justice 'spatially', in this sense, implies reworking the accepted coordinates of theoretical thinking. It means throwing justice into what Doreen Massey termed the 'terrifying simultaneity', and thus unavoidable conflictuality, of co-existence.[25] This also entails, incidentally, to let a properly post-human and material understanding of space emerge, in the face of the heavily anthropocentric connotation that all the just discussed approaches to spatial justice betray. In a sentence, this means simultaneously *doing* justice to space (i.e. addressing its complex ontology) as well as *rescuing* justice from the threefold betrayal that the concept usually suffers.

We saw it before. First, justice is made transcendent, teleological, absolute. Second, it is reduced to the administration of justice. Third, it is de-materialised into a quasi-mystical, yet-to-come (im)possibility, a synonym for paradox and deconstruction lacking strategic edge, and as such ultimately impotent. Instead, spatial justice is meant to restore, in a deeply material sense, the original meaning encapsulated in the Greek notion of *dike*, as a persistent incompatibility with a given state of affairs: never simply a matter of rearranging the status quo (e.g. distributive justice), but rather of opening *and* reorienting it towards alternative configurations. Spatial justice is not the 'antidote' to spatial injustice that many wish for, but a *pharmakon*.[26] Neither is the 'ultimate goal' of urban planning, an under-

23 As for instance the case of urban sustainability, a term that increasingly 'occupies the ground that alternative environmental politics of the city could occupy' (Whitehead, 2011: 30).

24 Hence the task to survey 'existing and emerging spatial and territorial inequalities and evaluate them normatively from perspectives of justice and fairness'. Available at http://ec.europa.eu/research/participants/portal/desktop/en/opportunities/h2020/topics/rev-inequal-07-2016.html

25 Massey, 2005.

26 As it was defined in the description of a dedicated conference on New Urban Languages: Tales and Images of Spatial Justice, Delft, 24–26 June 2015. Available at https://nulconference.wordpress.com/new-urban-languages/

standing that instrumentally reduces it to a solution to be achieved, de-spatialising it into the linearity of a better time to come.[27] Instead, in the more modest but strategic formulation Philippopoulos-Mihalopoulos makes the following proposal:

> while acknowledging and working through the impossibility of a solution, spatial justice brings forth the conditions of such an impossibility, thereby allowing a flicker of possibility to stream through.[28]

1.3 A politics of emancipation does not seek the happiness of people but rather seeks universal disquiet.[29]

'"Spatial justice" is not an end, however defined, to be achieved', argues Dikeç.[30] Spatial justice, he argues, is a critique of systematic forms of spatially produced domination and oppression, 'aimed at cultivating new sensibilities' towards the spatial dynamics of injustice or, as he puts it, to the 'spatial dialectics of injustice', defined as the interplay between the 'spatiality of injustice' and 'the injustice of spatiality'.[31] Accordingly, spatial justice is neither an instrument to be used by replicating tactical operations into the city,[32] nor a pacific and inclusionary tool for allowing more participation within the given order. Instead, it is meant to *wrong* the given order itself.

Dikeç develops his argument by drawing from the work of three key French thinkers: Henri Lefebvre, Etienne Balibar and Jacques Rancière. From the first two he takes, respectively, the notions of *differential space* and *égaliberté*. Spatial justice is thus conceived as a way to address the spatial dialectics of injustice, in order to achieve both a right to the city and a right to difference. Here the problems begin. First, we already observed the limits of Lefebvre's notion of differential space, insofar as projecting of a post-conflictual space of consensual deliberation that neutralises pre-emptively the radicality of his own proposal. Second, Balibar's notion of *égaliberté* problematically seeks to re-surface the anachronistic model of the *polis*: 'a political collectivity, a place where public interest is defined and realized'.[33] Notwithstanding its complexity, which cautions against quickly reducing it to just another instance of urban idealism, there remains a

27 Marcuse, 2010.
28 Philippopoulos-Mihalopoulos, 2015: 184.
29 Meillassoux, 2010: 475.
30 Dikeç, 2002: 96.
31 Dikeç, 2002: 96; 2001.
32 For a piercing account on the perils the trendy notion of Tactical Urbanism falls into, see Mould, 2014.
33 Balibar, quoted in Dikeç, 2001: 1800.

discomforting Kantian flavour in this notion, which Bailbar understands as a universal and unconditional push towards equality (as non-discrimination) and freedom (as non-constraint). It is a regulative ideal that risks functioning like those 'bad utopias' Cacciari refers to, namely those approaches that seek to overcome urban contradictions, instead of understanding them as ontologically constitutive of the city itself.[34] Another problem, far from being merely stylistic, is the *grand* overtone these approaches encapsulate.

As I will explain further below, my understanding of spatial justice eschews such 'eschatologically nomic desire', typical of revolutionary enterprises, although certainly does not limit itself to the naive exaltation of everyday acts of resistance. Instead, I am closer to Brighenti's notion of *diavolution*, namely a strategy of inhabiting and traversing the problematic fields of a given historical configuration, dismantling them by remaining within, rather then postulating their future overcoming,[35] to repeat, a simultaneously modest and strategic approach. It is modest, not as a renunciation to act, but in the sense of asserting the awareness of our positional (ethical) responsibility vis-à-vis the assemblages in which we are. It is strategic, because it requires a situated praxis aimed to *act* on the asymmetries, disparities and conflicts of urban, rather than pretending to transcend them into post-conflictual utopias, or indeed shatter them through hubristic ruptures: 'spatial justice is the movement out of this conflict while delving deeper into it'.[36]

It is exactly this pretence that remains, I believe, implicit in Dikeç's use of Rancière's notion of the *political*, understood as the proper moment of politics: namely the irruption of an event that *wrongs* the given order (what Rancière terms the *police*), and which 'makes visible what had no business being seen, and makes heard a discourse where once there was only place for noise'.[37] According to Dikeç, spatial justice would correspond to the event of the political. Two considerations may follow. First, following Žižek, this conception appears to rely on, to ultimately 'need' (and, I would say, presuppose) the reality of a monolithic order (the police), which functions as a comfortable point of reference to build resistance against, that is, to *wrong*.[38] Yet, is not the reality of control a configuration of power whose main characteristic is exactly the fact of not presenting anything tangible to

34 Cacciari, 2009.

35 Diavolution is 'the cross-breed term replaces the Latin prefix re- with the Greek prefix dià-, which means "through". The Latin root volvo, - re, which means "to turn", remains ... Revolution is an eschatologically nomic desire which kathectically needs the anomic to prepare for its own occurrence: it thus produces extrinsic, vertical deterritorialization' (Brighenti, 2008: 797).

36 Philippopoulos-Mihalopoulos, 2015: 41.

37 Rancière, 1995: 30.

38 Žižek, 2000: 171–245.

oppose? 'Why proclaim the need for a right to difference', as in the already quoted rhetorical question by Noys, if this is what capitalism quintessentially supplies 'in far more radical, a-subjective, and inhuman forms than any mutated subject?'[39] Second, the emphasis on the moment of rupture risks fetishising it as the political moment *per se*, a dangerous path indeed. Again, does not capitalism itself proceed through constant shocks and ruptures? As we noted, control is flexible, experimental and open-ended. It 'tolerates all transgressions, provided they remain soft': any resistance provided it remains micro, any 'autonomous zone' provided it remains *temporary*, any re-appropriation provided it does not provoke challenges to the *status quo*, any event provided it falls short of becoming eventful.[40] In this sense, by implicitly mirroring Rancière's deprioritisation of power relations, Dikeç runs the risk of falling into a spatial romanticism, with problematic strategic outcomes.

A telling example is when he maintains that, whilst the 'given order' 'excludes the possibility of two things being in the same location' (as the police confine 'everything at the right place'), the space of the *political* (i.e. of spatial justice), with its unstable and non-univocal quality, is what allows for such a possibility to occur.[41] If this is the case, however, does not spatial justice risk being rarefied into a merely epistemological tool to 're-imagine' urban contradictions, rather than facing the task of addressing them in their materiality? Let us compare that passage with Philippopoulos-Mihalopoulos':

> all space is violent on account of the fact that only one body (assemblage) can occupy a specific space at a specific time … Every body is obliged by its nature as both intensive (symbolic and ideal) and extensive (corporeal and spatial) to occupy a certain space at a certain time … *spatial justice emerges from the fact that only one body can occupy a specific space at any specific time*. In other words, *spatial justice is the struggle between bodies to be in a specific space at a specific time*.[42]

On the one hand, this more strategic elaboration explains the constant necessity of violently delimiting space, by producing the safe and the unsafe, the familiar and the strange, the habitable and the hostile, that is, to *police* everything into a *right place*. On the other hand, it makes clear that once the given order is challenged, disrupted or removed, a new one is to be produced. Power asymmetries and conflict won't disappear. They need to be retuned, and this must occur within, rather than beyond, the

39 Noys, 2012: 71.
40 Tiqqun, 2010, 170.
41 Dikeç, 2005: 182.
42 Philippopoulos-Mihalopoulos, 2015: 176, 198.

constraints of spatiality. The right to the city, Chris Butler argues after Lefebvre, is 'neither a natural nor a contractual right but is grounded in the entitlement to physically occupy urban space'.[43] If this is what spatial justice addresses, then this cannot rest on the mystical presupposition of a *political* space where bodies would be able to occupy the same space at the same time, but rather on the strategic task to find a 'better' way of being-together within this impossibility.

There is no escape from the materiality of the urban, no possibility of occupying the same place at the same time: inhabiting means displacement, inequality and conflict, and it is only by accepting, addressing and traversing such a dense complexity that justice may be conceived. Since space is violent, 'the problem now is not how to end violence but to understand why it occurs in the ways it does'.[44] Neither equality nor freedom are universal, but inequality, asymmetry, constraint are. Hence Philippopoulos-Mihalopoulos' Spinozian definition of freedom is:

> the actualisation of one's situatedness ... This is a distinctly collective freedom that operates as the enabling bondage of the responsibility of being situated with regards to other bodies. Freedom is a responsibility, and the responsibility of freedom is to unveil the illusion of freedom (in the sense of free will) and allow this to inform our knowledge of the causes for which bodies move the way they do.[45]

Likewise, spatial justice is never only a question of rupturing, but also of reorienting, never only a question of dismantling, but also of counter-effectuating. *Contra* Badiou, it is not an event 'popping out of emptiness', but rather from 'an intensive variation in a full and continuous *spatium*', in which the rupturing of the transcendental conditions of possibility of a situation (what 'holds a situation together') is not the end point but only a seismic tremor, a promising potential.[46] Its possibility of collapsing the given situation depends on its intensity and on the anti-seismic quality of the situation itself, and yet even this collapse is far from being emancipatory *per se*. The problem passes through a point of physical, material resolution, a point of crisis. It never calls for a solution to be solved, but it calls us to reorient our configuration to allocate its powers. As Charles Péguy observed, this is what occurs when a problem that seemed to have no solution, a problem against which the entire world had failed, suddenly does not exist anymore: we have been reoriented and we are no longer shaken by its telluric shock. We are ready to face the next one.[47]

43 Butler, 2009: 325.
44 Whitehead, 2007: 41.
45 Philippopoulos-Mihalopoulos, 2015: 62.
46 Laerke, 1999: 91–2.
47 Péguy, 1917.

It is such a *reorientation* that spatial justice points to. In the way I conceive strategically this crucial instance, my perspective slightly diverges from Philippopoulos-Mihalopoulos'. Where he focuses on the notion of withdrawal, I employ that of profanation, to explain how such a combination of rupture (as deactivation) and reorientation (as counter-effectuation) is to occur. Here, the role played by law will be crucial. Incidentally, one may ask, where is the law in the accounts of spatial justice so far discussed? Of course, the fact that all of them come from the field of geography minimises the presence of a legal perspective. And yet, is not the legal, or indeed spatiolegal question a fundamental one when discussing justice? I believe so.[48]

1.4 Suddenly, we felt that we were no longer the same convicts. Nothing had happened. Yet a problem in which a whole world collided, a problem without issue, in which no end could be seen, suddenly ceased to exist and we asked ourselves what we had been talking about. Instead of an ordinary solution, a found solution, this problem, this difficulty, this impossibility had just passed what seemed like a physical point of resolution. A crisis point. At the same time, the whole world had passed what seemed like a physical crisis point. There are critical points of the event just as there are critical points of temperature: points of fusion, freezing and boiling points, points of coagulation and crystallization. There are even in the case of events states of superfusion which are precipitated, crystallized or determined only by the introduction of a fragment of some future event.[49]

In his conceptualisation of spatial justice as withdrawal, Philippopoulos-Mihalopoulos depicts it as the production of micro-ruptures in the spatiolegal atmospherics that hold the potential to reorient it, potentially shifting the unavoidable conflict of being-together towards different registers.[50] This reorientation, or retuning, is the crucial ethico-political dimension opened up by spatial justice, in the two interrelated senses somewhat left unaccounted for by Rancière. A rupture, accordingly, is just a rupture which is immediately re-absorbed within the situation, if not followed by a retuning, a collective and post-human endeavour that always occurs within the same dense contingency. We never enter a neutral, non-tuned space. Always 'we return to the law, not to conserve it and its institutional fantasies, but to reorient it'.[51]

48 For a similar call to explore the legal dimension vis-à-vis the notion of right to the city, see Fernandes, 2007.
49 Péguy, 1917: 269.
50 Philippopoulos-Mihalopoulos, 2015.
51 Philippopoulos-Mihalopoulos, 2015: 215.

Focusing on law's production of legal subjects, Goodrich argues that we should not understand it only negatively, as a simple 'extraction' of abstract figures (*personae*) from the social, but as the ontological production of 'the spectacular space of the social' in which the 'persons [are] catapulted'.[52] Incidentally, whether or not taken in its material sense, Guy Debord's notion of *Society of Spectacle* expresses nothing but this: a society in which the mediation of the real abstraction of the juridico-economical *persona* gains full ontological reality.[53] In this respect, it is obviously possible (indeed simple) to charge the notion of *legal persona* for being an illusionary construct that, insofar as postulating a 'methodical abstraction from every situation', neglects the vibrant complexity and heterogeneity of social life.[54]

This is perhaps a necessary step, yet hardly a sufficient one. Taking legal abstractions seriously means to assume them as 'social facts and objects of practical struggle',[55] and thus to explore the assemblages they produce regardless of our attempt to deconstruct them. In *Terza Persona*, after a brilliant genealogy of the notion of persona, Esposito sets out to remove this juridico-political mask (the Latin meaning of the word *persona*) in the direction of the 'impersonal'.[56] Beyond the law and the mechanism of personification, he argues, lies the emancipatory potential of an impersonal life that 'cannot but resist whatever power, or knowledge, is arranged to divide it'.[57] However, pretending to have done with abstraction in the name of the creative praxis of multitudes, the post-human relationalism of networks, the vibrant vitalism of matter, is a deeply problematic approach that runs the risk of de facto remaining stuck within – as well as reproducing – the ontological reality it set up to challenge in the first place.[58] Goodrich's assessment is accurate:

> Saying 'let's exit,' 'new words must be devised,' 'time to escape' is simply, well, no avoiding it, escapist … not so much impersonality that needs to be sought but rather and more aggressively it is the process of emblematization, the inhabitation of the roles, the apparatuses. Regimes and machines that institute and induct that deserve to be revolved … As with any functioning machine, it is dubious to treat it as

52 Goodrich, 2012: 59.

53 That is, a 'social relation among people, mediated by images' (Debord, 1983: 4). Debord refers to the persona of the capital, whose ties to the legal persona are indissoluble. In fact, the capitalistic abstraction cannot be detached from the legal scaffolding that sustains it, and that indeed provides it with ontological reality.

54 Tiqqun, 2010: 25.

55 Toscano, 2011b: 91.

56 Esposito, 2007.

57 Esposito, 2011: 218.

58 Toscano, 2008: 283.

> junk, better to take it apart, piece by piece, frame by frame to see what can be used, what jettisoned, how to improve on the show.[59]

Rather than remaining hypnotised by its aura, or embarking on a quest for some more genuine, authentic or impersonal substratum lying beneath, the point is to ontologically engage with the reality produced by the juridico-economical abstraction of persona, and thus with the machinery and apparatuses which establish and keep it in place (i.e. rituals, practices, techniques, technologies, etc.). We should be suspicious about iconoclastic urges to have done with law. Such an anti-normative stance is marred by inconsistencies, as we discussed already. True, we should follow Deleuze's famous injunction to 'have done with judgement'. However, without misunderstanding it as a call to 'have done with law', but rather to have done with the mechanism of exception which grounds law's judgement, that is, with its exceptional operation through which law reduces the world to a *world for law*.

There is a sibylline sentence in the book Deleuze and Guattari dedicated to Kafka: '*the transcendence of the law was an abstract machine, but the law exists only in the immanence of the machinic assemblage of justice*'.[60] Law and justice, in other words, occupy the same ontological space. This sanctions both the impossibility to actually 'exit' the spatiality of a situation, as well as the eventful materiality of its haunting excess. Notwithstanding his awareness of the necessary link between justice and (the calculation of) law, Derrida ultimately missed this point by situating justice in a pre-ontological dimension, assuming it as an impossible possibility, reducing it to a 'temporal' instance *à venir*. Justice is not to come however, but always-already here: an 'absolute horizon, independent from any observer', which is at the same time here and now, that is, a '*local absolute*, an absolute that is manifested locally', and that is never reducible to a configuration *for us*, or to a world *yet-to-come* according to our desires.[61] In the words of Cunningham, therefore,

> a politics adequate to the contemporary must always go beyond the terrain of the 'legal', but equally cannot afford to 'eradicate' it, for this would risk merely reinscribing rights, in an illusory desire for the 'concrete', as a purely 'moral' category divided from questions of political accountability or enforceability.[62]

'Going beyond the terrain of the legal' does not mean to abandon law, since 'the law is not just legalistic ... the law is both legalistic *and* just'.[63]

59 Goodrich, 2012: 64–7.
60 Deleuze and Guattari, 1986: 51 (italics in original).
61 Deleuze, and Guattari, 1994: 36; 2004[1980]: 422.
62 Cunningham, 2008: 467.
63 Philippopoulos-Mihalopoulos, 2010b: 10.

Surely, justice cannot come *only* through law. It cannot come without law either though, since the negation of law would only reinstate it in an implicit and potentially more dangerous form. This is not, of course, an attempt to preserve the *grandeur* and mystical aura of law. Paraphrasing Jessica Whyte, what this entails is thinking law beyond the false alternative between its glorification and its dismissal, 'beyond the reactionary desire to re-instil law with a lost meaning, the nihilistic embrace of law's emptiness, and the dialectic of constituent and constituted power',[64] in other words, justice, 'through and despite the law', that is.[65]

At the same time, this account must be firmly situated within the peculiar socio-historical configuration I defined as the spatiolegal architecture of control. It is vis-à-vis this configuration that spatial justice assumes a cogent relevance. Control, we saw it extensively, is tied to the surfacing of exceptional tunings whose effects are simultaneously responsibilising and de-responsibilising. In the context of security for instance, we saw how responsibility is rhetorically outsourced onto the individual (*do not become a crime victim*) whilst at the same time an ever-wider opportunity is provided, for delegating this very responsibility to socio-technological and legal protocols. Thus responsibility, so to speak, is reduced to the task of carving out spaces of delegation from the very need to be responsible: a condition of *horizontal separation via vertical delegation,* which systematically immunises the urban against the ethical necessity to perform 'responsible gestures' in reaction to unexpected occurrences. This is how the logic of comfort functions, physically, legally, aesthetically, tuning the urban into spaces of consensual de-responsibilisation.[66]

Reasserting the situated, collective, post-human, relational quality of responsibility, spatial justice incorporates a direct challenge to this very logic. Strategically, this may be actualised via dismantling the spatiolegal atmosphere of a situation (its exceptional tuning), thus opening the potential for its retuning. In Agamben's terms, 'what opens a gateway towards justice is not the elimination of law, but its deactivation and inoperosity – that is, another use of law'.[67] What is dismantled is not law, but its exceptional, juridifying operation, thus disclosing the geo-legal fact of its real contiguity with justice.

How is this to be (un)done? It cannot be undone through all-encompassing principles or vague yearnings for a world beyond. Elaborating on Benjamin, Agamben observes that the 'state of the world in which the world appears as a good that absolutely cannot be appropriated or made juridical', is not another world but rather a potential that any situation *in*

64 Whyte, 2009: 320.
65 Philippopoulos-Mihalopoulos, 2010a: 9.
66 Brighenti and Pavoni, 2017.
67 Agamben, 2005a: 64 (modified translation).

this world harbours.[68] This implies engaging at every moment in an ever-new struggle, not acting beyond, outside or without law, but rather *forcing* law to transform *sur place,* making space for the possibility of the properly creative, un-authorised emergence of justice. What kind of ethico-political action does such an understanding envisage? What kind of urban politics does it entail? Indeed, what does 'action' mean in this sense, and how can we rescue it from the reduction into the compromised paradigm of operation? Prior to coming back to the law/justice relation, we must confront such an 'inoperose' dimension of acting.

2.1 What deed would man be capable of if he had not first entered that vaporous region of the unhistorical?[69]

The urban presents a level of complexity that advises against more or less well-intended faith in unilateral solutions, or post-political beliefs in the possibility of impartial actions oriented by pragmatic and non-ideological ideas that work, spaces that fix, hence the need to assume one's inescapable placed-ness (the unavoidable fact of occupying one place, of *taking place*) as a body amongst other bodies. A being-there that is irreducible to (although not independent from) physical, representational or phenomenological 'states of affair', i.e. to an actual relationalism traceable via socio-legal-empirical means. A singular positioning, within an always excessive assemblage.

Yes, we are within a dense materiality in which every movement is fraught with consequences, and as the dichotomy of action and inaction loses meaning, the question of whether this ultimately leads to an inescapable political impasse cannot be easily dismissed. Could not such a perspective be assumed as atrophying the possibility for ethico-political action, entangling agency within such a dense and complex web of indefinite consequences to the point of rendering it pointless? According to some, in fact, this is an 'intensely demotivating' position, conducive to either passive renunciation or resignation to low-profile and innocuous tactics of small-scale transgressions that in the end become 'comforting substitutes for effective success'.[70] This is not necessarily the case. The approach developed here does not imply resignation or renunciation, but rather a motivation to act within this world, rejecting the assumption that only a negative and actually external position would provide the ground for

68 'Law that becomes indistinguishable from life in a *real* state of exception is confronted by life that, in a symmetrical but *inverse* gesture, is entirely transformed into law … Only at this point are the two terms distinguished and kept united by the [sovereign] relation of ban (bare life and the form of law) abolish each other and enter into a new dimension' (Agamben, 1998a: 55).

69 Nietzsche, 1997[1876].

70 Barnett 2011b: 252; Williams and Srnicek, 2013.

action. It prefigures an *interventionism* disarticulated from the hubris of activism: *inoperose acting*. Zourabichvili once defined Deleuze's ethico-political stance as 'involuntarism'.[71] Provided it is not assumed as passive inaction, but rather as incompatible with the 'voluntarism' of a subjective will, I take it as a good approximation of the stance I am here discussing. To define the act of thinking away from intentionality, subjectivity, voluntarism and any conception of thought as generated *ex nihilo* by a *cogito*, Deleuze and Guattari proposed understanding it as an act of diving, or surfing. This is what intervention means: *inter-venire*, i.e. to come between, entering the flow of things, always beginning in the middle, being forced to coordinating 'one's body with other modi', always '"get[ting] into something" instead of being the origin of an effort'.[72] Surfing, that is.

Of course, it is not *that* simple. Legitimate critiques cannot be shunned just by resorting to adventurous analogies. In fact, how can surfing be a viable model for ethico-political action in the age of control? How can we differentiate between the flexible capacity to 'flow between things', and the precarious vulnerability to the flows of capital? Incidentally, does not the rather unorthodox way in which Deleuze deals with control (often 'laterally', in variously different and unconventional formats) testify for his uneasiness with a notion which seems able to seriously compromise his whole project?[73]

2.2 The enemy interprets space in a traditional, classical manner, and I do not want to obey this interpretation and fall into his traps. Not only do I not want to fall into his traps, I want to surprise him! ... I said to my troops, 'Friends'! This is not a matter of your choice! There is no other way of moving! If until

71 Zourabichvili, 1998.

72 Deleuze and Guattari, 1994: 71; see also Palmas, 2009.

73 Namely an interview (Deleuze and Negri, 1990); the final part of a talk (Deleuze, 2012[1987]); the last pages of *A Thousand Plateaus*, referring to the 'organisation of the Capital' no longer seeking to striate space but rather producing 'a sort of smooth space in which the destiny of human beings is recast ... in which capital reaches its 'absolute' speed, based on machinic components rather than the human component of labour' (Deleuze and Guattari, 2004[1980]: 543); the preface of a book by Serge Daney (Deleuze, 1986). To be sure, the fragmented way of approaching this concept was also caused by Deleuze's objective difficulty to make sense of an evolution in techniques and technologies of government which he was experiencing in-the-making. For instance, see the last, exciting pages of his book on Foucault, where he hints forcefully at a new 'configuration of forces' to come, whilst stressing that we are living exactly the phase of transition towards this new, still undefined diagram of power (Deleuze, 2006[1986]: 175).

> now you were used to move along roads and sidewalks, forget it! From now on we all walk through walls![74]

We have already encountered Badiou's critique of Deleuze and his supposedly a-political ambition to

> separate and dissolve oneself … to be a creator, what Deleuze calls a 'purified automaton', a surface more and more porous to the impersonal modalisation of being.[75]

As Peter Hallward argues, Deleuze's philosophy points to the ultimate task to dissolve 'limitations in order to become a more adequate or immaterial vehicle' to the undifferentiated flow of the virtual.[76] The political vulnerability of such an ascetic vitalism, Žižek maintains, following (and trivialising) Badiou's argument, will become explicit once it has turned, via Deleuze's encounter with Guattari, into a romantic, nomadic activism of becoming.[77] This strategy lacks a 'lever of agential intervention' from which to build the possibility of any resistance, and as a result ends up eventually replicating, rather than contrasting, the 'impersonal modalisation' of control.[78]

As Deleuze himself wrote in the *postscript*, 'the man of control is undulatory, in orbit, in a continuous network. Everywhere surfing has already replaced the older sports'.[79] Is not surfing then the perfect conceptual persona for expressing the compromised self-consumption of the subject of neo-liberallism, an apparently liberating 'going with the flow' that perfectly fits the accelerated ideology of late capitalism and its 'postmodern superego'? Yes, Žižek replies. Premised as it is on the renunciation to 'any attempts to retain control over what goes on, rejecting such efforts as expressions of the modern logic of domination', an ethos of surfing prompts one to '"let oneself go", drift along, while retaining an inner distance and indifference toward the mad dance of the accelerated process'.[80] Indeed 'we may be moving fast 'Alex Williams and Nick Srnicek observe in their critique of Nick Land' but only within a strictly defined set of capitalist parameters that themselves never waver'.[81] Stuck as we are

74 Aviv Kochavi, former commander of the Paratrooper Brigade, Israeli Army, quoted in Weizman, 2007.
75 Badiou, 2000: 196.
76 Hallward, 2006: 2.
77 Žižek, 2004.
78 Noys, 2012: 65.
79 Deleuze, 1992: 6.
80 Žižek, 2005.
81 Williams and Srnicek, 2013.

within waves we cannot challenge, then, is one confined to the resigned task of trying to surf them towards 'libertarian ends'?[82]

In the first chapter I sought to decouple some of the misunderstandings that inform these critiques. Some ambiguities however remain. The problematic convergence between some strands of Deleuzian thought and the smooth and preventing logic of control is undeniable. Solving this impasse is not simply an academic exercise in patrolling Deleuzian orthodoxy. It is more significantly a necessary step towards *the* most pressing ethico-political questions of contemporary critical theory: how to construct 'a political philosophy and practice adequate to the deterritorialising dynamic of global capitalism'?[83] Some further clarifications are thus needed. A brief Chinese detour will help. Taking inspiration from the main target of Žižek's last quote, i.e. the Westernised appropriation of Eastern philosophy (from 'pop-Buddhism' to Taoism), and employing François Jullien's compelling *Treatise on Efficacy*, in the next two sections I qualify how the inoperose 'surfing ethics' I am sketching, whilst avoiding the operational paradigm of action as well as the hubristic search for 'revolutionary' authenticity, at the same time does neither unfold into self-satisfied micro-resistance, nor succumb to the naivety of an already co-opted going with the flow.

2.3

> May I disappear in order that those things that I see may become perfect in their beauty from the very fact that they are no longer things that I see.[84]

In his *Treatise on Efficacy*, subtitled 'between Western and Chinese thinking', François Jullien embarks on a brief and engaging analysis of the Chinese concept of action by drawing on classical texts of Taoism. Taoism, he argues, is an immanent and eminently strategic philosophy, utterly alternative to the operational, project-oriented paradigm of Western action. In one of the most famous instances of Western strategic thinking, von Clausewitz lamented the ultimate impossibility for a theory of warfare to bridge the gap with the actual practice of war. Unfortunately, he complained, a strategy must always enter (and thus be dislocated by) the 'fog of war'.[85] What for Clausewitz is a major concern is a non-problem for Chinese thinkers. Untouched by the projectual anxiety of the 'plan', Chinese strategy is totally immanent to the situation in which it occurs. Theory and practice become one. The fog of war is not an atmospherics dislocating the war-plan. Instead, it is everything that war is about, i.e. a contingent config-

82 A 'compulsion towards liquidity, flow' which is 'the exact replica of the force which rules market value: capital must circulate; gravity and any fixed point must disappear' (Noys, 2012: 7).

83 Sinnerbrink, 2006: 85.

84 Weil, 2002: 42.

85 Jullien, 2004: 14; Clausewitz, 2008[1832].

uration of forces carrying an inherent and 'circumstantial' potential, which is the duty of the strategist to act upon in-the-moment.[86] There is neither determinism nor indeterminacy in this conception. Every situation is understood as an 'objective configuration' in which the *dao* – i.e. 'the natural course of things' – flows, guiding without determining, i.e. tuning the possibilities for action.[87] How these potentials unfold in the actual situation is the task of the good strategist to accurately evaluate, calibrating the action accordingly. Whilst adequate preparation is needed, abstracting 'projectuality' is of no use. As Jullien qualifies, in this 'phenomenology of effectiveness' one does not abstract from a situation in order to decide upon it, but rather seeks to *dissolve* oneself into the flow of things, 'harmonising' immanently with their becoming.[88] What counts is being able to act at the 'stage of pre-actualisation' where reality is more 'malleable' and 'flexible': i.e. acting 'upstream', that is, plugging into the unformatted, plasmatic dimension where the potential of a situation lies, and where vast transformations can be engendered with minimal effort, a *butterfly effect*. As Miguel Benasayag puts it, non-action within this perspective does not mean 'inaction' but rather indicates a way of 'non-acting in response to the accident, non-being in agitation, *non-reacting*, by means of resisting the urge to exercise some power to be'.[89] Action, yet 'freed' from activism and its prefigured objectives, the world is no longer an object *for us*, 'to be acted upon', but a reality in evolution to which we must *conform* through a process which is neither magical nor technical, neither goal-oriented nor chancy, and which 'instead of being willed ... stems from the conditions implied in a situation'.[90]

Jullien is heuristically simplifying Taoism here and, as some noted, also skipping the contemporary Chinese philosophical debate, thus risking to offer a frozen and almost mythical image of 'Chinese alterity'.[91] This is not relevant for the present discussion however, since I am employing Jullien's text (and his version of Taoism) as much heuristically, as a tool to build my own argument. What is relevant, in fact, is the evident similarity between the model of 'action' he is sketching and the one I am proposing. Jullien describes 'acting' as merging with the immanence of a situation in order to unfold its potentialities by 'impinging upon them' as well as, as he puts it, 'swerving from the aim of achieving' them; never 'saturating' an effect (i.e.

86 Jullien, 2004: 22. 'Instead of setting up a goal for our actions, we could allow ourselves to be carried along with the propensity of things ... instead of imposing our plan upon the world, we could rely on the potential inherent in a situation' (16).

87 Daoism or Taoism is a philosophy based on a conception of reality as continuous flow of becoming. Dao, or Tao, means the *way*, i.e. the 'spontaneous' and 'natural course of things', the 'flow of reality' which is the duty of the 'good man' to let unfold.

88 Jullien, 2004: 51.

89 Benasayag, 2005: 15 (my translation).

90 Jullien, 2004: 132.

91 See Billeter, 2006.

the inherent potential of a situation) and rather 'letting it grow', liberating it from its 'goals' and its operational apparatus: 'intending an effect kills it, dries it up, exhausts it'.[92] This seems very consistent with the 'surfing interventionism' I began to sketch above. Yet, two crucial differences should be emphasised, as many misunderstandings into which Deleuze's strategic thinking is often diluted.

First, Jullien understands the potential of a situation as a 'fund of potentiality', 'the undifferentiated basis of all things – which is also the basis of all their virtualities'.[93] Beings are thus denied consistency, insofar as posited as 'sterile' entities emanating from a deeper flux of becoming. Actuality is a limitation that must be overcome, dematerialising oneself to become, just as in Hallward's account of Deleuze's approach, an 'immaterial vehicle' to the undifferentiated flow of the virtual. Second, within this perspective the event disappears, 'dissolved' into 'silent transformations', sublimated into the flow of things.[94] This processual philosophy of becoming understands reality as a smooth, continuous and anti-evental movement into which we are called to conform and dissolve, thus fully justifying Žižek's remarks about the suspicious proximity between Taoism and the ethos of neo-capitalism. The key problem of assuming Taoism as an ethico-political model for the present, in fact, is the innocence of the *dao* on which it is premised, which crucially leads to overlooking the question of ontological production. There is no natural course of thing. Even the climate, as is dramatically evident today, is a socio-political object. Perfectly de-politicised, the Taoist stance instead overlooks the structures, processes and power asymmetries that produce, striate and tilt the 'flow of things', with the result of ending up being vulnerable to them. Something that was strikingly evident already in the sixth century BC.

At that time, Taoism was being co-opted within the authoritarian philosophy of so-called *Legalist* tradition. Legalist thinkers exploited Taoist teachings by taking to the extreme their underlining presuppositions, in order to build a model of despotic authoritarianism aimed at establishing a form of absolute and 'automatic', i.e. self-regulating, control over the population. Han Feizi's 'theory of impersonal sovereignty' is a textbook case of the logic of control. It proposes an absolutely immanent model of government in which the ruler must be depersonalised and de-humanised to the point of 'disappearing' into the flow of things, becoming a 'void without action'.[95] Here, the emptiness of sovereignty is not concealed behind a rhetoric of power, but directly assumed as the empty core of a

92 Jullien, 2004: 109, 122.
93 Jullien, 2004: 92; 'a great fund (of the processivity of things)' (183).
94 Jullien, 2004: 78–9.
95 Jullien, 2004: 30, 101, 151.

system able to 'run smoothly on its own accord', i.e. automatically: a cybernetic apparatus of power organised in

> a completely artificial fashion (it is completely independent from the sentiment of the ruler and rests solely on the norms that are imposed and the control that is exercised) ... [a system expected to] operate *on its own.*[96]

The ruler is like a ghost, 'as a perfect manipulator, he is dissolved within his manipulation'.[97] This theory of political manipulation, grounded on the 'reduction of all others to passivity ... as pure automatons', is a configuration aimed at defusing the eventful potentiality of being-together, 'manipulat[ing] the situation so as to influence one's adversary indirectly, progressively getting him to move in a particular direction'.[98]

Here at play we may see all the elements discussed above: a system of power which is self-justified by its own internal regularity, keeping alive a smooth and frictionless movement which does not offer anything tangible to oppose, 'defusing antagonism', 'disarticulating solidarity' and dissolving the 'possibility of event' according to a preventive logic in which *anticipation* supplants projection.[99] The recuperation of Taoism within the oppressive model of legalism mirrors the recuperation of naive vitalism within the oppressive model of control. In fact, *neotaoism* is the definition Tiqqun uses: an immanent and centre-less configuration of power, a *'mastery without masters'* thriving onto a global, deterritorialised and smooth space where it operates without friction.[100]

Equally telling is the counter-strategy Taoist thinkers envisaged against legalism. As ante-litteram accelerationists, Taoist thinkers suggested to let the tyrant follow 'his own inclinations and sink to the extremes', until self-destruction: liberation would not come through revolt, but from the 'self-regulation of reality'.[101] Yet conformation risks becoming conformism. The faithful reliance on the self-regulation of reality and the implicit assumption of its divine neutrality prefigure an endlessly postponed wait for the miraculous event of liberation, nothing but a-political inertia stuck within the horizon of a power-structured reality. *Never believe the smooth would suffice to save us.* Vitalistic accelerationism, horizontal relationalism

96 Jullien, 2004: 100–2.
97 Han Feizi quoted in Jullien, 2004: 164.
98 Jullien, 2004: 151–2, 168.
99 Jullien, 2004: 149, 173, 192.
100 Tiqqun, 2010: 152, 165.
101 Jullien, 2004: 118. This is the kind of accelerationism today often referred to as right-wing, as opposed to the left-wing brand coined by Alex Williams and Nick Srnicek. The former may be encapsulated in Noys' concise formula: 'if capitalism generates its own forces of dissolution then the necessity is to radicalise capitalism itself: the worse the better' (Noys, 2012: 5).

and Taoist ascesis eventually share the same 'lack of depth' that, we have already seen that 'assemblage urbanism' at times betrays: they are too *superficial.* They do overcome transcendent dichotomies, only to remain stuck to a flat and seamless ontological surface, at every point coinciding with the relational immanence of control. How is the verticality of 'heights' and 'depths' to be overcome without getting stranded on the horizontal closure of 'surfaces'?[102] A transcendental sensibility is required, one that does not take refuge into transcendent solution, avoids remaining stuck in the quicksand of the situation, and rather explores its conditions of possibility, where the eventful potential for its reconfiguration lies, that is, where spatial justice resides, as 'a position of reorientation from within' a given tuning, premised on the excessive lines of flight every situation harbours.[103]

A qualification is required. The approach developed so far, informed by a firm intention to de-centre the human-world correlation, betrays a sensibility that resonates with OOO's ethical injunction not to objectify objects, that is, to do 'justice to a world where objects are always more than they literally state'.[104] With respect to OOO's 'nomadic claustrophobia', however, my approach also decidedly gestures towards a constructive aperture to the notion of event, as encapsulated in Deleuze's famous injunction to be 'faithful to' and 'worthy of' the event, in the sense of being faithful to a world which is ultimately *not* 'for us'.[105] This is not, to be sure, a fideistic predisposition, but rather an ethical strategy, which rests on inhuman speculation, post-human embodiment, and a constructive and collective use of abstraction. Three notions that, I believe, are implicit in Deleuze's suggestion that an event must be *understood, willed* and *represented.* Following and perverting this suggestion, I unpack this strategy in the next section.

102 In the afterword to the Italian edition of the *Logique du Sens*, Deleuze writes: '*Difference and Repetition* still aspired to a sort of classical heights and even to an archaic depth … intensity was presented as coming from depth … In the *Logic of Sense* the novelty for me consisted in learning something about surfaces … [then, with Felix Guattari] I believe we looked for other directions since we wanted to do so. The Anti-Oedipus has neither heights nor depth, nor surfaces. There everything happens … intensities, multiplicities, events, in a sort of spherical body … a body without organs' (Deleuze, 2007: 294) (my translation).

103 Philippopoulos-Mihalopoulos, 2015: 195.

104 Harman, 2007: 212. 'I desire an ontology capable of doing justice to these strange nonhuman actors, capable of respecting these strange strangers on their own terms' (Bryant, 2011: 248).

105 As in Harman's ontology of 'being without event' touched upon in the first chapter. The subject of OOO, Masciandaro argues, 'appears to surf an exciting wave between terror and freedom that flows upon the sea of an endless *within,* dancing to gnostic jazz in a mood of mobile, nomadic claustrophobia' (Masciandaro, 2012b: 255).

> **3.1** There are instants that last no longer than five or six seconds, in which all of a sudden you hear the presence of eternal harmony, and in which you have reached it. It is not earthly. But I do not want to say that it is heavenly either; only that in his earthly form man is incapable of tolerating it. He must either be physically transformed or die.[106]

Understanding. The stoic sage '*understands the pure event* in its eternal truth, independently of its spatio-temporal actualisation'.[107] Not to be 'unworthy of what happens to us' means to be faithful to a world not for us, a world never fully reducible to the relations we trace.[108] It is an inhuman speculation: overcoming the limits of human knowing (i.e. *my* incapacity to know) and human sensing (i.e. *my* incapacity to escape the phenomenological circle), without however abdicating to knowledge, without dissolving into a post-human sensoriality, but rather opening 'to the inhuman and the superhuman durations ... beyond the human condition', the inhuman becomings that escape our phenomenological sentimentality and exactly for this reason are the condition of possibility for our own becoming.[109] The Anthropocene may be read exactly as such: an event that unfolds the openness and permeability of the human to cosmic and geological durations, exposing us to 'questions, powers, problems that are not of our own choosing, that affect us not as doers or performers but as barely adequate witnesses.'[110]

This is not a redeeming, restoring or healing *understanding*, but rather one that is 'destructive of the anthropomorphic sense we make of things', that is, of any attempt to 'make sense' of the post-human condition by resorting to the comforting images of a 'common (post)humanity'.[111] This is an ethical position which Meillassoux seeks to grasp, as a shift from the human *I don't know* to the inhuman knowledge of the real content of the real:

> transform our perspective on unreason, stop construing it as the form of our deficient grasp of the world and turn it into the veridical content of the world as such – we must project unreason into things themselves.[112]

This world constitutively 'without-reason' cannot be embraced by a common (human or post-human) gaze. It requires instead the cosmic

106 Kimura Bin, quoted in Agamben, 2000b: 127.
107 Deleuze, 2004[1969]: 146.
108 Deleuze, 2004[1969]: 149.
109 Deleuze, 1991a: 28.
110 Colebrook, 2014b: 48.
111 Colebrook, 2014a: 225.
112 Meillassoux, 2009: 82.

appreciation (rather than personal realisation) of the indifference of the world to our inescapable placed-ness in it, a world absolutely not for us, non-disposable, non-appropriable and non-juridifiable. From this inhuman gaze the earth does not appear as an 'exotic blue marble', but nothing more than 'a fractal clump'.[113]

Negarestani delineates the impasse of anti-humanist (post-human) thinking in the inability to escape the conservative horizon in which capitalism thrives, wherein any notion of excess risks being recaptured within a closed horizon of post-political calculation for the sake of conservation, because of 'capitalism's restless assimilation of every form of negativity so as to reintegrate it as another mode or style of life'.[114] Instead, he continues,

> being genuinely terrestrial demands presupposing the death and pure contingency of the Earth in each and every equation, thought, feat of creativity and political intervention. Earthly thought embraces perishability (i.e. cosmic contingency) as its immanent core.[115]

For some, this would mean nothing but a political standstill. If nothing has meaning, why bother? Yet it is exactly such an appreciation that releases the potential for an emancipatory and constructive politics: 'the poverty of our future is not a poverty of the future', as Bratton affirms.[116] Therefore the brutal materialisation of the truth of extinction actually becomes a potential for a novel vista into the real.[117] This means thinking the earth as radically external to 'us', that is, to our self-production, meaning, environment, projectuality, affect, life, embodiment and thinking the future as not our future but the future of something else, in which the human may disappear. Alien to this attitude are the hope of *égaliberté* and the promise of *differential space*. Instead, accepting, the contingent and senseless nature of the world would function as a cure against the 'hypocritical … impulse to "make the world a better place"', prompting us to strategically 'embrace dereliction, which is the only real way the world is actually improved'.[118]

Justice is accordingly here and now, not as a given condition but an ever-present, cosmic potential that requires a transcendental sensibility to be attuned to, and a strategic praxis to be turned into a constructive retuning of the situation itself. Justice is what does not belong to anyone, and yet can only be found in this world, not a yearning for a beyond, but a yearning for

113 Negarestani, 2010: 3.
114 Negarestani, 2011a: 196.
115 Negarestani, 2010: 7.
116 Bratton, 2013.
117 Of course this is not to say that these concepts are chronologically 'new'. New is their geological and cosmic unfolding.
118 Masciandaro, 2012a.

a now-here beyond appropriation: 'not a hope *for* anything, nor a hope *of* any value, but a hope *in* the immanent truth of its own situation'.[119]

3.2 The human beauty we're talking about here is beauty of a particular type; it might be called kinetic beauty. Its power and appeal are universal. It has nothing to do with sex or cultural norms. What it seems to have to do with, really, is human beings' reconciliation with the fact of having a body.[120]

Willing. Speculatively occupying the inhuman point of view of the event is only one step. The event must be willed. 'The sage also *wills the embodiment* and the actualisation of the pure incorporeal event in a state of affairs and in his or her body and flesh'.[121] A truly ethical stance entails not simply accepting, but responsibly willing one's singular positioning within an assemblage. This is the ethical, not moral, responsibility of 'being worthy of the event'. The surfer is the conceptual persona that expresses the will to 'give a body' to the event. Ontologically unable to transcend it, a surfer must stay in the water. 'Forced to coordinate one's body with other modi', he does not simply relinquish through spontaneous, reckless and naive affirmation to the smoothness of the sea, but rather rides through its materiality, always retaining a singular potency to swerve, with style.[122] Surfing is inconsistent with a politics of a-critical affirmation: not the one who joyfully utters YES to what occurs (acceleration bound to manipulation, 'empty enjoyment' fitting capitalist production of *juissance*, passive conformism), the surfer is the one that 'knows how to say "no"', the one who selects, able to detect and 'ride' the excesses, blind spots and contradictions that every system of power produces, exploiting the conflictual intensity that palpitates in the cracks and fault lines wrinkling the apparent smoothness of control.[123]

There is, in this praxis, no anxious demand for a negativity which would provide a 'lever for agential intervention', neither the hubristic *grandeur* of a revolutionary subject emerging *ex nihilo*. From this dense ontology

119 Masciandaro, 2012a.
120 Foster Wallace, 2006.
121 Deleuze, 2004[1969]: 146.
122 Once the operation is de-activated, it is the inoperose core of every action to unfold, i.e. what 'is on every act as a "style", almost the counter-force which, in the creation, resists to the creation and undoes it' (Agamben, 2009d: 14 (my translation)).
123 Deleuze, 1983: 108–13; Nunes, 2010: 121, 123. Brassier emphasises the role of reason by which 'the purposelessness of becoming would become intelligible as the enabling condition of action … this would be the rationalist alternative to Nietzsche's irrationalist solution, which is simply to affirm, rather than understand, the senselessness of becoming' (2015: 219). I argue that this is exactly the qualitative advancement of Deleuze's *selection* vis-à-vis Nietzsche's *affirmation*.

no-body can 'exit'. This would be just escapism. As a 'genuinely terrestrial' being, the surfer knows that 'staying with the earth is the means of not remaining stuck on it', and thus 'experiences rather than flees the earth … passes through by remaining with it': *voyage in place*.[124] There is no passivity or renunciation, no entrapment or suffocation. Willing one's own singular positioning is the Spinozan freedom *as* responsibility, the freedom to accept one's position within an assemblage, dismantling freedom by liberating the multiple, collective freedoms lying beneath.

Neither passive nor impassive, to surf means to be 'passable', not passively 'accepting a situation', but rather engaging in a constructive complicity with materials one cannot objectify, as a mere body among other bodies in a world ultimately independent from one's involvement. Surfing the waves, climbing the rocks. Antoine Hennion describes the activity of climbing as the encounter between – as well as a 'double erasure' of – the climbing body and the rock. Their 'separation' disappears in the 'zone of contact' in which the activity of climbing unfolds, through *gestures* which are no longer precisely ascribable to specific bodies.[125] For the climbing to occur it is necessary to experiment with the rock, 'in and through contact', yet this 'in no way does … signal a reduction to the here and now of the situation'.[126] The rock is 'a reservoir of differences' whose relation to the climber's body in no way exhausts it. Gestures are *counter-effectuations* which 'free' the climbing from its reduction to a phenomenological relation (or, worst, from its abstraction into a mere 'social construction'), and at the same time connect this here-and-now to other locales, overflowing abstractions and floating potentialities.

'The free man – Deleuze writes – is the one who caught the event itself, he doesn't allow the event to effectuate as such without "operating" in it, as an actor, its counter-effectuation'.[127] The quintessential task here is that of 'freeing' the situation from its 'state of affair', rupturing its tuning and releasing the possibility for a novel configuration, by counter-effectuating the potential thus unleashed into the constructive task of retuning. It is exactly this notion of counter-effectuation, Toscano observes, that allows for 'transforming Badiou's ascetic image [of Deleuze's concept] of the "purified automaton" into a constructivist one'.[128]

The surfer knows how to do justice to the sea just as the climber knows how to do justice to the rock. They neither transcend nor slide over, but rather inhabit the problematic field of a situation that cannot be escaped via transcendental ascesis, overcome via mad or authentic decisions, or

124 Masciandaro, 2010: 28.
125 Hennion, 2007.
126 Hennion, 2007: 101.
127 Deleuze, 2004[1969]: 136.
128 Toscano, 2000: 238.

simply solved and fixed through appropriate operations. The postmodern hubristic caricature does not hold here: every surfer knows that surfing is an 'art of dosages, since overdose is a danger'.[129] No 'wildly de-stratifying', no 'going underground' to flee the smooth spaces of control,[130] deactivation means perforation: a strategy of opening 'positive voids' in the urban texture, i.e. voids devoid of any negativist/nihilistic hubris, which allow for incorporating a non-negative negativity into a constructive approach.[131]

There is no seamless relationalism, but a *holey space*, which 'communicates' with the striated and the smooth, and yet exceeds them both, simultaneously dismantling the striating logic of sovereignty and the smooth logic of control.[132] If there is no normative prescription in this understanding, there is no anti-normative stance either. This approach neither deontologically indicates what ought to be done, nor simply leaves the stage to the spontaneity of the assemblage. Instead it actively *undoes*: the space cleared by unplugging its power relations, however, is not a space free of power relations, but rather a space of released conflict (a space of justice) in which a contested retuning must be responsibly carried out, one whose desirability cannot be guaranteed in advance, but rather assessed at every step. This is where the role of law becomes explicit.

3.3 This is what attracted me, a transitory imbalance between the traits, this unpredictable dimple in the homogenous surface.[133]

Representing. That events that must be represented may sound contradictory vis-à-vis a philosophy so explicitly nurtured by the task if challenging the notion of representation. However, the simple critique of representation is merely the critique of one correlation (representation) in the name of a more original (e.g. non-representational, post-human etc.) one.[134] An ethics of surfing, it should be clear, is not meant to champion a *return to*

129 Deleuze and Guattari, 2004[1980]: 162. There is a whole part of Deleuzoguattarian thought, often forgotten by their imprudent followers, dedicated to the themes of caution and sobriety (e.g. 7, 109, 116, 179, 308, 379).

130 'Now that States are able to create a smooth space of surveillance and global military intervention. Holey spaces have flourished for the only way to escape the spying eyes of State intelligence is to go underground' (Bonta and Protevi, 2004: 95).

131 *Contra* Noys, 2012: 53–60.

132 Deleuze and Guattari, 2004[1980]: 415. With the enigmatic notion of holey space, Deleuze and Guattari perform a 'perforating' appropriation of the Nietzschean geophilosophical cry of being true-to-the-earth, in the sense offered by Negarestani's own re-appropriation of the term, as an injunction to be true-to-the-universe (Negarestani, 2011b).

133 de Carlo, 1981: 121 (my translation).

134 Meillassoux, 2009.

body, sensoriality and more generally 'the concrete' as opposed to the cold forms of abstraction.

> This compulsion towards liquidity, flow, and an accelerated circulation of what is physics, sexual, or pertaining to the body is the exact replica of the force which rules market value; capital must circulate; gravity and any fixed point must disappear.[135]

Williams and Srnicek recently called for an alternative understanding of the notion of universal. This is not a homogenising and generalising totalisation, but rather

> an empty placeholder that hegemonic particulars (specific demands, ideals and collectives) come to occupy. It can operate as a subversive and emancipatory vector of change with respect to established universalisms, and it is heterogeneous and includes differences, rather than eliminating them.[136]

This resonates with Spinoza's understanding of *common notions* that, differently from classical conceptions of universality, point towards a strategic understanding of generality. In Merrifield's words, they 'are general rather than abstract, general in their practical and contextual applicability'.[137] This is the sense in which I propose to *use* law, by making it inoperose and thus turning it, from an ingesting exceptional machine, into an open structure. Using legal abstractions against their own determining, homogenising and preventing operation is a way to enact contingency, heterogeneity and eventfulness. This is a way, I argue, to avoid the perils that Williams and Srnicek refer to as the fetishism of 'direct action', and its consequent resigning to piecemeal attempts at carving temporary comfort-zones of 'radicalist' self-fulfilment. Instead, what is envisaged is a 'localised' political strategy that 'acts on the potentials of this actual' as well as on the 'abstraction of this real', simultaneously oriented to what is 'non-local, abstract, and rooted deep in our everyday infrastructure'.[138]

Representation may become an ally vis-à-vis this strategy, if appropriately used. Although the event by definition cannot be represented, representation may provide a vehicle in order for the event to be expressed, to 'liberate' the event by 'averting its sclerosis':

> representation envelops the event in another nature, it envelops at its borders, it stretches until this point, and it brings about this lining or

135 Baudrillard, 1987: 25.
136 Williams and Srnicek, 2016.
137 Merrifield, 2013: 33.
138 Williams and Srnicek, 2013.

> hem. This is the operation which defines living usage, to the extent that representation, when it does not reach this point, remains only a dead letter confronting that which it represents, and stupid in its representativeness.[139]

'There is a "use" of representation – Deleuze writes – without which representation would remain lifeless and senseless', without which its functioning is reduced to sclerotising the real. The 'sense' of representation, accordingly, is use, as Wittgenstein would say, yet

> such use is not defined through a function of representation in relation to the represented, not even through representativeness as in the form of possibility ... use is in the relation between representation and something extra-representative.[140]

What this suggests then is a strategy that uses representation to unfold the event it envelops, an open structure that makes space for the event to occur, by deactivating the exceptional operation of representation itself, an inoperose use of representation, that is, that opens it up to its extra-representative event. Could we in this sense suggest a strategy that *uses* law, by making it inoperose, in this way opening it to something extra-juridical, namely: the event of spatial justice?

Santiago Cirugeda is a self-defined *social architect* whose projects often involve spatial explorations in the city and engagement with its spatiolegal mechanisms. In Seville, for the project *Scaffolding*, he covered a wall with graffiti and then sued himself so as to be able to install a temporary scaffolding on the street, which then became for several months a new (abusive) room for the adjacent house. Deactivating legal abstractions from their operations (the exclusionary repression of the anti-graffiti law, the separating delegation of litigation), he showed how their residual power may be reoriented to generate alternative assemblages of urban bodies, digging positive voids for action within the urban itself.

In Vigo, for the project *Alegal Benches*, he set up six benches in a residual patch of ground of a peripheral neighbourhood. The authorities first reacted negatively, because the lack of authorisation, yet subsequently cleaned the patch and provided it with public illumination.[141] By positioning himself in the 'alegal' threshold, again, Cirugeda disoriented the

139 Deleuze, 2004[1969]: 146.
140 Deleuze, 2004[1969]: 146.
141 Cirugeda's project can be explored on his website: www.recetasurbanas.net

spatiolegal apparatus, forcing it to reorient towards urban bodies lying beyond its appropriating operations. These are minor examples of course, and yet interesting for their paradigmatic value. Philippopoulos-Mihalopoulos writes that the mission of a truly radical right to the city should be 'to dig holes in the urban texture and to make the city ... a "holey space with holes"'.[142] Cirugeda's works likewise expose a simultaneously abstract and concrete, vermicular way of acting within and without the law, by 'exploiting the loopholes and legal voids in city planning legislation', perforating the membrane of its spatiolegal apparatus of exception, detecting and exploiting frictions between the legal abstractions and the physical landscape in which they are inscribed, and in this way indicating the eventful potential for other, 'inoperose uses' of spaces, objects and laws, which reside in any urban assemblage.[143]

3.4 Justice without law is not the negation of the law, but the realization and fulfillment, the pleroma, of the law.[144]

The possibility of simply *using* things beyond any possession was at the core of the thought of St Francis of Assisi. Convinced of the need to overcome the conception of man as *dominus sui actus* (i.e. proprietor of his own actions), which he saw as an original sin, St Francis proposed a notion of life in 'absolute poverty' (*altissima povertà*). Not simply a life *in* poverty, but a life in *non-proprietary* relation with the world and its objects.[145] Unsurprisingly the Church was not enthusiastic about the idea, and was worried about the destabilising potential it might have on its vast possessions. Facing the Church's mounting pressure, Franciscan theologians thus introduced the notion of *usus facti* (factual use), seeking to carve a space of action 'outside' of the grasp of law's proprietary mechanism. The factual use of things indicates a series of acts (e.g. a minimum amount of eating, drinking, wearing clothes) supposedly without juridical implications. Use in this conception is defined *negatively*, as a dimension of 'life and human praxis absolutely outside the determinations of law' and its proprietary mechanism.[146] Any quest for exhuming a dimension of (bare) life or praxis 'outside' of law, however, implicitly confirms the very presupposition (the separation of law and life) on which the legal mechanism of exception rests. It is a contradictory strategy bound to be eventually re-appropriated.[147]

142 Philippopoulos-Mihalopoulos, 2012b: 131.
143 MAS Context, 2012.
144 Agamben, 2005b: 107.
145 Agamben, 2011a: 171 (my translation).
146 Agamben, 2011a: 137 (my translation).
147 '[T]he factual character of use is not sufficient to warrant an exteriority with respect to law, since every fact can be transformed into usus' (Agamben, 2011a: 170) (my translation).

The Franciscan nemesis, Pope John XXII, did lucidly address the source of this contradiction: the condition of possibility for *using* a thing is to possess it, he argued, since any use *necessarily* implies a 'proprietary subject', and thus any non-proprietary use is, simply, impossible.[148] In fact, by defining a notion of use understood as 'a series of operations performed by a subject', the Franciscans themselves had reasserted the notion of *dominus sui actus* their founder intended to challenge in the first place. As an *ante-litteram* Kant, the Pope thus reframed the notion of use into a *de jure* problem, postulating that the reality of any object is exhausted into its proprietary correlation with a subject: an object can only be an object *for us*. The impossibility of using an 'object', i.e. its systematic reduction to (proprietary) relations, sanctions the impossibility to 'do justice' to it. The complicity of relationalism with capitalism finds here a correlationist archetype: as Agamben observes, capitalism thrives on conceiving any non-proprietary use as impossible, that is, in reducing every use to consumption or ab-use.[149] The importance of this question cannot be overstated: to emancipate life from law into a plane of pure (bare) praxis equates exposing life to the realm of control – which is, arguably, the contradiction the 'Franciscan' attempt of Hardt and Negri falls into.[150]

Yet as we saw, an alternative non-negative conception of use was already encapsulated in St Francis' message: not a praxis outside of law's reach (a *usus facti*), but rather one able to put the very notions of subject, object and praxis into question. A key dispositif in this strategy was a peculiar and eminently 'legal' apparatus, the Franciscan '*regola*' (i.e. rule). The *regola* was centred on the St Francis' dictum: *vivere secundum formam sancti Vangeli* (to live according to the form of the Holy Gospels). In this sense it was not meant to be a set of rules to be followed, but a paradigmatic model – the life of Jesus – to be differentially repeated, i.e. embodied, or 'willed', into a style of living: not a matter of 'applying a norm to a life, but rather of *living* according to that form'.[151] It did not function through the logic of the norm, but that of the model.

The exceptional logic of the norm is based on a given sameness to which legal subjects must constantly approximate. They *ought* to respect a law, a compliance enforced by surveillance and control, judgement and punishment, expectations and reward. Qualitatively different is the logic of the 'model'. As Sutter explains,

148 As stated in the pontifical bull *Ad Conditorem Canonum*, where the Pope argued that a use without possession would be an 'act in becoming', as such different from being, therefore equal to non-being, and thus non-existent (Agamben, 2011a: 159–61) (my translation).

149 Agamben, 2000a.

150 St Francis is the one who 'pos[es] against the misery of power the joy of being', the bare joy of the multitude. Hardt and Negri, 2001: 413.

151 Agamben, 2011a: 124 (my translation).

> every rule requires, in absolute terms, its observance (or the penalty of sanction for inobservance); while each model demands, in its own way, its betrayal (or the penalty of ridicule for imitation).[152]

As example of the latter Sutter mentions the *kare-sansui*, the sand and rock garden in Kyoto's Ryoan-ji temple. This 'simple assemblage of gravels and rocks, not representing anything other than itself', provides a minimal set of elements, whose potentially infinite variation will always betray and yet never deny the open structure of the garden itself.[153] The highly normative Western art of gardening is based on the constant judgement between a here-and-now and an ideal sameness to which the garden ought to approximate, according to the logic of obligation, control and sanction. The Japanese art of gardening instead relies on a differential model that does not entail an always incomplete (guilty) reiteration but an always-new repetition, not a matter of abstract (exceptional) compliance but of embodied, stylistic variation.

This is how the *regola* functions, by opening a paradoxical space of non-law within law, which does not abandon law but rather profanates its operation and thus releases the possibility of it being *used,* that is, put in relation 'with something extra-juridical'. Agamben defines profanation as the strategy according to which

> something – a power, a function, a human operation – is made inoperose without being simply destroyed, but rather freeing the potentialities that there remained non-actualised, in this way allowing a different use of them.[154]

This is a strategy that digs a void within law, by reorienting it towards a world *not for law,* that is, towards the very event of its encounter with a non-juridifiable world from which law is 'inseparable' nonetheless. It is neither pursued technically *with* law by seeking to remedy the problems once and for all, nor mystically, madly or pragmatically *without* law: the releasing of spatial justice is here pursued as *without* law.

The scene takes place in the 'food department' of an upmarket department store in Sydney. Eating at a 'common table', Gassan Hage notes an old woman who sits down and begins 'to mark a space of her own', placing

152 de Sutter, 2012.
153 de Sutter, 2012.
154 Agamben, 2013: 345 (my translation).

serviette, food and cutlery on the table.[155] To his surprise, soon after the woman abruptly addresses him saying, 'do you mind putting your hand on your mouth when you cough'? Hage is unnerved, finding the woman's complaint 'unpleasant', disproportionately 'aggressive' and even, on a second thought, racist. After a quick hesitation he resorts to counter-attack: 'look, if you are old and lonely, there must be better ways of socializing'. A few seconds pass. The woman begins to quietly sob. The people at the table look at Hage with reproach. Uncomfortable and embarrassed, finding 'unbearable' the suffocating normative atmosphere of the common table, he gets up and leaves.

The common table is typical of a certain contemporary aesthetics. Designed to stage a sense of communality, this often remains played out simply at a superficial level: people *share* a common space without actually eating *in common*. As such, the common table makes explicit the inherent tension between the urge to be in a community and the danger that such a common entails for the co-immunity of the individuals. Here, 'protection' from an explicitly engineered commonality is sought by means of legal abstractions (e.g. one's right to be left alone) and relative practices of territorialisation. At the common table, every human being is an island, projecting a legal subjectivity on an assemblage of objects, postures, protocols and mutual assumptions, through which being in public is performed whilst the expectations about one's right to be left alone remain intact. At the table, the other materialises on our radar, for the most part, only as the potential carrier of polluting atmospherics. 'The law creates a relationality between people', Hage observes, 'a relationality of subjects who have been abstracted from their particularity'. As a result, it 'always seems to stage a tension between the libidinal and the abstract, the particular and the universal, dimensions of people'. At the common table, this tension is played out between one's sensual, bodily enjoyment of food and the protection, 'from one's own libidinality as well as the libidinality of others', granted by the abstract legal self. Yet, are immunity and protection necessarily reactive? Is law necessarily opposed, negatively, to the bodily, the sensorial, the libidinal? Sacher Masoch would certainly disagree.

Hage sees the old woman as 'an unreflexive enactor of an alienated form of seriality: happy with her individuality, happy with her sovereignty that can afford her the space of a serviette on a public table, happy to protect the sanctity of her abstract self in the face of the cough/libidinality of the other'. Happiness here is only in the negative form. Namely, what results from the successful self-immunisation from a sociality that, it is implied, is somewhat more genuine and real than the one the woman is enjoying within the sanctity of her abstract self. Yet, could not the woman also be

155 Hage, 2013. All the quotes in this section, unless specified, are from this piece. This is a reworked version of a discussion I made in Pavoni, 2017b.

happy to libidinously enjoy the cosy comfort that the right to be left alone provides her whilst being-in-common with others? Should not her pleasure be understood as simultaneously abstract and concrete, rational and sensual, rather than *a priori* 'alienated' from a more authentic sociality?

According to Hage, the woman is seeking to reassert her immunity as a legal persona from the libidinal and literally infecting promiscuity of the situation, by claiming her abstract 'right not to be coughed at'. Yet, he continues, there is maybe more that this gesture conceals. Perhaps hers is an attempt to breach the atomised sociality of the table: a sort of 'perverse gift', offering the others the possibility for another form of sociality, that is, an ambivalent 'offering made with the only shareable means of relationality left to her, taken from the space of legality: the assertion of her entitlement to be free of bodily relationality'. In the sterilised alienation of public life, the reassertion of one's entitlement *to be left alone* paradoxically becomes a tool to affect and be affected (i.e. not to be left alone) by others: 'telling you "don't interact with me" is the only thing left for me to offer as a means to interact with you and squeeze a bit of sociality from such a sociality-free situation'. Stuck within this alienated space, the woman resorted to challenge alienation paradoxically using the very device (the right to be left alone) that was constitutive of it in the first place. As 'an unhappy and desperate strategist', Hage continues, she was trying to express 'a desire for sociality in a space where sociality was at its minimum'. In this sense, she was 'perhaps the radical one on the table, unaccepting of existing forms of un-sociality and still hoping for the possibility for some other form of relationality'.

Hage has a significant intuition, when emphasising the woman's strategic *use* of abstraction. The way she turns her right to be left alone against itself, she turns it into a tool to reassert a contradictory hope *not to be left alone*. Yet, in the light of what has been written so far, we may suggest a different understanding of the 'radicalism' of the woman's gesture.

What the woman shakes with her sudden demand is not simply Hage's personal space, nor the supposed dichotomy between social and unsocial space, but rather the post-conflictual atmosphere of systematic de-responsibilisation of control societies. By doing so, the woman exposes her vulnerability, an emotionally demanding effort, as her subsequent burst into sobbing testifies. As Philippopoulos-Mihalopoulos reminds, 'a particular kind of courage is needed to leave behind one's bubble of comfort, however defined'.[156] This is where her 'perverse' way to deal with the atomism of legal immunisation lies: not in denying the immunitary notion of legal persona for the sake of a non-conflictual opening to a sociality of reciprocity and exchange. The public is not a homogenous and authentic 'social' space lying beneath alienation, but a heterogeneous space always tilted by power

156 Philippopoulos-Mihalopoulos, 2016: 162.

relations and normative asymmetries, and as such always conflictual. This is what the woman's gesture suggests, by *using* the abstraction of legal persona beyond (i.e. by deactivating) its mechanism of de-responsibilisation: that is, by *profanating* it. A necessary, though insufficient step, to generate an alternative a retuning: the deactivation of the separating legal atmosphere of 'vertical' delegation, and the use of the legal abstraction (the right not to be left alone) to (responsibly) unfold the conflictual substance of the common being-together: its spatial justice. Not a way to 'snatch a bit of optimism within society's cruelty', this was rather a 'pessimistic' affirmation of conflict as the inescapable 'reality' of being-together.

3.5 To learn more and more how to see what is necessary in things as what is beautiful in them –- thus I will be one of those who make things beautiful.[157]

Whiteout is a weather condition which always occurs in the *middle*. An exceptional fog, low clouds, a snowstorm and a three-dimensional whiteness dematerialise bodies into a dense continuum, plunging them into the tactile materiality of a vortex.[158] Prior to 'what is to be done', the whiteout prompts the question: 'what has been undone'? To be temporarily dismantled is the anthropological machine of exception: separation, recognition, possession: all these operations are deactivated, and seeking to reassert control over them only produces more disorientation, dizziness, nausea.[159] Yet, as Sapienza reminds us, the nausea we experience in the middle of the whiteout is 'the sign that we are fraught with becoming'.[160] Here phenomenological experience wedded to transcendental speculation, as the 'felt absence' of our coordinating apparatus, is not in fact an emptiness to be filled by revolutionary subjects or mad decisions, not the nothingness of a non-being but a fullness: the consequent blindness is an obscurity that the excess of light provokes.[161] Liu Bolin, artist of environmental camouflage, expresses precisely this condition:

157 Nietzsche, 2001[1882]: 157.

158 The whiteout is 'a condition of diffuse light when no shadows are cast, due to a continuous white cloud layer appearing to merge with the white snow surface. No surface irregularities of the snow are visible, but a dark object may be clearly seen. There is no visible horizon', retrieved from http://en.wikipedia.org/wiki/Whiteout_(weather)

159 'The traumatic force catches up and, as it were, shakes the ego down from the high tree or the tower. This is described as a frightening whirlwind, ending in the complete dissolution of connexions and a terrible vertigo, until finally the ability, or even the attempt, to resist the force is given up as hopeless, and the function of self-preservation declares itself bankrupt' (Ferenczi, 1994: 222–3).

160 Sapienza, 2011: 32 (my translation).

161 Ronchi, 2011: 14.

> Instead of saying that I simply disappear into the background, it would be better to say that the environment has engulfed me and that I cannot afford to choose to be either active or passive.[162]

Evidently there is no place here for joyful affirmation, nihilistic negation, reactionary escape, revolutionary overcoming, authentic decision, technical solution: all different ways to deny the whiteout, or to get lost forever in its sweeping turmoil. Like the sudden explosion of an aeroplane window, the whiteout signals the turbulent encounter with a radical exteriority which, however, is not a transcendent outside, but rather the transcendental, 'vaporous region' that keeps the situation alive, the 'real' condition of possibility of our being-there. The whiteout is experienced as an overwhelming condition only from the coordinates of the situation that is being ruptured, whilst it simultaneously indicates the only 'way out' as being unavoidably 'within', that is, a constructive and collective task of retuning.

The composer John Cage was extremely interested in the *kare-sansui*. In this ordered composition of sand and rocks he saw the potential of the model as an open structure able to profane the normative logic of rhythm so as to unleash the contingency of sound. His strategy accordingly involved generating and traversing sonorous whiteouts through 'de-familiarising techniques', that is techniques aimed at deactivating the (Western) normativity of authoring, composing and producing music. This did not entail a simple withdrawal from the position of producer. Refusing to control sounds did not imply abandonment to non-control, but the construction of an apparatus (the model) through which the unlearning normativity could be enacted, and the irruption of 'unruly' chance unleashed. As Mohaghegh and Golestaneh put it,

> the composer here neither resists the unrest of this sensorial chasm nor asserts himself with the hegemony of an outside agent, no longer anchored by the tyranny of presence through which he might intrude as an autonomous, knowing subject, but rather assumes the status of a trigger, a catalyst, that which clears space for the infiltration of sound's unruly wilting.[163]

In the manner of a post-structural Franciscan, John Cage suggests that 'no one loses nothing because nothing is securely possessed'.[164] No longer

162 Liu Bolin, quoted in Mattei, 2013.
163 Mohaghegh and Golestaneh, 2011: 490.
164 Cage, 1969: 108.

'possessing' and 'producing' sounds, one would simply resort to *use* them. Beyond the revelatory critique, anarchic dismissal and faithful observance of law, there lies the possibility of its profanation.

3.6 How is it possible to dismantle this infernal hegemony without eradicating it?[165]

Neither complying *with* the excepting machine of law, nor having done with law, at the threshold of this seemingly unavoidable alternative is the inseparable contiguity of law and justice: the legal whiteout is *the necessary (yet insufficient) condition for the unfolding of justice*: the *place* of a law which refuses to be completed through the relentless actualisation of its potentialities into a given state of affairs. It is the place in which law is opened to the 'geo-legal' fact of a non-juridifiable world, from which it is 'inseparable' nonetheless. This signals the beginning of a new legal modesty.

The whiteout in fact indicates the aperture in which we are called to responsibly, ethically and creatively counter-effectuate, by entering in relation with other objects as objects amongst them, building necessarily common, more abstract and more concrete ways of being-together, not simply for the sake of mutual synchronisation, but to avert further closures, so as to keep each situation open to the immanent presence of its justice.[166] To 'whiteout' law means to make law inoperose, not eliminating law and its potentialities, but rather the purposes and modalities in which it is inscribed.[167] Thus repurposed, law is 'forced' to acknowledge its 'complicity with anonymous materials' which are independent of its juridification, and that it cannot objectify (and thus immunise from) either representationally or empirically, theoretically or practically.[168] This is a technique of legal 'de-

165 Negarestani, 2008: 19.

166 Meillassoux proposes to think justice as a superior and yet immanent order of 'universal equality' that is opened by a truly emancipatory politics that is simultaneously aimed at its self overcoming (i.e. to a world after the end of politics) insofar as projected towards justice, and yet unable to actually reach such an end. This is because 'the *finality* of politics … cannot be the *product* of a politics, except that of a totalitarian fantasy'. Thus the 'end of politics is that which proceeds from an ontological uprising that is independent of our action, an uprising whose hypothesis contributes at present to the shaping of the subjectivity of the vectoral militant' (Meillassoux, 2010: 477). Although sympathetic with his attempt, the understanding of justice I am proposing is dependent from our 'actions', even though it cannot be their 'product'. This is what an inoperose acting gestures to. The opening of the whiteout is exactly the locus of an emancipatory politics whose purpose is not to 'produce justice', but rather to open the space to its cosmic event, by deactivating the exceptional apparatuses that prevent and neutralise its potential, as well as counter-effectuating it to produce alternative spatialities.

167 That is, 'all the purposes that separate life and living' (Agamben, 2009d: 144) (my translation).

168 Negarestani, 2008.

familiarisation', by 'experimentally allowing the law to be affected by an encounter', as Lefebvre proposes or, in Zartaloudis' words, by exposing law to

> the experience of encountering the limit of the law, where one encounters the possibilities *of* the law (its own juridical potentiality) and all other non-juridical possibilities *to* law.[169]

A geo-legal approach underlines simultaneously law's situated-ness in the spatio-temporal here and now, as well as its immersion into the 'unhistorical vapour' of justice, the cosmic excess through which alone can law be fulfilled, applied, *used.* Justice cannot be assumed as what 'irritates or sabotages the law'. It is the state of exception to systematically sabotage the law, making it 'function' by dis-applying it, and thus it is this separating machine that needs to be made inoperose, at least temporary, tentatively, contingently, so as to unfold the *inseparable contiguity* of law and justice. There is no separation: law and justice are always in a vermicular zone of contact: a hollow law, a holey justice. In legal parlance the term 'hollow law' is usually employed to refer to a specific law so ridden with contradictions to be unenforceable. My use of the term is consistent with this interpretation, yet unenforceability in this case is no reason for discomfort. Hollow law is not a law we have got rid of, an endlessly dislocated law, or a law which must be enforced: it is rather a law that can be 'commonly' and constructively *used.*

Faced with the need to improve the safety and vitality of public roads, the 'traffic philosopher' Hans Monderman coined the notion of *shared space.* Introduced and experimented in the 1980s in villages in the northeast of the Netherlands, shared space contrasts the principle of segregation which traditionally organises the street by keeping strictly separated its different practices and users (e.g. car drivers, pedestrians, cyclists). Shared space removes separation and hierarchical differentiation between road users not only by lowering pavement to street level but also eliminating traditional traffic-control signs and devices (signs, street lights, zebra crossings), substituted with visual and tactile cues on the surface, such as different colours and textures. The task, as the leading UK proponents Ben Hamilton-Baillie puts it, is 're-writing the language of separation' by modifying the approach to planning, design, decision making, and more

169 Lefebvre, 2008: 235–6; Zartaloudis, 2010: 279.

importantly to develop, in Monderman terms, 'a common vision about how public space can work.'[170]

The urban space is a governed space pervaded by regulations, protocols, norms, security design and software-encoded technologies. These technological and legal proxies function as *actants* to which the responsibility to react under unexpected circumstances can be, and in fact is, delegated. The preventive logic of security is thus coupled with the systematic discouraging of counter-effectuation, as the necessity to 'take responsibility' vis-à-vis one's singular position within an assemblage is delegated to higher authorities (law, security, technology etc.). The exceptional tunings of control, as explained, function by immunising anyone from the risk of being 'held responsible'. This is a de-responsibilising and pre-empting movement of legal self-immunisation that systematically neutralises the potential for justice to emerge, since defusing its constitutive material: conflict.[171]

In the model proposed by Monderman, this logic is directly challenged via the de-activation of the spatiolegal mechanism of exception and thus the removal of its operational devices (signs and physical barriers, but obviously also the legal scaffolding which reinforces them). Legal abstractions are deactivated from their separating, de-responsibilising, litigation-bound operations, and thus restored to a 'common use', i.e. the possibility of being employed as tools to retune the urban and build alternative spatiolegal normativities. Elsewhere I have discussed the limits of this approach.[172] Particularly in its UK application, for instance, the tendency has been that of fetishising the model as a sort of panacea for the *solution* of street conflict, standardising into a replicable formula which de-prioritises its subversive potential in favour of a superficial and costly aesthetic device easily co-opted by neo-liberal logics of place valorisation.

Re-inserting a logic of solution, as well as idealistically presupposing that the removal of 'segregating devices' would remove power asymmetries as well, shared space proponents often fail to capitalise on its promising potential: namely, as a strategy aimed at pursuing a 'more just' urban space neither through law, nor through its elimination, but rather *whiteouting* law, that is, by dismantling and making it inoperose. Unplugging the spatial apparatus of segregation is not the end point but rather the beginning of an urban praxis that must be necessarily followed by a strategic approach

170 Quoted in Clarke, 2006.

171 Brighent and Pavoni, 2017.

172 First, it tends to underestimate power relations and thus the potential for certain categories to be excluded and discriminated (most notably blind people, evidently disadvantaged by a model that strongly relies on visual clues). Second, it tackles the effect of traffic politics disparities such as spatial segregation without challenging directly its main cause, namely the predominance of car-culture. Third, its de-politicised understanding of the urban often leads to prioritise de-contextualised aesthetic principles over strategic and contextual political questions. Pavoni, 2017a.

able to address the situation thus unleashed, and constructively reconfigure it towards potentially emancipatory outcomes. Notwithstanding its flaws, and the related danger of shared space being co-opted into capitalistic processes of urban valorisation, shared space remains a valuable experiment in urban normativity, at the conceptual and strategic level, to rethink the relation between law, space, and justice against the perils of the current neo-liberal condition.

Decolonising Architecture (DA) is a project set up in Palestine by Eyal Weizman, together with Alessandro Petti and Sandi Hilal. In an interview, Weizman explains that the project has been inspired by the need to overcome the claustrophobic logic of the 'Occupied Territories', that is, the logic of the *solution* (one-state, two-state, etc.) that traps them 'in an "endless present", a historical process without culmination'.[173] The quest for the solution freezes the potentialities of the situation, leaving 'intact' its oppressive configuration, in the eternal wait for a yet-to/never-to-come salvation.[174] DA eschews problem-solving anxieties and is rather concerned with inhabiting this problematic field, challenging the present situation from within, opening a 'new political temporality' in which to operate or, in other terms, reorienting a temporal yearning (*à venir*) into a spatially situated strategy.[175]

The questions nurturing this enterprise are strategic, namely whether there 'could be something in excess' in the order of occupation, an excess that could be employed in order to use the power of colonial architecture, once its apparatus of domination has been deactivated (de-colonised).[176] The term 'decolonisation' in fact indicates the attempt of 'undoing' the existent system of inequalities, by depotentiating and defusing colonial relations of power, and thus reorienting them towards different uses, 'articulated differently, inhabited differently'.[177] DA does so strategising Agamben's concept of

173 Weizman, 2010: 279.

174 I refer to Noys' above quoted critique to Derrida's strategy that 'leaves capitalism intact while we await the grand and shattering arrival of the spectral event "to come", which never truly materialises as such' (Noys, 2012: 45).

175 This is what Weizman expresses in temporal terms 'one might open a way to operate in the present in relation to a future that is much further away than the one-state/two-state thing. So it's both immediate and very far.' That is, in the absolute situatedness of a contingency and yet open to a potentiality far away and yet absolutely here and now (Weizman, 2010: 293).

176 '[D]oes the power that exists in the architecture of colonial exclusion remain in it like a residue, when it is unplugged? … The task is to identify this power that remains, this charge, and to attempt to reorient it' (Weizman, 2010: 282–3).

177 Weizman, 2010: 282.

profanation. As Weizman qualifies, profanation means 'the deactivation of the spatial apparatus of exclusion ... the dismantling of the power that exists ... a restoration of things to the common use'.[178] Yet, does not this strategy imply the 'dangerous assumption', the interviewer asks, that 'matter is ultimately innocent, that matter, at some level, can be decoupled from power'?[179]

Weizman's answer exposes the double strategy so far presented. The aim, he explains, is

> not to simply undo the power and techniques of the occupation but to reorient them ... if resistance is not complete withdrawal, if it is articulated through some form of action, the question is whether there is a mode of action that might contain the possibility of a break rather than the constant elasticity of material organisation and political evolutions.[180]

In the sense of the 'surfing interventionism' presented above, this implies detecting and exploiting the frictions in the smooth surface of control, opening up the space to inoperose uses, so that to 'use it in a way that does not reproduce, that really breaks, this relationship of power and its forms'.[181] According to Weizman,

> the city is not spatially governed so much by its structures and buildings but rather by the way it organises and divides the surface ... [its] ground is a certain code, both at the operational and symbolic levels: the code of the city – its operational logic and its ideology ... a 'thick surface' in which occurs the designation of private and public, walk/drive/no walk, the relation between figure and ground, between the object and the surface on which it relies.[182]

The question then becomes that of *ungrounding* the city, as he puts it, making inoperose its structures of power and domination by perforating the smooth surface of its spatiolegality, and thus counter-effectuating this eventful potential in order to make space for the emergence of novel concatenations.

The abandoned military base of Oush Grab (crowd's nest) has neither been destroyed by the retreating Israeli army, nor by the re-appropriating Palestinians, as usually occurs in these cases. The DA project was assigned

178 Weizman, 2010: 296.

179 Weizman, 2010: 283.

180 Weizman, 2010: 294, 277.

181 'So the spaces despoiled by power represent an opportunity in so far as they become depotentiated in terms of the existing politics, and operate within this new political temporality' (Weizman, 2010: 293).

182 Weizman, 2010: 296, 298.

with the task of envisaging a way to deal with the building. The question here was not only that of thinking of new ways to re-use it. At the same time, there was the necessity of preventing it from being re-appropriated by the army. In fact, within the regime of

> 'revolving door occupation', in which the danger of the place's appropriation by settlers always exists, it is important to first render the building less amenable to be used, before allowing for new functions to inhabit them.[183]

For this purpose, DA devised a strategy consisting in 'perforat[ing] the buildings of the military base by drilling holes into their walls.'[184] Through this profanation by perforation, the structure of power entangled in the building is literally hollowed out, by dismantling its appropriating, violent and exclusionary mechanism and thus creating an 'absence of occupation' that prevents its re-occupation, in this way restoring the building to a common use, i.e. to the potential for conjuring complicities between human and non-human bodies.

In the introduction, I concluded by mentioning Lars Lerup's concept of 'building the unfinished' as an instance, I suggested, of inoperose building that is oriented to build works able to 'make space' for the irruption of the eventful potential of being-together, rather than preventively closing them off into a pre-determined result.[185] In this sense, through the inoperose deactivation of the spatiolegal apparatus of exception DA opens 'a space that escape[s] the grasp of power and its laws, without entering into conflict with them yet rendering them inoperative'.[186] A holey space, that is opened to the cosmic justice of its taking place in a world that is ultimately irreducible to its mechanism of exclusion, immunisation and juridification. Oush Grab is an important stop for thousands of migrating birds on their way to Africa, for whom the cavities excavated through the building function as temporary nests. In this holey space, a novel, impersonal, posthuman tuning surfaces.[187]

183 Retrieved from www.decolonizing.ps/site/texts/

184 Retrieved from www.decolonizing.ps/site/texts/

185 Lerup, 1977. In Weizman's words, the military base is redesigned 'on behalf of nature… design not for a construction but for the controlled disintegration of the building, we accelerate or intervene in the process of its disintegration' (Weizman, 2010: 295).

186 Agamben, 2005b: 27.

187 Pictures of the 'hollowed' building can be seen at www.decolonizing.ps/site/texts/

Conclusion

An exhibition

Through the book I addressed the relationship between law, space and control, how it unfolds in the contemporary city – with particular attention to how this occurs in the extraordinary spatio-temporal context of mega events – and what ethico-political strategy may be adequate to it. This was done in three overlapping steps.

The first consisted in tracing two theoretical trajectories: the elaboration of an original ontology of the urban, culminated in the notion of urban tunings; and the investigation of the spatiolegal architecture of control, culminated in the notion of brandscaping. The second tested the theoretical framework through an ethnographic exploration set in Johannesburg during the FIFA 2010 South Africa World Cup. Here, I dealt with Johannesburg through the notion of urban tuning – hence: the Joburg Tune – and that of brandscaping – hence, the World Cup Brandscaping. The third addressed the dimension of justice, first genealogically, then strategically, through the notions of spatial justice and profanation. Neither a set of new principles nor a panacea for social injustices, what I suggested is a situated strategy aimed at dismantling the exceptional tunings of control and counter-effectuating their residual power so as to retune the urban into alternative, hopefully more 'just' configurations.

This endeavour provided a tentative answer to the questions that prompted this book. Yet, the problematic field they generated is not going to disappear: it is to be traversed each time. The conceptual tools here proposed are meant to be helpful in this regard. This conclusion has no feeling of completion. In fact, whether introductions provide cartographies to orient the reader through the narration, conclusions should venture towards unknown territories for which cartographies still need to be drawn. They conclude a text, by opening it up to what is outside. Faithful to this intention, this conclusion explores a paradigmatic example, by performing a transversal recognition of the main argument of the book, its lines of thought, and lines of flight.

Agamben provides a different notion of paradigm to that of Thomas Kuhn. Thomas Kuhn defines the paradigm as not only a set of rules and savoirs, but a fundamental worldview or framework which members of a scientific community consensually share by more or less consciously adhering to it, and which guides and shapes the boundaries of the scientific research of a certain epoch.[1] Digging through philosophy in his typical archaeological fashion, Agamben exhumes a different meaning: not the *de jure* condition of possibilities of a science, but its *de facto* existence.[2] The paradigm can be understood as a special kind of norm, one that cannot be posited or verified from outside, but rather exists and subsists only in the exhibition of the paradigmatic case, by which it is generated and produced. As for the Franciscan *regula*, the paradigm is a norm that cannot be applied or enunciated, but only exposed, performed, and lived. An always contingent example (e.g. an architectural project: the panopticon), that is, and yet one that, through the 'suspension from its immediate factual reference', is at the same time able to expose the 'canon' or abstract form which it shares with the other instances to which it is paradigmatically related (e.g. *panopticism*, i.e. a diagrammatic function detached from any use).[3] There is, in other words, always an *analogical* relation between a singularity and its paradigmatic suspension, one that avoids and neutralises the binary correspondence between particular and general.[4] Understood as such, the paradigm assumes an immanent and generative quality with respect to a problematic field:

> the intelligibility of the paradigm is never presupposed, on the contrary, the specificity of the paradigm resides precisely in the suspension of its immediate factual reference and in the exhibition of its intelligibility as such in order to give life to a new problematic context.[5]

It is in this sense that the paradigm of *operation* I referred to throughout the book should be understood: a problematic field in which the operation is assumed as the necessary mode of action, grounded on the presupposition of an undifferentiated something (void, chaos, substance, life…) which such operation should simultaneously manage and immunise from. Accordingly, Parmenides' split between Being and non-Being is not to be understood as an original cause, but a paradigmatic example able to expose such a problematic field, which is what the book sought to traverse

1 Kuhn, 1977.
2 '[N]ot its right to be a science, but the fact that it exists' (Agamben, 2009b: 7).
3 As in the grammatical example, where in order for a rule to be made explicit, an actual, singular instance must be performed (for instance, the imperative 'go away') and at the same time 'suspended' from its contextual signification (the injunction for somebody to 'go away') in order to 'exhibit' its paradigmatic value, its norm (in this case, the imperative form) (Agamben, 2009b: 26).
4 Agamben, 2009b: 31.
5 Agamben, 2002.

and dissect. In the following pages, I deal again with such a paradigm from an eccentric perspective, with the aim to reshuffle and possibly shine new light on the main questions raised through the book. Most importantly, the questions of how to detach radical thought and thus ethico-political action from its exceptional recuperation; how to generate tunings which are truly alternative to the urban brandscaping, beyond reactive opposition, fleeting spontaneity or technical synchronisation; how to keep the space open to its spatial justice, once the deactivation of its exceptional tunings has been carried out.

This is done in two steps. First, I dig through the notion of *gardening*, neither a lazy and unoriginal metaphor nor a redundant and pretentious digression but, taken analogically as well as to some extent allegorically, a paradigm through which the canon of the spatiolegal operation may be exposed. Whereas this allows me to come back and clarify the exceptional relation between law, space and control, at the same time also permits me to focus more in depth (through the conceptual figure of the 'weeds') on the issue of the complicity between radical thought and contemporary neo-liberalism. Thus I set the stage for a rather unorthodox instance of gardening, Ai Weiwei's art installation *Kui Hua Zi* (Sunflower Seeds), which offers me the chance to wrap up, and push forward, the discussion developed in the final chapter.

1.1 By its existence alone, the lily of the field sings the glory of the heavens.[6]

All begins with a garden, the locus where the encounter between the human and the divine is mediated into a paradisiac normativity (*pairi-daeza*: 'enclosed space', from wall [*daeza*] and around [*pairi*]).[7] Here, the utopian dream of an all-encompassing law merges with that of pure happiness in freedom, an ever-receding origin which will subsequently ground and justify the human gardening enterprise. In fact, as the human is thrown into the Earth by the original gardener, this creature of lack will be condemned to compensate for the ontological poverty of its *fallen* condition, by involving himself in an operation. Here we find again the prototypical 'reduction of human beings into praxis', as the fallen human being becomes the sovereign gardener of the world, tasked with the duty to tame its unruly wilderness into a productive order. As Gilles Clement reminds in his *brève histoire du jardin*, the first garden was an alimentary one, the *hortus* (From the Latin root *GHAR-* or *HAR-*: to enclose). Culture begins as agriculture, out of an original urge to 'transform Earth into an agricultural

6 Deleuze, 2004[1968]: 75.

7 This trope appears, albeit in different ways, in the three main monotheisms.

space ... agriculture turns reality into domination-ready chunks of parcelled out space'.[8]

Thus the distinction was instituted between 'those organisms contained, managed and bred for the benefit of the humans, and those which are "wild", continuing to live in their own territories on, more or less, their own terms', and whose presence would testify the immoral idleness of its savage inhabitants. In the eighteenth century the Scottish botanist and garden designer John Claudius Loudon invited readers 'to compare plants with men, consider aboriginal species [i.e. wild plants] as mere savages, and botanical species [i.e. cultivars] as civilised beings'.[9] Civilisation is cultivation, cultivation is colonisation: it is those who cultivate, civilise and make the land *productive*, according to John Locke, that will be granted the right to property over those undeserving hands living the *terra nullius* of the New World: 'wild woods and uncultivated waste ... left to nature, without any improvement, tillage or husbandry' will have thus to be expropriated so as to be gardened into productivity.[10]

Gardening equates with establishing the quintessential separation (culture/nature), and articulates it into an immunising operation. The garden is the 'homogenous medium' in which a stable order of being is projected, by simultaneously *erasing* the complexity from space – extirpated, eradicated and weeded into a bare space – and then *partitioning*, i.e. ploughing, sowing and fencing this bare substratum into a precise and productive order. Beneath its seemingly rational, peaceful and ordered gesture, in fact, always lies the violence of extirpation: the sovereign gardener must constantly *decide upon* i.e. 'cut off' (*decision*: *de-* 'off'; *caedere* 'to cut') the weeds (although of course, the gardener more precisely extirpates the weeds, so as not to leave roots on the ground) in order to re-establish the exceptional order, which his spectacular authority alone is unable to maintain. Every garden is a garden of exception. Its foundations are shaky, its perimeters vulnerable, sooner or later to be invaded by those beings whose very existence the garden obstinately denies. Every garden always contains 'the seeds of its own deconstruction'.[11]

1.2 Without a master, one cannot be cleaned. Purification... requires submission to the law.[12]

One millennium ago, Arab philosophers employed the figure of weeds (*al-*

8 Morton, 2012: 16.

9 Mabey, 2012: 9.

10 'As much land as a man tills, plants, improves, cultivates, and can use the product of, so much is his property. He by his labour does, as it were, inclose it from the common' (Locke, 1690: ch. V).

11 de Sutter, 2011: 56 (my translation).

12 Laporte, 2002: 2.

naw bit) as a metaphor to indicate the 'oppositionists', i.e. 'those who oppose the rulers and their doctrine'.[13] This was no negative understanding. Although at times in significantly different ways, Al Farabi, Ibn Bajjah and Ibn Tufayl saw a potential in the weeds' opposition to the common *doxa*, provided it was cultivated and gardened within the space of the 'virtuous city', that is, provided the unruly weeds could be channelled by the philosopher towards the higher truth. Yet, a weed is by definition incompatible with this effort. Its 'untameable' nature does not derive from its 'wilderness', but rather because it dislocates the very dichotomy on which the logic of taming rests. As Richard Mabey writes,

> The weeds occur when this tidy compartmentalisation [cultivated/wild] breaks down. The wild gatecrashes our civilised domains, the domesticated escapes and runs riot.[14]

The weed does not belong to a wilderness comfortably situated outside of the gardening endeavour. It does not deny the space of gardening, but more precisely *wrongs* it. Paralleling Mary Douglas' famous definition of dirt as *matter out of place*, Mabey observes, 'the best-known and simplest definition is that a weed is a plant in the wrong place'.[15] The weed is useless, parasitic and thus immoral, ugly, savage, toxic: all the ideals that make up our society, from aesthetics to morality, from utilitarianism to health, are challenged by these dirty, swarming, incomprehensible beings, whose continuous and rhizomatic proliferation aptly expresses the ineradicable conflictuality which lies within, and constantly dislocates, any order.[16]

Able to proliferate where all other forms of life disappear, from post-conflict ruins to abandoned cemeteries, from desert land to asphalt roads, covering and erasing the *holzwege* of our confortable wanderings, the weeds expose the reality of a world 'not for us', populated by bodies which cannot be reduced to our relation to them: 'the weed is the Nemesis of human endeavour … exists only to fill the waste spaces left by cultivated areas. It *grows between*, among other things.'[17] The anarchic, rhizomatic vitalism of weeds exposes the impotence and nakedness of the sovereign gardeners, whilst showing the permeability and fragility of its disciplinary fences, as well as (apparently) running counter the utilitarianism of the operational paradigm: 'of course they don't have a "purpose"', thus Mabey exclaims; 'they just "are"'.[18] Is it perhaps in their just being that their being 'just' lies?

13 Kochin, 1999.
14 Mabey, 2012: 21.
15 Mabey, 2012: 5.
16 Mabey, 2012: 9.
17 Henri Miller, quoted in Deleuze and Guattari, 2004[1980]: 20.
18 Mabey, 2012: 14.

1.3 Being truly terrestrial is not the same as being superficial.[19]

Just as weeds appear as nomads embodying a rhizomatic challenge to the agricultural paradigm, as much rhizomatic and weed-like are the roots of contemporary *radical* thought whose task, it seems, writes Colebrook, is the 'annihilation of the self-gathering subject and a becoming one with a broader inhuman ecology'.[20] An ecology of hybrids, cyborgs, networks, assemblages, rhizomes, multitudes... What if, however, the anarchic nomadism these figures express embody the very form of the paradigm it sets up to contest? What if the weeds do not harbour the seeds for the de(con)struction of gardening, but are rather the allegory of its full postmodern unleashing, in a much more coherent, post-human and impersonal form?

At a first level, weeds embody the deconstruction of the exceptional gardening. By inserting a 'chaos within the garden', they unmask the sovereign impotence and disaggregate its stable order. Yet, do they stop the gardening operation? We may answer affirmatively, only by pretending the garden to be a rigid and arboreal structure, one which will therefore collapse before weedy chaos. However, we saw how chaos is not the limit, but rather the inherent justification, and unspoken projection, of control. Once the state of exception is deconstructed, its operation does not stop but rather folds onto itself, from a binary to a circular, all-ingesting exceptionality: no longer radiating from a given sovereign or enclosed within a precise location, control becomes boundless, planetary (i.e. fully deterritorialised) and impersonal (post-sovereign).

At a second level, by blurring the boundaries between cultivars and wild plants, but also parasitically dissolving the integrity of each plant, weeds *make explicit* the trans-individual mechanism and rhizomatic materiality of the molecular ontology of being together. In this sense they are the quintessential embodiment of post-human vitalism: the expression of life as an 'inherently positive, primal propulsive force that opposes domination and control'.[21] Yet, we know that whilst the 'static' mechanism of exception is based on the bionomical extirpation (abstraction) of individuals from the spatiality of being together, its 'dynamic' configuration introduces a different kind of abstraction, molecularising the static and self-contained individual into the dynamic machinism of re-combinable *dividuals*, internalising the dispositif of gardening, that is, *within* every being. This is a different sort of gardening, one that is not opposed, but rather thrives on the metamorphosis, translatability, movement and variation that the weeds embody. If weeds superficially sabotage the gardening project, more

19 Negarestani, 2010: 7.
20 Colebrook, 2014b: 59.
21 Hall *et al.*, 2010: 42.

profoundly they appear to *internalise* and fully unleash its exceptional operation.

1.4 The attempt to force Earth into self-consistency with the human agricultural project has resulted precisely in a more virulent form of miasma taking hold … the generation of, and scientific discovery of, beings that are far more virulently uncanny, far more obviously riddled with nothingness.[22]

In the hallucinated appendix to his book on Foucault, Deleuze sketches two great 'historical configurations'. First, is the vertical transcendence of the 'God-form' and the universal *unfolding* to which it centripetally attracted mankind: a 'continual need to unfold and "explain". What is God, if not the universal explanation and supreme unveiling?' Second, the 'Man-form', in which the infinite unfolding of God is reversed, i.e. folded back into the finitude of a 'horizontal transcendentalism', as novel *savoirs* (biology, political economy, linguistics, socio-empiricism, etc.) gradually provide an immanent *folding* to the vertical aspiration of the former era. What occurs when this form also begins to disintegrate? If life was imprisoned by man, as Nietzsche argued, the *Ubermensch* would 'free life *within man himself*, to the benefit of another form'. What form, though? No longer molar but molecular, no longer arboreal but rhizomatic, post-structural and post-human, this form would challenge and deterritorialise the realms of life, labour and language. This is no longer *unfolding*, not even a *folding*, but rather a *Superfold*, the unleashing of the proper forces of immanence that, Deleuze adds cautiously, 'it is hoped, will not prove worse than its two previous forms'.[23]

In the vast spaces of the central United States, a great horde of wandering nomads moves at a persistent, massing and contagious pace through the fences, barricades and bunkers of the agro-industrial project. Emerging as the unintentional outcome of the massive employment of war-like herbicides (e.g. products like Agent Orange which, acting like a vaccine, gradually stimulated in them massive herbicide-resistance capacities), and as direct or indirect result of widespread GM-cultivation (through mutation, cross-breeding or other indirect causes), these beings truly embody the revenge of 'the genetic components … over the organism' which Deleuze wrote about. They have been called *superweeds*.

Certainly of no use to the humans, these weeds are not 'without purpose' either. They rather embody a relentless, virulent *urge to grow*, explicit in their persistent (photosynthetic) operation of self-consumption: they produce energy, grow without limits, smooth out space into a homogeneous,

22 Morton, 2012: 19.
23 Deleuze, 2006[1986]: 124–32.

weedy surface, whilst suffocating and destroying other beings. Embodying a paradigm of productivity gone mad, they only superficially seem to sabotage the gardening project. More profoundly, they *internalise* and fully unleash its exceptional operation, in the form of a wildly de-stratifying 'gardening' that does no longer rely on a sovereign master or a disciplined space, but is now fully autonomous, impersonal, post-human: *gardening without gardeners, gardening without gardens.*[24]

The folding of the state of exception implies that there is no longer a static separation of a bare life from a life worth living, but rather the reduction of the whole life to a bare life, whole space to a bare space. This is what superweeds' parasitic and viral 'process of omnivorous immanentization' generate.[25] Here the ambiguity of vitalism finds its deadly (dis)embodiment, a dark and oppressive body without organs whose vitalistic proliferation is one with a necrocratic parasitism, producing a smooth space which deadly colonises any 'vital space', destroying crops and shrinking the cultivation area. *Never believe that the weeds would suffice to save us.*

1.5 ...excavate the land instead of striating it, bore holes in space instead of keeping it smooth, turn the earth into a Swiss cheese.[26]

Negarestani diagnoses the impasse of post-human thinking in the inability to escape the conservative horizon in which capitalism thrives. As a never-setting sun, capitalism functions as the necessary horizon, allowing every form of resistance, transgression and revolution to take place, provided its 'Solar Hegemony' remains unquestioned.[27] Thus ever-new ways of life are envisaged, that is, an abundance of possibility for self-realisation through self-consumption, possibilities which are provided within a horizon (within a world or possible worlds) which has already been (ontologically) posited by the capitalistic abstraction: a plurality of lifestyles, and a monism of death.[28] Whereas 'the positive stance of affirmation is an artless re-enactment of the conservative horizon', the merely oppositional stance, pretending to negate this system from an outside standpoint, is not only illusory. It reinforces the very system and it confirms it.[29] Within this framework any nomadic excess risks being recaptured. Both negative nihilism and positive vitalism remain stuck onto the surface of the earth, differently and yet equally unable to escape the modulation of capitalism, in fact

24 'You don't reach the BwO, and its plane of consistency, by wildly de-stratifying' (Deleuze and Guattari, 2004[1980]: 160).
25 Tiqqun, 2010: 132.
26 Deleuze and Guattari, 2004[1980]: 456.
27 Negarestani, 2010.
28 Negarestani, 2011a: 194 n. 20; 2010.
29 Negarestani, 2011a: 200.

contributing to produce the suffocating closure of its seamless and uneventful relationalism.

The superweeds' unstoppable immanentization testifies for their inability to escape such local horizons: just like other plants, although at an unrestrained 'warp speed', weeds remain sun-jects, subjects of the Sun and as such condemned to glorify its light.[30] What their ambiguous vitalism embodies is the suspicious superficiality of the political dimension of '(neo)liberation'. They 'may be moving fast, but only within a strictly defined set of capitalist parameters that themselves never waver'.[31]

This is the impasse that the geo-legal position I proposed in the final chapter sought to avoid. Evidently, the absolute deterritorialisation of superweeds cannot be contrasted through (since constituted by) the accelerated overdose of the ambiguous vitalism of GM-crops and the lethal nihilism of herbicides. Yet, if acceleration is not a solution, neither is the mere inertia of an 'onto-phenomenological letting-be'.[32] Beyond the false dichotomy of action and inertia, lies the art of profanation, that is, the contingent dismantling of the apparatus of control, and the counter-effectuation of the eventful potential thus unleashed: *inoperose gardening*.

2.1 I act in a way more or less as programmed by an uncertain force.[33]

Ai Weiwei's art installation *Kui Hua Zi* (Sunflower Seeds) took place between 2010 and 2011 in the gigantic Turbine Hall of the Tate Modern Gallery, in London. It consists of 100 million hand-crafted porcelain seeds made in Jingdezhen, China.[34] An uneven surface to dive into, a haptic space of undulating vision, rustling steps, and unusual horizontality, a meaningless quicksand where the separation between artwork and spectator is engulfed, the immunity of distant contemplation denied.

Doing justice to this 'garden of stones', I believe, means not to treat it as a 'box' with some hidden meaning inside to be uncovered and interpreted.[35] What does it signify? A legitimate question, yet a pacifying one, that reduces the work to a self-contained object and dissolves the intensity

30 Glorification, I argued above, is the operation of ontological *production* of the sovereign: the glorifying subject ultimately *coincides* with the operation of glorification.

31 Williams and Srnicek, 2013.

32 Marder, 2013: 3. Marder proposes 'doing justice to them [plants] by means of this very onto-phenomenological letting-be'. I think letting-be is not enough. See Morton, 2010, for a critique of the principle of letting-be in ecology.

33 In Rauch, 2010.

34 The installation included: 100 million porcelain sunflower seeds; a short 'making-of' documentary; a 'OnetoOne With the Artist', where visitors could record themselves asking/answering questions. I have discussed this exhibition in Pavoni, 2015b.

35 In Weiwei's neighbouring Japan the art of gardening is defined as the *ishi wo taten koto*, literally 'the art of setting stones'.

it can generate into a differential space of interpretations. How does it work? This is a more significant, strategic question, that allows us to connect the work to its outside, thus to keep its intensity alive by following the concatenations produced in the contingency of its taking place: 'there's nothing to explain, nothing to understand, nothing to interpret. It's like plugging into an electric circuit.'[36]

Modulation through immersion: this is how Paul Valéry famously defined architecture. Control is modulation, Deleuze reminded us. Above, I elaborated on the concept of brandscaping in the attempt to understand and explore this process vis-à-vis urban tunings. The mega event offered a significant example: a urban installation simultaneously aimed at stimulating and exploiting the eventfulness of the urban, by producing pervasive entertainment and frenetic festival rhythms, whilst at the same time seeking to defuse any conflict, intensity and friction which could roughen its smooth, secured and capitalised circulation: a machine for the *pre-emptive production of events*. *Kui Hua Zi,* instead, seems to function as a machine for generating encounters, producing intensities, a machine that makes space for the eventful potential of its taking place by generating a whiteout in the spatiolegal surface of the gallery.

This is not an explanation or an interpretation. Neither is directly relevant with respect to the author's intentions. If anything, the 'sense' of artistic composition resides in its capacity to hold together, on the concatenations it generates, on the disseminations through which it proliferates. The intentions of the author are always exceeded by the taking place of the work and the machines it is captured by. 'Machines don't explain anything, you have to analyze the collective arrangements of which the machines are just one component.'[37] You have to follow the concatenations, attend to them, report the effects.

2.2 One must follow what the rock demands.[38]

The contemporary art gallery is the quintessential atmospheric illusion, Philippopoulos Mihalopoulos argues. It is in itself an event-defusing installation that ingests ever controversial, disturbing, transgressive works, whilst neutralising their conflictual quality in order for them to be equally enjoyed by everybody as objects of (an)aesthetic experience. It is a safe,

36 Deleuze, 1995: 8–9.

37 Deleuze and Negri, 1990. Incidentally, in the short making-of video accompanying the exhibition Weiwei explains how he was interested at the unpredictable outcome generated by the encounter between visitors and seeds: 'Because they are fake seeds, it takes them a while to adjust their minds. They would always say: is that possible? Then they would pick up a few, some would even want to put them in their mouth to try' (retrieved from www.youtube.com/watch?v=PueYywpkJW8)

38 Takei and Keane, 2008.

consensual and egalitarian space that dissimulates itself as the materialisation of an absolute freedom of intellectual enjoyment, whilst it is 'completely populated by property lines, health and safety regulations, consumer protection barriers, public morality risks, insurance diktats and so on'.[39] This is the space *Kui Hua Zi* profaned.

What an object can do? This is the question the installation prompts and performs, by 'freeing' the seeds from their function, 'not simply restor[ing] something like a natural use that existed before being separated', but rather opening them to a common and post-human use.[40] This was not done, in guerrilla-art fashion, by directly transgressing (and thus implicitly reasserting) this space in the name of a libertarian striving for unbounded artistic freedom. Neither was it done by seeking to impose control over contingency, but rather by making space for its unruly irruption, 'demodulating the immersion', extracting intensity from the waves of being together, rather than defusing them.[41] This was no simple improvisation but a calibrated experiment in 'building the unfinished', an inoperose gardening, that is, that instead of prescribing any peculiar interaction to the human and non-human bodies involved, lets 'them hold together without wounding their disjointure and their becoming otherwise'.[42]

Contrary to the weeds' accelerationist hubris, the 'urge to grow' is foreign to these seeds. What they express is not the propulsive movement of naive vitalism, but the impotentiality of demonic vitalism, a retreat from the 'evil' urge to exercise some power to be.[43] Let us not be distracted by the seeming inconsistency of this analogy. Let us instead follow the intensive lines of flight it generates. Doing justice to objects is freeing them from our interpretation and appropriation, understanding them as double-structures, never fully graspable, reducible, manipulatable, always situated within a relational here-and-now, and yet never actually resolved, i.e. exhausted into that. What the porcelain seeds express is such 'inoperose potency to swerve', allegorically symbolised by the deactivation of the condition of being 'constantly enrolled into activity' expressed by the photo-synthesis of a Mao-Sun.[44] Whereas the viral molecularisation of the

39 Philippopoulos-Mihalopoulos, 2013: 3.

40 Agamben, 2007: 77–86.

41 'Demodulation is the act of extracting the original information-bearing signal from a modulated carrier wave' (from Wikipedia entry: 'demodulation').

42 The 'ethical task is to become worthy of one's encounter with these forces of affectation: not to force constancy on them, but to lend them consistency. To let them hold together without wounding their disjointure and their becoming otherwise' (Doel, 1999: 6).

43 Weiwei himself emphasises such deactivation of purpose as an element of this artwork: 'it's a work about mass production and repeatedly accumulating the small effort of individuals to become a massive, useless piece of work' (retrieved from www.tate.org.uk/whats-on/tate-modern/exhibition/unilever-series-ai-weiwei/interpretation-text)

weeds embodied a suspicious politics of reckless 'liberation', the 'inoperose acting' of the seeds may represent a more radical direction.

What keeps a body 'alive' is not a 'capacity to do', but more importantly a 'capacity to undo'. An 'inoperose potentiality' that, by 'making inoperose' the operational mechanism of appropriation, unleashes the excessive eventfulness of the materiality of being together, piercing the exceptional horizon by opening space to the uncorrelated event of its *taking place*. The seeds' 'de-sun-jectification' is the preamble for the production of the spatiolegal whiteout that the installation triggers, unleashing the demonic potentialities of bodies that, liberated from exceptional captures, are free to enter into novel relations, producing new power configurations. Let us not be fooled by their static, passive, a-political appearance. Seeds are 'nomads by dint of not moving', escaping the closure of brandscaping by remaining within, complicitous with anonymous bodies with which they enter in unpredictable and unauthorised compositions, causing friction with abstract and concrete structures, unleashing their demonic, chaotic, immoral, illegal and poisonous potentialities, producing alternative normativities: 'accomplishing nothing [they] become *capable* of everything'.[45]

Specifically, the seeds were capable of generating toxic atmospherics by entering in frictional relation with human bodies and their shoes. They produced resonant noise across the aural space of the gallery, through multi-sensorial interaction with people, in this way polluting the normative ideal of anaesthetic contemplation. Finally, they entered into an incontrollable circulation among visitors' pockets and further locales, destabilising the abstract scaffolding of property, and disaggregating the artwork's authorial integrity.

What they (un)did then, what they pierced through is the seemingly impenetrable smoothness of the safe, controlled and capitalised brandscape of the gallery. Firmly situated within its boundaries, and yet renouncing to prescribe any pre-determined *ought* to its fruition, the installation polluted the atmosphere of the gallery itself. Not eradicated, but rather dismantled was the event-defusing spatiolegal apparatus of exception, made *inoperose* by its immunitary operations. Thus excavated, within the space of the gallery, was another 'space that escape[s] the grasp of power and its laws, without entering in conflict with them yet rendering them inoperative'.[46] Thus a holy space of sanitised and authorial insulation

44 In the making-of video Weiwei suggests a political inspiration for his work: 'In the political area all the paintings have sunflower seeds. Whenever Chairman Mao comes out there are sunflowers around him, that means that Chairman Mao is the sun and all the ordinary people loyal to the party are the sunflowers. Sunflowers supported the whole revolution, spiritually and in material ways' (Retrieved from www.youtube.com/watch?v=PueYywpkJW8).

45 Paraphrasing Masciandaro, 2010: 52.

was turned into a perforated space of unpredictable occurrences. After only five days *Kui Hua Zi,* was cordoned off and quarantined behind a fence for the rest of its duration.[47]

2.3 Sunflower Seeds is contingent, oddly moving and beautiful. It is like quicksand.[48]

Unpredictably, by wandering over this grey matter the visitors' footsteps raised an impalpable dust, the by-product of the black paint used to decorate the seeds. Prolonged exposition may prove hazardous, the experts said. Although dust masks could have been a more than sufficient compromise, this meant exposing Tate to tricky matters of insurance and liability.[49] Much to Weiwei's disappointment, the gallery in the end, as a staff member put it, 'chose to be on the safe side'.[50]

'The enthusiastic interaction of visitors has resulted in a greater than expected level of dust in the Turbine Hall',[51] read the official statement. Incidentally, to some, this very interaction, the sight of visitors running around, lying down, throwing seeds, was just a 'distracting eccentricity'.[52] The implicit normativity of art's (an)aesthetic experience was voiced out by those lamenting the 'unruly behaviour' of the visitors: the seeds, it seems, were also polluting the normative atmosphere of the gallery. Not only.

The invisible property lines striating the exhibition space were being contaminated as well. Walking over a carpet of 100 million seeds was too much of a temptation, taking some of the seeds home seemed, to many, an obvious action, not carrying any moral or legal implications. Whilst the Tate was busy 'encouraging people not to',[53] Weiwei did not specify any protocol in this regard and, when asked, replied:

> for the museum, it is a total work, and taking a seed would affect the work. Institutions have their own policies. But I know I would want to take a seed.[54]

46 Agamben, 2005b: 27.
47 The 'fenced' exhibition is pictured here: www.flickr.com/photos/appelogen/5179744040/
48 Searle, 2010.
49 'Are the Tate's sunflower seeds a risk to health?.' *Recognition, Evaluation, Control* blog, 18 October 2010. Available at http://diamondenv.wordpress.com/2010/10/18/are-the-tates-sunflower-seeds-a-risk-to-health/
50 In Higgins, 2010b.
51 Retrieved from www.tate.org.uk/whats-on/tate-modern/exhibition/unilever-series-ai-weiwei-sunflower-seeds
52 Jones, 2010.
53 As reported by Higgins, 2010a.
54 Retrieved from www.theguardian.com/artanddesign/charlottehigginsblog/2010/oct/12/ai-weiwei-sunflower-seeds

Art needs to make us sense the invisible forces that are the conditions of possibility of sensation itself, Deleuze once wrote.[55] In an increasingly capitalised world, art needs also to make us sense the conditions of possibility for aesthetic experience in the neo-liberal condition. Here, like a thick smoke revealing otherwise invisible laser beams, the dust raised by *Kui Hua Zi* made visible the invisible threads holding together the immunitary operations of the gallery: security, order, property.

2.4 Architecture is a delicate method to produce accidents.[56]

Arguing with a member of the staff, I found myself suggesting whether 'stealing' the seeds was part of the artistic experience of *Sunflower Seeds,* romantically pointing to the possibility of it being spread around the world. He replied to me with a grin: 'as you'll surely know there are works which explicitly contemplate the possibility of bringing home a part of them, not this one'.[57] This reminded me of an anecdote narrated by Jeremy Till in *Architecture Depends,* a compelling reflection on the relation between architecture and contingency, and the constant attempt by architects to avoid, control or deny it. Till narrates the story of an architect's despair at coming home every night into the house he himself designed, only to find '"rogue objects" disturbing his ordered interior': his children's toys.[58]

Pretending to overcome the proprietary separation between artwork and spectator by simply articulating it into an internalised encounter to be 'explicitly contemplated' in advance, is an as much contradictory practice as those preached by the post-political rhetoric of 'community participation', where disagreement is warmly welcomed as long as it is pre-emptively neutralised of any real dissensus, i.e. safely de-politicised: a space in which *uneventful events* are free to occur. It is instructive to see how Tate Modern's curator justified *a posteriori* the decision to fence in the exhibition:

> The thinking behind the work lies in far more than just the idea of walking on it. The precious nature of the material, the effort of production and the narrative and personal content create a powerful commentary on the human condition.[59]

55 Deleuze, 2005a.
56 Fujimoto, 2008.
57 Member of Tate Staff, interviewed by the author.
58 Till, 2009: 31.
59 'The Unilever Series: Ai Weiwei: Sunflower Seeds.' *Tate Modern* website. Available at www.tate.org.uk/whats-on/tate-modern/exhibition/unilever-series-ai-weiweisunflower-seeds

Sensible words where, however, the contingent potentialities of the installation are ultimately defused, are explained away into layers of socio-anthropological supra-structures.

Facing bodies that are *not for us* – that is, bodies that cannot be framed within the normative structure of the gallery, the categories of property, the requirement of security – the immunitary apparatus *de facto* re-configured itself. Thus the seeds were re-objectified, and neutralised, into inert matter amenable to safe interpretation, preventive control, and capitalistic appropriation.

Sure, I am not suggesting that elaborating a theoretical reflection on the seeds is less a material activity than walking over them. Nor am I arguing that a representational relation is less material that a physical one. Finally, I am not implying that Weiwei did not take into account this aspect. Obviously, art is also a way to reflect on the human condition, as well as the political situation in which an artist lives, and it is certainly possible that Weiwei did intend to produce the 'commentary' the Tate's curator hints at. Yet in this case it is evident that, by being representationally reduced to a mere metaphor, and physically secluded within the immunitary and proprietary cage of a self-contained box, the seeds were ontologically erased from the picture, deprived of their capacity to generate concatenations, reduced to an epistemological tool for the creative re-imagining of a critic.

2.5 Exhaustion is something entirely different: one combines the set of variables of a situation, on the condition that one renounce any order of preference, any organization in relation to a goal, any signification. The goal is no longer to go out or stay in, and one no longer makes use of the days and nights. One no longer realizes, even though one accomplishes something. Shoes, one stays in; slippers, one goes out. Yet one does not fall into the undifferentiated, or into the famous unity of contradictories, nor is one passive: one remains active, but for nothing.[60]

Kui Hua Zi performs a spatiolegal whiteout. Again, this is no explanation or interpretation. Neither is there any intention to attach a 'political' meaning to what occurred in the Tate. Yet, a spatiolegal whiteout is what the invisible fog produced by the seeds generated. In this vortex the law is exposed to events that are no longer defused by its exceptional operations, before bodies it cannot objectify and whose demonic potentialities it cannot prevent, internalise or immunise from. Among those bodies, spaces, scales and laws, non-immunitary and non-proprietary complicities surface, engendering frictions that are more than phenomenological and that pierce the smooth texture of the spatiolegal. The aperture thus provoked harbours

60 Deleuze, 1998: 15.

the potential for the emergence of immanent tunings in which the abstract and concrete relations between bodies, spaces, scales and laws are reconfigured in ways that cannot be known, and thus valued, in advance. In an indirect, imaginative and allegorical sense, *Kui Hua Zi* sketches the contours of a promising strategic praxis: making space for the eventful contingency of a situation by perforating the superficial coherence of an apparatus, letting emerge conflict where it has been suppressed, frictions where they had been smoothed out: spatial justice, that is. Tate's reaction is also a reminder of how quick the system is to re-configure and re-ingest spaces of resistance. Temporary autonomous zones, whether left to themselves, are innocuous niches of self-satisfaction, bound to be sooner or later recuperated within the system itself. Some final suggestions follow.

First, 'unleashing the eventful potential' of being together is not simply a matter of going with the flow, self-indulging in evocative language and drunken wanderings. The weeds symbolise a wildly de-stratifying gardening that has done with structures, gardens, abstractions: a reckless smoothing out of space whose hubristic vitalism borders into a parasitic nihilism. *Kui Hua Zi* expresses another praxis, neither seeking to restore sovereign gardens nor indulging in an iconoclastic post-gardening inoperose gardening. It shows that an intensive and eventful politics is not an improvised praxis but rather requires a situated, careful and informed strategy of deactivation. It is not a simplistic renunciation to build something, but an attempt at doing so 'inoperosely': (un)building, or more precisely, unplugging the apparatus that exists, 'freeing' a given situation from its 'state of affairs' by deactivating its exclusionary configuration, and retuning its residual power towards other possibilities.

Second, the desirability of any re-tunings is not to be taken for granted. It must be assessed every time in the contextual unfolding of their situation, where justice is an ever-present potential, never a pre-given guarantee or a justifying goal.

Third, this is still not enough. Space can be always re-appropriated. On the one hand, this is an important ethical reminder: whether no longer 'respected on their own terms', bodies become again the prey of preventive neutralisation, capitalisation, de-materialisation and safe interpretation.[61] On the other, this is a precise strategic suggestion. Temporary autonomous zones are insufficient, innocuous and always bound to be re-ingested. Not only an opening then, the ethico-political task is that of counter-effectuating the potentialities thus unleashed, constructively turning 'absences of occupation' into novel configurations that would prevent the ever-present risk of re-appropriation.

61 Bryant, 2011: 248.

Twofold, therefore, appears the task of any praxis that wishes to challenge appears twofold, rather than simply reproduce the purifying logics of the dominating paradigm. On the one hand is 'the deactivation of the spatial apparatus of exclusion' and thus the 'restoration of things to the common use'.[62] On the other, is the counter-effectuation of the potentialities thus unleashed, constructively turning 'absences of occupation' into novel configurations that would prevent the ever-present risk of re-appropriation by the system itself.

This is what *Kui Hua Zi* exposes, the contours of a radical urban politics, whose task is to make space for the eventful contingency of a situation through a work of de-activation, perforating the superficial coherence of the spatiolegal architecture of control by letting conflict emerge where it has been suppressed and generating frictions where they had been smoothed out. Producing urban whiteouts, that is, accepting and traversing constructively the immersion in their contingent and inescapable materiality, the 'cosmic' dimension in which justice is to be found, in this world is not for us.

62 Weizman, 2010: 296.

Bibliography

Accarino, Bruno. 2009, 'Peter Sloterdijk Filosofo dell'Estasi', introduction to Italian translation of Peter Sloterdijk. *Sfere I, Bolle:* 1 (Meltemi).

Adams, Ross. 2014, 'Natura Urbans, Natura Urbanata: Ecological Urbanism, Circulation, and the Immunization of Nature'. *Environment and Planning D: Society and Space,* 32: 12–29.

Adey, Peter. 2009, 'Facing Airport Security: Affect, Biopolitics, and the Preemptive Securitisation of the Mobile Body'. *Environment and Planning D: Society and Space,* 27 (2): 274–95.

Adey, Peter, Laure Brayer, Damien Masson, Patrick Murphy, Paul Simpson and Nicolas Tixier. 2013, '"Pour votre Tranquillité": Ambiance, Atmosphere, and Surveillance'. *Geoforum,* 49: 299–309.

Adranovich, Greg, Matthew J. Burbank and Charles H. Heying. 2001, 'Olympic Cities: Lessons Learned from Mega Events Politics'. *Urban Affairs,* 23 (2): 113–31.

Agamben, Giorgio. 1993, 'Bartleby o della Contingenza', in Gilles Deleuze and Giorgio Agamben, *Bartleby, la Formula della Creazione* (Quodlibet).

Agamben, Giorgio. 1995, *Idea of Prose* (State University of New York Press).

Agamben, Giorgio. 1996, *Mezzi Senza Fine: Note sulla Politica* (Bollati Boringhieri).

Agamben, Giorgio. 1998a, *Homo Sacer: Sovereign Power and Bare Life* (Stanford University Press).

Agamben, Giorgio. 1998b, *Quel Che Resta di Auschwitz: L'Archivio e il Testimone* (Bollati Boringhieri).

Agamben, Giorgio. 1999a, *Potentialities: Collected Essays in Philosophy* (Stanford University Press).

Agamben, Giorgio. 1999b, *The Man Without Content* (Stanford University Press).

Agamben, Giorgio. 2000a, *Means Without End: Notes on Politics* (University of Minnesota Press).

Agamben, Giorgio. 2000b, *Remnants of Auschwitz: The Witness and the Archive* (Zone Books).

Agamben, Giorgio. 2001a, 'On Security and Terror'. *Frankfurter Allgemeine Zeitung,* 20 September.

Agamben, Giorgio. 2001b, *Infanzia e Storia: Distruzione dell'Esperienza e Origine della Storia* (Einaudi).

Agamben, Giorgio. 2001c, *La Comunità Che Viene* (Bollati Boringhieri).

Agamben, Giorgio. 2002, 'What is a Paradigm?' lecture at European Graduate School, August. Available at: www.egs.edu/faculty/giorgio-agamben/articles/what-is-a-paradigm/

Agamben, Giorgio. 2005a, *State of Exception* (University of Chicago Press).

Agamben, Giorgio. 2005b, *The Time That Remains: A Commentary on the Letter to the Romans*(Stanford University Press).

Agamben, Giorgio. 2006[1982], *Language and Death: The Place of Negativity* (University of Minnesota Press).

Agamben, Giorgio. 2007, *Profanations* (Zone Books).

Agamben, Giorgio. 2008, 'K', in Justin Clemens, Nicholas Heron and Alex Murray (eds). *The Work of Giorgio Agamben: Law, Literature, Life*, 13–18 (Edinburgh University Press).

Agamben, Giorgio. 2009a, *Il Regno e La Gloria: Per Una Genealogia Teologica dell'Economia e del Governo* (Bollati Boringhieri).

Agamben, Giorgio. 2009b, *The Signature of All Things: On Method* (Zone Books).

Agamben, Giorgio. 2009c, *What is an Apparatus? and Other Essays* (Stanford University Press).

Agamben, Giorgio. 2009d, *Nudità* (Nottetempo).

Agamben, Giorgio. 2011a, *Altissima Povertà. Regole Monastiche e Forme di Vita* (Neri Pozza).

Agamben, Giorgio. 2011b, *The Kingdom and the Glory: for a Theological Genealogy of Economy and Government* (Stanford University Press).

Agamben, Giorgio. 2012, *La Potenza del Pensiero: Saggi e Conferenze* (Neri Pozza).

Agamben, Giorgio. 2013, *Opus Dei: An Archaeology of Duty* (Stanford University Press).

Alexander, Harriet. 2009, 'South Africa Unveils World Cup 2010 Security Measures'. *Telegraph*, 1 December. Available at: www.telegraph.co.uk/sport/football/world-cup-2010/6700199/South-Africa-unveils-World-Cup-2010-security-measures. html

Alkemeyer, Thomas and Alfred Richartz. 1993, 'The Olympic Games: from Ceremony to Show'. *Olympika*, 2: 79–89.

Allen, John. 2006, 'Ambient Power: Berlin's Potsdamer Platz and the Seductive Logic of Public Spaces'. *Urban Studies*, 43(2): 441–55.

Alliez, Eric. 2006, 'Anti-Oedipus: Thirty Years On (Between Art and Politics)', in Martin Fuglsgang, and Bent Meier Sorensen (eds). *Deleuze and the Social*, 151–68 (Edinburgh University Press).

Altbeker, Antony. 2007, *A Country at War with Itself: South Africa's Crisis of Crime* (Jonathan Ball).

Amin, Ash. 2007, 'Rethinking the Urban Social'. *City*, 11 (1): 100–14.

Amin, Ash and Nigel Thrift. 2002, *Cities: Reimagining the Urban* (Polity).

Anderson, Ben. 2006, 'Becoming and Being Hopeful: Towards a Theory of Affect'. *Environment and Planning D: Society and Space*, 24 (5): 733–52.

Anderson, Ben. 2009, 'Affective Atmospheres'. *Emotion, Space and Society*, 2: 77–81.

Anderson, Ben. 2010, 'Modulating the Excess of Affect: Morale in a State of Total War', in Melissa Gregg and Gregory J. Seigworth (eds). *The Affect Theory Reader*, 161–85 (Duke University Press).

Anderson, Ben and Adam Holden. 2008, 'Affective Urbanism and the Event of Hope'. *Space and Culture*, 11: 142–59.

Anderson, Ben and Paul Harrison (eds). 2010, *Taking-Place: Non-Representational Theories and Geography* (Ashgate).

Anderson, Ben and Colin McFarlane. 2011, 'Assemblage and Geography'. *Area*, 43 (2): 124–7.

Anderson, Ben and John Wylie. 2009, 'On Geography and Materiality'. *Environment and Planning A*, 41 (2): 318–35.

Andrejevic, Mark. 2007, *iSpy: Surveillance and Power in the Interactive Era* (University Press of Kansas).

Arendt, Hannah. 2007, *The Promise of Politics* (Schocken Books).

Armstrong, Philip. 2009, *Reticulations: Jean-Luc Nancy and the Networks of the Political* (University of Minnesota Press).

Atkinson, Michael and Kevin Young. 2005, 'Political Violence, Terrorism, and Security at the Olympic Games', in Kevin Young and Kevin B. Wamsley (eds). *Global Olympics: Historical and Sociological Studies of the Modern Games*, 269–94 (Elsevier).

Aureli, Pier Vittorio. 2011, *The Possibility of an Absolute Architecture* (MIT Press).

Bachelard, Gaston. 2000[1936], *The Dialectic of Duration* (Clinamen).

Badiou, Alain. 1999, *Deleuze: The Clamour of Being* (University of Minnesota Press).

Badiou, Alain. 2000, 'Of Life as a Name of Being, or, Deleuze's Vitalist Ontology'. *PLI: The Warwick Journal of Philosophy*, 10: 191–99.

Badiou, Alain. 2007, 'The Event in Deleuze'. *Parrhesia*, 2: 37–44.

Baeten, Guy. 2000, 'The Tragedy of the Highway: Empowerment, Disempowerment and the Politics of Sustainability Discourses and Practices'. *European Planning Studies*, 8 (1): 69–86.

Bajc, Vida. 2007, 'Surveillance in Public Rituals'. *American Behavioral Scientist*, 50 (12): 1648–73.

Baldwin, David. 1997, 'The Concept of Security'. *Review of International Studies*, 23 (1): 5–26.

Bale, John. 1988, 'Virtual Fandoms: Futurescapes of Football', in Adam Brown (ed.). *Fanatics: Power, Identity and Fandom in Football*, 265–78 (Routledge). Available at: www.efdeportes.com/efd10/jbale1.htm

Bale, John. 2001, *Sport, Space and the City* (The Blackburn Press).

Ball, Kirstie and David Murakami Wood. 2008, 'Brandscapes of Control', paper presented at the 3rd Surveillance and Society Conference, Sheffield.

Ball, Kirstie and David Murakami Wood. 2013, 'Brandscapes of control? Surveillance, Marketing and the Co-construction of Subjectivity and Space in Neo-liberal Capitalism'. *Marketing Theory*, 13: 47–67.

Barnett, Clive. 2011a, 'Theory and Events'. *Geoforum*, 42 (3): 263–5. Available at: http://oro.open.ac.uk/29008/2/Theory_and_events.pdf

Barnett, Clive. 2011b, 'Geography and Ethics: Justice Unbound'. *Progress in Human Geography*, 35 (2): 246–55.

Barnett, Clive. 2012, 'Geography and Ethics: Placing Life in the Space of Reasons'. *Progress in Human Geography*, 36 (3): 379–88.

Barry, Andrew and Nigel Thrift. 2007, 'Gabriel Tarde: Imitation, Invention and Economy'. *Economy and Society*, 36 (4): 509–25.

Bataille, George. 1929, 'Architecture', in *Dictionnaire Critique* 2. Available at: https://lepelikan.files.wordpress.com/2014/03/bataille-architecture_ordi.pdf

Baudrillard, Jean. 1987, 'Forget Foucault', in Jean Baudrillard, *Forget Foucault & Forget Baudrillard: An Interview with Sylvère Lotringer*, 27–70 (Semiotext(e)).

Baudrillard, Jean. 2009, *The Transparency of Evil: Essays on Extreme Phenomena* (Verso).

Beck, Ulrich. 2002, 'The Terrorist Threat: World Risk Society Revisited'. *Theory, Culture and Society*, 19 (4): 39–55.

Benasayag, Miguel. 2005, *Contro il niente: ABC dell'impegno* (Feltrinelli).

Bender, Thomas. 2010, 'Reassembling the City: Networks and Urban Imaginaries', in I. Farías and T. Bender (eds). *Urban Assemblages: How Actor-Network Theory Changes Urban Research*, 303–24 (Routledge).

Benjamin, Walter. 1999, 'Critique of Violence'. *Selected Writings, 1, 1923–1926* (Harvard University Press).

Bennett, Jane. 2010, *Vibrant Matter: A Political Ecology of Things* (Duke University Press).

Bennett, Jane. 2011, 'Author Response'. *Dialogues in Human Geography*, 1(3): 404–6.

Berardi, Marco. 2010, *Essere e oblio dell'essere nei Beitrage zur Philosophie di Martin Heidegger*, PhD Thesis, Università di Perugia.

Berger, Sebastien. 2009, 'World Cup 2010: England Fans "Virtually Certain" to Die in South Africa'. *Telegraph*, 11 September.

Bergson, Henri. 2008[1898], *Matière et Mémoire* (PUF).

Bergson, Henri. 2011[1907], *Creative Evolution* (Digireads.com).

Berlant, Laurent 2011, *Cruel Optimism* (Duke University Press).

Berressem, Hanjo. 2005, '"Is it Possible Not to Love Žižek?" on Slavoj Žižek's Missed Encounter with Deleuze'. *Electronic Book Review*. Available at: www.uni-koeln.de/phil-fak/englisch/abteilungen/berressem/zizek/zizek.html

Berry, David. 2012, 'The Uses of Object-Oriented Ontology'. *Stunlaw* blog, 25 May. Available at: http://stunlaw.blogspot.it/2012/05/uses-of-object-oriented-ontology.html?m=1

Bey, Hakim. 1985/1991, *T. A. Z. The Temporary Autonomous Zone, Ontological Anarchy, Poetic Terrorism* (Autonomedia).

Bille, Mikkel, Peter Bjerregaard and Tim Flohr Sørensen. 2015, 'Staging Atmospheres: Materiality, Culture, and the Texture of the In-between'. *Emotion, Space and Society*, 14: 31–8.

Billeter, Jean-François. 2006, *Contre François Jullien* (Allia).

Birchall, Clare, Gary Hall and Peter Woodbridge. 2010, 'Deleuze's Postscript on the Societies of Control'. *Liquid Theory TV Project Video*, 22: 45, 28 January. Available at: www.youtube.com/watch_popup?v=GIus7lm_ZK0

Bissell, David. 2010a, 'Passenger Mobilities: Affective Atmospheres and the Sociality of Public Transport'. *Environment and Planning D: Society and Space*, 28 (2): 270–89.

Bissell, David. 2010b, 'Placing Affective Relations: Uncertain Geographies of Pain', in Ben Anderson and Paul Harrison (eds). *Taking-Place: Non-Representational Theories and Geography*, 79–98 (Ashgate).

Bissell, David, Maria Hynes and Scott Sharpe. 2012, 'Unveiling Seductions Beyond Societies of Control: Affect, Security, and Humour in Spaces of Aeromobility'. *Environment and Planning D: Society and Space*, 30 (4): 694–710.

Blackman, Lisa. 2007, 'Reinventing Psychological Matters: The Importance of the Suggestive Realm of Tarde's Ontology'. *Economy and Society*, 36 (4): 574–96.

Blackman, Lisa. 2008, 'Affect, Relationality and the "Problem of Personality"'. *Theory, Culture & Society*, 25 (1): 23–47.

Blecher, Max. 2007[1936], *Adventures in Immediate Unreality*, trans. Jeanie Han. Available at: https://archive.org/details/AdventuresInImmediateUnreality

Blomley, Nicholas. 1994, *Law, Space and the Geographies of Power* (Guilford Press).

Blomley, Nicholas. 2002, 'From "What" to "So What?": Law and Geography in Retrospect', in J. Holder and C. Harrison (eds). *Law and Geography: Current Legal Issues,* 5: 17–33 (Oxford University Press).

Blomley, Nicholas, David Delaney and Richard T. Ford (eds). 2001, *The Legal Geographies Reader* (Blackwell).

Böhme, Gernot. 1993, 'Atmosphere as the Fundamental Concept of a New Aesthetics'. *Thesis Eleven,* 36: 113–26.

Böhme, Gernot. 1995, *Atmosphare: Essays zur ein neuen Ästhetik* (Suhrkamp Verlag).

Böhme, Gernot. 2003, 'Contribution to the Critique of the Aesthetic Economy'. *Thesis Eleven,* 73 (1): 71–82.

Bond, Patrick. 2010, 'Fifa Forbids Free Speech at World Cup Fan Fest'. *ZSpace,* 9 July. Available at: www.zcommunications.org/fifa-forbids-free-speech-at-world-cup-fan-fest-by-patrick-bond.html

Bonta, Mark and John Protevi. 2004, *Deleuze and Geophilosophy: A Guide and Glossary* (Edinburgh University Press).

Borch, Christian. 2005, 'Urban Imitations: Tarde's Sociology Revisited'. *Theory, Culture & Society,* 22 (3): 81–100.

Borch, Christian. 2008, 'Foam Architecture: Managing Co-Isolated Associations'. *Economy and Society,* 37 (4): 548–71.

Borch, Christian. 2010, 'Organizational Atmospheres: Foam, Affect and Architecture'. *Organization: The Critical Journal of Organization, Theory and Society,* 17 (2): 223–41.

Borch, Christian. 2012, *The Politics of Crowds* (Cambridge University Press).

Bos, René ten. 2009, 'Towards an Amphibious Anthropology: Water, and Peter Sloterdijk'. *Environment and Planning D: Society and Space,* 27 (1): 73–86.

Boullier, Dominique. 2010, *La ville évenement. Foule et public urbains* (PUF).

Boullier, Dominique. 2011, 'Méthodes de tri des foules et des publics dans le parc humain Lors des événements/ Metodi di ordinamento delle folle e dei pubblici all'interno del parco umano in occasione degli eventi urbani'. *Lo Squaderno,* 19: 9–14.

Boundas. Constantin V. 2011a, 'Laurent de Sutter, Deleuze: La pratique du droit' (Book Review). *Symposium: Canadian Journal of Continental Philosophy/Revue canadienne de philosophie continentale,* 15 (1): 201–7.

Boundas, Constantin V. 2011b, 'Review of Alexandre Lefebvre, *The Image of Law: Deleuze, Bergson, Spinoza*'. *Symposium,* 15 (2). Available at: www.c-scp.org/en/2011/07/12/alexandre-lefebvre-the-image-of-law.html

Bourdieu, Pierre and Loic Wacquant. 2001, 'New Liberal Speak: Notes on the New Planetary Vulgate'. *Radical Philosophy,* 105: 2–5.

Bourriaud, Nicolas. 1998, *Relational Aesthetics* (Les Presse Du Reel).

Boycoff, Jules. 2011, 'Space Matters: The 2010 Winter Olympics and Its Discontents'. *Human Geography,* 4 (2): 48–60.

Boycoff, Jules and Pete Fussey. 2014, 'London's Shadow Legacies: Security and Activism at the 2012 Olympics'. *Contemporary Social Science,* 9 (2): 253–70.

Boyle, Philip and Kevin D. Haggerty. 2009, 'Spectacular Security: Mega-Events and the Security Complex'. *International Political Sociology,* 3: 257–74.

Braidotti, Rosi and Patricia Pisters. 2012, 'Introduction', in Rosi Braidotti and Patricia Pisters (eds). *Revisiting Normativity with Deleuze,* 1–10 (Bloomsbury Academic).

Brassier, Ray. 2015, 'Reason Is Inconsolable and Non-Conciliatory: Ray Brassier in Conversation with Suhail Malik', in Suhail Malik, Christoph Cox and Jenny Jaskey (eds). *Realism Materialism Art*, 213–30 (Sternberg Press).

Bratton, Benjamin H. 2013, 'Some Trace Effects of the Post-Anthropocene: On Accelerationist Geopolitical Aesthetics', *e-flux*, 46. Available at: www.e-flux.com/journal/46/60076/some-trace-effects-of-the-post-anthropocene-on-accelerationist-geopolitical-aesthetics/

Braun, Bruce. 2011, 'Book Review Forum: Vibrant Matter: A Political Ecology of Things'. *Dialogues in Human Geography*, 1 (3): 390–3.

Braverman, Irus. 2013, 'Animal Mobilegalities: The Regulation of Animal Movement in the American City'. *Humanimalia*, 5 (1): 104–35.

Braverman, Irus, Nicholas Blomley, David Delaney and Alexandre Kedar. 2014, *The Expanding Spaces of Law: A Timely Legal Geography* (Stanford University Press).

Brennan, Teresa. 2004, *The Transmission of Affect* (Cornell University Press).

Brenner, Neil. 2009, 'What Is Critical Urban Theory?'. *City*, 13 (2–3): 198–207.

Brenner, Neil. 2013, 'Theses On Urbanization'. *Public Culture*, 25 (1): 85–114.

Brenner, Neil, David J. Madden and David Wachsmuth. 2011, 'Assemblage Urbanism and the Challenges of Critical Urban Theory'. *City: Analysis of Urban Trends, Culture, Theory, Policy, Action*, 15 (2): 225–40.

Brenner, Neil, Peter Marcuse and Margit Mayer (eds). 2012, *Cities for People, Not for Profit: Critical Urban Theory and the Right to the City* (Routledge).

Brighenti, Andrea Mubi. 2006a, 'Did We Really Get Rid of Commands? Thoughts on a Theme from Elias Canetti'. *Law and Critique*, 17 (1): 47–71.

Brighenti, Andrea Mubi. 2006b, 'On Territory as Relationship and Law as Territory'. *Canadian Journal of Law and Society*, 21 (2): 65–86.

Brighenti, Andrea Mubi. 2008, 'Revolution and Diavolution: What Is the Difference?'. *Critical Sociology*, 34 (6): 787–802.

Brighenti, Andrea Mubi. 2009, 'Le voci del diritto. Elias Canetti', in Giuseppe Campesi, Ivan Pupolizio and Nicola Riva (eds). *Diritto e teoria sociale* (Carocci): 65–86.

Brighenti, Andrea Mubi. 2010a, *Visibility in Social Theory and Social Research* (Palgrave Macmillan).

Brighenti, Andrea Mubi. 2010b, 'On Territorology: Towards a general science of territory'. *Theory, Culture & Society*, 27 (1): 52–72.

Brighenti, Andrea Mubi. 2010c, 'Tarde, Canetti and Deleuze on Crowds and Packs'. *Journal of Classical Sociology*, 10 (4): 291–314.

Brighenti, Andrea Mubi. 2010d, 'The Publicness of Public Space: On the Public Domain'. *Quaderni del Dipartimento di Sociologia e Ricerca Sociale*, 49 (Università di Trento).

Brighenti, Andrea Mubi and Cristina Mattiucci. 2008, 'Editing Urban Environments. Territories, Prolongations, Visibilities', in Frank Eckardt, Jens Geelhaar and Laura Colini (eds). *Mediacity. Situations, Practices, and Encounters* (Frank & Timme).

Brighenti, Andrea Mubi and Cristina Mattiucci. 2015, 'The Ground before the Battle', in Massimiliano Guareschi and Federico Rahola (eds). *Forme della città. Sociologia dell'urbanizzazione*, 199–212 (Agenzia X).

Brighenti, Andrea Mubi and Andrea Pavoni. 2017, 'City of Unpleasant Feelings: Stress, Comfort and Animosity in Urban Life'. *Social and Cultural Geography*. Available at: http://dx.doi.org/10.1080/14649365.2017.1355065

Broudehoux, Anne-Marie. 2007, 'Delirious Beijing: Euphoria and Despair in the Olympic Metropolis', in Mike Davis and Daniel Bertrand Monk (eds). *Evil Paradises: Dreamworlds of Neo-Liberalism* (The New Press).

Brown, Mark. 2010, 'Tate Modern Rethinks Sunflower Seeds Show after Health Fears'. *Guardian,* 15 October. Available at: www.guardian.co.uk/artanddesign/2010/oct/15/tate-modern-sunflower-seeds-ban

Bryant, Levi. 2011, *The Democracy of Objects* (Open Humanities Press).

Bryant, Levi, Nick Srnicek and Graham Harman. 2011, *The Speculative Turn: Continental Materialism and Realism* (Re.press).

Burbank, Matthew J., Charles H. Heying and Greg Andranovich. 2000, 'Antigrowth Politics or Piecemeal Resistance? Citizen Opposition to Olympic-Related Economic Growth'. *Urban Affairs Review,* 35 (3): 334–57.

Burger, Johan. 2007, 'A Golden Goal for South Africa – Security Arrangements for the 2010 FIFA Soccer World Cup'. *SA Crime Quarterly,* 19: 1–6.

Burocco, Laura and Andrea Pavoni. 2016, 'Recriar o legado a partir das periferias', in *Mapa/Jornal de Informação Critica,* 14 (September–November).

Burroughs, William S. 1961, Interview Conducted by Gregory Corso and Allen Ginsberg, originally in *Journal for the Protection of All People.* Available at: http://realitystudio.org/interviews/1961-interview-with-william-s-burroughs-by-gregory-corso-and-allen-ginsberg/

Butler, Chris. 2008, 'Slicing through Space: Mobility, Rhythm and the Abstraction of Modernist Transport Planning'. *Griffith Law Review,* 17 (2): 470–88.

Butler, Chris. 2009, 'Critical Legal Studies and the Politics of Space'. *Social and Legal Studies,* 18 (3): 313–32.

Butler, Judith. 1997, *Excitable Speech: A Politics of the Performative* (Routledge).

Byrne, Clare. 2010, 'Speedy Justice in World Cup Courts'. *Mail and Guardian,* 16 June. Available at: www.mg.co.za/article/2010-06-16-speedy-justice-in-world-cup-courts

Cacciari, Massimo. 1995, *Architecture and Nihilism On the Philosophy of Modern Architecture* (Yale University Press).

Cacciari, Massimo. 1997, *L'arcipelago* (Adelphi).

Cacciari, Massimo. 2009, *La città* (Pazzini).

Cage, John. 1969, *A Year from Monday: New Lectures and Writings* (Wesleyan University Press).

Caldeira, Teresa P.R. 2001, *City of Walls: Crime, Segregation, and Citizenship in São Paulo* (University of California Press).

Callon, Michel. 1986, 'Some Elements of a Sociology of Translation: Domestication of the Scallops and the Fishermen of St. Brieuc Bay', in J. Law (ed.). *Power, Action and Belief: A New Sociology of Knowledge?,* 196–233 (Routledge).

Campbell, Heather. 2006, 'Just Planning'. *Journal of Planning Education and Research,* 26 (1): 92–106.

Campbell, Timothy C. 2011, *Improper Life: Technology and Biopolitics from Heidegger to Agamben* (University of Minnesota Press).

Canetti, Elias. 1994, *Massa e Potere* (Adelphi).

Casey, Edward S. 2007, *The World at a Glance* (Indiana University Press).

Cashman, R. 2003, 'What is Olympic Legacy', in Miguel de Moragas, Christopher Kennett and Nuria Puig (eds). *The Legacy of the Olympic Games, 1984–2002,* 31–42 (International Olympic Committee).

Castree, Noel. 2014, 'The Anthropocene and Geography I: The Back Story'. *Geography Compass*, 8: 436–49.

Cerdá, Ildefons. 1867, *Teoría general de la urbanización, y aplicación de sus principios y doctrinas a la reforma y ensanche de Barcelona* (Imprenta Española).

Chappelet, Jean-Loup. 2012, 'Mega Sporting Event Legacies: A Multifaceted Concept', in *Papeles de Europa*, 25: 76–86.

Chasse, Robert, Bruce Elwell, Jonathon Horelick and Tony Verlaan. 1969, 'Faces of Recuperation'. *Situationist International*, 1. Available at: www.cddc.vt.edu/si online/si/faces.html

Chisholm, Dianne. 2007, 'Rhizome, Ecology, Geophilosophy (A Map to this Issue)'. *Rhizomes*, 15 (4). Available at: www.rhizomes.net/issue15/chisholm.html

Citroni, Sebastiano and Andrea Pavoni. 2016, 'An Ethnographic Approach to the Taking Place of the Event', in Ian R. Lamond and Louise Platt (eds). *Critical Event Studies: Approaches to Research*, 231–52 (Palgrave Macmillan).

Clarke, Emma. 2006, 'Shared Space – The Alternative Approach to Calming Traffic', *TEC*. Available at: www.hamilton-baillie.co.uk/_files/_publications/18-1.pdf

Clarke, R.V. 1983, 'Situational Crime Prevention: Its Theoretical Basis and Practical Scope'. *Crime and Justice: An Annual Review of Research*, 4: 225–56.

Clausewitz, Carl von. 2008, *On War* (Wilder Publications).

Clear, Todd and Eric Cadora. 2001, 'Risk and Community Practice', in Kevin Stenson and Robert R. Sullivan (eds). *Crime, Risk and Justice: The Politics of Crime Control in Liberal Democracies* (Willan Publishing).

Coimbra, Leonardo. 1912, *O criacionismo. Esboço de um sistema filosófico* (Renascença Portuguesa).

COJ (City of Johannesburg). 2008, *Summary Submission. Host City Transport Operations Plan*. Available at: www.docstoc.com/docs/90679805/WC2010-FIFA-Submission-Host-City-TOP—CoJ

COJ (City of Johannesburg). 2010a, *Delivering a Promise, Creating a Legacy*.

COJ (City of Johannesburg). 2010b, *Safety and Protection Information Guidelines*.

Colebrook, Claire. 2009, 'Legal theory after Deleuze', in Rosy Braidotti, Claire Colebrook and Patrick Hanafin (eds). *Deleuze and Law: Forensic Futures*, 6–23 (Palgrave Macmillan).

Colebrook, Claire. 2014a, *Death of the PostHuman: Essays on Extinction, Vol. 1* (Open Humanities Press).

Colebrook, Claire. 2014b, *Sex After Life. Essays on Extinction, Vol. 2* (Open Humanities Press).

COM (Commission of the European Communities). 2000, 'The Prevention of Crime in the European Union – Reflection on Common Guidelines and Proposals for Community Financial Support', Brussels, 29 November. Available at: http://eur-lex.europa.eu/LexUriServ/LexUriServ.do?uri=COM:2000:0786:FIN:EN:PDF

Comitato no Expo and Laboratorio Off-Topic. 2012, *Exit Expo 2015 | come uscire da Expo e vivere felici*. Milano: Comitato no Expo and Laboratorio Off-Topic (self-published).

Conradson, David and Adam Latham. 2007, 'The Affective Possibilities of London: Antipodean Transnationals and the Overseas Experience'. *Mobilities*, 2 (2): 231–54.

Constable, Marianne. 2007, *Just Silences: The Limits and Possibilities of Modern Law* (Princeton University Press).

Cooper, Davina. 1998, *Governing Out of Order: Space, Law and the Politics of Belonging* (Rivers Oram).

Costa, Giuliana. 2014, 'Impatti e legacy sociali dei grandi eventi, esperienze internazionali, sfide e opportunità per Milano 2015', in Rosangela Lodigiani (ed.). *Rapporto sulla città Milano 2014: Expo, Laboratorio Metropolitano, Cantiere Per Un Mondo Nuovo*, 111–34 (Franco Angeli).

Council of Europe. 1985, *European Convention on Spectator Violence and Misbehaviour at Sports Events and in particular at Football Matches* CETS no 120.

Cover, Robert M. 1986, 'Violence and the Word'. *Yale Law Journal*, 95: 1601–29.

CPCORJ [Comitê Popular da Copa e Olimpíadas do Rio de Janeiro]. 2015, *Megaeventos e violações dos direitos humanos no Rio. Olimpíada Rio 2016, os Jogos da Exclusão.* Available at: https://comitepopulario.files.wordpress.com/2016/03/dossiecomiterio2015.pdf

Craig, Martin. 2011, 'Fog-bound: Aerial Space and the Elemental Entanglements of Body-with-world'. *Environment and Planning D: Society and Space*, 29 (3): 454–68.

Crary, David. 2010, 'World Cup Security Raises Concerns'. *Huffington Post*, 13 June. Available at: www.huffingtonpost.com/2010/06/13/world-cup-security-raises_n_610593.html

Crutzen, Paul J. and Eugene F. Stoermer. 2000, 'The Anthropocene'. *IGBP Newsletter*, 41 (17): 17–18.

CSI (Consorzio Suonatori Indipendenti). 1996, 'Linea Gotica'. (Polygram).

Culf, Andrew. 2007, 'Capital Will Need 9,000 Officers a Day to Police 2012 Olympics'. *Guardian*, 17 March. Available at: www.theguardian.com/uk/2007/mar/17/ukcrime.olympics2012

Cunha, R.S. 2009, 'A filosofia do ritmo portuguesa: da monadologia rítmica de Leonardo Coimbra a Lúcio Ponheiro dos Santos e a Ritmanálise', in *O pensamento luso-galaico-brasileiro (1850–2000). Actas do I Congresso Internacional, vol. III* (Casa da Moeda).

Cunningham, David. 2005, 'The Concept of Metropolis: Philosophy and Urban form'. *Radical Philosophy*, 133: 13–25.

Cunningham, David. 2008, 'Spacing Abstraction: Capitalism, Law and the Metropolis'. *Griffith Law Review*, 17 (2): 454–85.

Dansero, Egidio, Barbara Del Corpo, Alfredo Mela and Irene Ropolo. 2011, 'Olympic Games, Conflicts and Social Movements: The Case of Torino 2006', in Graeme Hayes and John Karamichas (eds). *Olympic Games, Mega-Events and Civil Societies. Globalization, Environment, Resistance*, 195–218 (Palgrave Macmillan).

de Carlo, Andrea. 1981, *Treno di panna* (Einaudi).

de Certeau, Michel. 1984, *The Practice of Everyday Life* (University of California Press).

Degen, Monica. 2008, *Sensing Cities: Regenerating Public Life in Barcelona and Manchester* (Routledge).

de Sutter, Laurent. 2005, 'How to Get Rid of Legal Theory: Epistemology and Ontology', in Zénon Bankowski (ed.). *Proceedings of the XXI° IVR World Congress, Lund, 2003.*

de Sutter, Laurent. 2011, *Deleuze e la pratica del diritto* (Ombre Corte).

de Sutter, Laurent. 2012, 'Gardening the Law: Rules and Models in the Japanese Art of Gardening', paper presented during Gardens of Justice: The Critical Legal

Conference 2012, Kungligla Teknikska Högskolan, Stockholm (Sweden), 14–16 September.

de Sutter, Laurent and Kyle McGee. 2012, 'Postscript: A Brief Reflection on the Universality of Jurisprudence', in L. de Sutter and K. McGee (eds). *Deleuze and Law*, 204–12 (Edinburgh University Press).

Dean, Jodi. 2014, 'After Post-Politics: Occupation and the Return of Communism', in Japhy Wilson and Erik Swyngedouw (eds). *The Post-political and its Discontents: Spaces of Depoliticisation, Spectres of Radical Politics*, 261–78 (Edinburgh University Press).

Dean, Mitchell M. 1999, *Governmentality: Power and Rule in Modern Society* (Thousand Oaks).

Dear, Michael. 2000, *The Postmodern Urban Condition* (Blackwell).

Debord, Guy. 1983, *Society of the Spectacle* (Black & Red).

Debray, Regis. 1983, *Critique of Political Reason* (New Left Books).

DeLanda, Manuel. 2005, 'Space: Extensive and Intensive, Actual and Virtual', in Ian Buchanan and Gregg Lambert (eds). *Deleuze and Space*, 80–88 (Edinburgh University Press).

DeLanda, Manuel. 2016, *Assemblage Theory* (Edinburgh University Press).

Delaney, David. 1998, *Race, Place, and the Law, 1836–1948* (University of Texas Press).

Delaney, David. 2002, 'Beyond the World: Law as a Thing of this World', in Jane Holder and Carolyn Harrison (eds). *Law and Geography*, 67–83 (Oxford University Press).

Delaney, David. 2010, *The Spatial, the Legal and the Pragmatics of World-Making: Nomospheric Investigations* (Routledge).

Deleuze, Gilles. 1978, 'Cours Vincennes, deuxième leçon sur Kant 21/03/1978'. Available at: www.le-terrier.net/deleuze/16kant21-03-78.htm

Deleuze, Gilles. 1983, *Nietzsche and Philosophy* (Columbia University Press).

Deleuze, Gilles. 1985, *Kant's Critical Philosophy: The Doctrine of the Faculties* (University of Minnesota Press).

Deleuze, Gilles. 1986, 'Optimisme, pessimisme et coyage: Lettre à Serge Daney', in Serge Daney, *Ciné Journal 1981–1986*, Cahiers du Cinéma; then reprinted as 'Letter to Serge Daney: Optimism, Pessimism, and Travel'. *Negotiations 1972–1990*, Columbia University Press, 1995, trans. Martin Joughin: 68–79.

Deleuze, Gilles. 1988, *Spinoza: Practical Philosophy* (City Lights Books).

Deleuze, Gilles. 1989, *Cinema 2. The Time-Image* (University of Minnesota Press)

Deleuze, Gilles. 1991a, *Bergsonism* (MIT Press).

Deleuze, Gilles. 1991b, *Masochism: Coldness and Cruelty* (Zone Books).

Deleuze, Gilles. 1992, 'Postscript on the Societies of Control'. *October*, 59: 3–7.

Deleuze, Gilles. 1995, *Negotiations: 1972–1990* (Columbia University Press).

Deleuze, Gilles. 1997, 'Desire and Pleasure', translation of 'Désir et plaisir'. *Magazine Littéraire*, 325, October 1994: 59–65. Available at: www.artdes.monash.edu.au/globe/delfou.html#1

Deleuze, Gilles. 1998, 'The Exhausted', in Gilles Deleuze, *Essays Critical and Clinical*, trans. Daniel W. Smith and Michael A. Greco, 152–74 (Verso).

Deleuze, Gilles. 2003, 'Qu'est-ce que l'acte de création?', in David Lapoujade (ed.). *Gilles Deleuze, deux régimes de fous. Textes et Entretiens 1975–1995*, e-book (Minuit).

Deleuze, Gilles. 2004, *Fuori dai cardini del tempo. Lezioni su Kant* (Mimesis).

Deleuze, Gilles. 2004[1968], *Difference and Repetition* (Continuum).

Deleuze, Gilles. 2004[1969], *The Logic of Sense* (Continuum).

Deleuze, Gilles. 2005a, *Francis Bacon: The Logic of Sensation* (University of Minnesota Press).

Deleuze, Gilles. 2005b, *Pure Immanence: Essays on a Life* (Zone).

Deleuze, Gilles. 2006, 'Desire and Pleasure', in David Lapoujade (ed.). *Two Regimes of Madness* (Semiotext(e)).

Deleuze, Gilles. 2006[1986], *Foucault* (Continuum).

Deleuze, Gilles. 2007, *Logica del senso* (Feltrinelli) afterword to the Italian edition.

Deleuze, Gilles. 2009, *La filosofia critica di Kant* (Cronopio).

Deleuze, Gilles. 2012[1987], 'Que-est ce que l'acte de creation? What is the Creative Act? (1987). 'Youtube video, 46:59, posted by 'tw19751' 13 November. Available at: www.youtube.com/watch?v=7DskjRer95s

Deleuze, Gilles and Félix Guattari. 1986, *Kafka* (University of Minnesota Press).

Deleuze, Gilles and Félix Guattari. 1994, *What Is Philosophy?* (Verso).

Deleuze, Gilles and Félix Guattari. 2004[1980], *A Thousand Plateaus: Capitalism and Schizophrenia* (Continuum).

Deleuze, Gilles and Antonio (Toni) Negri. 1990, 'Control and Becoming: Conversation with Toni Negri', trans. Martin Joughin. *Futur Anterieur*, 1. Available at: www.generation-online.org/p/fpdeleuze3.htm

Deleuze, Gilles and Claire Parnet. 1987, *Dialogues* (Columbia University Press).

della Porta, Donatella. 2008, 'Eventful Protests, Global Conflicts'. *Distinktion. Scandinavian Journal of Social Theory*, 17: 27–56.

Department of Community Safety and Liaison [KwaZulu-Natal]. 2010, *Traveller Tips*.

Department of Tourism. 2010, *Visitor Guide, Republic of South Africa*.

Derrida, Jacques. 1976, *Of Grammatology* (Johns Hopkins University Press).

Derrida, Jacques. 1990, '*Force de Loi*: Le "Fondement Mystique de l'Autorité"'. *Cardozo Law Review*, 11 (5–6): 919–1045.

Derrida, Jacques. 2005, *Rogues: Two Essays on Reason* (Stanford University Press).

Dewsbury, John D. and Nigel Thrift. 2005, '"Genesis Eternal": After Paul Klee', in Ian Buchanan and Gregg Lambert (eds). *Deleuze and Space* (University of Toronto Press).

Dikeç, Mustafa. 2001, 'Justice and the Spatial Imagination'. *Environment and Planning A*, 33 (10): 1785–805.

Dikeç, Mustafa. 2002, 'Police, Politics, and the Right to the City'. *GeoJournal*, 58 ([illegible]). 91–[illegible].

Dikeç, Mustafa. 2005, 'Space, Politics, and the Political'. *Environment and Planning D: Society and Space*, 23 (2): 171–88.

Dikeç, Mustafa. 2009, 'Space, Politics and (In)Justice'. *Justice spatiale | Spatial Justice*, 1. Available at: www.jssj.org/article/lespace-le-politique-et-linjustice/

Doel, Marcus A. 1999, *Poststructuralist Geographies: The Diabolical Art of Spatial Science* (Rowman & Littlefield).

Doherty, Joe, Volker Busch-Geertsema, Vita Karpuskiene, Jukka Korhonen, Eoin O'Sullivan, Ingrid Sahlin, Antonio Tosi, Agostino Petrillo and Julia Wygnańska. 2008, 'Homelessness and Exclusion: Regulating Public Space in European Cities'. *Surveillance & Society*, 5 (3): 290–314.

Douglas, Mary. 1966, *Purity and Danger: An Analysis of Concepts of Pollution and Taboo* (Frederick A. Praeger).

Douzinas, Costas. 2014, 'The "Right to the Event": The Legality and Morality of Revolution and Resistance'. *Metodo: International Studies in Phenomenology and Philosophy*, 2 (1): 151–67.

Douzinas, Costas, Peter Goodrich and Yifat Hachamovitch. 1994, *Politics, Postmodernity and Critical Legal Studies: The Legality of the Contingent* (Routledge).

Dovey, Kim. 2011, 'Uprooting Critical Urbanism'. *City*, 15 (3–4): 347–54.

Doyle, Arthur Conan. 2001[1890], *The Sign of Four* (Penguin Classics).

Dracula. 1992. Directed by Francis Ford Coppola. Written by James V. Hart (based on the novel by Bram Stoker).

Drummond de Andrade, Carlos. 2012[1936], *A rosa do povo* (Companhias das Letras).

Duffy, Michelle, Gordon Waitt, Andrew Gorman-Murray and Chris Gibson. 2011, 'Bodily Rhythms: Corporeal Capacities to Engage with Festival Spaces'. *Emotion, Space and Society*, 4 (1): 17–24.

Durkheim, Émile. 2008[1912], *The Elementary Forms of Religious Life* (Oxford University Press).

Eco, Umberto. 2007, *Dall'albero al labirinto. Studi storici sul segno e l'Interpretazione* (Bompiani).

Edensor, Tim. 2015. 'Producing Atmospheres at the Match: Fan Cultures, Commercialisation and Mood Management in English Football'. *Emotion, Space and Society*, 15: 82–9.

Eick, Volker. 2011, 'Secure Our Profits! The FIFATM in Germany 2006', in Colin J. Bennett and Kevin Haggerty (eds). *Security Games: Surveillance and Control at Mega-Events*, 87–102 (Routledge).

Eisenman, Peter. 2008, *Ten Canonical Buildings: 1950–2000* (Rizzoli International Publications).

Elden, Stuart. 2005, 'Contributions to Geography? The Spaces of Heidegger's Beiträge'. *Environment and Planning D: Society and Space*, 23 (6): 811–27.

Elias, Norbert and Eric Dunning. 1971, 'Leisure in the Sparetime Spectrum', in R. Albonic and K. Pfister-Binz (eds). *Sociology of Sport*, 27–34 (Birkhäuser).

Esposito, Roberto. 1999, *Categorie dell'impolitico* (Il mulino).

Esposito, Roberto. 2002, *Immunitas: protezione e negazione della cita* (Einaudi).

Esposito, Roberto. 2007, *Terza persona. Politica della vita e filosofia dell'impersonale* (Biblioteca Einaudi).

Esposito, Roberto. 2011, 'The Person and Human Life', in Jane Elliott and Derek Attridge (eds). '*Theory after Theory*', 205–20 (Routledge).

Fainstein, Susan. 2011, *The Just City* (Cornell University Press).

Farías, Ignacio. 2010, 'Introduction: Decentring the Object of Urban Studies', in I. Farías and T. Bender (eds). *Urban Assemblages: How Actor-Network Theory Changes Urban Research*, 1–24 (Routledge).

Farías, Ignacio and Thomas Bender (eds). 2010, *Urban Assemblages: How Actor-Network Theory Changes Urban Research* (Routledge).

Farinelli, Franco. 2003, *Geografia: un'introduzione ai modelli del mondo* (Einaudi).

Farmer, Paul. 2004, 'An Anthropology of Structural Violence'. *Current Anthropology*, 45 (3): 305–25.

Feeley, Malcom M. and Jonathan Simon. 1992, 'The New Penology: Notes on the Emerging Strategy of Corrections and its Implications'. *Criminology*, 30 (4): 449–74.

Ferenczi, Sándor. 1994, *Final Contributions to the Problems and Methods of Psycho-analysis* (Karnac Books).

Fernandes, Edesio. 2007, '"Constructing the "Right to the City" in Brazil'. *Social & Legal Studies*, 16 (2): 210–19.

Ferrell, Jeff. 2009, 'Kill Method: A Provocation'. *Journal of Theoretical and Philosophical Criminology*, 1 (1). Available online.

Ferrell, Jeff and Robert Weide. 2010, 'Spot Theory'. *City Journal*, 14 (1–2): 48–62.

Fieldman, Gregory. 2011, 'If Ethnography is More than Participant-observation, then Relations Are More than Connections: The Case for Nonlocal Ethnography in a World of Apparatuses'. *Anthropological Theory*, 11: 375–95.

FIFA. 2010, Stadium Code of Conduct. Available at: www.fifa.com/worldcup/archive/southafrica2010/organisation/ticketing/stadiumcodeofconduct.htm]

FIFA. 2010, FIFA World Cup South Africa™ Rights Protection Programme. Available at: www.fifa.com/mm/document/affederation/marketing/01/18/98/99/march 2010rightsprotection_a5_20100308.pdf

FIFA. 2010, FIFA Fan Fest Information Pack. Available at: www.fifa.com/mm/document/tournament/fanfest/01/20/88/48/fifafanfest_infopack.pdf

FIFA. 2012, World Cup South Africa™ Regulation for Public Viewing Exhibition. Available at: www.fifa.com/mm/document/tournament/loc/01/12/91/88/fwc2010_regulations_for_commercial_public_viewing_exhibitions_100330.pdf

FIFA. 2010, Durban Fan Guide 2010. Available at: http://fifaworldcup.durban.gov.za/Documents/DurbanFanGuide2010.pdf

FIFA. 2012, 'FIFA Fan Fest™ concept takes shape in the Host Cities'. 31 January. Available at: www.fifa.com/worldcup/news/newsid=1576927/index.html

FIFA. 2012, FIFA Fan Fest for the 2010 FIFA World Cup South Africa. Frequently Asked Questions. Available at: www.fifa.com/mm/document/tournament/fanfest/01/14/09/88/fifafanfest-faqs.pdf

Fisher, Mark. 2009, *Capitalist Realism: Is There No Alternative?* (Zero Books).

Foster Wallace, David. 1998, *A Supposedly Fun Thing I'll Never Do Again: Essays and Arguments* (Abacus).

Foster Wallace, David. 2006, 'Roger Federer as Religious Experience', *New York Times*, 20 August.

Foucault, Michel. 1979, *The History of Sexuality* (Penguin).

Foucault, Michel. 1981, 'The Order of Discourse', in R. Young (ed.). *Untying the Text: A Post-Structural Anthology*, 48–78 (Routledge).

Foucault, Michel. 1984, 'Of Other Spaces, Heterotopias'. *Architecture, Mouvement, Continuité*, 5: 46–9.

Foucault, Michel. 1995, *Discipline & Punish: The Birth of the Prison* (Vintage).

Foucault, Michel. 1997, 'The Birth of Biopolitics', in Paul Rabinow (ed.). *Michel Foucault, Ethics: Subjectivity and Truth*, 73–80 (The New Press).

Foucault, Michel. 1998, *The History of Sexuality Vol. 1: The Will to Knowledge* (Penguin).

Foucault, Michel. 2003, *Society Must be Defended: Lectures at the Collège de France, 1975–76* (Penguin).

Foucault, Michel. 2008, *The Birth of Biopolitics: Lectures at the Collège de France, 1978–1979* (Palgrave Macmillan).

Foucault, Michel. 2009, *Security, Territory, Population: Lectures at the Collège de France, 1977–1978* (Palgrave Macmillan).

Frew, Matt and David McGillivray. 2008, 'Exploring Hyper-Experiences: Performing the Fan at Germany 2006'. *Journal of Sport & Tourism*, 13 (3): 181–98.

Frew, Matt and David McGillivray. 2014, 'From Fan Parks to Live Sites: Mega Events and the Territorialisation of Urban Space'. *Urban Studies*, 52 (14): 1–15.

FSF (Football Supporters Federations), 2010, *Free Lions: England Fans' Guide to South Africa* (A19 Ltd).

Fujimoto, Sou. 2008, *Primitive Future* (INAX-Shuppan).

Furani, Khaled. 2014, 'State of Exception, Ethics and New Beginnings in Middle East Politics'. *International Journal of Postcolonial Studies*, 16 (3): 346–64.

Gadebe, Themba. 2007, 'Strong Police Presence for 2010'. *SouthAfrica.Info*, 14 May. Available at: www.southafrica.info/2010/police-140507.htm

Galli, Carlo. 2001, *Spazi politici. L'età moderna e l'età globale* (Il Mulino).

Galloway, Alexander. 2012, 'A Response to Graham Harman's "Marginalia on Radical Thinking"'. *An Und Fur Sich* blog, 3 June. Available at: http://itself.wordpress.com/2012/06/03/a-response-to-graham-harmans-marginalia-on-radical-thinking/]

Gandy, Matthew. 2004, 'Rethinking Urban Metabolism: Water, Space and the Modern City'. *City*, 8 (3): 363–79.

Gandy, Matthew. 2006, 'Planning, Anti-planning and the Infrastructure Crisis Facing Metropolitan Lagos'. *Urban Studies*, 43 (2): 371–96.

Garland, David. 1996, 'The Limits of the *Sovereign State*: Strategies of Crime Control in Contemporary Society'. *British Journal of Criminology*, 36 (4): 445–71.

Garland, David. 2001, *The Culture of Control: Crime and Social Order in Contemporary Society* (University of Chicago Press).

Garland, David. 2003, 'Risk', in Richard V. Ericson and Aaron Doyle (eds). *Risk and Morality* (University of Toronto Press).

Gastaldi, Jean Luis. 2009, 'La politique avant l'être. Deleuze, ontologie et politique'. *Cités*, 4 (40): 59–73.

Gauteng Tourism Authority. *Visitor Guide: Safety*. Available at: www.gauteng.net/guide/safety/

Gehring, Petra. 2005, 'Force and the Mystical Foundation of Law: How Jacques Derrida Addresses Legal Discourse'. *German Law Journal*, 6: 151–69.

Gibson, Owen. 2010, '"Fan Embassies" to help England Supporters at World Cup'. *Guardian*, 3 May. Available at: www.guardian.co.uk/world/2010/may/03/world-cup-football-fan-support

Girginov, Vassil and Laura Hills. 2008, 'A Sustainable Sports Legacy: Creating a Link between the London Olympics and Sports Participation'. *The International Journal of the History of Sport*, 25 (14): 2091–3117.

Girginov, Vassil and Jim Parry. 2004, *The Olympic Games Explained: A Student Guide to the Evolution of the Modern Olympic Games* (Routledge).

Giulianotti, Richard. 2011, 'Sport Mega Events, Urban Football Carnivals and Securitized Commodification: the Case of the English Premier League'. *Journal of Sport Social Issues*, 35 (1): 50–71.

Giulianotti, Richard and Francisco R. Klauser. 2009, 'Security Governance and Sport Mega-Events: Toward an Interdisciplinary Research Agenda'. *Journal of Sport and Social Issues*, 34 (1): 49–61.

Goffman, Erwin. 1971, *Relations in Public. Microstudies of the Public Order* (Basic Books).

Gold, John R. and Margaret M. Gold. 2009, 'Future Indefinite? London 2012, the Spectre of Retrenchment and the Challenge of Olympic Sports Legacy'. *The London Journal,* 34 (2): 180–97.

Goodrich, Peter. 2012, 'The Theatre of Emblems: On the Optical Apparatus and the Investiture of Persons'. *Law, Culture and the Humanities,* 8 (1): 47–67.

Goonewardena, Kanishka. 2008, 'Marxism and Everyday Life: On Henri Lefebvre, Guy Debord and Some Others', in Kanishka Goonewardena, Stefan Kipfer and Richard Milgrom (eds). *Space, Difference, Everyday Life: Reading Henri Lefebvre* (Routledge).

Gotham, Kevin Fox. 2011, 'Resisting Urban Spectacle: The 1984 Louisiana Exposition and the Contradictions of Mega Events'. *Urban Studies,* 48 (1): 197–214.

Graeber, David. 2012, *Debt: The First 5,000 Years* (Melville House).

Graham, Stephen. 2010, *Disrupted Cities: When Infrastructure Fails* (Routledge).

Graham, Stephen and Simon Marvin. 2001, *Splintering Urbanism* (Routledge).

Gray, Kevin and Susan F. Gray. 1999, 'Civil Rights, Civil Wrongs and Quasi-Public Space'. *European Human Rights Law Review,* 1: 46–102.

Greenfield, Steve and Guy Osborn. 1997, 'Enough Is Enough: Race, Cricket and Protest in the UK'. *Sociological Focus,* 30 (4): 373–83.

Grix, Jonathan and Donna Lee. 2013, 'Soft Power, Sports Mega-Events and Emerging States: The Lure of the Politics of Attraction'. *Global Society,* 27 (4): 521–36.

Grusin, Richard. 2015, 'Radical Mediation'. *Critical Inquiry,* 42 (1): 124–31.

Hacking, Ian. 2003, 'Risk and Dirt', in Richard V. Ericson and Aaron Doyle (eds). *Risk and Morality,* 22–47 (University of Toronto Press).

Haferburg, Christoph, Theresa Golka and Marie Selter. 2009, 'Public Viewing Areas: Urban Interventions in the Context of Mega-Events', in Udesh Pillay, Richard Tomlinson and Orli Bass (eds). *Development and Dreams: The Urban Legacy of the 2010 Football World Cup,* 174–99 (HSRC Press).

Hage, Ghassan. 2013, 'Coughing out the Law: Perversity and Sociality around an Eating Table'. *Critical Legal Thinking* blog, 18 January. Available at: http://criticallegalthinking.com/2013/01/18/coughing-out-the-law-perversity-and-sociality-around-an-eating-table/

Hagemann, Anke. 2010, 'From the Stadium to the Fan Zone: Host Cities in a State of Emergency'. *Soccer & Society,* 11 (6): 723–36.

Haggerty, Kevin and Richard V. Ericson. 2000, 'The Surveillant Assemblage'. *British Journal of Sociology,* 51: 605–22.

Hall, C. Michael and Stephen J. Page. 2012, 'Geography and the Study of Events', in Stephen J. Page and Joanne Connell (eds). *The Routledge Handbook of Events,* 148–64 (Routledge).

Hall, Gary, Clare Birchall and Peter Woodbridge. 2010, 'Deleuze's "Postscript in The Society of Control"'. *Culture Machine,* 11.

Hallward, Peter. 2006, *Out of This World: Deleuze and the Philosophy of Creation* (Verso).

Hamilton-Baillie, Ben. 'What is Shared Space?' Available at: www.hamilton-baillie.co.uk/_files/_publications/6-1.pdf

Hancox, Simone. 2012, 'Art, Activism and the Geopolitical Imagination: Ai Weiwei's "Sunflower Seeds"'. *Journal of Media Practice,* 12 (3): 279–90.

Hannah, Matthew G. 2013, 'Attention and the Phenomenological Politics of Landscape'. *Geografiska Annaler: Series B, Human Geography,* 95 (3): 235–50.

Hardt, Michael and Antonio (Toni) Negri. 2001, *Empire* (Harvard University Press).

Harman, Graham. 2007, 'On Vicarious Causation', in Robin Mackay (ed.). *Collapse, II: Speculative Realism*, 171–206 (Urbanomic).

Harman, Graham. 2009, *Prince of Networks: Bruno Latour and Metaphysics* (re.press).

Harman, Graham. 2011, *The Quadruple Object* (National Book Network).

Hart, H.L.A. 1997, *The Concept of Law* (Oxford University Press).

Harvey, David. 1973, *Social Justice and the City* (Johns Hopkins University Press).

Harvey, David. 1996, *Justice, Nature and the Geography of Difference* (Blackwell).

Harvey, David. 2008, 'The Right to the City'. *New Left Review*, 53, September–October. Available at: http://newleftreview.org/II/53/david-harvey-the-right-to-the-city

Harvey, David. 2009, *Social Justice and the City* (University of Georgia Press).

Harvey, David, with Cuz Potter. 2009, 'The Right to the Just City', in Peter Marcuse, James Connolly, Johannes Navy, Ingrid Olivo, Cuz Potter and Justin Steil (eds). *Searching for the Just City* (Routledge).

Harvey, Jean, John Horne and Parissa Safay. 2013, *Sport and Social Movements: From the Local to the Global* (Bloomsbury).

Hastings, Annette. 1999, 'Discourse and Urban Change: Introduction to the Special Issue'. *Urban Studies*, 36 (January): 7–12.

Hay, James. 2006, 'Designing Homes to Be the First Line of Defense'. *Cultural Studies*, 20 (4): 349–77.

Heidegger, Martin. 2008[1927], *Being and Time* (Harper Perennial Modern Classic).

Hennion, Antoine. 2007, 'Those Things that Hold Us Together: Taste and Sociology'. *Cultural Sociology*, 1, 97–114.

Hentschel, Christine. 2010, *The Spatial Life of Security: Durban, South Africa*, PhD Thesis, School of Social Sciences and Philosophy, University of Leipzig.

Heynen, Nick, Maria Kaika and Erik Swyngedouw (eds). 2006, *In the Nature of Cities: Urban Political Ecology and the Politics of Urban Metabolism* (Routledge).

Higgins, Charlotte. 2010a, 'People Power comes to the Turbine Hall: Ai Weiwei's Sunflower Seeds'. *Guardian*, 11 October. Available at: www.theguardian.com/artanddesign/2010/oct/11/tate-modern-sunflower-seeds-turbine

Higgins, Charlotte. 2010b, 'Sunflower Seeds Raise a Quintessence of Dust in the Turbine Hall'. *On Culture* blog, 19 October. Available at: www.guardian.co.uk/culture/charlottehigginsblog/2010/oct/19/sunflower-seeds-dust-turbine-hall

Hirvonen, Ari. 2011, 'The Politics of Revolt: On Benjamin and Critique of Law'. *Law and Critique*, 22 (2): 101–18.

Holston, James. 1998, 'Spaces of Insurgent Citizenship', in Leonie Sandercock (ed.). *Making the Invisible Visible: A Multicultural Planning History* (University of California Press).

Horne, John. 2011, 'The Four "Cs" of Sports Mega-Events: Capitalism, Connections, Citizenship and Contradictions', in Graeme Hayes and John Karamichas (eds). *Olympic Games, Mega-Events and Civil Societies: Globalization, Environment, Resistance.* (Palgrave Macmillan).

Husak, Douglas. 2008, *Overcriminalization: The Limits of the Criminal Law* (Oxford University Press).

Hyde, Marina. 2010, 'World Cup 2010: Fans, Robbers and a Marketing Stunt Face Justice, Fifa Style'. *Guardian*, 20 June. Available at: www.guardian.co.uk/football/2010/jun/20/world-cup-2010-fans-marketing-justice-fifa

ICHRP (International Council on Human Rights Policy). 2010, 'Modes and Patterns of Social Control: Implications for Human Rights Policy'. Available at: www.ichrp.org/files/reports/61/Social_Control_and_Human_Rights_ICHRP_Electronic_Final.pdf

Iles, Anthony. 2009, *Legislating for Enthusiasm from Fun Palace to Creative Prison* (Arcade – Sacrifice Zone).

Jacob, Doreen. 2013, 'The Eventification of Place: Urban Development and Experience Consumption in Berlin and New York City'. *European Urban and Regional Studies,* 20 (4): 447–59.

Jacobson, Eric. 2003, *Metaphysics of the Profane: The Political Theology of Walter Benjamin and Gershom Scholem* (Columbia University Press).

Jansson, André. 2005, 'Re-encoding the Spectacle: Urban Fatefulness and Mediated Stigmatisation in the "City of Tomorrow"'. *Urban Studies,* 42 (10): 1671–91.

Jazz. Directed by Ken Burns. Written by Geoffrey Ward. PBS Broadcasting, 2001.

Jeffery, C.R. 1971, *Crime Prevention Through Environmental Design* (Sage Publications).

Jones, Jonathan. 2010, 'Turbine Hall's Sunflower Seeds: Does it Matter If They're Closed Off?'. *Jonathan Jones on Art* blog, 15 October. Available at: www.guardian.co.uk/artanddesign/jonathanjonesblog/2010/oct/15/turbine-hall-sunflower-seeds?intcmp=239

Jullien, François. 2004, *A Treatise on Efficacy: Between Western and Chinese Thinking* (University of Hawaii Press).

Kacem, Mehdi Belhaj. 2011, 'A Tunisian Renaissance'. Available at: www.lacan.com/thesymptom/?page_id=1046

Kaika, Maria. 2005, *City of Flows: Modernity, Nature and the City* (Routledge).

Kant, Immanuel. 1987[1790], *Critique of Judgment* (Hackett Publishing).

Kant, Immanuel. 2012[1785], *Groundwork of the Metaphysics of Morals* (Cambridge University Press).

Kärrholm, Mattias. 2009, 'To the Rhythm of Shopping – On Synchronisation in Urban Landscapes of Consumption'. *Social & Cultural Geography,* 10 (4): 421–40.

Keepile, Karabo. 2010, 'Cape Traders to be Moved Ahead of World Cup'. *Mail and Guardian,* 26 April. Available at: www.mg.co.za/article/2010-04-26-cape-traders-to-be-moved-ahead-of-world-cup

Kempa, Michael, Philip Stenning and Jennifer Wood. 2004, 'Policing Communal Spaces: A Reconfiguration of the Mass Private Property Hypothesis'. *British Journal of Criminology,* 44 (4): 562–81.

Khumalo, Sibongile. 2010, 'S. Africa Rounds Up Poor, Prostitutes Ahead of World Cup'. *AFP,* 18 May.

Klauser, Francisco. 2009, 'Spatial Articulations of Surveillance at the FIFA World Cup 2006 in Germany', in Katja Franko Aas, Helene Oppen Gundhus and Heidi Mork Lomell (eds). *Technologies of (In)security: The Surveillance of Everyday Life* (Routledge).

Klauser, Francisco. 2010, 'Splintering Spheres of Security: Peter Sloterdijk and the Contemporary Fortress City'. *Environment and Planning D: Society and Space,* 28 (2): 326–40.

Klingmann, Anna. 2007, *Brandscapes: Architecture in the Experience Economy* (MIT Press).

Kochin, Michael S. 1999, 'Weeds: Cultivating the Imagination in Medieval Arabic Political Philosophy'. *Journal of the History of Ideas,* 60 (3): 399–416.

Koolhass, Rem. 2002, 'Junkspace'. *October*, 100: 175–90.

Kracauer, Siegfried. 1995[1963], *Das Ornament der Masse: Essays*, English edn, Thomas Y. Levin (ed.). *The Mass Ornament: Weimar Essays*. (Harvard University Press).

Kracauer, Siegfried. 1997, 'Employment Agencies: The Construction of a Space', in Neil Leach (ed.). *Rethinking Architecture: A Reader in Cultural Theory*, 57–62 (Routledge).

Kubheka, Anelisa. 2010, 'Fan Park Stall Holders Feel Short-changed'. *Daily News*, 17 June.

Kuhn, Thomas S. 1977, *The Essential Tension: Selected Studies in Scientific Tradition and Change* (University of Chicago Press).

Kullenberg, Christopher and Karl Palmås. 2009, 'Contagiontology'. *Eurozine*, 3 September. Available at: www.eurozine.com/articles/2009-03-09-kullenberg-en.html

Laerke, Mogens. 1999, 'The Voice and the Name: Spinoza in the Badioudian Critique of Deleuze'. *Pli: The Warwick Journal of Philosophy*, 8: 86–99.

Land, Nick. 2011, 'After the Law', in Robin Mackay and Ray Brassier (eds). *Fanged Noumena: Collected Writings 1987–2007*, 229–60 (Urbanomic/Sequence).

Laporte, Dominique. 2002, *History of Shit* (MIT Press).

Latham, Alan and Derek P. McCormack. 2004, 'Moving Cities: Rethinking the Materialities of Urban Geographies'. *Progress in Human Geography*, 28 (6): 701–24.

Latham, Alan and Derek P. McCormack. 2009, 'Globalizations Big and Small: Notes on Urban Studies, Actor Network Theory, and Geographical Scale', in Ignacio Farias and Thomas Bender (eds). *Urban Assemblages: How Actor-Network Theory Changes Urban Studies*, 53–72 (Routledge).

Lamond, Ian and Karl Spracklen. 2014, *Protests as Events Politics, Activism and Leisure* (Rowman & Littlefield International).

Latour, Bruno. 2002, 'Gabriel Tarde and the End of the Social', in Patrick Joyce (ed.). *The Social in Question. New Bearings in History and the Social Sciences*, 117–32 (Routledge).

Latour, Bruno. 2004, *Politics of Nature: How to Bring the Sciences into Democracy* (Harvard University Press).

Latour, Bruno. 2005, *Reassembling the Social: An Introduction to Actor-Network-Theory* (Oxford University Press).

Latour, Bruno. 2007, 'Can We Get Our Materialism Back, Please?'. *Isis*, 98 (1): 138–42.

Latour, Bruno. 2009a, 'Spheres and Networks: Two Ways to Reinterpret Globalization'. *Harvard Design Magazine*, 30.

Latour, Bruno. 2009b, *The Making of the Law: An Ethnography of the Conseil d'État* (Polity).

Latour, Bruno and Emilie Hermant. 1998, *Paris ville invisible* (Institut Synthélabo).

Law, John. 2004, *After Method* (Routledge).

Lawton, David. 1993, *Blasphemy* (Harvester Wheatsheaf).

Lazzarato, Maurizio. 2004a, *La Politica dell'Evento* (Rubbettino).

Lazzarato, Maurizio. 2004b, 'From Capital Labour to Capital Life'. *Ephemera*, 4 (3): 187–208.

Lazzarato, Maurizio, 2006a, 'The Machine'. Available at: http://eipcp.net/transversal/1106/lazzarato/en

Lazzarato, Maurizio. 2006b, 'The Concepts of Life and the Living in the Societies of Control', in Martin Fuglsang (ed.). *Deleuze and the Social* (Edinburgh University Press).

Lazzarato, Maurizio. 2012, *The Making of Indebted Man, An Essay on the Neoliberal Condition*, 171–90 (Semiotext(e)).

Lees, Loretta. 2002, 'Rematerializing Geography: The "New" Urban Geography'. *Progress in Human Geography*, 26: 101–12.

Lefebvre, Alexandre. 2008, *The Image of Law: Deleuze, Bergson, Spinoza* (Stanford University Press).

Lefebvre, Henri. 1965, *La Proclamation de la Commune: 26 Mars 1871* (Gallimard).

Lefebvre, Henri. 1991 [1974], *The Production of Space* (Wiley-Blackwell).

Lefebvre, Henri. 1996, *Writings on Cities*, ed. and trans. Eleonore Kofman and Elizabeth Lebas (Blackwell).

Lefebvre, Henri. 2004, *Rhythmanalysis: Space, Time and Everyday Life* (Continuum).

Lefebvre, Henri and Catherine Regulier. 1999, 'The Rhythmanalytical Project'. *Rethinking Marxism*, 11 (1): 5–13.

Lerup, Lars. 1977, *Building the Unfinished: Architecture and Human Action* (Sage Publications).

Lianos, Michalis. 2003, 'Social Control After Foucault'. *Surveillance & Society*, 1 (3): 412–30.

Lianos, Michaelis and Mary Douglas. 2000, 'Dangerization and the End of Deviance: The Institutional Environment'. *British Journal of Criminology*, 40: 261–78.

Lingis, Alphonso. 1998, *The Imperative* (Indiana University Press).

Loader, Ian. 2009, 'Ice Cream and Incarceration On Appetites for Security and Punishment'. *Punishment & Society*, 11 (2): 241–57.

Locke, John. 1690, *Second Treatise of Civil Government*. Available at: www.constitution.org/jl/2ndtreat.htm

London. 1994, Directed and written by Patrick Keiller (documentary film).

Löw, Martina. 2008, 'The Constitution of Space: The Structuration of Spaces Through the Simultaneity of Effects and Perception'. *European Journal of Social Theory*, 1 (11): 25–49.

Mabey, Richard. 2012, *Weeds: The Story of Outlaw Plants: A Cultural History* (Profile Books).

Mabuse, Nkepile. 2010, 'FIFA Criticized for Over-protecting 2010 World Cup Sponsors'. CNN, 29 April. Available at: http://edition.cnn.com/2010/SPORT/football/04/29/football.fifa.world.cup.africa/

Macrury, Iain and Gary Poynter. 2008, 'The Regeneration Games: Commodities, Gifts and the Economics of London 2012'. *International Journal of the History of Sport*, 25 (14): 2072–90.

McGillivray, David. 2014, 'Digital Cultures, Acceleration and Mega Sporting Event Narratives'. *Leisure Studies*, 33 (1): 96–109.

Madden, David J. 2010, 'Urban ANTs: A Review Essay'. *Qualitative Sociology*, 33 (4): 583–90.

Malpas, Jeff. 2006, *Heidegger's Topology: Being, Place, World* (MIT Press).

Mandic, Danilo, Caterina Nirta, Andrea Pavoni and Andreas Philippopoulos-Mihalopoulos. 2013, 'Introduction: Law and Taste'. *Non Licet: The Westminster Online Working Papers Series, Law and the Senses Series: The Taste Issue*, 3.

Marcuse, Peter. 2009, 'From Critical Urban Theory to the Right to the City'. *City*, 13 (2–3): 185–97.

Marcuse, Peter. 2010, 'Spatial Justice: Derivative but Causal of Social Injustice'. *Justice et Injustice Spatiales* (Presses universitaires de Paris Nanterre). Available at: http://books.openedition.org/pupo/420

Marder, Michael. 2013, *Plant-Thinking: A Philosophy of Vegetal Life* (Columbia University Press).

Marivoet, Salomé. 2006, 'UEFA Euro 2004™ Portugal: The Social Construction of a Sports Mega-event and Spectacle', in John Horne and Wolfram Manzenreiter (eds). *Sports Mega-events: Social Scientific Analyses of a Global Phenomenon*, 127–43 (Blackwell).

MAS Context. 2012. Negotiating Legality. Projects by Santiago Cirugeda, *MAS Context*, 13: 118–31.

Masciandaro, Nicola. 2010, 'Becoming Spice: Commentary as Geophilosophy', in Robin Mackay (ed.). *Collapse, VI: Geo/Philosophy*, 20–56 (Urbanomic).

Masciandaro, Nicola. 2012a, 'Comments on Eugene Thacker's "Cosmic Pessimism". *Continent*, 2 (2): 76–81. Available at: www.continentcontinent.com/index.php/continent/article/view/96

Masciandaro, Nicola. 2012b, 'Mysticism or Mystification? Against Subject-Creationism'. *English Language Notes*, spring/summer, 50 (1).

Masciandaro, Nicola. 2013, 'The Sweetness (of the Law)'. *Non Licet: The Westminster Online Working Papers Series, Law and the Senses Series: The Taste Issue*, 40–60.

Massey, Doreen, John Allen and Phil Sarre (eds). 1999, *Human Geography Today* (Polity).

Massumi, Brian. 2005, 'Fear (The Spectrum Said)'. *Positions*, 13 (1): 31–48.

Massumi, Brian. 2009, 'National Enterprise Emergency: Steps Toward an Ecology of Powers'. *Theory, Culture and Society*, 26: 153–85.

Matshikiza, John. 2008, 'Instant City', in Sarah Nuttall and Achille Mbembé (eds). *Johannesburg: The Elusive Metropolis*, 221–38 (Duke University Press Books).

Mattei, Silvia. 2013, 'Camouflage Revealed: Liu Bolin and the Art of Mimetic Performance'. *Liu Bolin. Hiding in the City*, exhibition catalogue, Galerie Paris-Beijing.

Mbembé, Achille. 2001, *On the Postcolony* (University of California Press).

Mbembé, Achille. 2004, 'Aesthetics of Superfluity'. *Public Culture*, 16 (3): 373–405.

McCormack, Derek. 2002, 'A Paper with an Interest in Rhythm'. *Geoforum*, 33: 469–548.

McCormack, Derek. 2008, 'Engineering Affective Atmospheres. On the Moving Geographies of the 1897 Andrée Expedition'. *Cultural Geographies*, 15 (4): 413–30.

McCormack, Derek. 2012, 'Geography and Abstraction: Towards an Affirmative Critique'. *Progress in Human Geography*, 36 (6): 715–34.

McCormack, Derek. 2013, *Refrains for Moving Bodies* (Duke University Press).

McCrea, Barbara, Tony Pinchuck, Donald Reid and Greg Salter. 2002, *The Rough Guide to South Africa* (Rough Guides).

McFarlane, Colin. 2008, 'Urban Shadows: Materiality, the "Southern City" and Urban Theory'. *Geography Compass*, 2 (2): 340–58.

McFarlane, Colin. 2011a, 'Assemblage and Critical Urbanism'. *City*, 15 (2): 204–24.

McFarlane, Colin. 2011b, 'The City as Assemblage: Dwelling and Urban Space'. *Environment and Planning D: Society and Space*, 29: 649–71.

McIntosh, Martha J. 2003, 'The Olympic Bid Process as a Starting Point of the Legacy Development', in Miguel de Moragas, Christopher Kennett and Nuria Puig (eds). *The Legacy of the Olympic Games 1984–2000.* (International Olympic Committee), 450–6.

McMichael, Christopher. 2010, 'Querying the Benefits of "Corporate Theme Parks" to Locals'. *The Mercury,* 10 June. Available at: www.abahlali.org/node/7046

Meillassoux, Quentin. 2007, 'Subtraction and Contraction: Deleuze, Immanence and Matter and Memory', in Robin Mackay (ed.). *Collapse, III: Unknown Deleuze,* 63–107 (Urbanomic).

Meillassoux, Quentin. 2009, *After Finitude an Essay on the Necessity of Contingency* (Continuum).

Meillassoux, Quentin. 2010, 'The Immanence of the World Beyond', in Peter. M. Candler and Conor Cunningham (eds). *The Grandeur of Reason,* 444–78 (SCM).

Merleau-Ponty, Maurice. 1968, *The Visible and the Invisible: Followed by Working Notes* (Northwestern University Press).

Merleau-Ponty, Maurice. 1995[1945], *Phenomenology of Perception: An Introduction* (Routledge).

Merrifield, Andy. 2013, 'Citizen's Agora. The New Urban Question'. *Radical Philosophy,* 179: 31–5.

Merrifield, Mary P. 1851, 'The Harmony of Colours as exemplified in the Exhibition', in *The Art-Journal Illustrated Catalogue of the Industry of All Nations 1851* (G. Virtue).

Michaux, Henri. 1966, *L'espace du dedans* (Gallimard).

Mieville, China. 2009, *The City and The City* (Del Rey).

Mill, John Stuart. 1869, *On Liberty* (Longmans).

Millward, Peter. 2009, 'Glasgow Rangers Supporters in the City of Manchester: The Degeneration of a "Fan Party" into a "Hooligan Riot"'. *International Review for the Sociology of Sport,* 44 (4): 381–98.

Minca, Claudio. 2006, 'Giorgio Agamben and the New Biopolitical Nomos'. *Geografiska Annaler: Series B, Human Geography,* 88 (4): 387–403.

Minnaar, Anthony and Leandri Van Jaarsveld. 2010, 'International Event Security: The Case of the Security Plan for the Fifa Soccer World Cup, South Africa 2010'. *Annual International Police Executive Symposium: Tourism, Strategic Locations & Major Events,* 17, Valletta.

Miraftab, Faranak. 2009, 'Insurgent Planning: Situating Radical Planning in the Global South'. *Planning Theory,* 8 (1): 32–50.

Mitchener-Nissen, T. 2014, 'Failure to Collectively Assess Surveillance-oriented Security Technologies will Inevitably Lead to an Absolute Surveillance Society'. *Surveillance and Society,* 12 (1): 73–88.

Mohaghegh, Jason B. and Seema Golestaneh. 2011, 'Haunted Sound: Nothingness, Movement, and the Minimalist Imagination'. *Environment and Planning D: Society and Space,* 29 (3): 485–98.

Moore, Jason W. 2015, *Capitalism in the Web of Life: Ecology and the Accumulation of Capital* (Verso).

Moore, Nathan. 2007a, 'Nova Law: William S. Burroughs and the Logic of Control'. *Law and Literature,* 19 (3): 435–70.

Moore, Nathan. 2007b, 'Icons of Control: Deleuze, Signs, Law'. *International Journal for the Semiotics of Law,* 20 (1): 33–54.

Moragas, Miquel de., Chrisopher Kennett and Nuria Puig, (eds). 2003, *The Legacy of the Olympic Games 1984–2000* (International Olympic Committee)

Morin, Marie-Eve. 2009, 'Cohabitating in the Globalised World: Peter Sloterdijk's Global Foams and Bruno Latour's Cosmopolitics'. *Environment and Planning D: Society and Space,* 27 (1): 58–72.

Morton, Timothy. 2010, 'Thinking Ecology: The Mesh, the Strange Stranger and the Beautiful Soul', in Robin Mackay (ed.). *Collapse, VI: Geo/Philosophy* , 265–93 (Urbanomics).

Morton, Timothy. 2012, 'The Oedipal Logic of Ecological Awareness'. *Environmental Humanities,* 1: 7–21.

Mould, Oli. 2014, 'Tactical Urbanism: The New Vernacular of the Creative City'. *Geography Compass,* 8: 529–39.

Mpe, Phaswane. 2002, *Welcome to Our Hillbrow* (University of KwaZulu-Natal Press).

Mules, Trevor and Bill Faulner. 1996, 'An Economic Perspective on Major Events'. *Tourism Economics,* 2 (2): 107–117.

Murray, Martin J. 2008, *Taming the Disorderly City: The Spatial Landscape of Johannesburg After Apartheid* (Cornell University Press).

Naidoo, Irene. 2010, 'Special courts ready for World Cup'. *SouthAfrica.Info,* 27 May. Available at: www.southafrica.info/2010/wccourts-260510.htm

Nancy, Jean-Luc. 1991, *The Inoperative Community* (University of Minnesota Press).

Negarestani, Reza. 2008, *Cyclonopedia: Complicity with Anonymous Materials* (re.press).

Negarestani, Reza. 2010, 'Solar Inferno and the Earthbound Abyss', in Pamela Rosenkranz. *Our Sun,* 3–8 (Mousse Publishing).

Negarestani, Reza. 2011a, 'Drafting the Inhuman: Conjectures on Capitalism and Organic Necrocracy', in Levi R. Bryant, Nick Srnicek and Graham Harman (eds). *The Speculative Turn: Continental Materialism and Realism* (re.press).

Negarestani, Reza. 2011b, 'Globe of Revolution: An Afterthought on Geophilosophical Realism'. *Identities,* 17: 25–54.

Negri, Antonio (Toni). 2008, *Reflections on Empire* (Polity).

Newman, Harvey K. 1999, 'Neighborhood Impacts of Atlanta's Olympic Games'. *Community Development Journal,* 34 (2): 151–9.

Newman, O. 1973, *Defensible Space; Crime Prevention Through Urban Design.* (Palgrave Macmillan).

Nietzsche, Friedrich. 1989[1886], *Beyond Good and Evil: Prelude to a Philosophy of the Future* (Vintage Books).

Nietzsche, Friedrich. 1997[1876], *Untimely Meditations* (Cambridge University Press).

Nietzsche, Friedrich. 2001[1882], *Gay Science* (Cambridge University Press).

Nietzsche, Friedrich. 2008[1887], *On the Genealogy of Morals* (Oxford Paperbacks).

Noys, Benjamin. 2012, *The Persistence of the Negative* (Edinburgh University Press).

Nunes, Rodrigo. 2010, 'Politics in the Middle: For a Political Interpretation of the Dualisms in Deleuze and Guattari'. *Deleuze Studies,* 4: 124–6.

Nuttall, Sarah and Achille Mbembé. 2004, 'Writing the World from an African Metropolis'. *Public Culture,* 16 (3): 347–72.

Nuttall, Sarah and Achille Mbembé. 2005, 'A Blasé Attitude: A Response to Michael Watts'. *Public Culture,* 17 (1): 193–202.

Olds, Kris. 1998, 'Urban Mega-Events, Evictions and Housing Rights: The Canadian Case'. *Current Issues in Tourism,* 1: 2–46.

Osborn, Guy and Andrew Smith. 2015, 'Olympic Brandscapes: London 2012 and the Seeping Commercialisation of Public Space', in Gavin Poynter, Valerie Viehoff and Yang Li, (eds). *The London Olympics and Urban Development: The Mega-Event City* (Routledge).

Osborne, Peter. 2004, 'The Reproach of Abstraction'. *Radical Philosophy,* 127: 21–8.

Page, Stephen J. and Connell, Joanne. 2012, *The Routledge Handbook of Events* (Routledge).

Palmås, Karl. 2009, 'Bodies without Bodhis'. *Eurozine,* 13. Available at: www.eurozine.com/articles/2009-11-13-palmas-en.html

Palmås, Karl. 2010, 'The Defence Minister's New Philosophy'. *Eurozine.* Available at: www.eurozine.com/articles/2010-02-12-palmas-en.html

Pasquinelli, Matteo. 2014, 'The Labour of Abstraction: Seven Transitional Theses on Marxism and Accelerationism'. Available at: http://matteopasquinelli.com/labour-of-abstraction-theses/

Patton, Paul. 2012, 'Immanence, Transcendence and the Creation of Rights', in L. de Sutter and K. McGee (eds). *Deleuze and Law,* 15–31 (Edinburgh University Press).

Pavoni, Andrea. 2010a, 'Erasing Space from Places. Brandscapes, Art and the (de)valorisation of the Olympic Space'. *Lo Squaderno,* 18: 9–14.

Pavoni, Andrea. 2010b, 'Looking for Spatial Justice', *Critical Legal Thinking* blog, 1 December. Available at: http://criticallegalthinking.com/2010/12/01/looking-for-spatial-justice/

Pavoni, Andrea. 2011, 'Tuning the City: Johannesburg and the 2010 World Cup'. *Urbe,* 2 (3): 191–209.

Pavoni, Andrea. 2015a, 'Resistant Legacies', *Annals of Leisure Research,* Special Issue on 'Sporting and Cultural Events: Contested Legacies'.

Pavoni, Andrea. 2015b, 'Seeds of Impurity'. *Lo Squaderno,* 36: 31–6.

Pavoni, Andrea. 2017a, 'Sharing Conflict. Law, Justice and the Street', in Sarah Marusek and John Brigham (eds). *Street Level Sovereignty: A Jurisprudence of the Everyday* (Lexington Books).

Pavoni, Andrea. 2017b, 'Abstracting Method: Taking Legal Abstractions Seriously', in Andreas Philippopoulos-Mihalopoulos and Victoria Brooks (eds). *Handbook on Research Methods in Environmental Law* (Edward Elgar Publishing).

Pearson, Keith Ansell. 1999, *Germinal Life: The Difference and Repetition of Deleuze* (Routledge).

Pedroncelli, Peter. 2010, 'The Countdown to the World Cup has Begun and an Atmosphere of Expectation is Settling over Cape Town'. *Goal,* 1 June. Available at: www.goal.com/en/news/1863/world-cup-2010/2010/06/01/1952230/world-cup-2010-cape-town-fifa-fan-festival-gears-up-for-carnival

Péguy, Charles. 1917, *Clio* (NRF).

Philippopoulos-Mihalopoulos, Andreas. 2007a, 'Fear in the Lawscape', in Jiri Priban (ed.). *Liquid Society and Its Law,* 79–100 (Ashgate).

Philippopoulos-Mihalopoulos, Andreas. 2007b, 'In the Lawscape', in Andreas Philippopoulos-Mihalopoulos (ed.). *Law and the City,* 1–19 (Routledge-Cavendish).

Philippopoulos-Mihalopoulos, Andreas. 2010a, 'Spatial Justice: Law and the Geography of Withdrawal'. *International Journal of Law in Context,* 6 (3): 201–16.

Philippopoulos-Mihalopoulos, Andreas. 2010b, 'Repetition: Deleuze and Kierkegaard on Law, Justice and Art'. *University of Westminster School of Law Legal Studies Research Paper Series.*

Philippopoulos-Mihalopoulos, Andreas. 2011a, 'Law's Spatial Turn: Geography, Justice and a Certain Fear of Space'. *Law, Culture and the Humanities*, 7 (2): 1–16.

Philippopoulos-Mihalopoulos, Andreas. 2011b, '"...The Sound of a Breaking String" – Critical Environmental Law and Ontological Vulnerability'. *Journal of Human Rights and the Environment*, 2 (1): 5–22.

Philippopoulos-Mihalopoulos, Andreas. 2012, 'Mapping the Lawscape: Spatial Law and the Body', in Zenon Bankowski, Maksymilian Del Mar and Paul Maharg (eds). *Beyond Text in Legal Education*, 119–34 (Edinburgh University Press).

Philippopoulos-Mihalopoulos, Andreas. 2013, 'Atmospheres of Law: Senses, Affects, Lawscapes' in *Emotion, Space and Society*, 7(1): 35–44.

Philippopoulos-Mihalopoulos, Andreas. 2015, *Spatial Justice: Body, Lawscape, Atmosphere* (Routledge).

Philippopoulos-Mihalopoulos, Andreas. 2016, 'Withdrawing from Atmosphere: An Ontology of Air Partitioning and Affective Engineering'. *Environment and Planning D: Society and Space*, 34 (1): 150–67.

Philippopulos-Mihalopoulos, Andreas and Sharron FitzGerald. 2008, 'From Space Immaterial – The Invisibility of the Lawscape'. *Griffith Law Review*, 17 (2): 438–54.

Pieterse, Edgar. 2006, 'Building with Ruins and Dreams: Exploratory Thoughts on Realising Integrated Urban Development Through Crises'. *Urban Studies*, 43 (2): 285–304.

Pile, Steve. 2005, *Real Cities: Modernity, Space and The Phantasmagorias of City Life* (Sage Publications).

Pillay, Kamcilla. 2010, 'Marchers Protest against World Cup'. *Daily News*, 17 June. Available at: www.abahlali.org/node/7086

Pine, Joseph and James Gilmore. 1999, *The Experience Economy* (Harvard Business School Press).

Pirie, Gordon H. 1983, 'On Spatial Justice'. *Environment and Planning A*, 15 (4): 465–73.

Pløger, John. 2010, 'Presence Experiences: The Eventalisation of Urban Space'. *Environment and Planning D: Society and Space*, 28 (5): 848–65.

Poole, Matthew. 2015, 'Specificities of Sitedness', in Robin Mackay (ed.). *When the Site lost the Plot* (Urbanomic).

Porter, Libby, Margaret Jaconelli, Julian Cheyne, David Eby and Hendrik Wagenaar. 2009, 'Planning Displacement: The Real Legacy of Major Sporting Events'. *Planning Theory & Practice*, 10 (2): 395–418.

Pottage, Alain. 1998, 'Power as an Art of Contingency: Luhmann, Deleuze, Foucault'. *Economy and Society*, 27 (1): 1–27.

Pottage, Alain. 2012, 'The Materiality of What?'. *Journal of Law and Society*, 39 (1): 167–83.

Powell, Hilary and Isaac Marrero-Guillamón. 2012, *The Art of Dissent: Adventures in London's Olympic State* (Marshgate Press).

Pramod, C.R. 2008, 'The "Spectacle" of the Beijing Olympics and the Dynamics of State–Society Relationship in PRC'. *China Report*, 44 (2): 111–37.

Preuss, Holger. 2007, 'The Conceptualisation and Measurement of Mega Sport Event Legacies'. *Journal of Sport & Tourism*, 12 (4): 207–28.

Preuss, Holger. 2013, 'The Contribution of the FIFA World Cup and the Olympic Games to Green Economy'. *Sustainability* (Special Issue 'Sustainable Mega-Events'), 5 (8): 3581–600.

Prior, Nick. 2011, 'Speed, Rhythm and Time-Space: Museums and Cities'. *Space and Culture*, 14 (2): 197–213.

Raco, Mike and Emma Tunney. 2010, 'Visibilities and Invisibilities in Urban Development: Small Business Communities and the London Olympics 2012'. *Urban Studies*, 47 (10): 2069–91.

Rahola, Federico. 2014, 'Urban at Large: Notes for an Ethnography of Urbanization and Its Frictious Sites'. *Etnografia e Ricerca Qualitativa*, 3: 379–400.

Rametta, Gaetano. 2006, 'Biopolitica e Coscienza. Riflessioni Intorno all'Ultimo Deleuze'. *Filosofia Politica*, 1: 29–42.

Ramsay, Peter. 2008, 'The Theory of Vulnerable Autonomy and the Legitimacy of the Civil Preventative Order'. *LSE Law, Society and Economy Working Paper Series*, 1.

Ramsay, Peter. 2010, 'Overcriminalization as Vulnerable Citizenship'. *New Criminal Law Review*, 13 (2): 262–85.

Rancière, Jacques. 1995, *Disagreement: Politics and Philosophy* (University of Minnesota Press).

Rancière, Jacques. 2001, 'Ten Theses on Politics'. *Theory & Event*, 5 (3): n.p.

Rauch, Alex. 2010, 'No Fake: An Interview with Ai Weiwei'. *Portland Art*, 9 August. Available at: www.portlandart.net/archives/2010/08/no_fake_an_inte.html

Raunig, Gerald. 2010, *A Thousand Machines: A Concise Philosophy of the Machine as Social Movement* (Semiotext(e)).

Richards, Anthony, Pete Fussey and Andrew Silke (eds). 2011, *Terrorism and the Olympics: Major Event Security and Lessons for the Future* (Routledge).

Richards, Greg. 2010, *Eventful Cities: Cultural Management and Urban Revitalisation* (Routledge).

Rilke, Rainer Maria. 1967, *Sonnets to Orpheus* (University of California Press).

Roberts, David. 2010, 'Durban's Future? Rebranding Through the Production/Policing of Event-Specific Spaces at the 2010 World Cup'. *Sport in Society*, 13 (10): 1486–9.

Robinson, Jennifer. 2006, *Ordinary Cities: Between Modernity and Development* (Routledge).

Roche, Maurice. 2000, *Mega-Events and Modernity: Olympics and Expos in the Growth of Global Culture* (Routledge).

Rodgers, Dennis. 2004, '"Disembedding" the City: Crime, Insecurity and Spatial Organization in Managua, Nicaragua'. *Environment and Urbanization*, 16 (2): 113–24.

Ronchi, Rocco. 2011, 'Introduction to Jean Paul Sartre', *La trascendenza dell'ego: una descrizione fenomenologica* (Marinotti).

Ronchi, Rocco. 2015, *Gilles Deleuze* (Feltrinelli).

Ruedin, Isaac. 2002, 'Bodies of Responsibility: Merleau-Ponty and Derrida'. *Philosophy Today*, 46 (3): 243–54.

Sadd, Debbie. 2013, 'Olympic Protest', in Vassil Girginov (ed.). *The Routledge 2012 Olympics Special Issue*. Routledge Online Studies on the Olympic and Paralympic Games (Routledge).

Salzer-Mörling, Miriam and Lars Strannegård. 2007, 'Ain't Misbehavin': Consumption in a Moralized Brandscape'. *Marketing Theory*, 7 (4): 407–25.

Samatas, Minas. 2007, 'Security and Surveillance in the Athens 2004 Olympics: Some Lessons from a Troubled Story'. *International Criminal Justice Review*, 17 (3): 220–38.

Sapienza, Davide. 2011, *La musica della neve: piccole variazioni sulla materia bianca* (Ediciclo).

Sartre, Jean-Paul. 1957, *The Transcendence of the Ego: An Existentialist Theory of Consciousness* (Noonday Press).

Sassen, Saskia. 2006, *Territory, Authority, Rights: From Medieval to Global Assemblages* (Princeton University Press).

Schatzki, Theodore R. 2007, *Martin Heidegger: Theorist of Space* (Franz Steiner Verlag).

Schmidt, James. 1985, *Maurice Merleau-Ponty: Between Phenomenology and Structuralism* (Palgrave Macmillan).

Schmitt, Carl. 2006, *Political Theology: Four Chapters on the Concept of Sovereignty* (University of Chicago Press).

Schmitz, Herman. 1969, *System der Philosophie 3: Der Gefuhlsraum* (Bouvier).

Schreiber, Martina and Otto Adang. 2010, 'The Poles Are Coming! Fan Behaviour and Police Tactics Around the World Cup Match Germany vs. Poland'. *Sport in Society*, 13 (3): 470–88.

Schütz, Anton. 2009, 'Imperatives Without Imperator'. *Law and Critique*, 20 (3): 233–43.

Schütz, Anton. 2011, 'A Quandary Concerning Immanence'. *Law and Critique*, 22 (2): 189–203.

Seabrock, Jeremy. 1996, *In the Cities of the South: Scenes from a Developing World* (Verso).

Searle, Adrian. 2010, 'What Happened Next? Sunflower Seeds'. *The Guardian*, 27 December. Available at: www.theguardian.com/lifeandstyle/2010/dec/27/ al-weiwei-sunflower-seeds-tate

Sennett, Richard. 1992, *The Uses of Disorder: Personal Identity and City Life* (W.W. Norton).

The Serpent's Egg. 1977, Directed and written by Ingmar Bergman (Columbia).

Serres, Michel. 1990, *The Natural Contract* (University of Michigan Press).

Serres, Michel. 1999, *Variations sur le corps* (Le Pommier).

Serres, Michel. 2009, *The Five Senses: A Philosophy of Mingled Bodies* (Continuum).

Severino, Emanuele. 1972, *Essenza del Nichilismo* (Paideia).

Severino, Emanuele. 1979, *Legge e Caso* (Adelphi).

Severino, Emanuele. 1980, *Destino Della Necessità* (Adelphi Edizioni).

Severino, Emanuele. 2009, *Il Destino della Tecnica* (Rizzoli).

Sewell, William H., Jr. 1996, 'Three Temporalities: Toward a Sociology of the Event', in Terence J. McDonald (ed.). *The Historic Turn in the Human Sciences*, 245–80 (University of Michigan Press).

Shah-Shuja, Mastaneh. 2008, *Shah-Shuja Zones of Proletarian Development.* (Openmute).

Sharma, N. 2006, *Home Economics: Nationalism and the Making of Migrant Workers in Canada.* (University of Toronto Press).

Sharpley, Richard and Philip Stone. 2012, 'Socio-cultural Impacts of Events. Meanings, Authorized Transgression and Social Capital', in Stephen J. Page and Joanne Connell (eds). *The Routledge Handbook of Events*, 347–60 (Routledge).

Shaw, Christopher A. 2008, *Five Ring Circus: Myths and Realities of the Olympic Games* (New Society Publishers).

Shearing, Clifford D. and Phillip C. Stenning. 1984, 'From the Panopticon to

Disneyworld: The Development of Discipline', in Anthony N. Doob and Edward L. Greenspan (eds). *Perspectives in Criminal Law: Essays in Honour of John Ll. J. Edwards*, 335–49 (Canada Law).

Shen, Aviva. 2012, 'Superweeds Lead to Heavier Pesticide Use On Crops'. *ThinkProgress*, 3 October. Available at: http://thinkprogress.org/health/2012/10/03/946801/superweeds-pesticides/?mobile=nc

Sherry, John F. 1998, 'The Soul of the Company Store: Nike Town Chicago and the Emplaced Brandscape', in John F. Sherry (ed.). *ServiceScapes: The Concept of Place in Contemporary Markets*, 109–46 (NTC Business Books).

Simmel, Georg. 1908, *Soziologie Untersuchungen über die Formen der Vergesellschaftung* (Duncker & Humblot). Available at: http://socio.ch/sim/soziologie/

Simmel, Georg. 2002[1903], 'The Metropolis and Mental Life' in Gary Bridge and Sophie Watson (eds). *The Blackwell City Reader*, 103–10 (Wiley-Blackwell).

Simone, AbdouMaliq. 2004, 'People as Infrastructure: Intersecting Fragments in Johannesburg'. *Public Culture*, 16 (3): 407–29.

Sinnerbrink, Robert. 2006, 'Nomadology or Ideology? Žižek's Critique of Deleuze'. *Parrhesia*, 1: 62–87.

Sloterdijk, Peter. 1999, *Spharen II: Globen, Makrospharrologie* (Suhrkamp).

Sloterdijk, Peter. 2005, 'Foreword to the Theory of Spheres', in Melik Ohanian and Jean-Christophe Royoux (eds). *Cosmograms*, 223–40 (Lukas and Sternberg).

Sloterdijk, Peter. 2006, *Sphères: Tome 3, Ecumes, Sphérologie plurielle* (Hachette Littératures).

Sloterdijk, Peter. 2009, *Sfere I, Bolle* (Meltemi).

Sloterdijk, Peter. 2011, *Bubbles: Microspherology* (Semiotext(e)).

Sloterdijk, Peter. 2013, *In the World Interior of Capital: For a Philosophical Theory of Globalization* (Polity Press).

Smart, Alan. 2001, 'Unruly Places: Urban Governance and the Persistence of Illegality in Hong Kong's Urban Squatter Areas'. *American Anthropologist*, 103: 30–44.

Smith, David. 2010, 'World Cup Kicks Violent South African Crime into Touch'. *Guardian*, 9 July. Available at: www.guardian.co.uk/football/2010/jul/09/world-cup-football-south-africa-crime-falls

Smith, Neil. 2004, 'Scale Bending and the Fate of the National', in Eric Sheppard and Robert B. McMaster (eds). *Scale and Geographic Inquiry: Nature, Society, and Method* (Blackwell), 192–212.

Smith, Richard G. 2010, 'Urban Studies without "Scale": Localizing the Global through Singapore', in I. Farías and T. Bender (eds). *Urban Assemblages: How Actor-Network Theory Changes Urban Research*, 73–90 (Routledge).

Smith, Richard G. and Marcus Doel. 2011, 'Questioning the Theoretical Basis of Current Global-City Research: Structures, Networks and Actor-Networks'. *International Journal of Urban and Regional Research*, 35 (1): 24–39.

Soja, Edward W. 1996, *Thirdspace* (Blackwell).

Soja, Edward W. 2010, *Seeking Spatial Justice* (University of Minnesota Press).

Spencer, Douglas. 2011, 'Architectural Deleuzism: Neoliberal Space, Control and the "Univercity"'. *Radical Philosophy*, 168 (9): 9–21.

Stadler, Raphaela, Sacha Reid and Simone Fullagar. 2013, 'An ethnographic exploration of knowledge practices within the Queensland Music Festival'. *International Journal of Event and Festival Management*, 4 (2): 90–106.

Stanley, Anna. 2009, 'Just Space or Spatial Justice? Difference, Discourse, and Environmental Justice'. *Local Environment: The International Journal of Justice and Sustainability*, 14 (10): 999–1014.

Stavrides, Stavros. 2010, *Towards the City of Thresholds* (Professionaldreamers).

Stephens, Angharad Closs. 2015, 'The Affective Atmospheres of Nationalism'. *Cultural Geographies*, 23 (2): 181–98.

Stewart, Katie. 2011, 'Atmospheric Attunements'. *Environment and Planning D: Society and Space*, 29 (3): 445–53.

Storper, Michael. 2001, 'The Poverty of Radical Theory Today: From the False Promises of Marxism to the Mirage of the Cultural Turn'. *International Journal of Urban and Regional Research*, 25 (1): 155–79.

Stramignoni, Igor. 2004, 'Francesco's Devilish Venus: Notations on the Matter of Legal Space'. *California Western Law Review*, 41: 147–240.

Sugranyes, Ana and Charlotte Mathivet. 2010, *Cities for All: Experiences and Proposals for the Right to the City* (Habitat International Coalition).

Sützl, Wolfgang. 2009, 'Languages of Surprise', in Wolfgang Sutzl and Geoff Cox (eds). *Creating Insecurity: Art and Culture in the Age of Security*, 67–82 (Autonomedia).

Swyngedouw, Erik. 2006, 'Metabolic Urbanization: The Making of Cyborg Cities', in Nick Heynen, Maria Kaika and Erik Swyngedouw (eds). *In the Nature of Cities: Urban Political Ecology and the Politics of Urban Metabolism*, 21–40 (Routledge).

Swyngedouw, Erik. 2011, *Designing the Post-Political City and the Insurgent Polis* (Bedford Press).

Takei, Jiro and Marc P. Keane. 2008, *Sakuteiki: Visions of the Japanese Garden* (Tuttle Publishing).

Tarde, Gabriel. 1903, *The Laws of Imitation* (H. Holt and Company).

Tarde, Gabriel. 2012[1893], *Monadology and Sociology* (re.press).

Taussig, Michael. 2013, *I Swear I Saw This: Drawings in Fieldwork Notebooks, Namely My Own* (University of Chicago Press).

Taylor, Louise. 2009, 'Why Going to South Africa for the World Cup Terrifies Me'. *Guardian*, 7 July. Available at: www.guardian.co.uk/football/blog/2009/jul/07/louise-taylor-south-africa-2010-world-cup

Teixeira Pinto, Ana. 2013, 'The Whole Earth: In Conversation with Diedrich Diederichsen and Anselm Franke'. *E-Flux*, 45. Available at: www.e-flux.com/journal/the-whole-earth-in-conversation-with-diedrich-diederichsen-and-anselm-franke/

Thacker, Eugene. 2012, 'Cosmic Pessimism'. *Continent*, 2.2. Available at: http://continentcontinent.cc/index.php/continent/article/view/84

Thacker, Eugene. 2013, 'Nekros; or, The Poetics of Biopolitics'. *foucaultblog*. Available at: www.fsw.uzh.ch/foucaultblog/featured/20/nekros-or-the-poetics-of-biopolitics

The Invisible Committee. 2009, *The Coming Insurrection* (Semiotext(e)).

Thibaud, Jean-Paul. 2011, 'The Sensory Fabric of Urban Ambiances'. *The Senses and Society*, 6: 203–15.

Thibaud, Jean-Paul. 2012. 'Petite archéologie de la notion d'ambiance'. *Communications*, 90 (1): 155–74.

Thoreau, Henry, D. 1962, *The Variorum Walden* (Twayne Publishers).

Thörn, Catharina. 2011, 'Soft Policies of Exclusion: Entrepreneurial Strategies of Ambience and Control of Public Space in Gothenburg, Sweden'. *Urban Geography*, 32: 989–1008.

Thrift, Nigel. 1993, 'An Urban Impasse?'. *Theory, Culture & Society*, 10: 229–38.

Thrift, Nigel. 2007, *Non-representational Theory: Space, Politics, Affect* (Routledge).

Thrift, Nigel. 2008, 'I Just Don't Know What Got into Me: Where is The Subject?'. *Subjectivity*, 22 (1): 82–9.

Thrift, Nigel. 2011, 'Lifeworld Inc—and What to Do About It'. *Environment and Planning D: Society and Space*, 29 (1): 5–26.

Thrift, Nigel and Jon May (eds). 2001, *TimeSpace: Geographies of Temporality* (Routledge).

Till, Jeremy. 2009, *Architecture Depends* (MIT Press).

Tiqqun. 2010, *Introduction to Civil War*, Alexander R. Galloway and Jason E. Smith (eds). (Semiotext(e)).

Toews, David. 2003, 'The New Tarde: Sociology After the End of the Social'. *Theory, Culture & Society*, 20: 81–98.

Toscano, Alberto. 2000, 'To Have Done with the End of Philosophy'. *Pli: The Warwick Journal of Philosophy*, 9: 220–38.

Toscano, Alberto. 2004, 'Factory, Territory, Metropolis, Empire'. *Angelaki: Journal of Theoretical Humanities*, 9: 197–216.

Toscano, Alberto. 2008, 'The Open Secret of Real Abstraction'. *Rethinking Marxism*, 20 (2): 273–87.

Toscano, Alberto. 2011a, 'Divine Management: Critical Remarks on Giorgio Agamben's *The Kingdom and the Glory*'. *Angelaki: Journal of Theoretical Humanities*, 16 (3): 125–36.

Toscano, Alberto. 2011b, 'Against Speculation, or, a Critique of the Critique of Critique: A Remark on Quentin Meillassoux's *After Finitude* (After Colletti)', in Levi R. Bryant, Nick Srnicek and Graham Harman (eds). *The Speculative Turn: Continental Materialism and Realism*, 84–91 (re.press).

Trost, Dolfi. 1953, *Visible et invisible* (Éditions Arcanes).

Tsing Lowenhaupt, Anna. 2004, *Friction: An Ethnography of Global Connection* (Princeton University Press).

Tsing Lowenhaupt, Anna. 2012, 'On Nonscalability. The Living World Is Not Amenable to Precision-Nested Scales'. *Common Knowledge*, 18 (3): 505–24.

Tsoukala, Anastassia. 2006, 'Combating Football Crowd Disorder at the European Level: An Ongoing Institutionalisation of the Control of Deviance'. *ESLJ*, 7 (2).

Tuppini, Tommaso. 2010, 'Ontologia della Comunità. Jean-Luc Nancy and Giorgio Agamben. Parte seconda: Agamben'. *Giornaledifilosofia.net*, January: 23–32. Available at: www.giornaledifilosofia.net/public/scheda.php?id=126

UNI Property Services and Alliance for Justice at Group 4 Securicor. 2007, *Who Protects the Guards? The Facts Behind G4S in Southern Africa*. Available at: www.globalexchange.org/sites/default/files/WhoProtectstheGuards.pdf

Urquhart, Craig. 2008, 'Building a Safe South Africa'. *SouthAfrica.Info*, 6 November. Available at: www.southafrica.info/2010/project2010column32.htm

Valéry, Paul. 1944, *Eupalinos or the Architect* (Oxford University Press).

van der Walt, Johan. 2007, 'Johannesburg: A Tale of Two Cases', in Andreas Philippopoulos-Mihalopoulos (ed.). *Law and the City*, 221–36 (Routledge).

van Gennep, Arnold. 1960[1909], *The Rites of Passage* (Routledge).

van Tuinen, Sjoerd. 2009, 'Air Conditioning Spaceship Earth: An Ethico-Aesthetic Paradigm'. *Society and Space*, 27 (1): 105–18.

Virno, Paolo. 2001, 'The Two Masks of Materialism'. *PLI: The Warwick Journal of Philosophy*, 12: 167–73.

Virno, Paolo. 2004, *A Grammar of the Multitude, For an Analysis of Contemporary Forms of Life* (Semiotext(e)).

Vladislavić, Ivan. 2009, *Portrait with Keys: The City of Johannesburg Unlocked* (W.W. Norton & Co).

Vos, Pierre de. 2010, 'On the Fifa World Cup by-laws'. *Constitutionally Speaking* blog, 17 June. Available at: http://constitutionallyspeaking.co.za/on-the-fifa-world-cup-by-laws/

Vries, Fred de. 2008, 'Megamalls, Generic City', in Sarah Nuttall and Achile Mbembé (eds). *Johannesburg: The Elusive Metropolis*, 297–306 (Wits University Press).

Wacquant, Loic. 2000, *Parola d'ordine: tolleranza Zero. La trasformazione dello stato penale nella società neoliberale* (Feltrinelli).

Waitt, Gordon. 2003, 'Social Impact of the Sydney Olympics'. *Annuals of Tourism Research*, 30 (1): 194–215.

Wakefield, Alison. 2003, *Selling Security: The Private Policing of Public Space* (Willan Publishing).

Warhol, Andy. 2007, *The Philosophy of Andy Warhol: From A to B and Back Again* (Penguin).

Wark, McKenzie. 2005, 'Securing Security'. *Kritikos*, 2: 3–13.

Watson, Sophie and Katherine Gibson (eds). 1995, *Postmodern Cities and Spaces* (Basil Blackwell).

Watts, Michael. 2005, 'Baudelaire over Berea, Simmel over Sandton?' *Public Culture*, 17 (1): 181–92.

Weber. Max. 2003[1905], *The Protestant Ethic and the Spirit of Capitalism* (Dover Publications).

Weil, Simone. 2002, *Gravity and Grace* (Routledge).

Weizman, Eyal. 2007, 'Walking Through Walls'. Available at: http://eipcp.net/transversal/0507/weizman/en/#_ftnref3

Weizman, Eyal. 2010, 'Political Plastic (Interview)', in Robin Mackay (ed.). *Collapse, VI: Geo/Philosophy*, 267–313 (Urbanomic).

Wells, Linda. 2013, 'Superweeds Spreading at Warp Speed'. *Ground Truth* blog, 7 February. Available at: www.panna.org/blog/superweeds-spreading-warp-speed

Wetherell, Margaret. 2013, 'Feeling Rules, Atmospheres and Affective Practice: Some Reflections on the Analysis of Emotional Episodes', in Clair Maxwell and Peter Aggleton (eds). *Privilege, Agency and Affect: Understanding the Production and Effects of Action*, 221–40 (Palgrave Macmillan).

Whatmore, Sarah. 2003, 'De/Re Territorialising Possession: The Shifting Spaces of Property Rights', in Jane Holder and Carolyn Harrison (eds). *Law and Geography*, 211–23 (Oxford University Press).

Whitehead, Mark. 2011, 'The Sustainable City: An Obituary? On the Future Form and Prospects of Sustainable Urbanism', in John Flint and Mike Raco (eds). *The Future of Sustainable Cities: Critical Reflections* (Policy Press).

Whitehead, Neil L. 2007, 'Violence and the Cultural Order'. *Daedalus*, 136 (1): 40–50.

Whyte, Jessica. 2009, "I Would Prefer Not to": Giorgio Agamben, Bartleby and the Potentiality of the Law'. *Law and Critique,* 20 (3): 309–24.

Wigley, Mark. 1998, *Constant's New Babylon: The Hyper-Architecture of Desire* (010 Publishers).

Williams, Alex and Nick Srnicek. 2013, 'Accelerate: Manifesto for an Accelerationist Politics'. *Speculative Heresy,* 3 (11). Available at: https://syntheticedifice.files.wordpress.com/2013/06/accelerate.pdf

Williams, Alex and Nick Srnicek. 2016, *Inventing the Future: Postcapitalism and a World Without Work* (Verso).

Wilson, James Q. and George L. Kelling. 1982, 'Broken Windows: The Police and Neighbourhood Safety'. *Atlantic Monthly,* 127: 29–38.

Wilson, Peter J. 2007, 'Agriculture or Architecture? The Beginnings of Domestication', in Rebecca Cassidy and Molly Mullin (eds). *Where the Wild Things Are Now: Domestication Reconsidered,* 101–22 (Berg).

Wolfendale, Pete. 2014, *Object-Oriented Philosophy: The Noumenon's New Clothes* (Urbanomic).

Woodward, Keith. 2010, 'Events, Spontaneity and Abrupt Conditions', in Ben Anderson and Paul Harrison (eds). *Taking-Place: Non-Representational Theories and Geography,* 321–40 (Ashgate).

Wright, Melissa, W. 2009, 'Justice and the Geographies of Moral Protest: Reflections from Mexico'. *Environment and Planning D: Society and Space,* 27 (2): 216–33.

Young, Iris Marion. 1990, *Justice and the Politics of Difference* (Princeton University Press).

Zaera-Polo, Alejandro. 2008, 'The Politics of the Envelope: A Political Critique of Materialism'. 17: 76–105.

Zartaloudis, Thanos. 2002, 'Without Negative Origins and Absolute Ends: A Jurisprudence of the Singular'. *Law and Critique,* 13 (2): 197–230.

Zartaloudis, Thanos. 2010, *Giorgio Agamben: Power, Law and the Uses of Criticism* (Routledge).

Zartaloudis, Thanos. 2011, 'On Justice'. *Law and Critique,* 22 (2): 135–53.

Zirin, Dave and Jules Boykoff. 2016, 'One Community's Resistance Will Be the Rio Olympics' Longest-Lasting Legacy'. *The Nation,* 17 August. Available at: https://comitepopulario.files.wordpress.com/2016/03/dossiecomiterio2015.pdf

Žižek, Slavoj. 1989, *The Sublime Object of Ideology* (Verso).

Žižek, Slavoj. 2000, *The Ticklish Subject: The Absent Centre of Political Ontology* (Verso).

Žižek, Slavoj. 2004, *Organs Without Bodies: Deleuze and Consequences* (Routledge).

Žižek, Slavoj. 2005, 'Revenge of Global Finance'. *In These Times,* 21 May. Available at: http://inthesetimes.com/article/2122/

Zourabichvili, François. 1998, 'Deleuze et le possible (de l'involuntarisme en politique)', in Eric Alliez (ed.). *Gilles Deleuze. Une Vie Philosophique,* 335–57 (Le Plessis-Robinson: Institut Synthélabo).

Zumthor, Peter. 2012, *Atmospheres* (Birkhäuser).

Index

Abstraction 24, 81, 96, 101–2, 222, 232, 236, 238, 244, 258, 260; control 117–19, 126; mega events 162, 164; real 108, 127–8, 133–4, 140, 143; techné/alienation 148–51; *see also* Legal abstraction
Acceleration/ism 231, 235, 261
Actor-network theory (ANT) 6, 11, 15–17, 20, 22–4, 28; assemblages 48–50, 53; atmospheres 58; methodology 171
Actual 28, 30, 32–3, 42, 44, 230; *see also* Virtual
Actualism 27
Affect 46, 54–5, 60–3, 166, 180; urban 142, 146, 146–7n185
Affection 60, 62–3
Agamben, Giorgio 5, 8; control/urban/event 111n10, 116, 124; law/profanation/justice 224, 225n68, 235n122, 240–2, 250–1; law/space/justice 72, 85, 87, 89–90; paradigm 253–4; space/matter/event 11, 30–4
Agencement 41, 46, 52, 103, 118; *see also* Assemblage
Agency 3–4, 12–13, 16, 41n135, 47–8, 61, 142, 154, 160, 225
Alertness 182–3, 187, 207, 209
Alienation 150–1, 243–4
Ambience 55–6, 59, 67; *see also* Atmosphere
Anthropocene 1, 55, 99, 233
Apartheid 177–8, 186–8, 202n228
Architecture 9–10, 50, 56, 112, 239; art and 262, 266; decolonising 250–2; *see also* Spatiolegal architecture of control
Aristotle 32, 111n10, 129
Art 135, 148, 245–6, 261–7; mega events 161–2
Assemblage 7, 41, 44, 50–5, 81, 118, 129n93; method 171, 176, assemblage urbanism 45, 47–50, 53–5, 232; *see also Agencement*
Atmo-rhythm/ical 68, 176, 181, 185, 198, 206–7n248; *see also* Tuning
Atmosphere 46, 54–64, 79; art/seeds 262, 264; Johannesburg 176, 181, 183; methodology 169; urban 134–5, 140, 144; World Cup 188, 190, 197–8, 210
Authenticity 3, 59, 127, 149, 203, 210

Badiou, Alain 23, 28, 38, 220, 227, 236
Bare life 31, 34, 71, 110–11, 117, 119, 260
Baudrillard, Jean 204, 238
Bausch, Pina 105n168
Becoming 29, 37–8, 40n132, 42, 65, 103–4, 174n102, 227, 235n123, 241n148, 245, 258, 263; da-sein 21–2; nihilistic 29–31; virtual 62; state of exception 90, 106; chaotic 92; urban 131; intense 148, 194; taoism 229–31
Being 18–9, 21, 28–9, 32, 34, 41–2, 86, 254
Being-there (*Da-sein*) 18–23, 30, 168, 225

Benjamin, Walter 2, 72, 75, 76n38, 92n114, 95, 103, 107, 211, 224
Bergson, Henri 14, 28, 39
Biopolitics 17, 35, 90, 94, 102, 138; control and 108, 110, 114–17, 122
Biopower 108, 111, 122, 151, 197
Bissel, David 61, 146, 146–7n185, 148, 183n148, 194
Body/bodies 2–7, 12–13, 20, 24, 26, 34–6, 38, 42–5, 48, 206, 209–10; art/seeds 261, 263–4, 267–8; atmosphere/rhythm 54, 57–8, 60–4, 66–8; control 111–13, 115, 117, 121, 125, 145; mega event/World Cup 152, 154–5, 162, 166, 169–84; law/justice 75, 81–2, 96, 99–101, 219–20, 225, 235, 238–40; profanation 243–5, 252; without organs 260, 260n24
Burroughs, William 5, 114, 159
Brandscape/ing 8, 108–9, 136–7, 144–8, 151, 253; art 262, 264; mega events 158, 160, 162–3, 165–6; World Cup 188, 191, 194–210
Brassier, Ray 23, 128, 235n123
Braverman, Irus 77–8, 79n52, 99
Brenner, Neil 1, 47–9, 54, 132–3, 214
Brighenti, Andrea Mubi 14–15, 20, 24n65, 124–5, 203, 218

Cacciari, Massimo 84, 218
Cape Town 192, 192n182–3, 198, 209
Capital/ism 1–2, 5–6, 8, 17, 25, 49, 51, 106–7, 164, 226n73, 260;
atmosphere/rhythm 54, 59, 65–6; control 111 10, 120, 131–2, 134,, law/profanation/justice 213, 219, 227–8, 230, 231n101, 234, 241; mega events 153, 155, 196; urban 150–1
Cerdà, Ildefons 1, 108, 130–2, 135, 145
Chaos 40n132, 67, 73–5, 92, 258
China 155–6, 189, 212, 261
Colebrook, Claire 23, 30, 62, 81, 258
Comfort 135, 143–5, 203, 224, 244
Commodification/commodified 5, 8, 109–10, 133, 135, 144, 153, 181, 203, 206–7
Conflict/confictual/ity, 3, 10, 14, 41, 45, 47, 63, 66–8, 71, 73, 80, 84, 98, 129, 132, 134, 144, 147, 154, 160, 165, 168–70, 173–4, 187, 195, 199, 203–4, 209, 213, 216–21, 235, 237, 244–5, 249, 257, 262, 264, 268–9
Consequentialism 160
Constructivism 45, 148, 236
Consumption 136–7, 199–200, 210
Contractualism 11–12, 20
Control 5, 7, 33, 94n121, 106–9, 114–22, 128, 262; Johannesburg 179–80; law/justice 218–19, 226–8, 230–2, 237; mega events 158–9; profanation 249, 253; spatiolegal architecture of 69, 106–8, 126, 224; urban 134, 139, 144–51; World Cup 198–9
Correlation/ism 5, 11, 22–3, 25–6, 40, 71, 241; *see also* Relationalism
Counter-effectuation 44, 236, 249, 268
Critical 2–3, 8, 12, 51, 80, 94, 123, 160, 166, 167, 182, 206, 210, 214, 221; legal geography (CLG) 7, 69, 78–80; sociology 16, 76; geography 46, 77; legal studies 78, 94n123; theory/thought 102, 127, 228
Critique 12, 15, 24, 29, 31–3, 46, 49–53, 61, 66, 73–4, 80, 90, 104, 120–1, 123–8, 150, 163, 178, 194, 215n20, 216–7, 227, 237, 247, 250n174

Dangerisation 139, 183
Da-sein (being-there) 18–23, 30, 168, 229201
Deconstruction 3, 69, 86–7, 89–94, 106, 258
Deleuze, Gilles 5–6, 8; atmosphere/rhythm/tuning 47, 52, 54, 65, 67; conclusions 259, 262, 266–7; control/urban/event 108, 112, 114–20, 125, 127, 145, 148; law/profanation/justice 223, 226–8, 230, 232, 236–9; law/space/justice 69, 85, 93n118, 95–7, 103–5; space/matter/event 12, 23–4, 27–9, 32, 34–5, 37–42, 44

Derrida, Jacques 7, 23, 44, 64, 69, 72, 83, 86–92, 94, 97, 223, 250n174
Descartes, René 18, 22, 39, 173
Deterritorialisation 93, 96–7, 128–9, 169, 177, 261; digital 160; mega events 155, 205; urban 133–4, 149
Desire 13, 34, 50, 52–3, 80, 106, 117, 171, 198, 218, 223–4, 244,
Diagram 41, 54, 106, 112–13, 115, 117–18, 131–2, 134, 226n73
Difference 13, 17, 64–5, 213, 219
Differential space 66, 66n105, 128–9, 217, 234
Dike 84, 86, 88, 216
Dikeç, Mustafa 212, 217–19
Doel, Marcus 17, 173, 215n20, 263n42
Durkheim, Émile 12, 155–6

Ecology/ical 2, 7, 20–1, 46, 51, 54, 58, 148, 151, 181, 258, 261n32
Embodiment/embodied/embody 2, 56, 59, 64, 80, 100, 162, 164, 190, 214, 232, 234–5, 241–2, 258–60, 264
Encounter 75, 103, 234, 236, 255, 262–3, 266; phenomenological 54, 63; agonistic 134; abstraction/contingency 133, 136, 154, 165–6, 169–70, 174, 188, 194, 208; alterity 177m122; law/space/justice 73, 105, 212, 242, 246, 248,
Engineering, atmospheric 56–8, 60, 62–3, 188
Erlebnisse 18–19; *see also* Everyday life
Esposito, Roberto 31n93, 101–5, 117, 222
Ethics/ethical/ly 5, 12, 59, 80, 87, 89, 92, 101, 160, 171–2, 218, 224, 232–3, 135, 171, 247, 248, 263, 268; atmospheric 62
Ethnography 8, 134, 166, 168–9, 172–4, 176
Event 5–6, 11–12, 17, 21–2, 37–8, 40, 42–4; law/space/justice 80–1, 83, 94–5, 97; methodology 167–70; understanding 232–3; urban 142–3, 147–8, 153–4; willing/representing 235–9; *see also* Mega events
Eventification 153, 199n210
Everyday Life 2–4, 18, 64–5, 133, 135–6, 148, 153, 156, 166, 179, 185
Exception: *see* State of exception
Excess 14, 44–7, 59–63, 83, 223
Explicitation 122, 135, 149, 152, 158

Fan zoning 195–8, 200–2, 204, 206–9
Fear 61–3, 139–42, 184
FIFA 159, 196–7, 199, 201–2, 205–6, 209; *see also* World Cup
Flat ontology 11, 16–17, 24, 44–5, 49, 119; law and 74–6, 95
Foam 20–2, 82, 129
Fold/ing 7, 18, 21n57, 35, 50, 97, 101, 105, 11, 119, 122, 151, 259–60; and unfolding 67
Foucault, Michel 17, 38, 54, 226n73, 259; on cities 131, 137–8; on control 108, 111–13, 115, 122
Franciscans 240–1, 246, 254
Freedom 101–2, 114, 143, 180, 220, 236
Friction 54, 68, 133–4, 173, 210; frictious sites 161–2

Geo-philosophy/geo-philosophical 98, 174, 237
Geography 4, 47, 54, 70, 184, 197, 212, 221; legal 7, 69, 77 psycho- 186; critical: *see* Critical; critical legal: *see* Critical
Germany 190, 194n190, 196, 197n199, 207–8n278
Goffman, Erwin 14n12, 67, 181, 185
Governmentality 113, 115, 118, 121–2, 138
Guattari, Félix 5–6, 119n50; atmosphere/rhythm 54, 67; law/profanation/justice 223, 226–7, 237n129n132; law/space/justice 69, 93n118, 95–7, 105; space/matter/event 23, 37, 40n132, 47, 52

Habermas, Jürgen 213
Harman, Graham 6, 11, 16, 22–8, 32n97, 232
Harvey, David 2, 213, 215

Hegel, Georg Wilhelm Friedrich 14, 23, 109, 127
Heidegger, Martin 6, 11, 17, 19–24, 27, 30, 70
Hobbes, Thomas 29, 45, 74
Holey space 237, 237n130n132, 240, 252
Human 26–7, 30, 40, 82–3, 111, 233–5, 255–6, 259; as operator 109–10; *see also* Inhuman; Post-human
Husserl, Edmund 18–19

Immanence/Immanent 1–2 6–7, 13–4, 20, 29n86, 31, 34, 41, 45, 133, 149, 162, 167, 191, 235, 247, 254, 259; plane of immanence 40, 40n132, 44n148; atmosphere 57, 59–60, 67–8; spatiolegal/normativity 71, 79, 81–5, 91, 99, 102–3, 105; control 107, 109, 111–13, 115, 118–19; law, 121–5; urban 130, 174 tuning 152, 178–82, 186, 188, 210, 268; taoism 228–34
Immaterial/ity 24, 36, 59, 80, 84, 86, 91, 227
Immunity/immunitary 64, 66, 70–1, 90; paradigm 100–1, 103; ethos 135; Johannesburg 180, 182, 186; ontology 27, 31; urban 135, 141, 148–9; World Cup 209–10; law 244, 264–7
Impotentiality 33–6, 111n10, 115–17
Inhuman 42–3, 62, 106, 233–4; *see also* Post-human
Inoperose/inoperosity 10, 33, 35–6; acting 221–6, building 201–2, gardening 261, 263–4, 268; law 212, 238–40, 242, 247–8; life 115–17
Installation 135, 148, 151–2, 202, 239, 262–5, 267
Interiorisation 7, 108, 134–5

Joburg Tune (JT) 152–3, 181–2, 185–95, 206, 208–9
Johannesburg 8, 173, 176–89; World Cup 192–3, 197, 206–8, 253
Juridification 5, 79, 81, 83–5, 203, 247, 252
Just city 213–14
Justice 69, 82–95, 211–21, 223–5, 234, 240, 247–50, 253, 268–9; Kafka 123; socio-empirical approach 75–6; transcendental 104; *see also* Spatial justice

Kafka, Franz 123, 223
Kant, Immanuel: 18, 22–3, 39, 39, 71, 73, 74n29, 75n34, 85, 89, 108, 124–5, 241
Kare-sansui 242, 246
Kracauer, Siegfried 2, 150, 165

Latour, Bruno 6, 11, 13, 15–17, 20–4, 27, 30–1, 32n97, 49–50, 76, 105
Lawscape 7, 69, 98, 129; *see also* Spatiolegal
Lazzarato, Maurizio 108n2, 116n36, 117n44, 144n174
Lefebvre, Henri 2, 3n11, 65–7, 131, 162, 173, 213, 217, 220, 248
Legacy (mega event) 158–61, 163, 180, 190, 193–4
Legal abstraction 74–7, 81, 101, 122–5, 143, 222–3, 238–40, 243–5, 249; *see also* Spatiolegal
Leibniz, Gottfried Wilhelm (von) 13
Leopardi, Giacomo 172
Liberalism 113–14, 143, 149
Libertarianism 140, 143, 148, 228
Life 23, 32–5, 101, 103, 106–7, 110–11, 115–17; *see also* Biopolitics; Vitalism
Line of flight 9, 23, 27, 44, 47 53–5, 61, 67, 83, 85, 87, 97, 165, 210, 232, 253, 263
Locke, John 256
Logos/nomos (logic/nomic) 69, 79, 84, 95–100, 129, 218
Luther, Martin 70

Mao Zedong 264n44
McCormack, Derek P. 58, 61, 168, 180, 210
McFarlane, Colin 47, 51, 106, 179
McGillivray, David 164, 170, 175, 198, 207

Machine/machinic 40n132, 41, 45, 54, 63, 67, 107, 115, 115n30, 118, 121, 125, 187, 222–3, 226, 262
Malls 135, 184n153, 185–6, 206, 208, 208n248
Marketing 7–8, 56, 136, 156, 199
Marx, Karl 108, 115, 117, 127–8
Materialism 24, 36; new 5, 36, 46, 55
Material/ity 4–10, 15, 19, 20, 24, 26–8, 36–8, 44, 46–8, 50–1, 53, 57–9, 62–4, 66–7, 69, 73, 75–6, 78–9, 81, 83, 92, 94–5, 97–101, 105, 108, 122–8, 130–1, 136, 147, 151–2, 154–5, 164, 165, 167, 169–70, 176, 182, 194–5, 198, 208, 213, 216, 220, 222, 225, 230, 249, 251
Matter 6, 12, 24, 31, 36, 43, 50–3, 56, 76, 80, 82, 99, 117, 149–50, 251, 257, 267–8
Mbembé, Achille 178, 181n138
Mega events 8, 147, 151–2, 154–67, 180, 262; ethnography 169–70; World Cup 188–92, 197–210
Meillassoux, Quentin 11, 22–3, 35, 174n102, 233, 247n166
Method assemblage 176
Methodology 48, 151, 167–9, 171–5
Microsociology 14
Milieu: *see Ambience*
Monadology 13–14, 35
Movement 9, 13, 19–20, 22, 29, 35, 37, 56, 64–6, 106–7, 109, 114–15, 119, 122, 126, 129n93, 130, 134, 158, 175, 180, 183–5, 198, 209–10, 225, 230–1, 258, 263; law/justice 86, 88, 93–4, 97, 99, 218,
Multiplicity 4, 27–8, 43, 46, 51, 65, 95, 100, 112, 115–17, 178, 186

Negarestani, Reza 23, 234, 237n132, 260
Negativity 31–2, 49n24, 89–90, 235, 237
Neo-liberalism 1–2, 5, 8, 12; atmosphere 54, 59; control 118–20; Johannesburg 186–7; law/ profanation/justice 227, 249–50; law/space/justice 105, 107; mega events 154–5, 157–8, 161, 166–8; urban 134, 144, 146
Neotaoism 231
Networks 11, 21–3; *see also* Actor-network theory (ANT)
New materialism 5, 36, 46, 55
Nietzsche, Friedrich 40n132, 103, 235n123, 237n132, 259
Nihilism 29–32, 110, 260
Nomad/ic/ism 95–6, 227, 232, 258–60, 264
Nomos 75, 84; see also Logos/Nomos
Nomosphere 78, 80–3, 100
Nomotop 81–2
Noys, Benjamin 31, 49n24, 59, 89, 106, 219, 228n82, 231n101, 250n174
Non-human 2, 4, 6, 13–4, 16, 20, 24, 26, 34, 46, 47, 49, 50–1, 57–9, 78, 81–2, 99–101, 111, 170, 173, 177, 188, 232n104, 252, 263

Object-Oriented Ontology (OOO) 22, 24, 33n101, 232
Olympics 7, 152–3, 157–9, 170, 189; brandscaping 160–4, 166, 198, 200
Ontology 5–6, 11–12, 15–32, 35–44, 48–9, 51–4, 68, 73–6, 83–4; of abstraction 125–7; of atmospheres 59, 61; deconstruction and 86, 92, 94; ethnography and 170–3; glorification 109–11; Olympian 162; Taoist 229–32
Operation 33–4, 71, 87, 90–1, 109–11, 117, 122–4, 131, 238–9, 254
Order 13, 45–6, 70–1, 95, 178–80
Organicism (holism) 11 12, 20
Outside 9, 20–1, 23, 36–7, 39, 40n132, 56n63, 63, 70, 73–5, 78, 86, 90–1, 94, 106, 113, 115, 126, 129, 135, 174, 186, 206–7n148, 225, 240–1, 246, 253–4, 257, 260, 262

Panopticon/panopticism 112, 115, 118, 179, 183, 254
Paradigm/atic 11, 90, 112, 120, 131, 151, 155, 203, 240, 241, 253–5
Parmenides 11, 28–30, 254
Phenomenology/ical/ly 7, 18–21, 23,

37, 39, 40–1, 43, 46, 54–61, 58, 67, 80–2, 101–2, 108, 135, 145, 150–1, 160, 172, 181–2, 203, 225, 233, 236, 245, 267,
Philippopoulos-Mihalopoulos, Andreas 7–8, 262; atmosphere/rhythm 57–9, 62; control/urban/event 126n77, 129, 146, 150–1; law/profanation/justice 215, 217–21, 240, 244; law/space/justice 69, 79–82, 98
Pessimism/pessimistic 172, 245
Plasma 31–2
Plato 29n86, 40n132, 70, 84n70, 86, 129
Police 183, 189, 191, 193–5, 198, 208–9, 218–19
Polis 3, 84, 95, 129, 217
Politics 109, 210–19; assemblage 50–3; justice 223, 225–7, 230–1, 234–5, 247n166, 268; mega events 201–3; ontology 11–12, 17, 25, 31; security 62–3; urban 130, 134, 210; *see also* Biopolitics
Possession 25, 27, 33, 246–7; and use 240–1
Post-human 260; atmosphere/rhythm 59, 67; law/justice 79, 83, 99, 216, 222, 233; ontology 22–3, 42, 46; *see also* Inhuman
Power 9, 50, 107, 111–18, 120–2, 211, 218–19, 237, 249; architecture 251–2; brandscaping 144, 146–7; Taoism 230–1
Praxis 30, 109, 218, 235, 241, 268
Prevention/preventive/pre-emptive 7, 141, 154
Profanation 8, 221, 242, 245–7, 251–2, 261
Property/proprietary 25, 27, 33–4, 39, 240–1, 256, 265–7
Protest 143n169, 162–4, 167, 202

Rancière, Jacque 153, 217–19, 221
Real abstraction 108, 127, 134, 222
Realism 37; speculative 22–3, 25–6, 35
Relation 16, 26, 34–6, 40, 43–4
Relational/ism 2, 5–6, 11, 16–17, 19, 21–8, 31–2, 35, 40, 46, 48, 50–2, 54, 57, 61, 63, 69, 81–3, 104, 119, 136, 213, 224–5, 232, 241, 263; methodology 171–3; urban 49–51; relational turn 5, 11, 142; non-relational 17, 22, 25–7, 32, 33, 40, 43, 63, 81, 97; aesthetics 59
Repetition 13, 64–5
Representation 36, 70–1, 237–9
Resistance 5, 83, 147, 151, 251, 260, 268; micro 146–8, 207n248, 219, 228; mega events 160–5, 167, 170, 187, 204, 214, 218
Responsibilisation 141, 224, 249
Reterritorialisation/reterritorialising 93, 97, 150, 155, 177, 183, 205
Rhizome/rhizomatic 9, 48, 82, 86, 93, 105–6, 108, 257–9
Rhythm 7, 14, 46, 54, 64–8, 84, 96, 131, 134, 153, 168, 172, 198, 205, 207n248, 208–9, 246; Johannesburg 180–1, 184–7; methodology 169, 172
Rhythmanalysis 65–6
Right to the city 213–14, 220, 240
Rimbaud, Arthur 39
Risk 103, 139, 142–3
Rupture 218–19, 221

Safety 181–2, 184–5, 188, 190–1, 194; *see also* Health and Safety
Sartre, Jean Paul 39, 40n130, 40n132
Schutz, A. 33n101, 126
Security 7–8, 113–14, 138–45, 224; Johannesburg 179–80, 186; mega events 157, 166–7; methodology 169–70; politics of 62–3; World Cup 188–98, 205–6, 209
Security-entertainment complex 144, 151, 167, 193, 198–9, 202, 206
Seeds 261, 262n37, 263–7
Serres, Michel 1
Severino, Emanuele 29–30, 92
Shared space 248–50
Simmel, Georg viii, 2, 131
Sloterdijk, Peter 5–7, 11, 17, 19–21; atmosphere 57, 59; cities 148–50, 176, 186; explicitation 122, 135, 149; interiorisation 108, 134–5; law/

space/justice 70, 81–2, 214; local 133
Smooth/smoothness 68, 93–7, 106–7, 126, 131–2, 163, 195, 208–9, 226n73, 228, 230–1, 235, 237, 251, 260, 262, 264, 267
Social 11–15, 17, 114, 149, 155
Social sciences 11, 16–17, 75, 77, 171
Socio-empiricism 75, 93, 259
Socio-legal 8, 75, 83, 99, 102, 162, 225
South Africa 8, 155–6, 180–1; World Cup 188–91, 195, 200, 205, 208n248, 209, 253; *see also* Johannesburg
Sovereignty 108–12, 120–2, 126, 138, 230, 237, 258
Space/spatial/spatiality 3–4, 17, 20, 38, 50, 58, 75, 95, 212, 237, 256; differential 66n105, 128–9, 217, 234; holey 237n130n132, 240, 252; law and 69–74, 77–80; ontology 17–20; rhythm and 65, 66n102; shared 248–50; urban 132, 137–8, 144–5
Spatial justice 5, 8–9, 97, 211, 214–21, 224, 232, 239, 242, 245, 268
Spatial turn 77–80, 215
Spatiolegal 69, 71–85, 89–102, 105–6, 129, 195, 249, 267
Spatiolegal architecture of control 69, 106–8, 126, 224
Spectacle 108, 112, 122, 139, 155, 157, 197, 222
Speculative Realism (SR) 22–3, 25–6, 35
Spinoza, Baruch 29n86, 43, 60, 102, 116, 238
Splice 78, 81
State of exception 69, 72–5, 77, 80, 83, 86–96, 100, 105–7; control 110–11, 119, 122; gardening 256, 258, 260; Kant 124–5; law/profanation/justice 223, 240, 249, 252; mega events 155, 158, 175; World Cup 200, 203
Strategy 5, 7–9, 97, 211–12, 234, 268; brandscaping 136; mega events 163–5; profanation 242, 251; spatial justice 216, 218–19, 239; taoism 228–30
Striate/striating/striation 54, 68, 93, 95–6, 106, 117, 226n73, 230, 237, 260, 265
Superweeds 259–61
Surfing 212, 226–8, 230, 235–7, 251
Swerving 21–2, 27–8, 33–5, 41, 43, 116, 229, 263

Tactical Urbanism 217n32
Tactics 164; *see also* Strategy
Taking place 36–8, 45, 65, 97, 116, 156, 264
Taoism 228–32
Tarde, Gabriel 6, 11–16, 20, 64, 66, 156
Techné 30–1, 90, 109–10, 126, 148–9
Temporary autonomous zone (TAZ) 211–12, 219, 268
Tensegrity 20, 20n49, 57, 68, 99, 129
Territorial justice 212, 214
Territorialisation 74, 96–7, 129, 133, 169, 243
Theology 73, 74n29, 109, 240–1
Thrift, N. 15, 17, 35n110, 144, 147
Transcend/ental/ence 6, 16, 18, 34, 39–40, 44, 73, 75, 79, 88, 90–1, 93, 96, 97, 102, 111, 115, 214, 220, 223, 232, 234, 236, 245, 246, 259; empiricism 44–6; field 40
Tuning 7, 13, 46, 54, 67–8, 143, 224, 253; conclusions 255, 262, 268; Johannesburg 178, 181–2, 187; mega events 152, 162, 165; methodology 169–70, 173–6; World Cup 191–2

Undecidability 72, 80–8, 90–1, 94
Undifferentiated 29, 31, 75, 230
United Kingdom (UK) 61, 141–2, 183n148, 202n228, 248–9
United States of America (USA) 142, 189, 208n248, 209, 215n18, 259
Unfolding 40, 67–8, 92, 109, 152, 157, 170, 234n117, 247, 259, 268; *see also* Fold/ing
Urban theory 3–4, 7, 45–50, 53–5, 64, 80, 132, 232
Urbanisation 1–2, 14n13, 130–1, 133, 161

Utopia/n 3, 98–9, 129, 218, 255

Violence 95, 112, 185, 187–8, 190, 219–20
Virtual 6, 81, 97, 100, 116, 143; ontology 12, 26–9, 32–4, 36, 42–4
Vitalism 23, 102, 107, 110, 149–50, 227; demonic 6, 12, 34–5, 263; gardening/weeds 257, 260–1; naïve 35, 117, 231

Weeds 256–61, 263–4, 268
Weiwei, AI 255, 261–8
Western thought: cities 178–9; law 104; life/body 66, 111; modernity 70; ontology 29–30, 39, 86; strategy 228
Whiteout 245–7, 249, 262, 264, 267
World Cup 8, 152, 157, 162, 166, 188–200, 209–10, 253
World Cup Brandscaping (WCB) 191, 194–5, 198–202, 205, 208–10, 253

Zartaloudis, Thanos 30, 77, 85, 89, 110n9, 248
Žižek, Slavoj 73, 218, 227–8, 230

For Product Safety Concerns and Information please contact our EU representative GPSR@taylorandfrancis.com
Taylor & Francis Verlag GmbH, Kaufingerstraße 24, 80331 München, Germany

www.ingramcontent.com/pod-product-compliance
Ingram Content Group UK Ltd.
Pitfield, Milton Keynes, MK11 3LW, UK
UKHW022012180926
475701UK00003B/317
* 9 7 8 0 3 6 7 2 6 4 3 5 2 *